# TRINITY BLOOD

ILLUSTRATOR
KIYO KYUJYO

AUTHOR
SUNAO YOSHIDA

CHARACTER DESIGN
THORES SHIBAMOTO

VOLUME
SEVEN

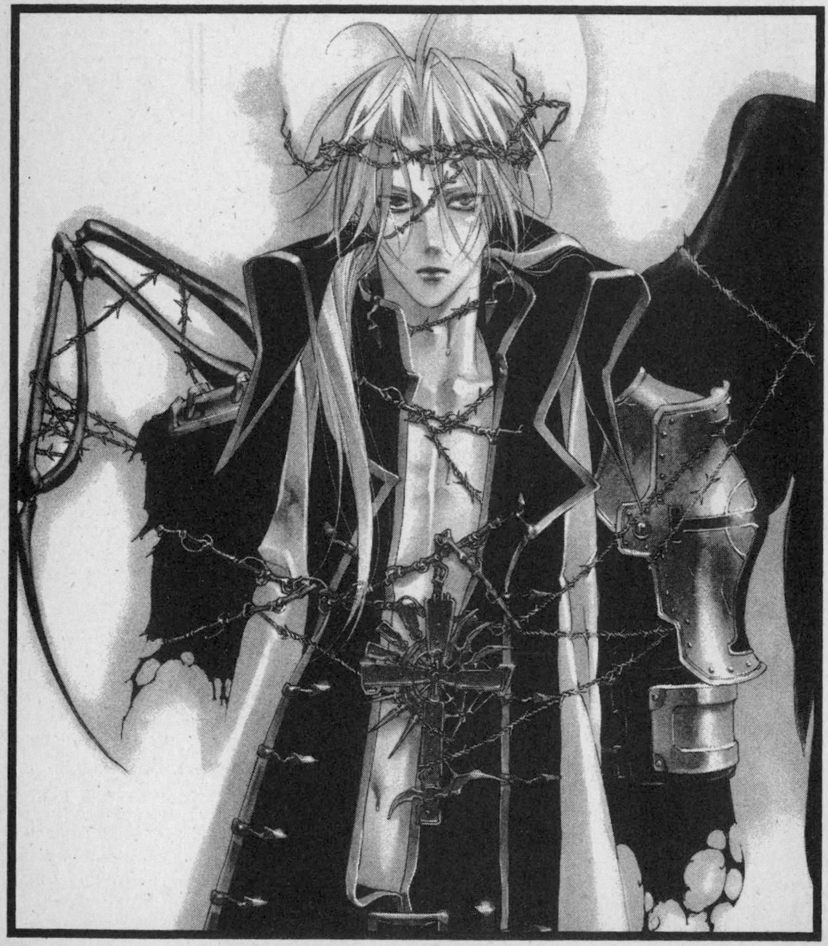

2869370

# Trinity Blood Volume 7
## Story By Sunao Yoshida
## Art By Kiyo Kyujyo
## Character Designs by Thores Shibamoto

Translation - Beni Axia Conrad
Englilsh Adaptation - Christine Boylan
Copy Editor - Jessica Chavez
Retouch and Lettering - Star Print Brokers
Production Artist - Mike Estacio
Graphic Designer - James Lee

Editor - Lillian Diaz-Przybyl
Digital Imaging Manager - Chris Buford
Pre-Production Supervisor - Vicente Rivera, Jr.
Production Specialist - Lucas Rivera
Managing Editor - Vy Nguyen
Art Director - Al-Insan Lashley
Editor-in-Chief - Rob Tokar
Publisher - Mike Kiley
President and C.O.O. - John Parker
C.E.O. and Chief Creative Officer - Stu Levy

A  Manga

TOKYOPOP Inc.
5900 Wilshire Blvd. Suite 2000
Los Angeles, CA 90036

E-mail: info@TOKYOPOP.com
Come visit us online at www.TOKYOPOP.com

ISBN: 978-1-4278-0177-7

First TOKYOPOP printing: August 2008
10  9  8  7  6  5  4  3  2  1
Printed in the USA

# TRINITY BLOOD™

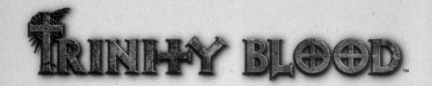

## VOLUME 7

WRITTEN BY
SUNAO YOSHIDA
ILLUSTRATED BY
KIYO KYUJYO

TOKYOPOP®

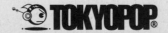

HAMBURG // LONDON // LOS ANGELES // TOKYO

Becomes

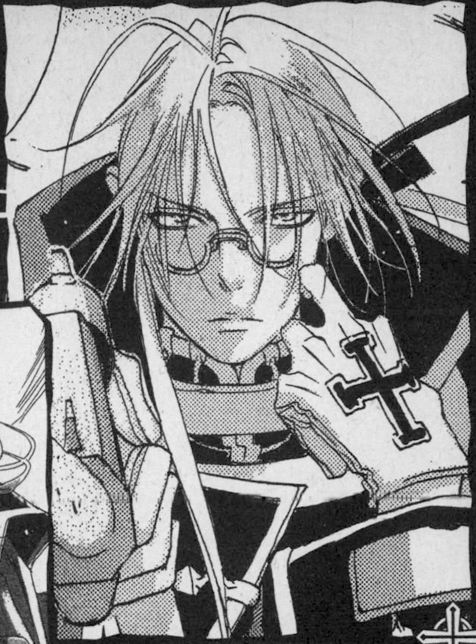

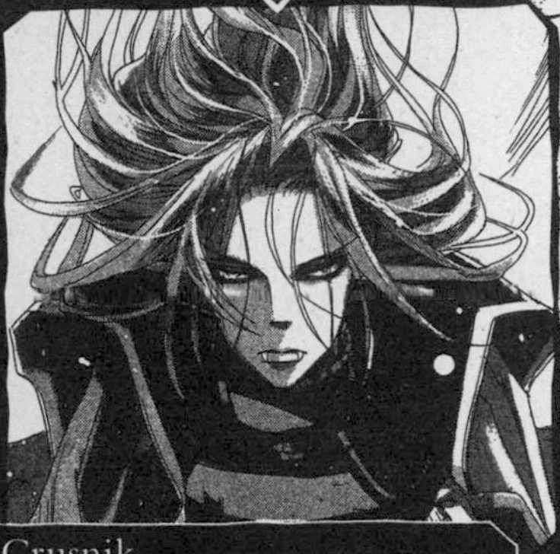

## Crusnik

When Abel's threatened and left with no other means of escape, he transforms into a crusnik, a mysterious vampire who drinks the blood of other vampires and possesses great power.

## Abel Nightroad

An absentminded, destitute traveling priest from the Vatican's secret AX organization. His official title is AX enforcement officer. His job is to arrest law-breaking vampires. And he takes 13 spoonfuls of sugar in his tea.

## Story

In the distant future, civilization has been destroyed by a catastrophe of epic proportions. Mankind is at war with vampires, an alien life form that appeared when the Earth changed. The Methuselah Empire and the Human Vatican attempted to negotiate peace, but were stopped by two forces: the betrayal of Ion, sent by the Emperor of the True Human Empire to parlay with Caterina Sforza, by his erstwhile best friend Radu, and by the martial intervention of the Human Inquisition. Sforza sends Abel and Esther as escorts to bring Ion back to the Empire. Upon his return, however, Ion is falsely accused of murdering his grandmother. To clear himself of the crime, he begs the help of Asthe, a noble of the Empire who is familiar with Abel, and seeks an audience at the highest assembly of the Empire. But it appears that Radu may not be quite as dead as previously believed...

# Characters & Story

## Ion Fortuna

He is the Earl of Memphis of the Tzara Methuselate; the vampire sent as a messenger of the Empire, who has a strong affection for Esther. After returning home, he was framed for the murder of his grandmother.

## Esther Blanchett

A novice nun with a strong sense of justice. After she lost her church and friends in a battle with vampires, she chose action over despair and followed Abel when he said, "I am on your side."

## Radu Barvon

He is the Baron of Luxor of the Tzara Methuselate. He was Ion's "tovarăş" but betrayed him and joined the Rosenkreuz Orden. After a battle with Ion, Radu was thought to be dead.

## Astharoshe Asran

She is the Marquis of Kiev of the Tzara Methuselate; she calls Abel, "tovarăş" since they worked an investigation together in the past. She's known in the Empire as a "Terran Lover."

# CONTENTS

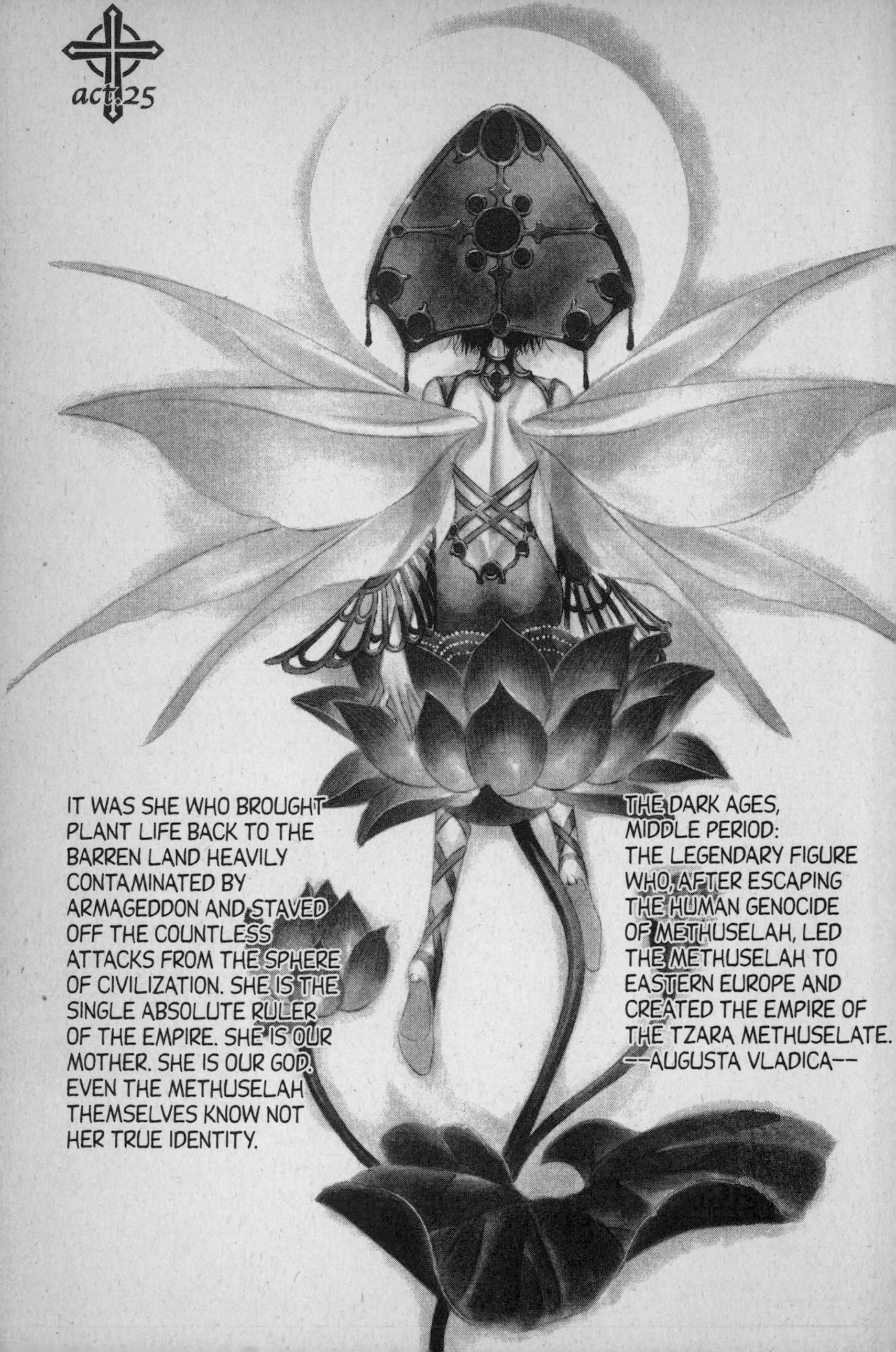
act.25
THE DARK AGES, MIDDLE PERIOD: THE LEGENDARY FIGURE WHO, AFTER ESCAPING THE HUMAN GENOCIDE OF METHUSELAH, LED THE METHUSELAH TO EASTERN EUROPE AND CREATED THE EMPIRE OF THE TZARA METHUSELATE.
--AUGUSTA VLADICA--
IT WAS SHE WHO BROUGHT PLANT LIFE BACK TO THE BARREN LAND HEAVILY CONTAMINATED BY ARMAGEDDON AND STAVED OFF THE COUNTLESS ATTACKS FROM THE SPHERE OF CIVILIZATION. SHE IS THE SINGLE ABSOLUTE RULER OF THE EMPIRE. SHE IS OUR MOTHER. SHE IS OUR GOD. EVEN THE METHUSELAH THEMSELVES KNOW NOT HER TRUE IDENTITY.

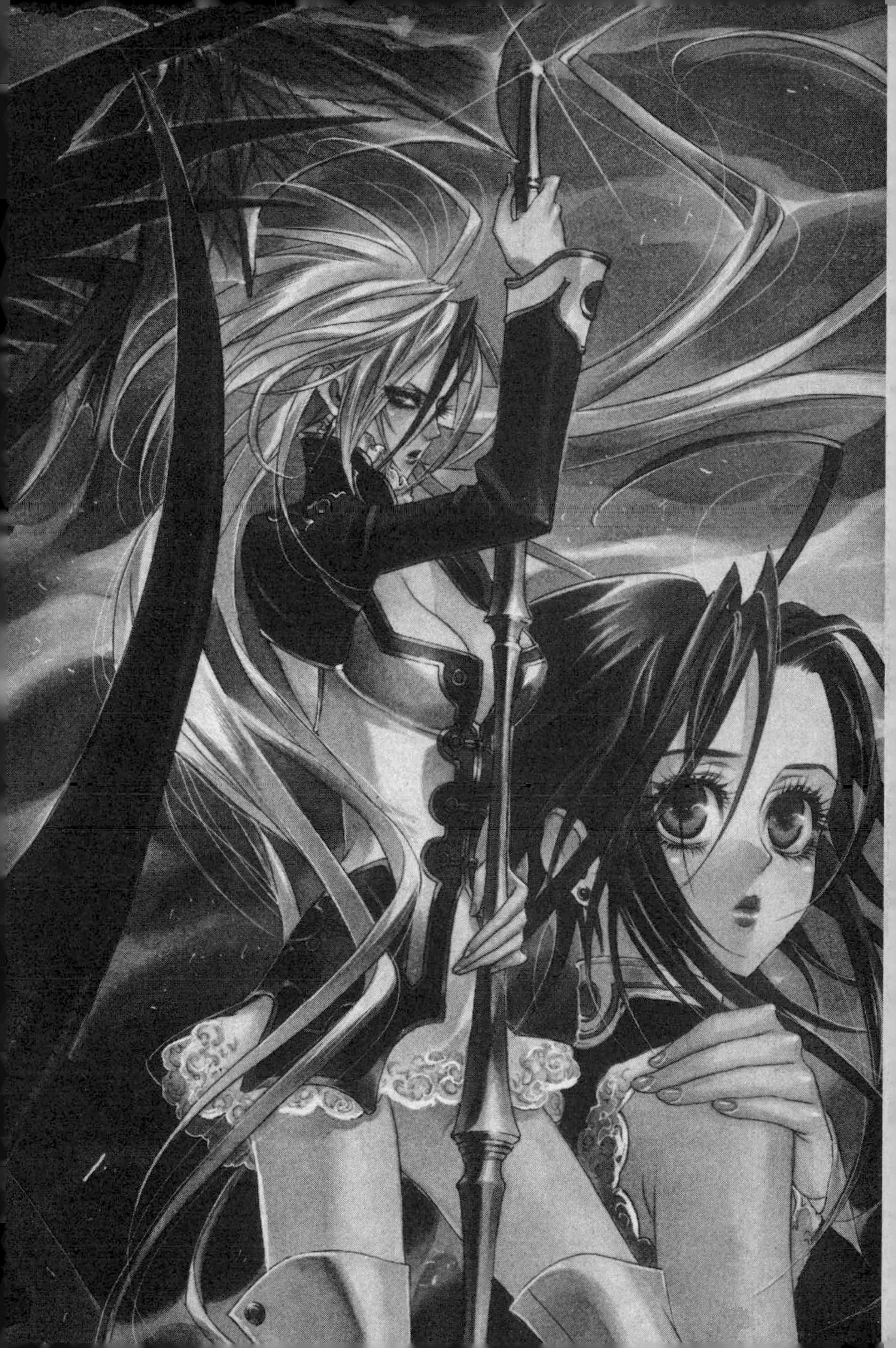

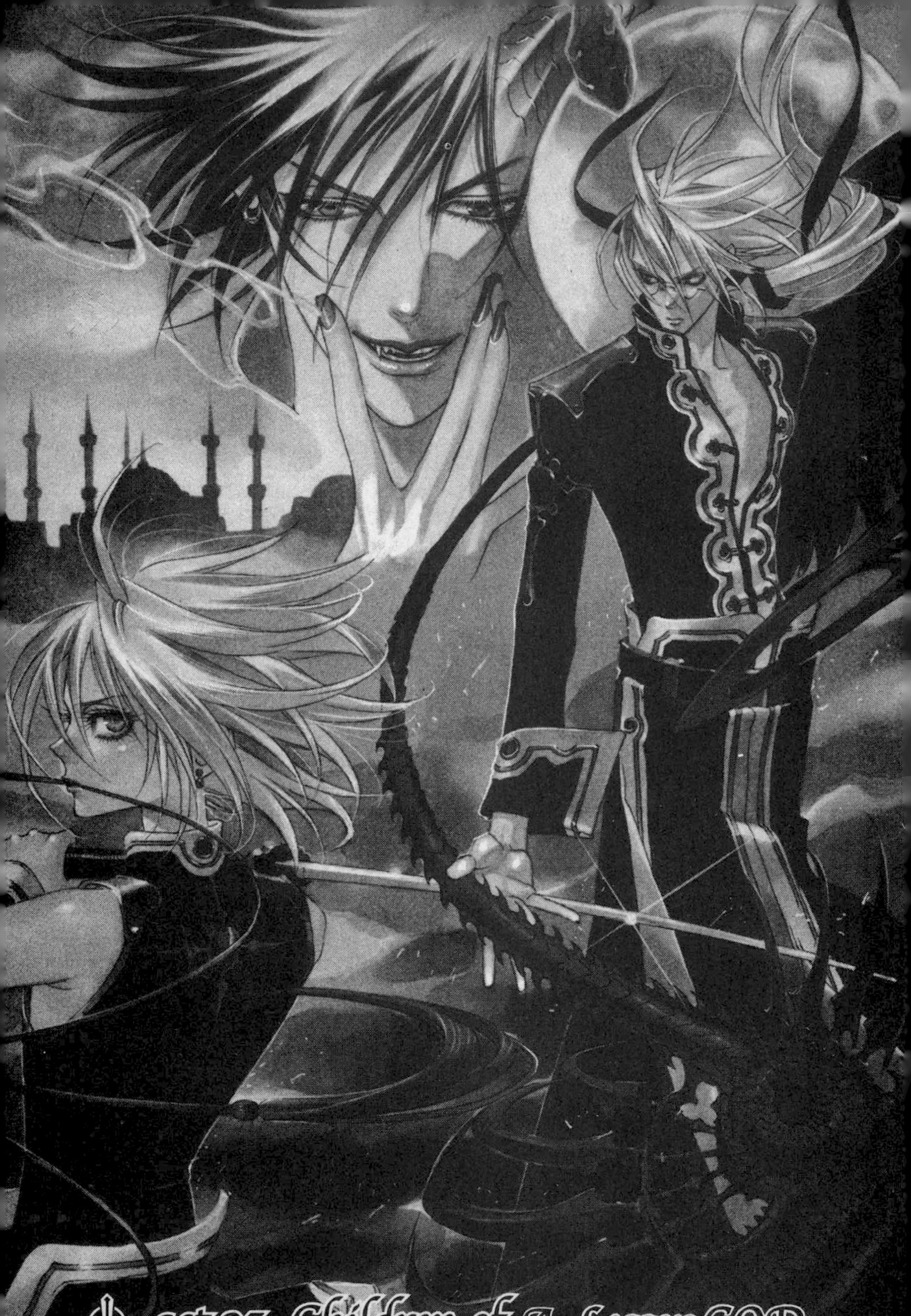

act.25 Children of A Lesser GOD

TRINITY BLOOD

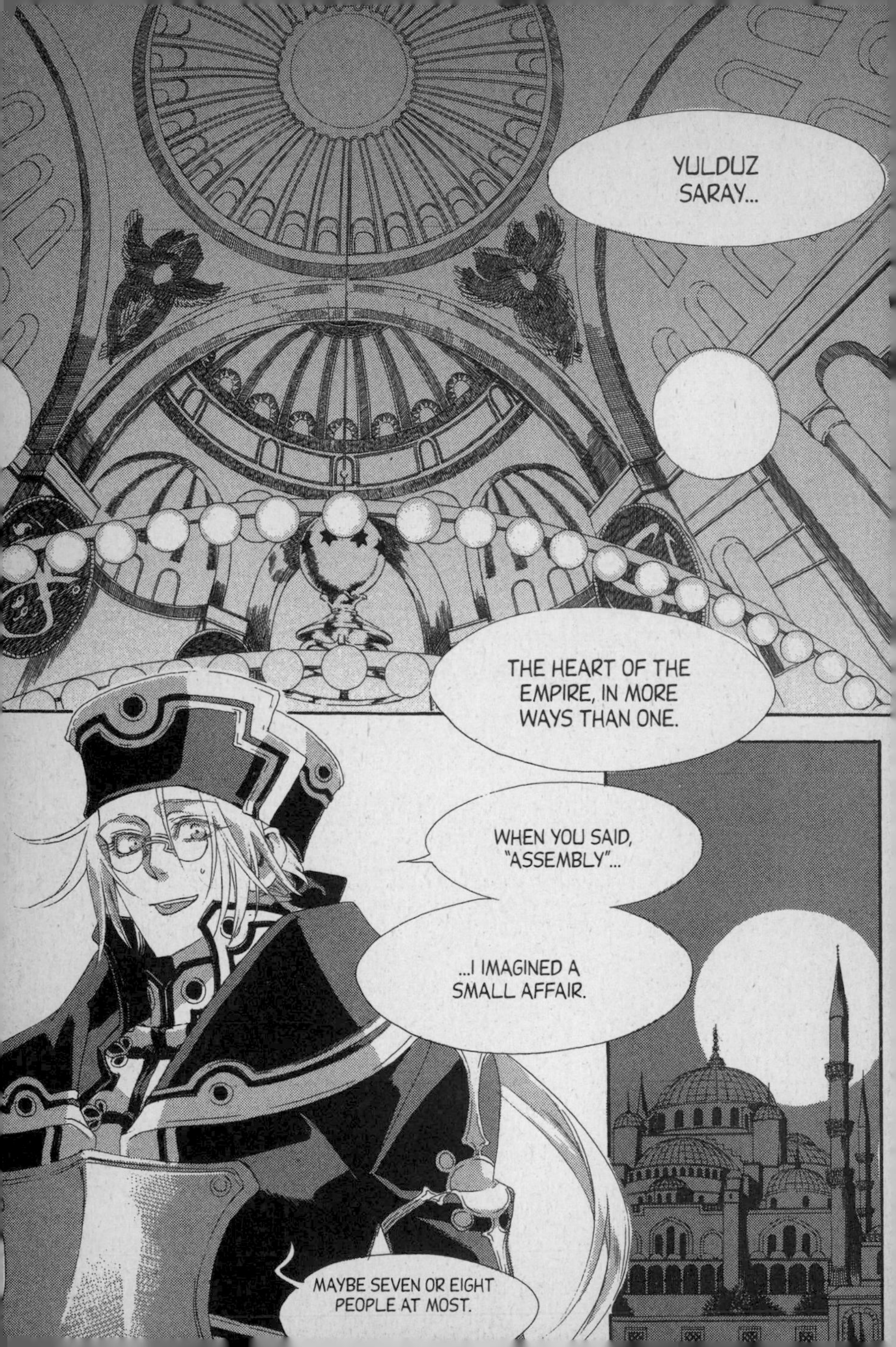
YULDUZ SARAY...
THE HEART OF THE EMPIRE, IN MORE WAYS THAN ONE.
WHEN YOU SAID, "ASSEMBLY"...
...I IMAGINED A SMALL AFFAIR.
MAYBE SEVEN OR EIGHT PEOPLE AT MOST.

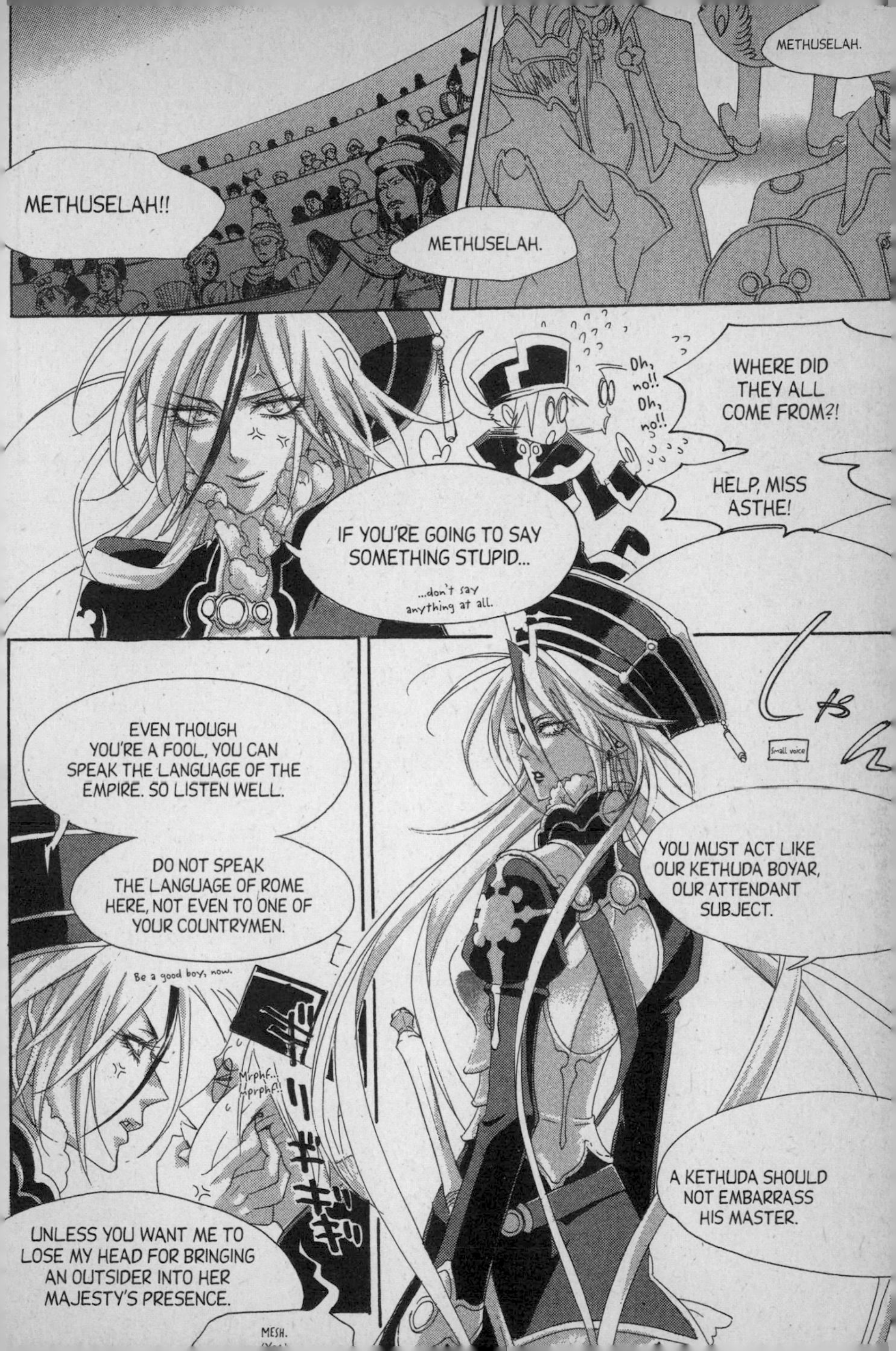
METHUSELAH.
METHUSELAH.
METHUSELAH!!
WHERE DID THEY ALL COME FROM?!
Oh, no!! Oh, no!!
HELP, MISS ASTHE!
IF YOU'RE GOING TO SAY SOMETHING STUPID...
...don't say anything at all.
Small voice
YOU MUST ACT LIKE OUR KETHUDA BOYAR, OUR ATTENDANT SUBJECT.
A KETHUDA SHOULD NOT EMBARRASS HIS MASTER.
EVEN THOUGH YOU'RE A FOOL, YOU CAN SPEAK THE LANGUAGE OF THE EMPIRE. SO LISTEN WELL.
DO NOT SPEAK THE LANGUAGE OF ROME HERE, NOT EVEN TO ONE OF YOUR COUNTRYMEN.
Be a good boy, now.
Mrphf... Mrphf!!
UNLESS YOU WANT ME TO LOSE MY HEAD FOR BRINGING AN OUTSIDER INTO HER MAJESTY'S PRESENCE.
MESH.

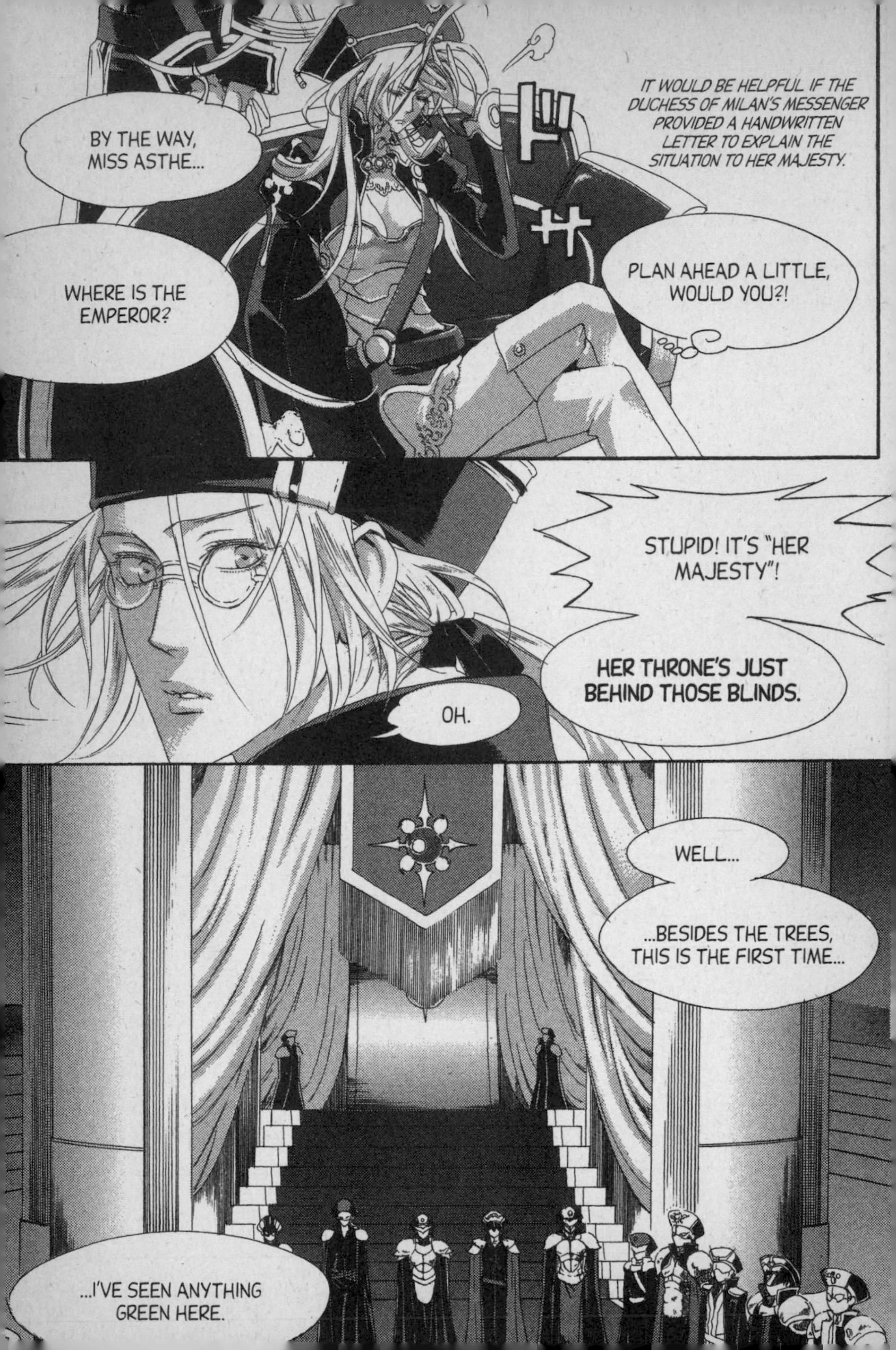
BY THE WAY, MISS ASTHE...
WHERE IS THE EMPEROR?
IT WOULD BE HELPFUL IF THE DUCHESS OF MILAN'S MESSENGER PROVIDED A HANDWRITTEN LETTER TO EXPLAIN THE SITUATION TO HER MAJESTY.
PLAN AHEAD A LITTLE, WOULD YOU?!
STUPID! IT'S "HER MAJESTY"!
HER THRONE'S JUST BEHIND THOSE BLINDS.
OH.
WELL...
...BESIDES THE TREES, THIS IS THE FIRST TIME...
...I'VE SEEN ANYTHING GREEN HERE.

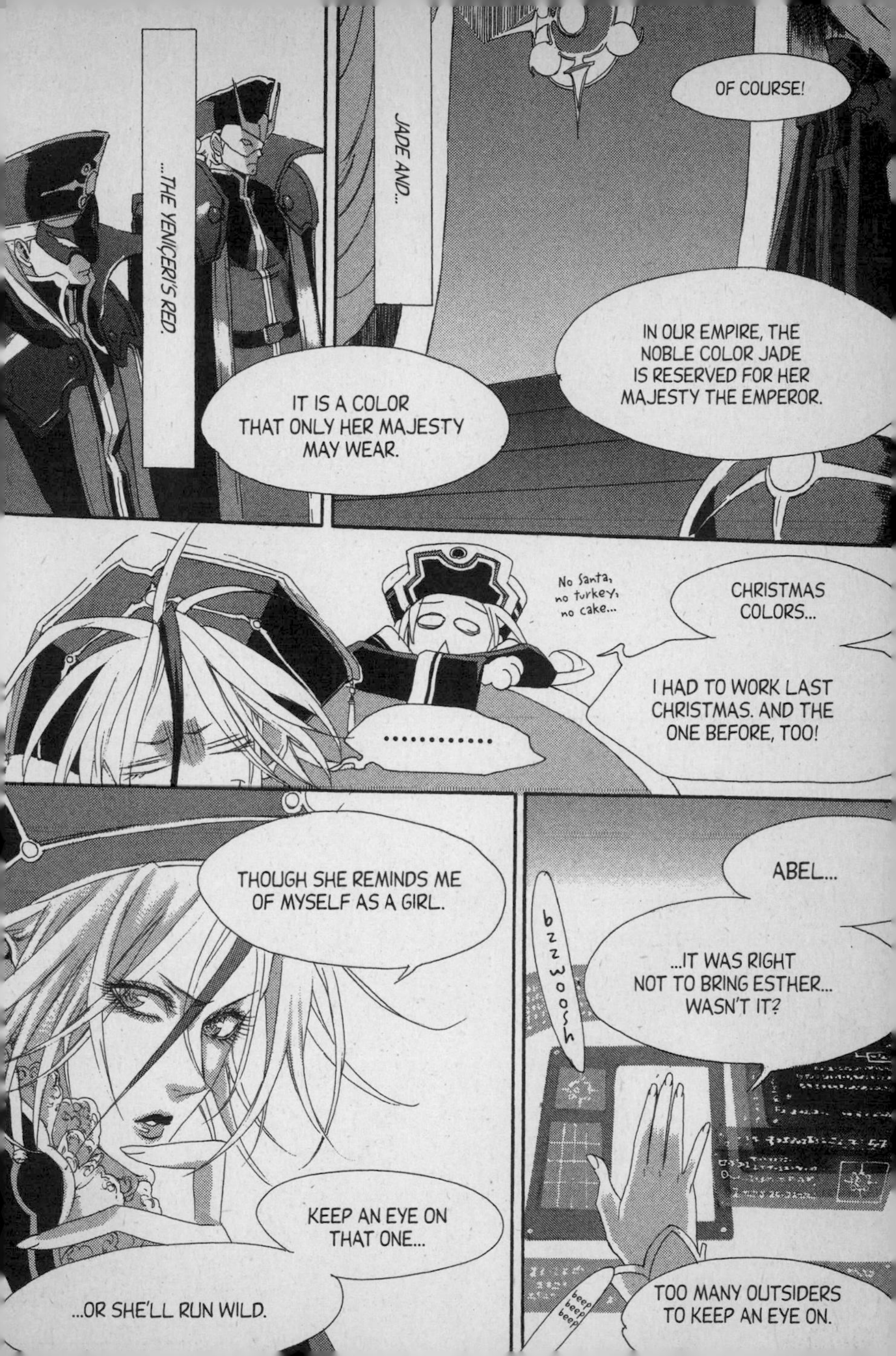
JADE AND...
...THE YENIÇERI'S RED.
OF COURSE!
IN OUR EMPIRE, THE NOBLE COLOR JADE IS RESERVED FOR HER MAJESTY THE EMPEROR.
IT IS A COLOR THAT ONLY HER MAJESTY MAY WEAR.
CHRISTMAS COLORS...
No Santa, no turkey, no cake...
I HAD TO WORK LAST CHRISTMAS. AND THE ONE BEFORE, TOO!
............
THOUGH SHE REMINDS ME OF MYSELF AS A GIRL.
KEEP AN EYE ON THAT ONE...
...OR SHE'LL RUN WILD.
ABEL...
bzzwoosh
...IT WAS RIGHT NOT TO BRING ESTHER... WASN'T IT?
beep beep beep
TOO MANY OUTSIDERS TO KEEP AN EYE ON.

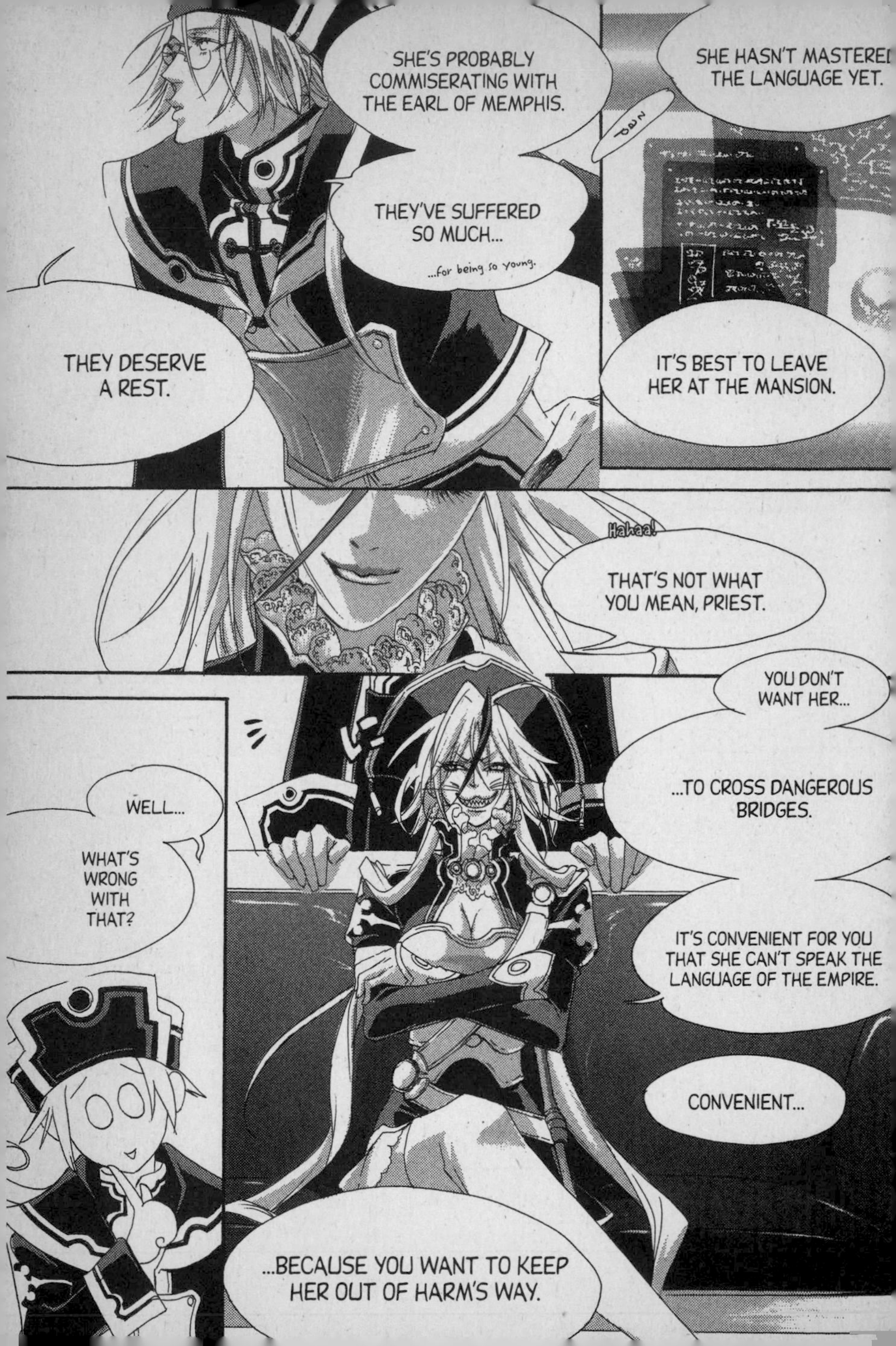

SHE HASN'T MASTERED THE LANGUAGE YET.
DOWN
IT'S BEST TO LEAVE HER AT THE MANSION.
SHE'S PROBABLY COMMISERATING WITH THE EARL OF MEMPHIS.
THEY'VE SUFFERED SO MUCH...
...for being so young.
THEY DESERVE A REST.
Hahaa!
THAT'S NOT WHAT YOU MEAN, PRIEST.
YOU DON'T WANT HER...
...TO CROSS DANGEROUS BRIDGES.
IT'S CONVENIENT FOR YOU THAT SHE CAN'T SPEAK THE LANGUAGE OF THE EMPIRE.
CONVENIENT...
...BECAUSE YOU WANT TO KEEP HER OUT OF HARM'S WAY.
WELL...
WHAT'S WRONG WITH THAT?

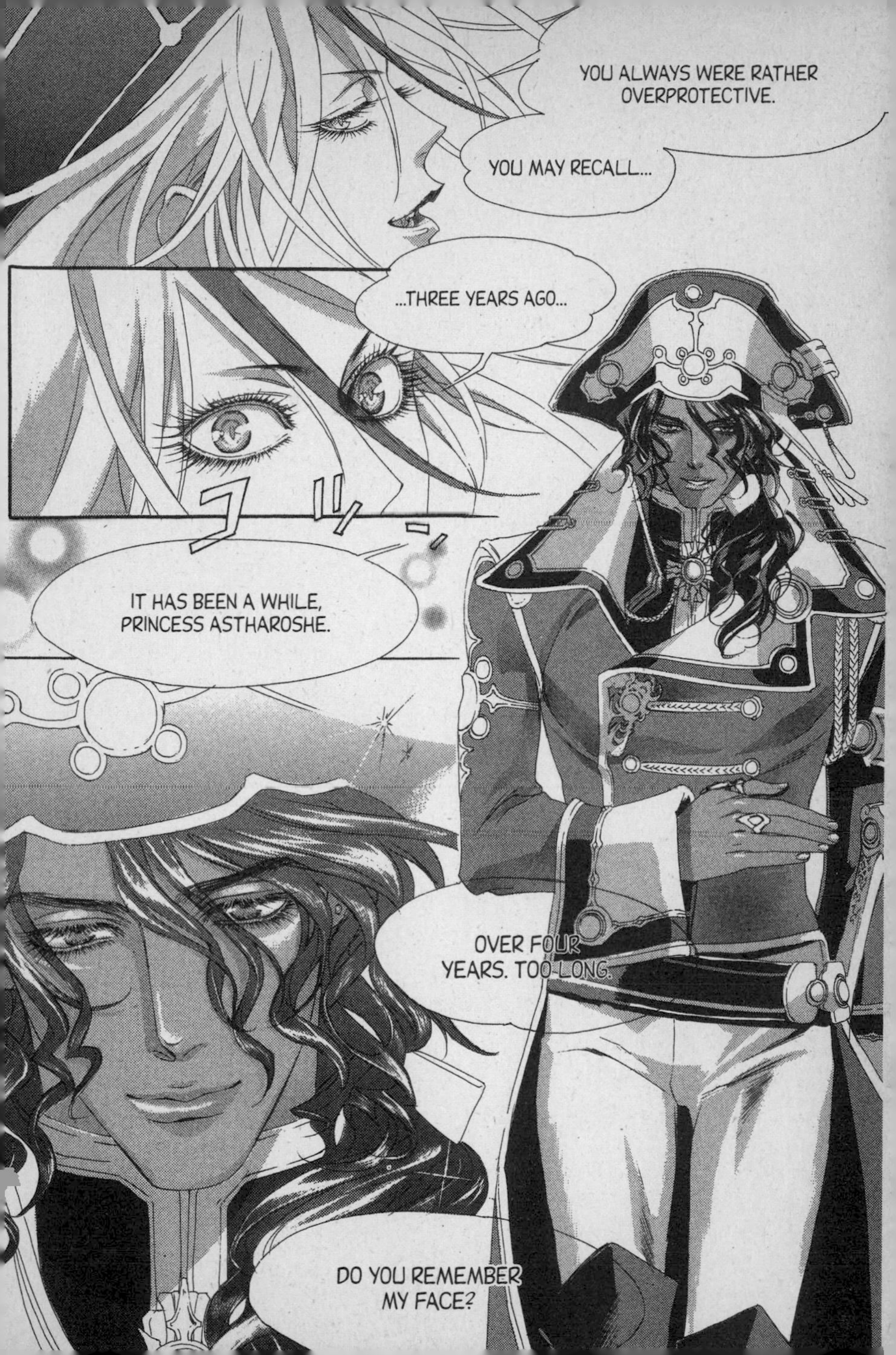
YOU ALWAYS WERE RATHER OVERPROTECTIVE.
YOU MAY RECALL...
...THREE YEARS AGO...
IT HAS BEEN A WHILE, PRINCESS ASTHAROSHE.
OVER FOUR YEARS. TOO LONG.
DO YOU REMEMBER MY FACE?

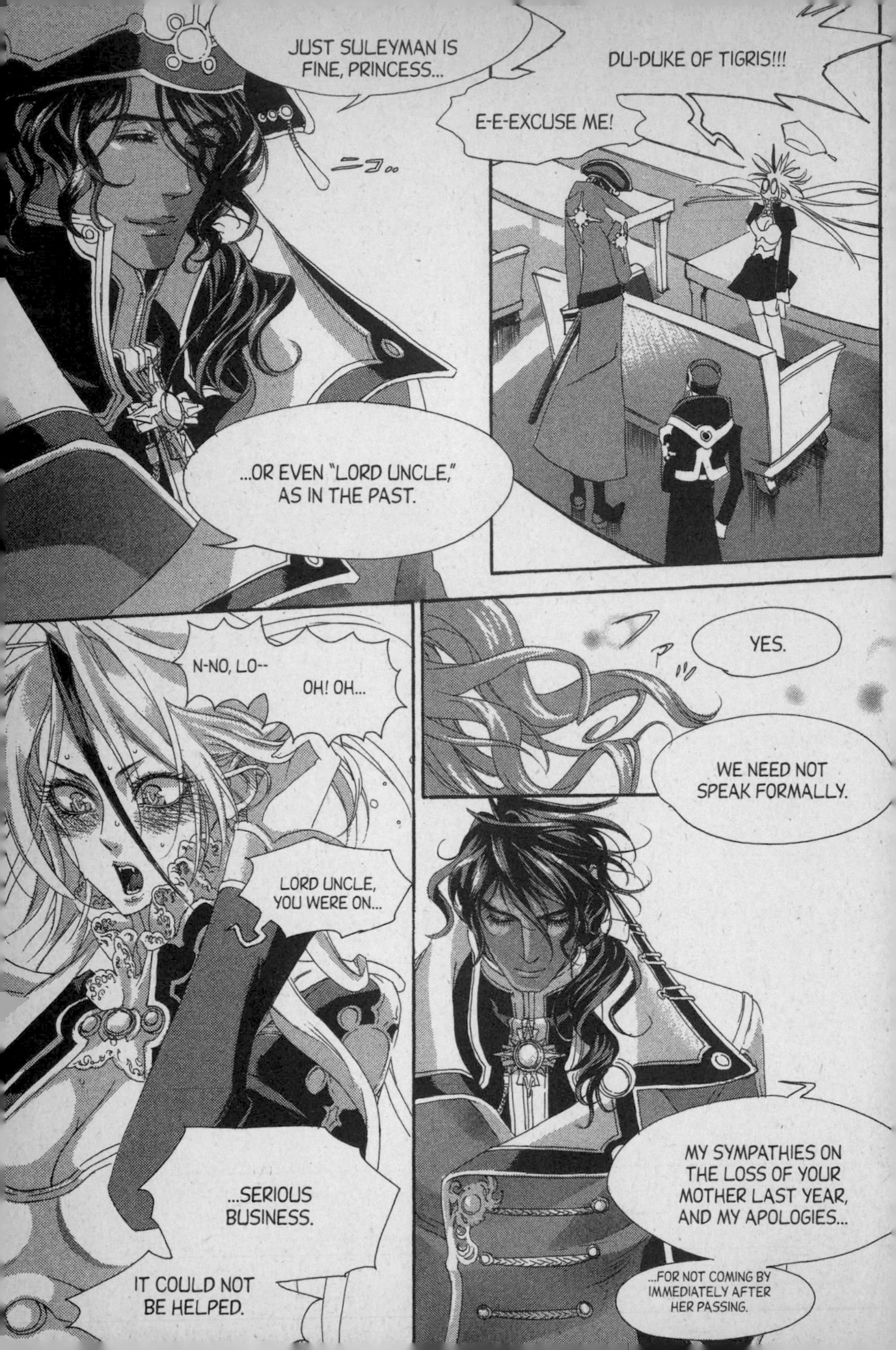
DU-DUKE OF TIGRIS!!!
E-E-EXCUSE ME!
JUST SULEYMAN IS FINE, PRINCESS...
...OR EVEN "LORD UNCLE," AS IN THE PAST.
N-NO, LO--
OH! OH...
YES.
WE NEED NOT SPEAK FORMALLY.
MY SYMPATHIES ON THE LOSS OF YOUR MOTHER LAST YEAR, AND MY APOLOGIES...
...FOR NOT COMING BY IMMEDIATELY AFTER HER PASSING.
LORD UNCLE, YOU WERE ON...
...SERIOUS BUSINESS.
IT COULD NOT BE HELPED.

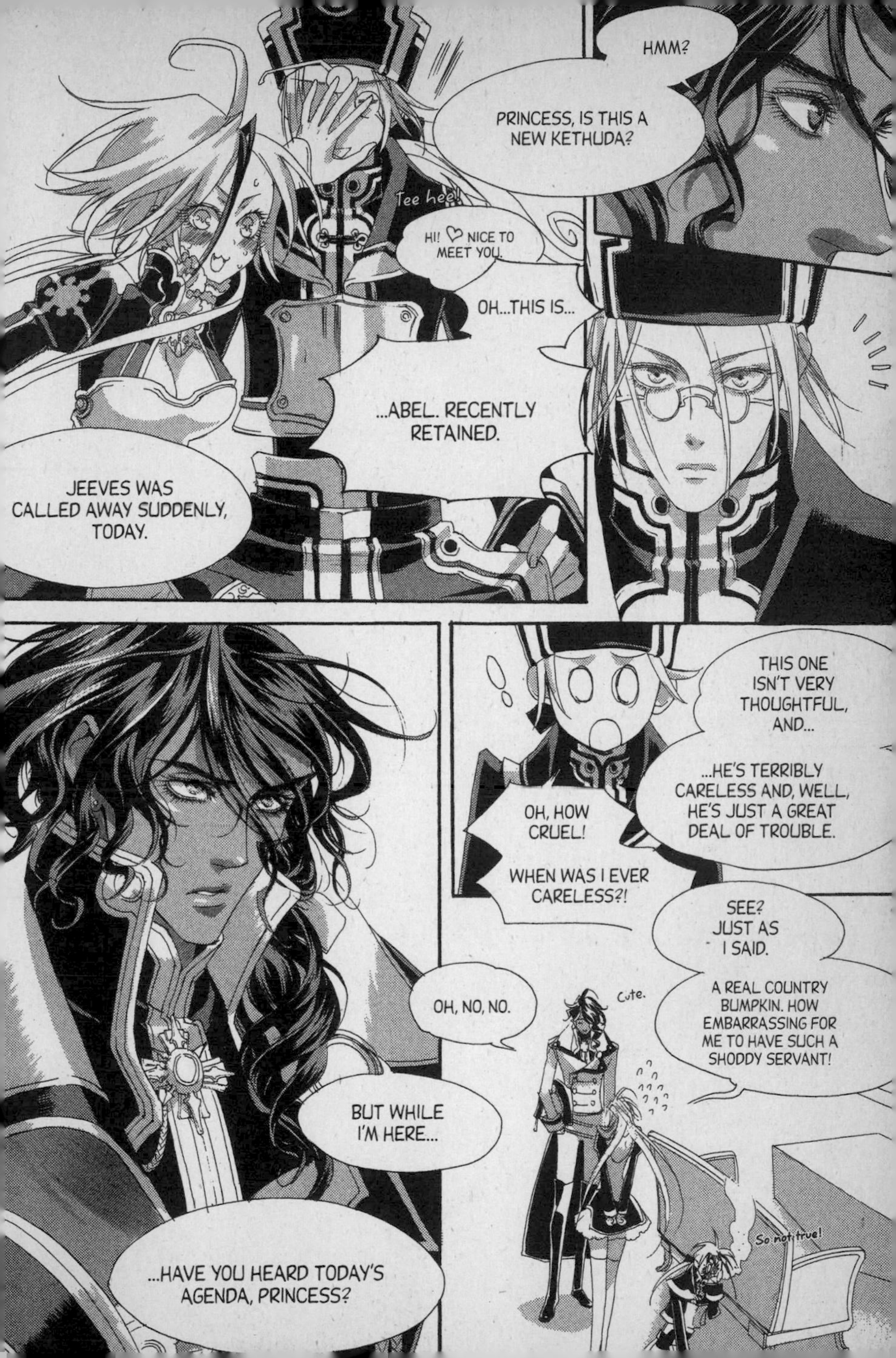
HMM?
PRINCESS, IS THIS A NEW KETHUDA?
OH...THIS IS...
...ABEL. RECENTLY RETAINED.
Tee hee!
HI! ♡ NICE TO MEET YOU.
JEEVES WAS CALLED AWAY SUDDENLY, TODAY.
THIS ONE ISN'T VERY THOUGHTFUL, AND...
...HE'S TERRIBLY CARELESS AND, WELL, HE'S JUST A GREAT DEAL OF TROUBLE.
OH, HOW CRUEL!
WHEN WAS I EVER CARELESS?!
SEE? JUST AS I SAID.
A REAL COUNTRY BUMPKIN. HOW EMBARRASSING FOR ME TO HAVE SUCH A SHODDY SERVANT!
Cute.
So not true!
OH, NO, NO.
BUT WHILE I'M HERE...
...HAVE YOU HEARD TODAY'S AGENDA, PRINCESS?

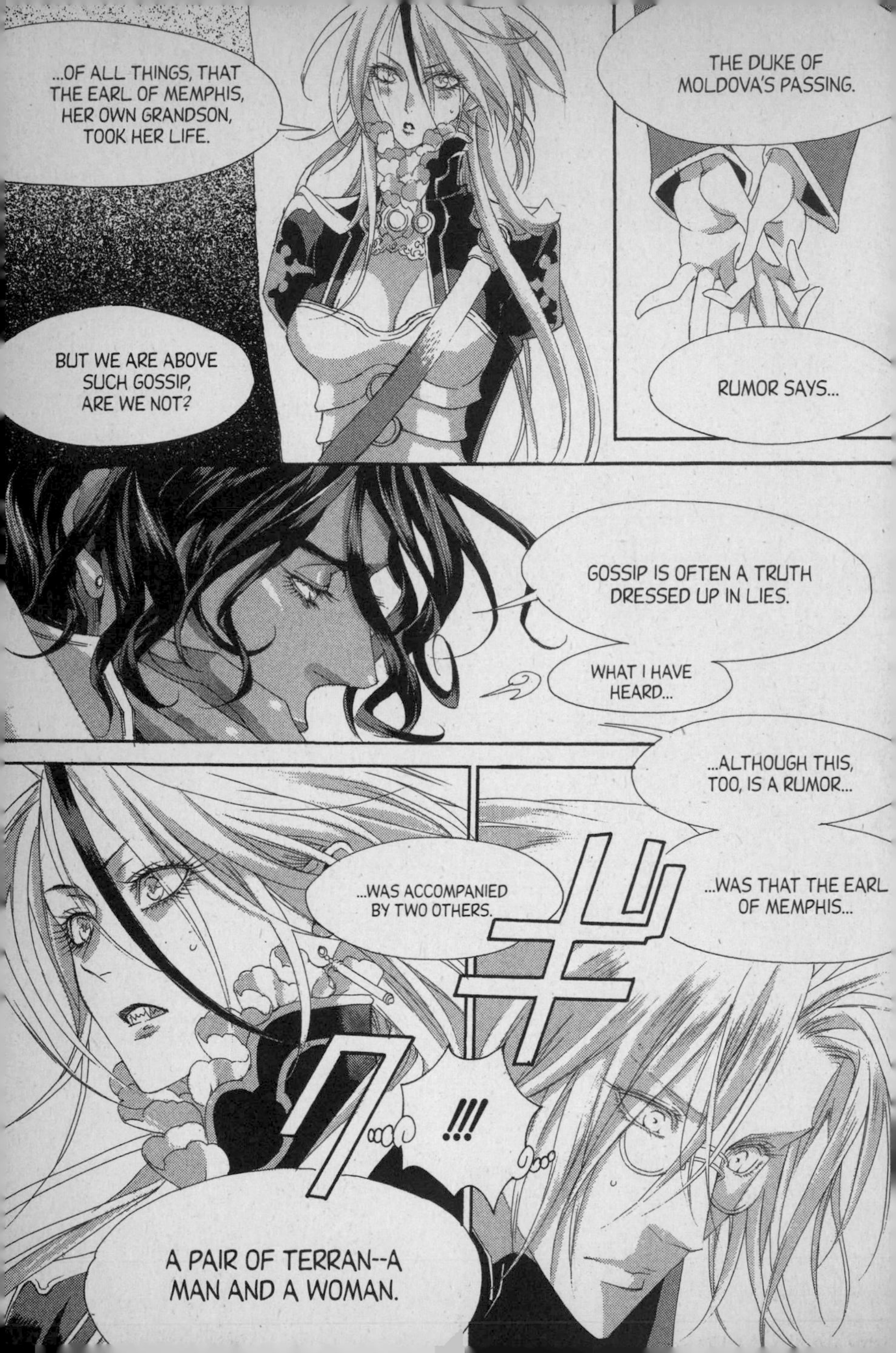
THE DUKE OF MOLDOVA'S PASSING.
RUMOR SAYS...
...OF ALL THINGS, THAT THE EARL OF MEMPHIS, HER OWN GRANDSON, TOOK HER LIFE.
BUT WE ARE ABOVE SUCH GOSSIP, ARE WE NOT?
GOSSIP IS OFTEN A TRUTH DRESSED UP IN LIES.
WHAT I HAVE HEARD...
...ALTHOUGH THIS, TOO, IS A RUMOR...
...WAS THAT THE EARL OF MEMPHIS...
...WAS ACCOMPANIED BY TWO OTHERS.
!!!
A PAIR OF TERRAN--A MAN AND A WOMAN.

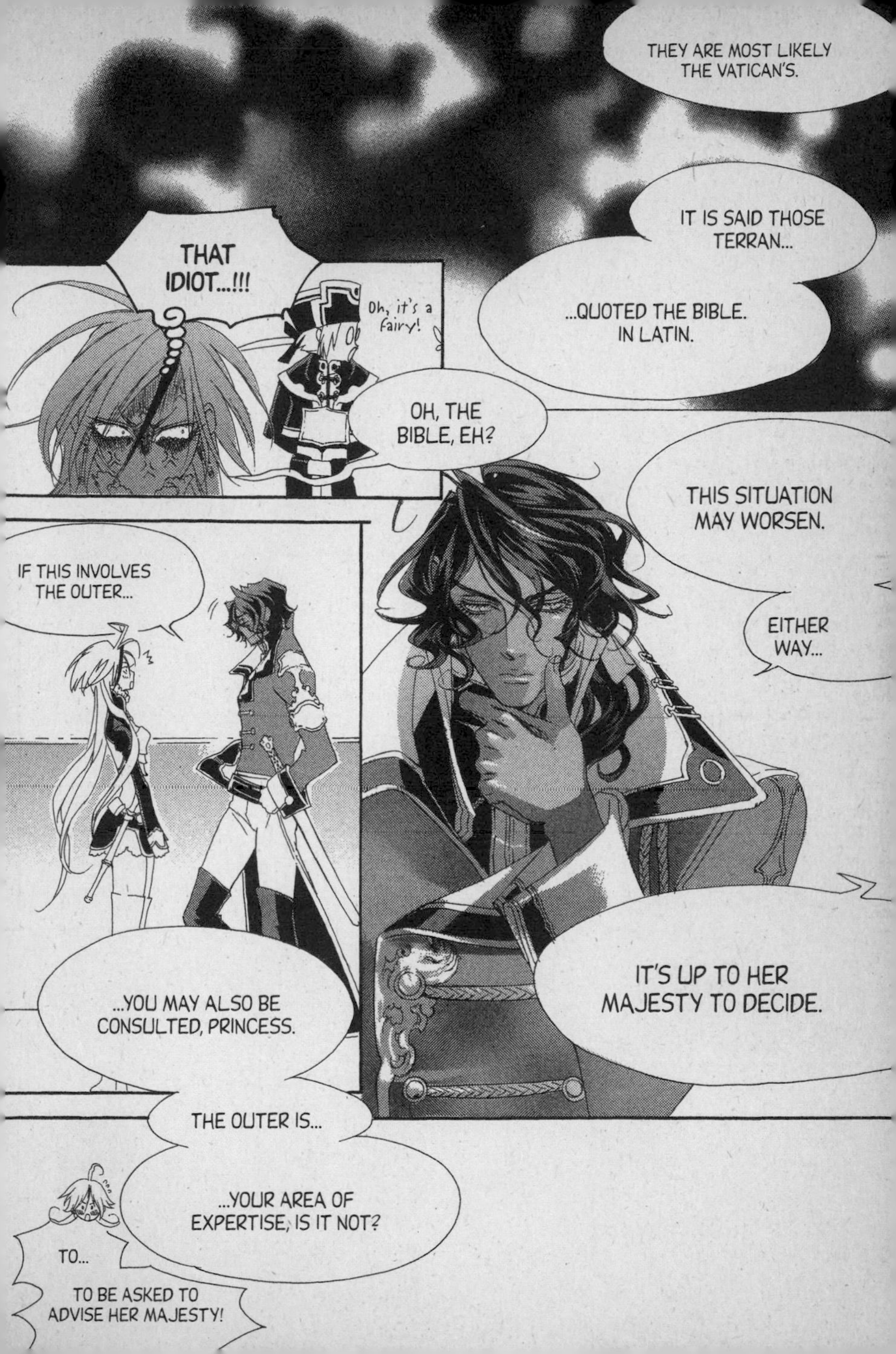
THEY ARE MOST LIKELY THE VATICAN'S.
IT IS SAID THOSE TERRAN...
...QUOTED THE BIBLE. IN LATIN.
THAT IDIOT...!!!
Oh, it's a fairy!
OH, THE BIBLE, EH?
THIS SITUATION MAY WORSEN.
EITHER WAY...
IT'S UP TO HER MAJESTY TO DECIDE.
IF THIS INVOLVES THE OUTER...
...YOU MAY ALSO BE CONSULTED, PRINCESS.
THE OUTER IS...
...YOUR AREA OF EXPERTISE, IS IT NOT?
TO...
TO BE ASKED TO ADVISE HER MAJESTY!

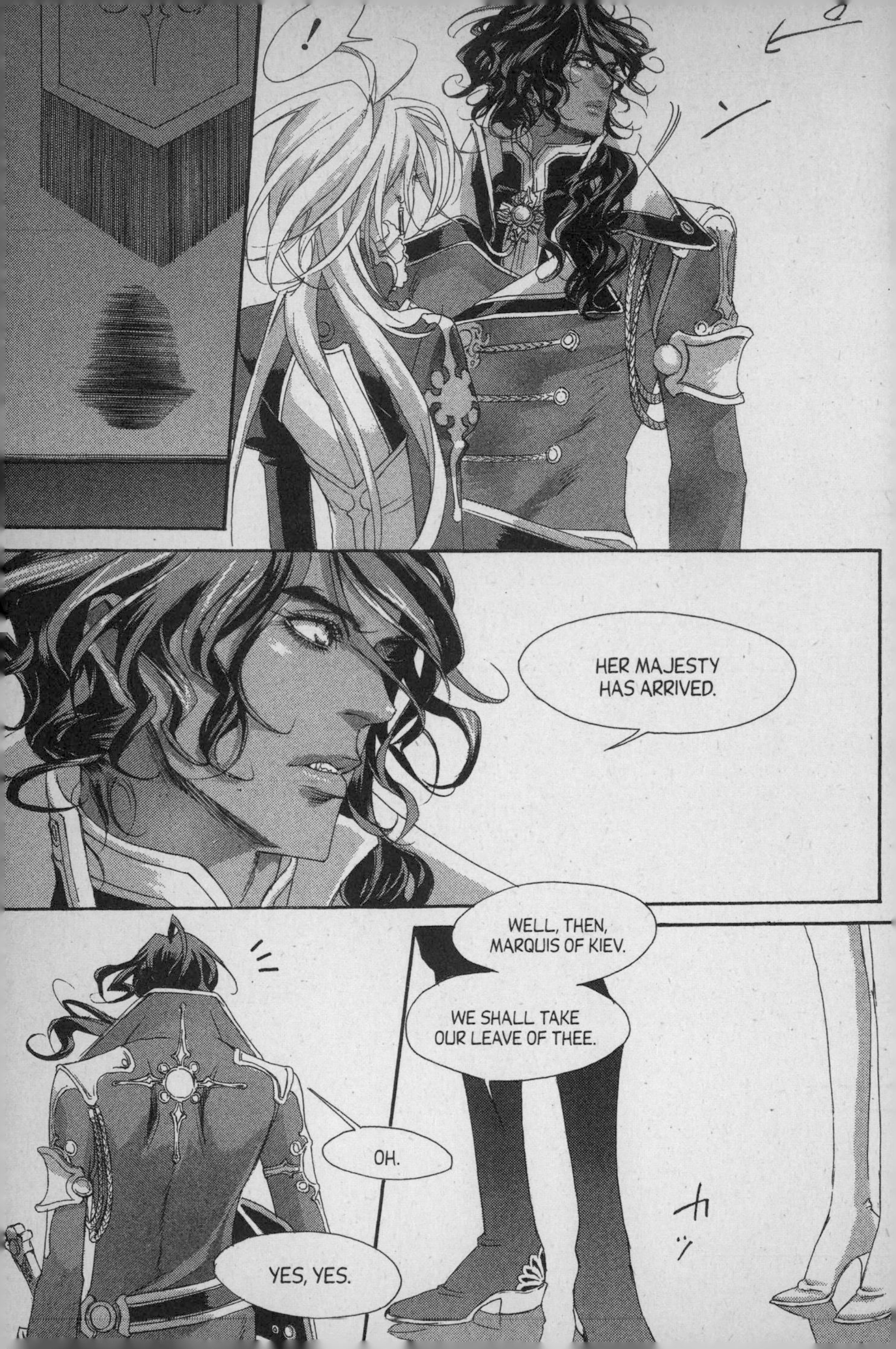
!
HER MAJESTY HAS ARRIVED.
WELL, THEN, MARQUIS OF KIEV.
WE SHALL TAKE OUR LEAVE OF THEE.
OH.
YES, YES.

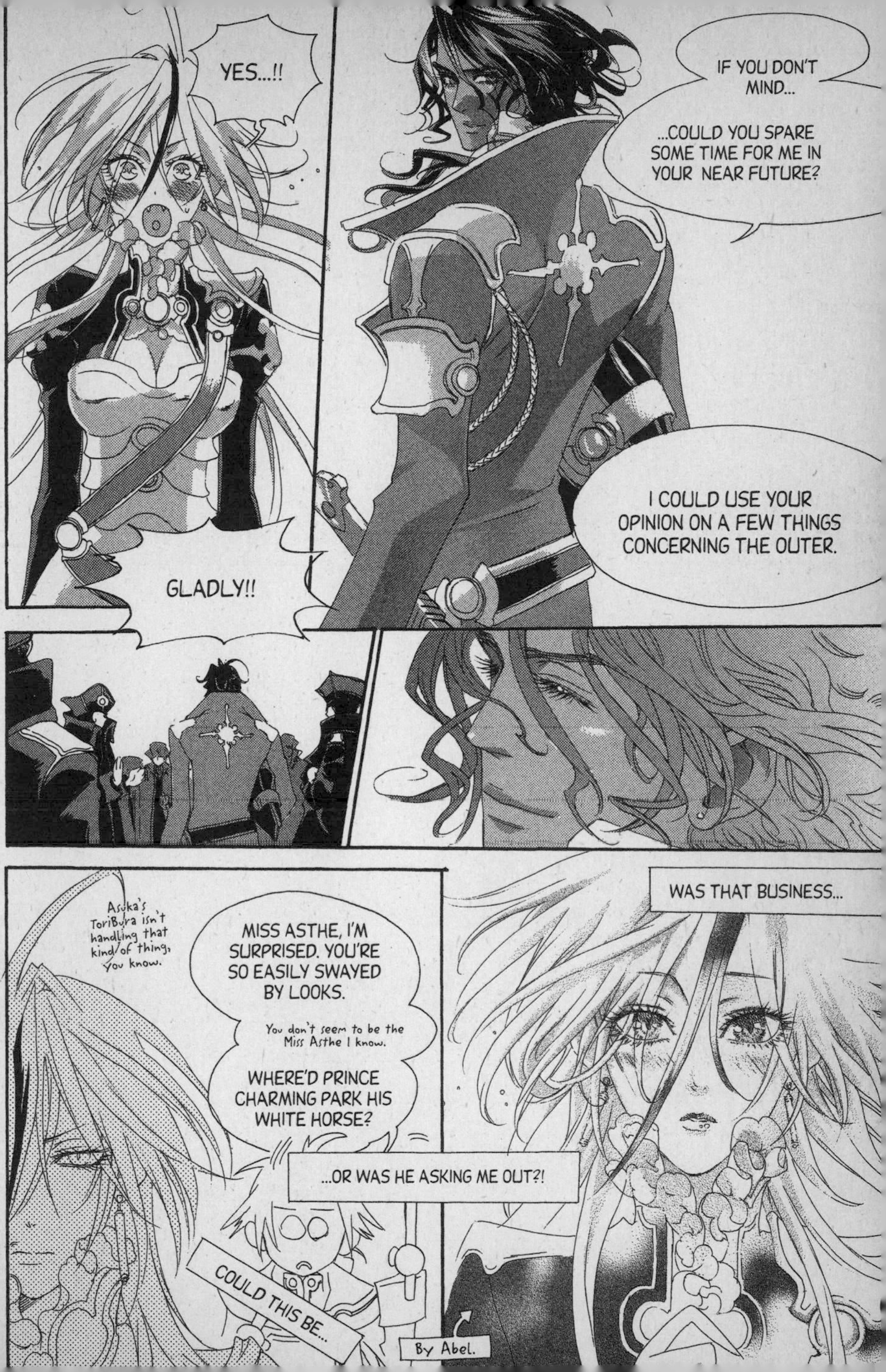
YES...!!
GLADLY!!
IF YOU DON'T MIND...
...COULD YOU SPARE SOME TIME FOR ME IN YOUR NEAR FUTURE?
I COULD USE YOUR OPINION ON A FEW THINGS CONCERNING THE OUTER.
Asuka's ToriBura isn't handling that kind of thing, you know.
MISS ASTHE, I'M SURPRISED. YOU'RE SO EASILY SWAYED BY LOOKS.
You don't seem to be the Miss Asthe I know.
WHERE'D PRINCE CHARMING PARK HIS WHITE HORSE?
COULD THIS BE...
By Abel.
WAS THAT BUSINESS...
...OR WAS HE ASKING ME OUT?!

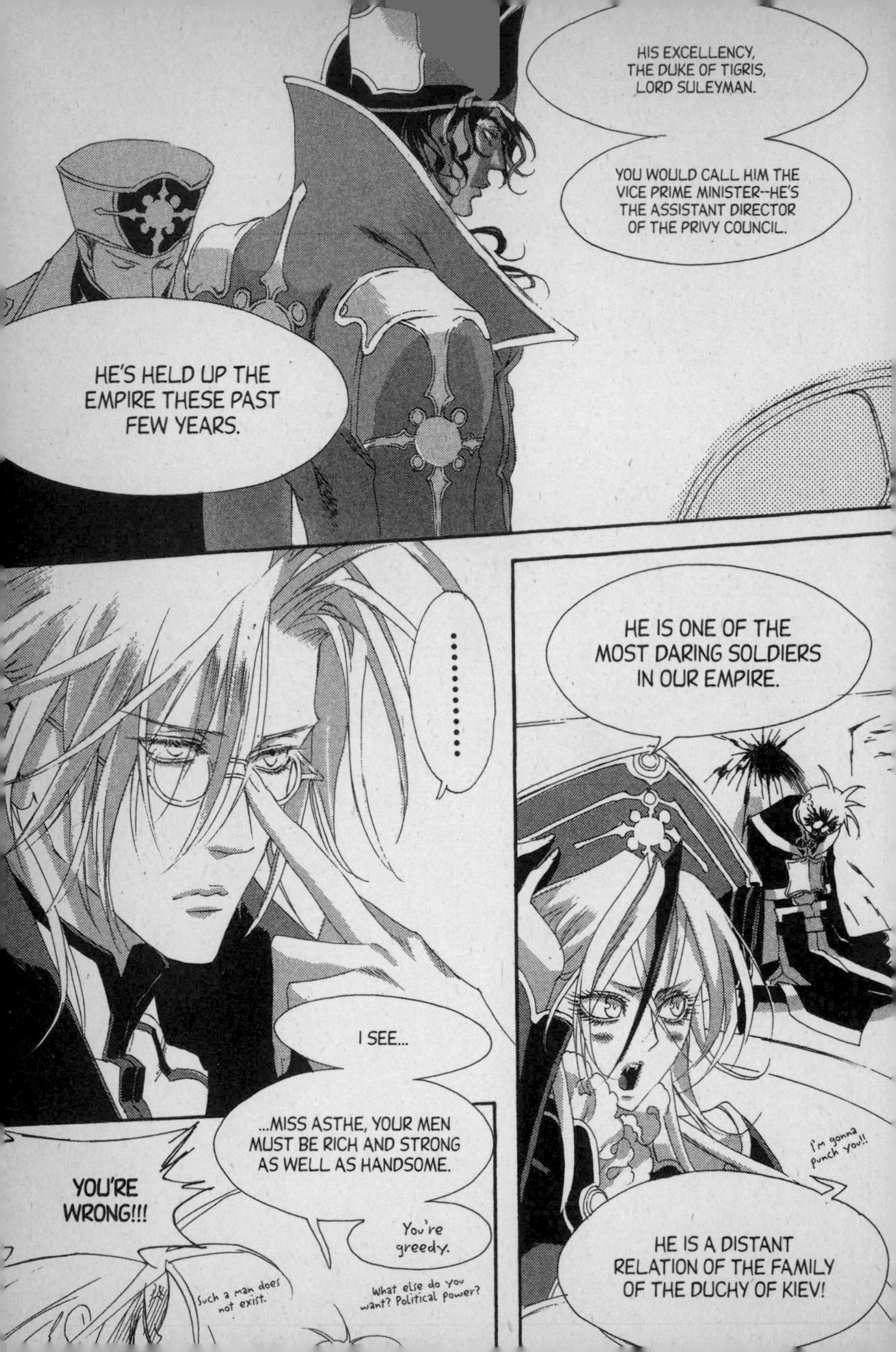
HIS EXCELLENCY, THE DUKE OF TIGRIS, LORD SULEYMAN.
YOU WOULD CALL HIM THE VICE PRIME MINISTER--HE'S THE ASSISTANT DIRECTOR OF THE PRIVY COUNCIL.
HE'S HELD UP THE EMPIRE THESE PAST FEW YEARS.
HE IS ONE OF THE MOST DARING SOLDIERS IN OUR EMPIRE.
.........
I SEE...
...MISS ASTHE, YOUR MEN MUST BE RICH AND STRONG AS WELL AS HANDSOME.
You're greedy.
What else do you want? Political power?
YOU'RE WRONG!!!
Such a man does not exist.
HE IS A DISTANT RELATION OF THE FAMILY OF THE DUCHY OF KIEV!
I'm gonna punch you!!

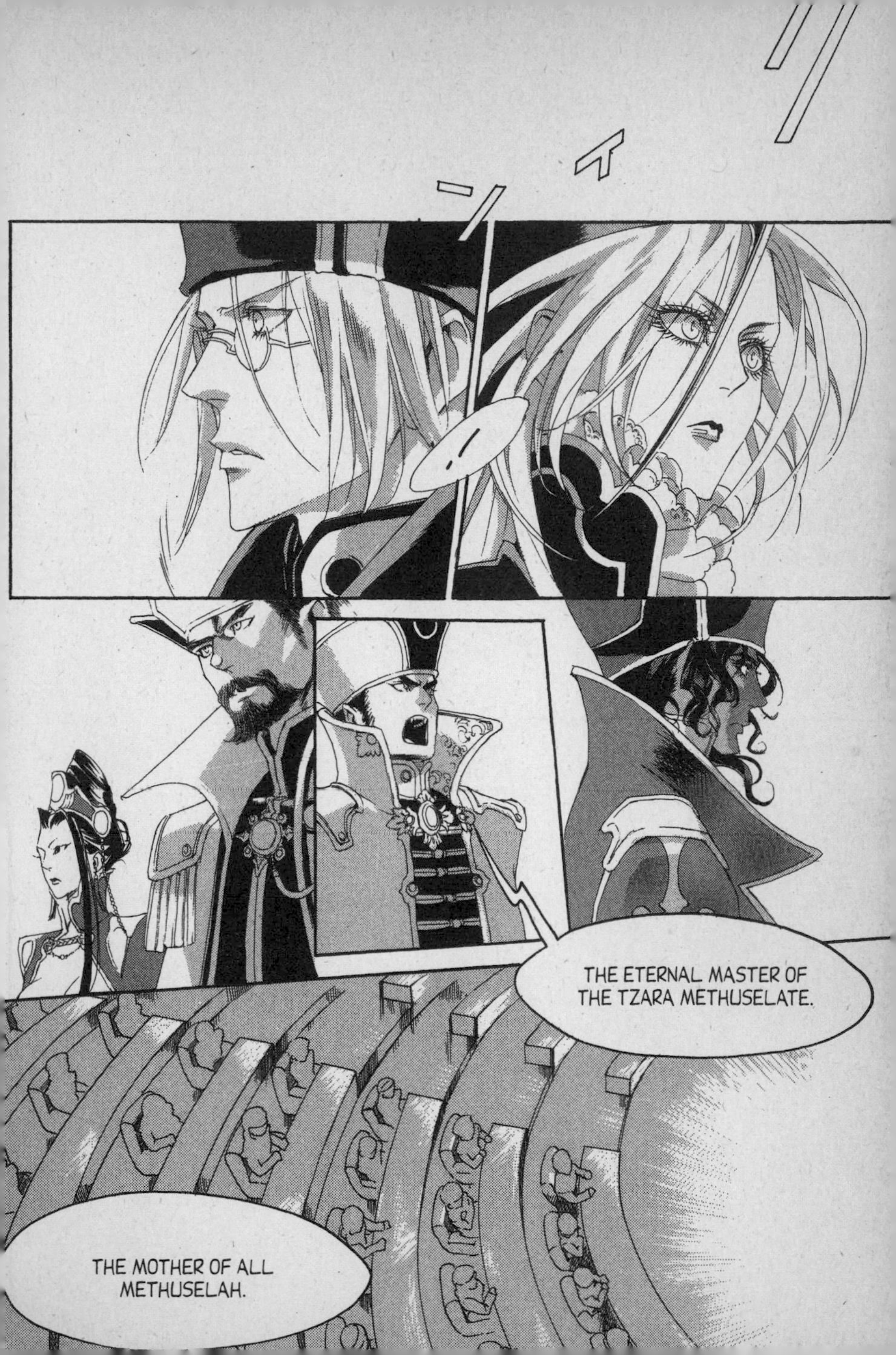
THE ETERNAL MASTER OF THE TZARA METHUSELATE.
THE MOTHER OF ALL METHUSELAH.

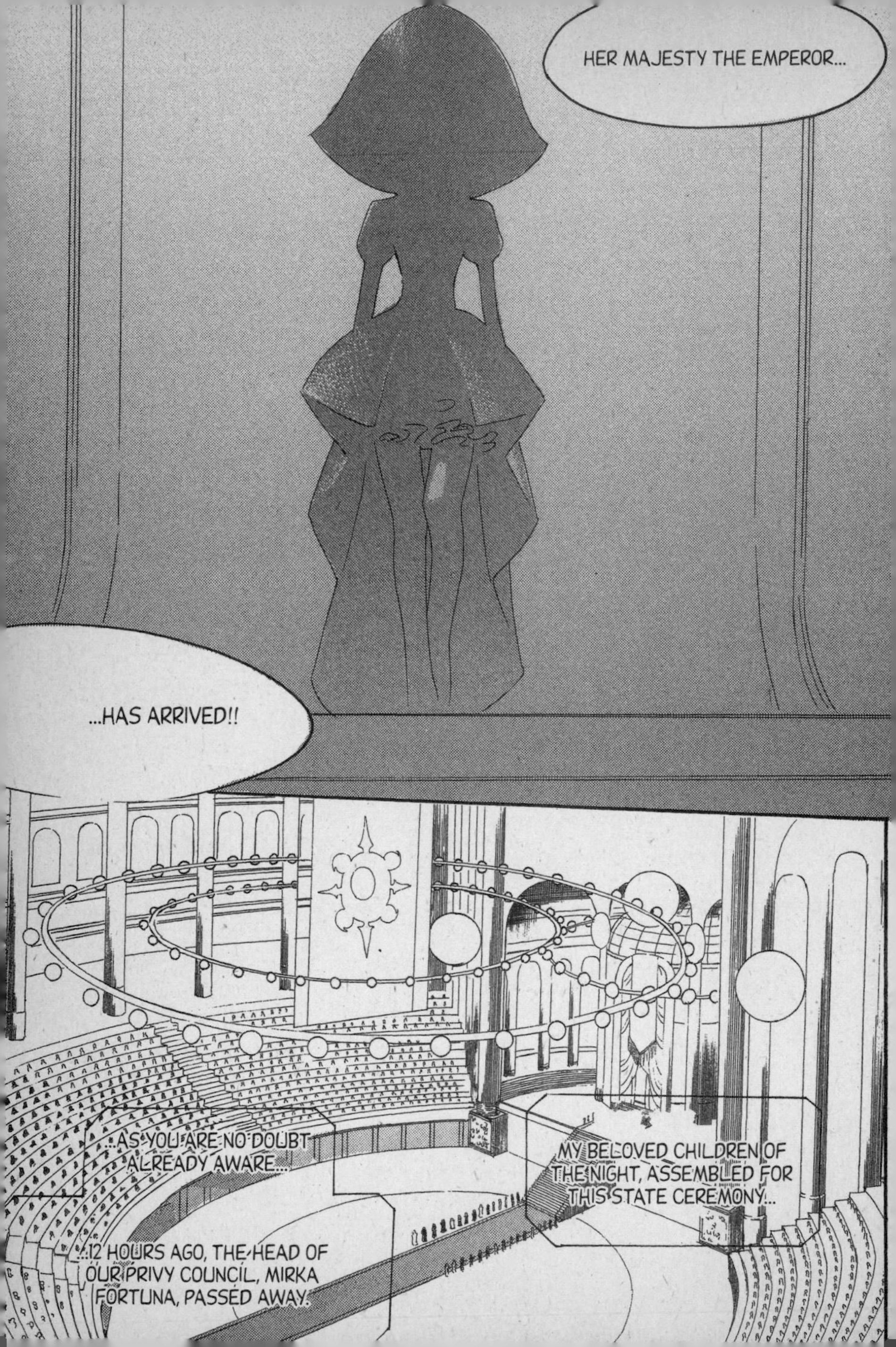
HER MAJESTY THE EMPEROR...
...HAS ARRIVED!!
MY BELOVED CHILDREN OF THE NIGHT, ASSEMBLED FOR THIS STATE CEREMONY...
...AS YOU ARE NO DOUBT ALREADY AWARE...
...12 HOURS AGO, THE HEAD OF OUR PRIVY COUNCIL, MIRKA FORTUNA, PASSED AWAY.

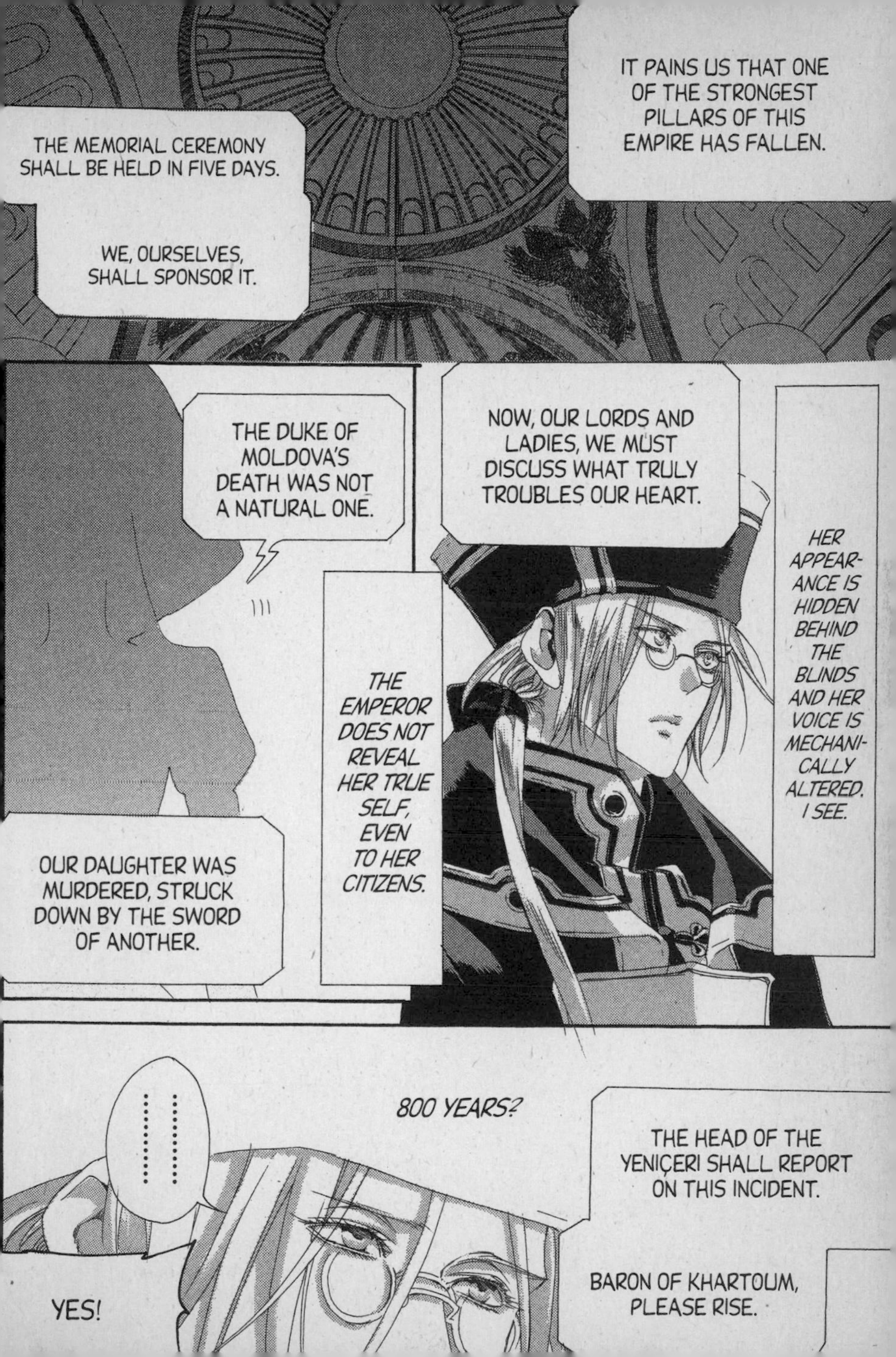
IT PAINS US THAT ONE OF THE STRONGEST PILLARS OF THIS EMPIRE HAS FALLEN.
THE MEMORIAL CEREMONY SHALL BE HELD IN FIVE DAYS.
WE, OURSELVES, SHALL SPONSOR IT.
HER APPEARANCE IS HIDDEN BEHIND THE BLINDS AND HER VOICE IS MECHANICALLY ALTERED. I SEE.
NOW, OUR LORDS AND LADIES, WE MUST DISCUSS WHAT TRULY TROUBLES OUR HEART.
THE EMPEROR DOES NOT REVEAL HER TRUE SELF, EVEN TO HER CITIZENS.
THE DUKE OF MOLDOVA'S DEATH WAS NOT A NATURAL ONE.
OUR DAUGHTER WAS MURDERED, STRUCK DOWN BY THE SWORD OF ANOTHER.
THE HEAD OF THE YENIÇERI SHALL REPORT ON THIS INCIDENT.
800 YEARS?
BARON OF KHARTOUM, PLEASE RISE.
......
YES!

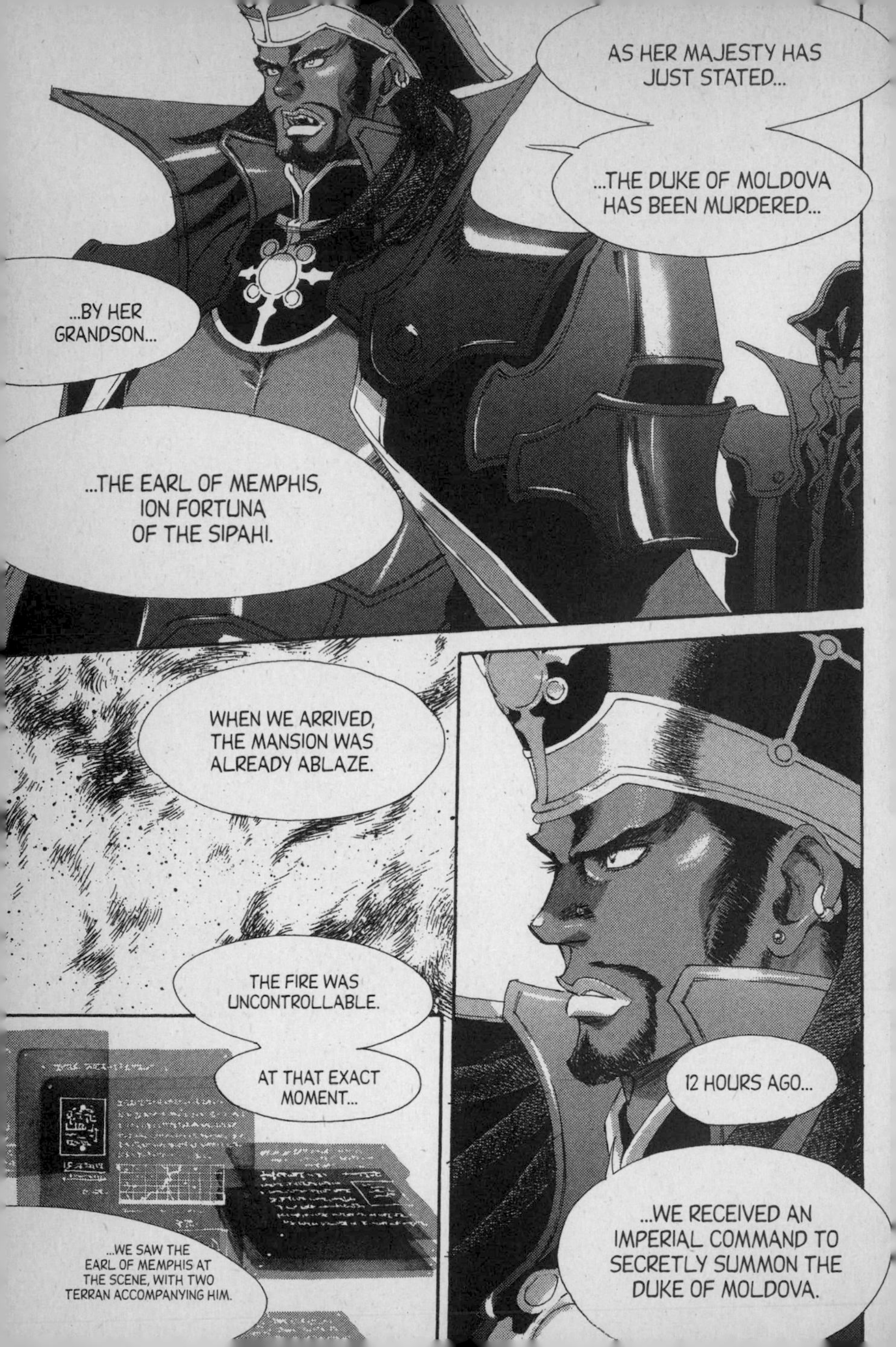
AS HER MAJESTY HAS JUST STATED...
...THE DUKE OF MOLDOVA HAS BEEN MURDERED...
...BY HER GRANDSON...
...THE EARL OF MEMPHIS, ION FORTUNA OF THE SIPAHI.
12 HOURS AGO...
...WE RECEIVED AN IMPERIAL COMMAND TO SECRETLY SUMMON THE DUKE OF MOLDOVA.
WHEN WE ARRIVED, THE MANSION WAS ALREADY ABLAZE.
THE FIRE WAS UNCONTROLLABLE.
AT THAT EXACT MOMENT...
...WE SAW THE EARL OF MEMPHIS AT THE SCENE, WITH TWO TERRAN ACCOMPANYING HIM.

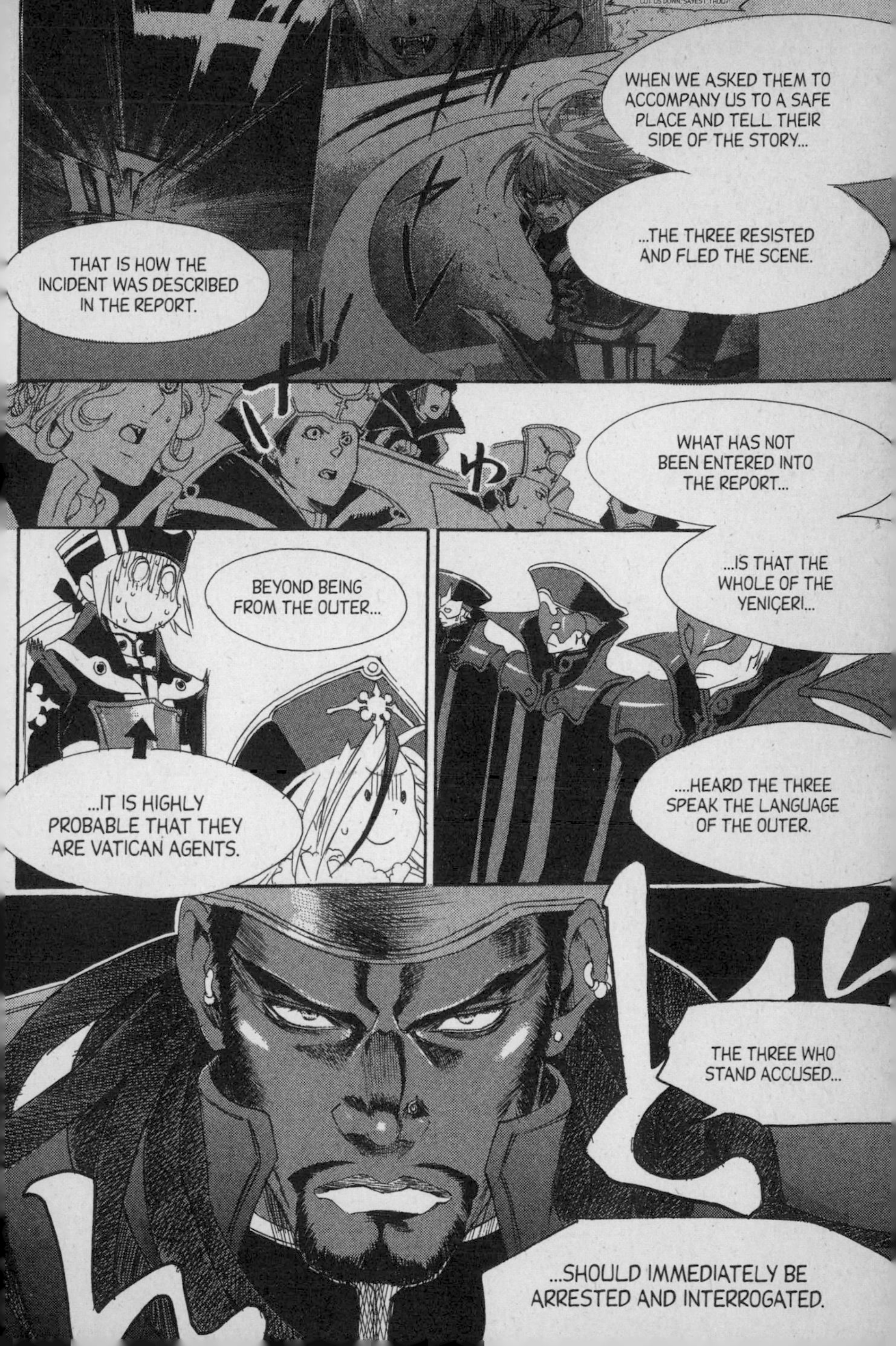
WHEN WE ASKED THEM TO ACCOMPANY US TO A SAFE PLACE AND TELL THEIR SIDE OF THE STORY...
...THE THREE RESISTED AND FLED THE SCENE.
THAT IS HOW THE INCIDENT WAS DESCRIBED IN THE REPORT.
WHAT HAS NOT BEEN ENTERED INTO THE REPORT...
...IS THAT THE WHOLE OF THE YENIÇERI...
....HEARD THE THREE SPEAK THE LANGUAGE OF THE OUTER.
BEYOND BEING FROM THE OUTER...
...IT IS HIGHLY PROBABLE THAT THEY ARE VATICAN AGENTS.
THE THREE WHO STAND ACCUSED...
...SHOULD IMMEDIATELY BE ARRESTED AND INTERROGATED.

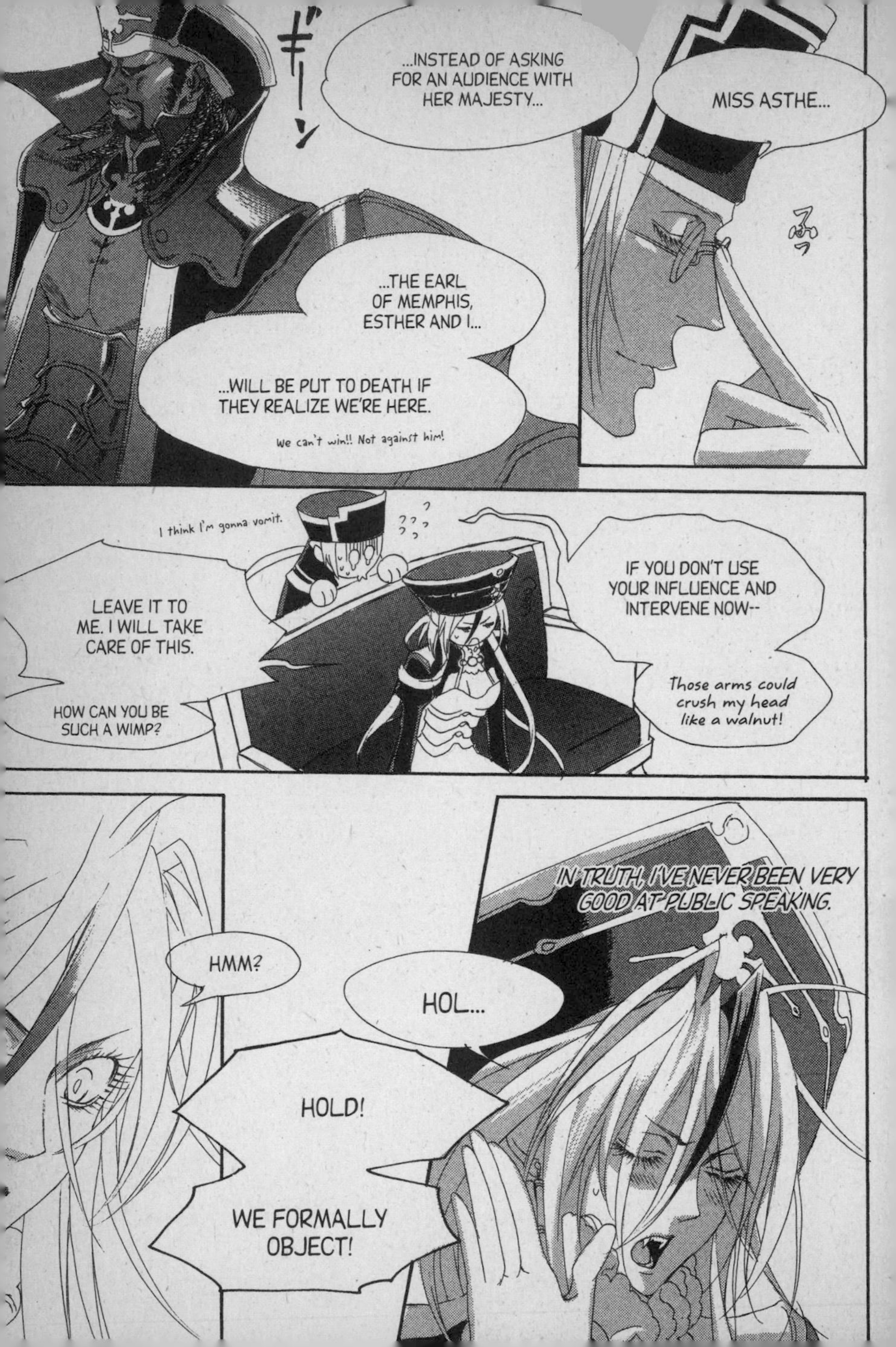
MISS ASTHE...
ふっ
...INSTEAD OF ASKING FOR AN AUDIENCE WITH HER MAJESTY...
ギーン
...THE EARL OF MEMPHIS, ESTHER AND I...
...WILL BE PUT TO DEATH IF THEY REALIZE WE'RE HERE.
We can't win!! Not against him!
IF YOU DON'T USE YOUR INFLUENCE AND INTERVENE NOW--
Those arms could crush my head like a walnut!
LEAVE IT TO ME. I WILL TAKE CARE OF THIS.
HOW CAN YOU BE SUCH A WIMP?
I think I'm gonna vomit.
IN TRUTH, I'VE NEVER BEEN VERY GOOD AT PUBLIC SPEAKING.
HOL...
HOLD!
WE FORMALLY OBJECT!
HMM?

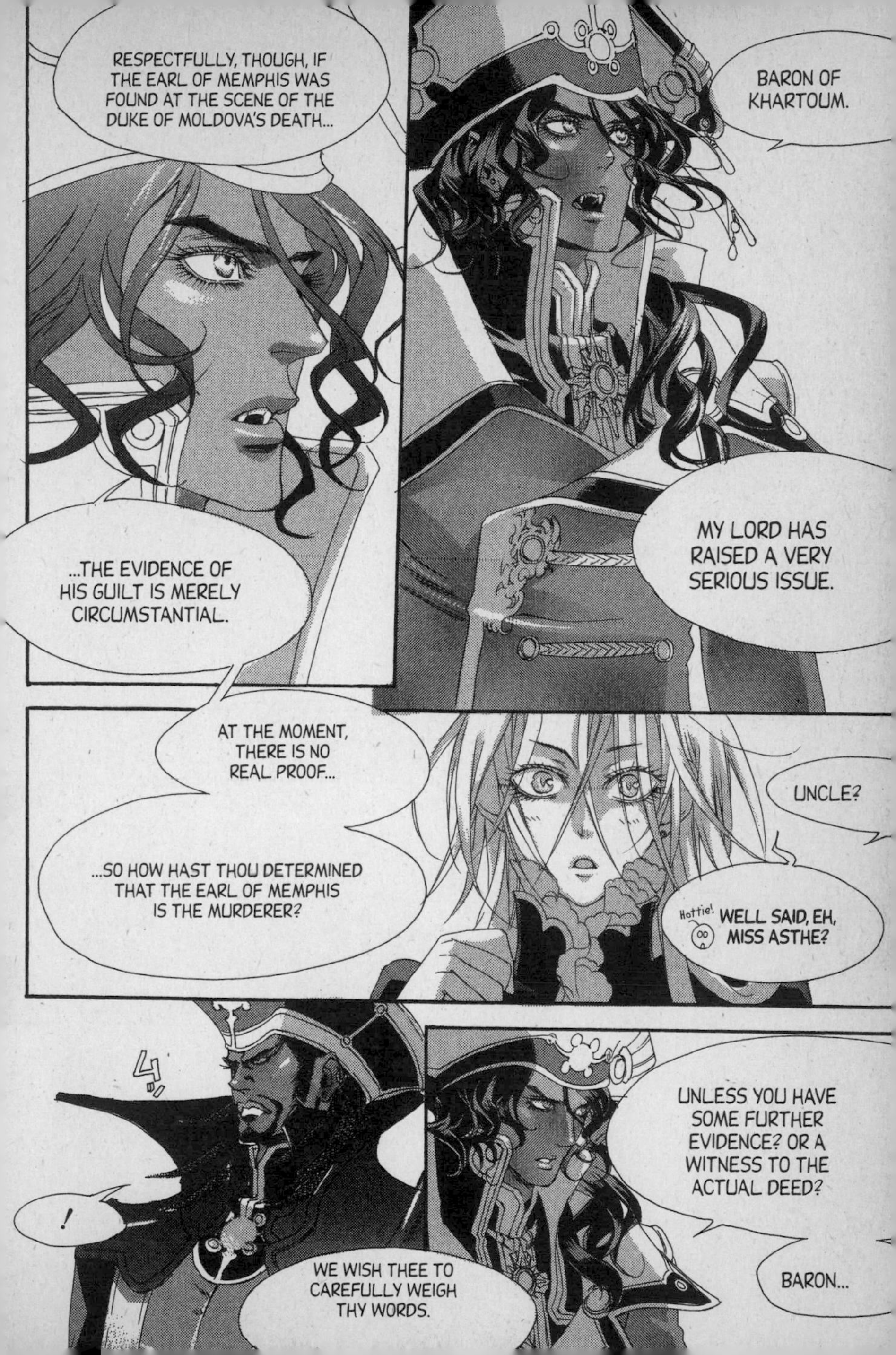
RESPECTFULLY, THOUGH, IF THE EARL OF MEMPHIS WAS FOUND AT THE SCENE OF THE DUKE OF MOLDOVA'S DEATH...
BARON OF KHARTOUM.
...THE EVIDENCE OF HIS GUILT IS MERELY CIRCUMSTANTIAL.
MY LORD HAS RAISED A VERY SERIOUS ISSUE.
AT THE MOMENT, THERE IS NO REAL PROOF...
...SO HOW HAST THOU DETERMINED THAT THE EARL OF MEMPHIS IS THE MURDERER?
UNCLE?
WELL SAID, EH, MISS ASTHE?
Hottie!
UNLESS YOU HAVE SOME FURTHER EVIDENCE? OR A WITNESS TO THE ACTUAL DEED?
!
WE WISH THEE TO CAREFULLY WEIGH THY WORDS.
BARON...

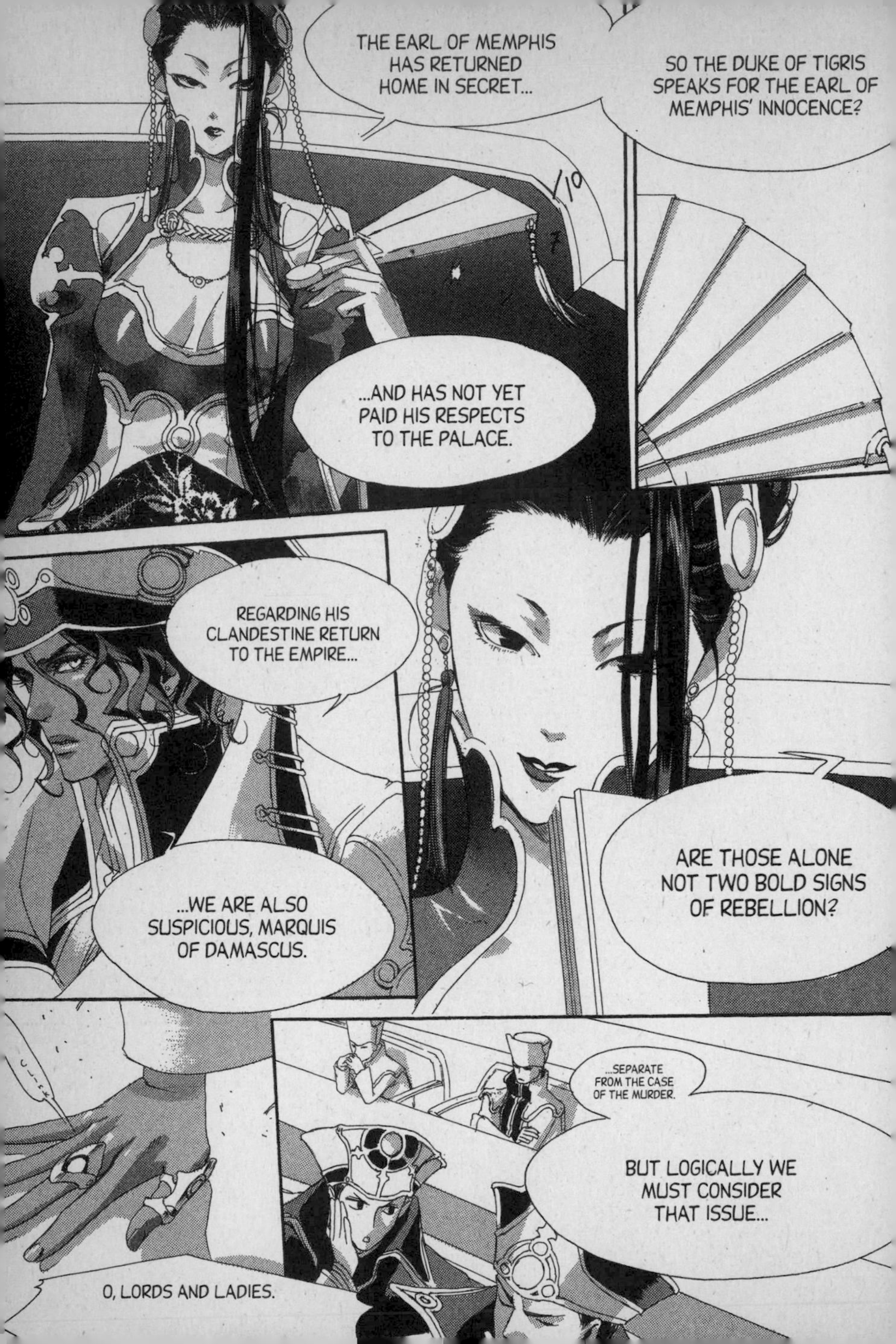
THE EARL OF MEMPHIS HAS RETURNED HOME IN SECRET...
...AND HAS NOT YET PAID HIS RESPECTS TO THE PALACE.
SO THE DUKE OF TIGRIS SPEAKS FOR THE EARL OF MEMPHIS' INNOCENCE?
REGARDING HIS CLANDESTINE RETURN TO THE EMPIRE...
...WE ARE ALSO SUSPICIOUS, MARQUIS OF DAMASCUS.
ARE THOSE ALONE NOT TWO BOLD SIGNS OF REBELLION?
...SEPARATE FROM THE CASE OF THE MURDER.
BUT LOGICALLY WE MUST CONSIDER THAT ISSUE...
O, LORDS AND LADIES.

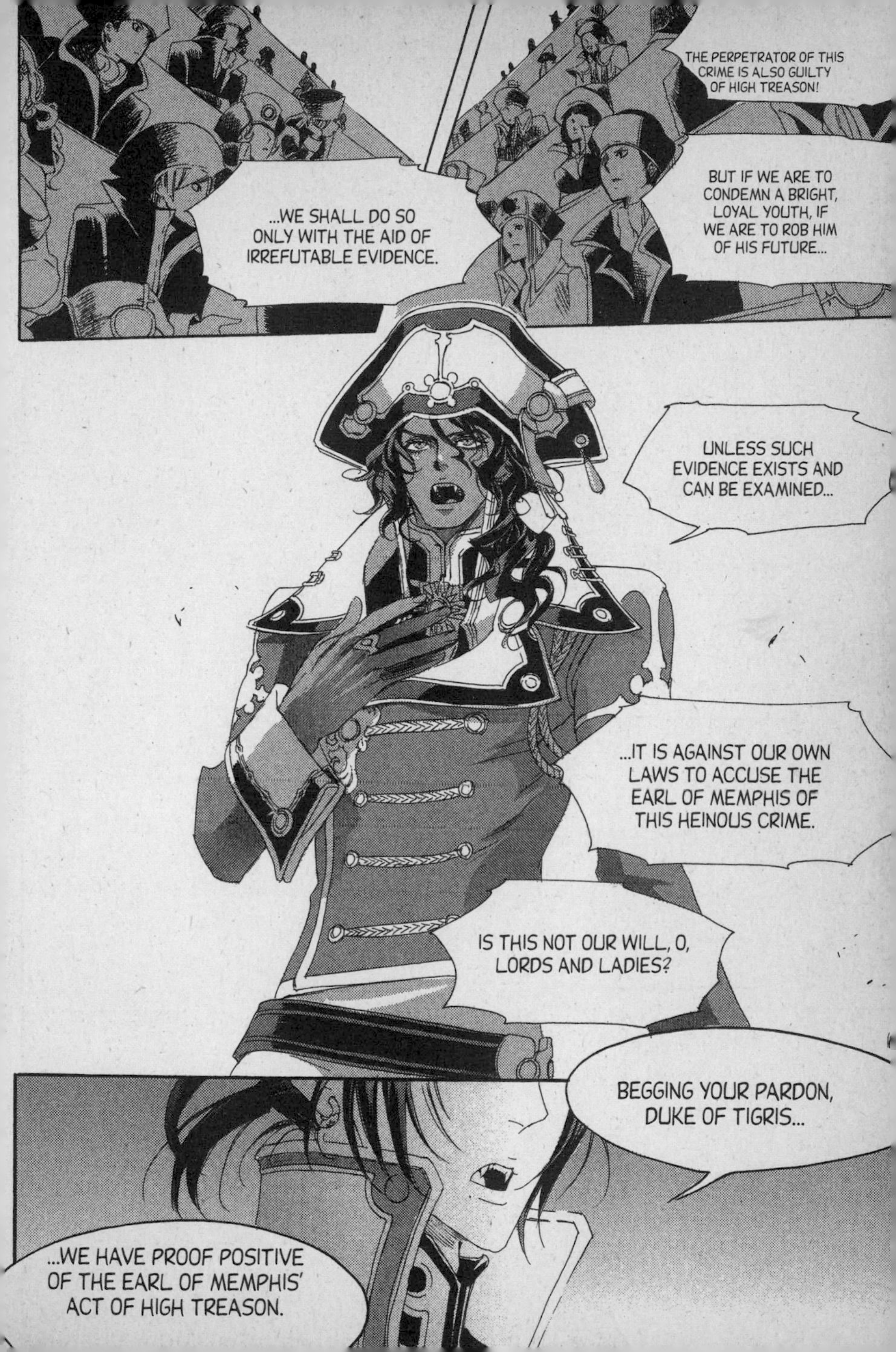
THE PERPETRATOR OF THIS CRIME IS ALSO GUILTY OF HIGH TREASON!
BUT IF WE ARE TO CONDEMN A BRIGHT, LOYAL YOUTH, IF WE ARE TO ROB HIM OF HIS FUTURE...
...WE SHALL DO SO ONLY WITH THE AID OF IRREFUTABLE EVIDENCE.
UNLESS SUCH EVIDENCE EXISTS AND CAN BE EXAMINED...
...IT IS AGAINST OUR OWN LAWS TO ACCUSE THE EARL OF MEMPHIS OF THIS HEINOUS CRIME.
IS THIS NOT OUR WILL, O, LORDS AND LADIES?
BEGGING YOUR PARDON, DUKE OF TIGRIS...
...WE HAVE PROOF POSITIVE OF THE EARL OF MEMPHIS' ACT OF HIGH TREASON.

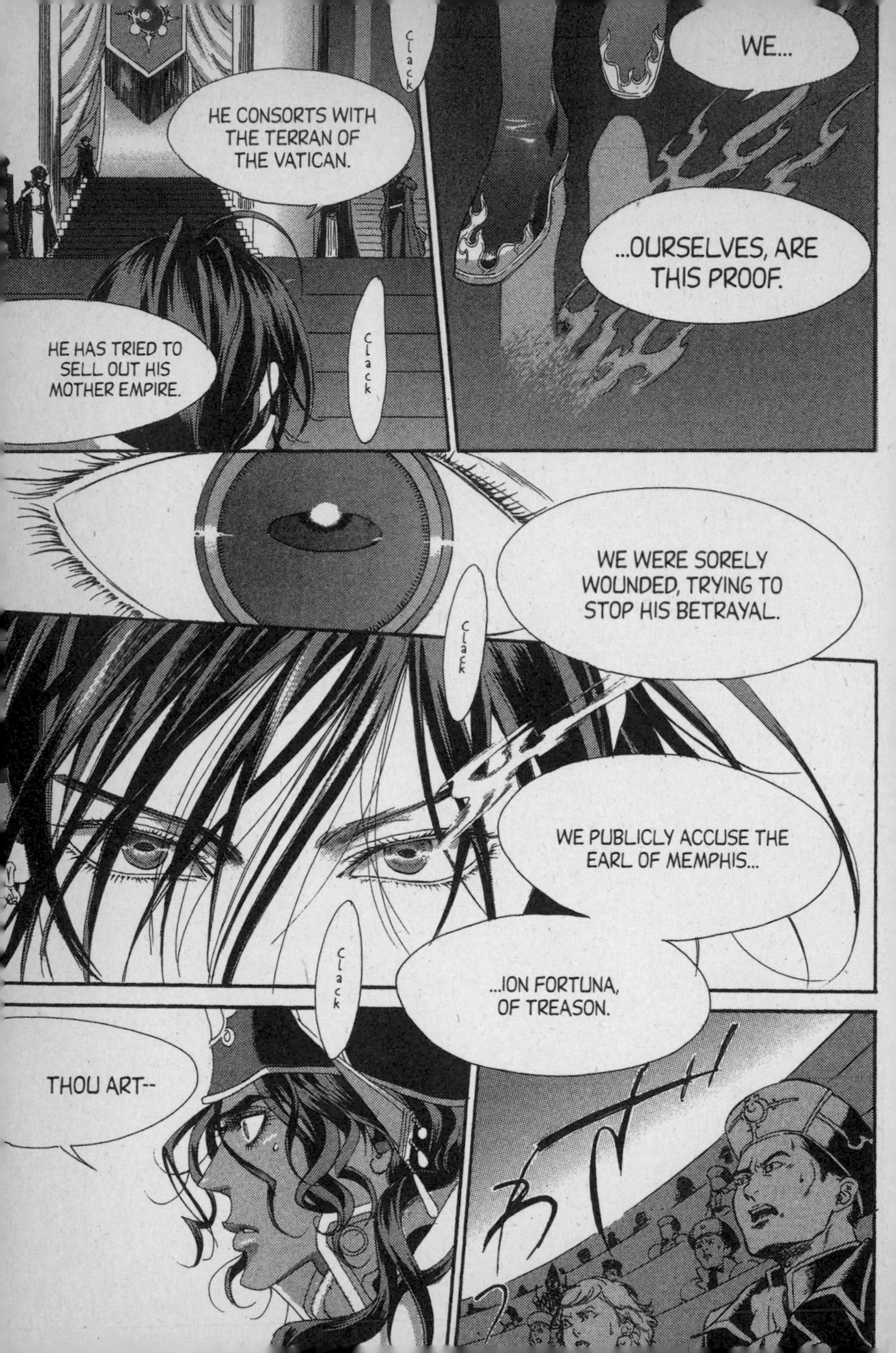
Clack
HE CONSORTS WITH THE TERRAN OF THE VATICAN.
WE...
...OURSELVES, ARE THIS PROOF.
HE HAS TRIED TO SELL OUT HIS MOTHER EMPIRE.
Clack
WE WERE SORELY WOUNDED, TRYING TO STOP HIS BETRAYAL.
Clack
WE PUBLICLY ACCUSE THE EARL OF MEMPHIS...
Clack
...ION FORTUNA, OF TREASON.
THOU ART--

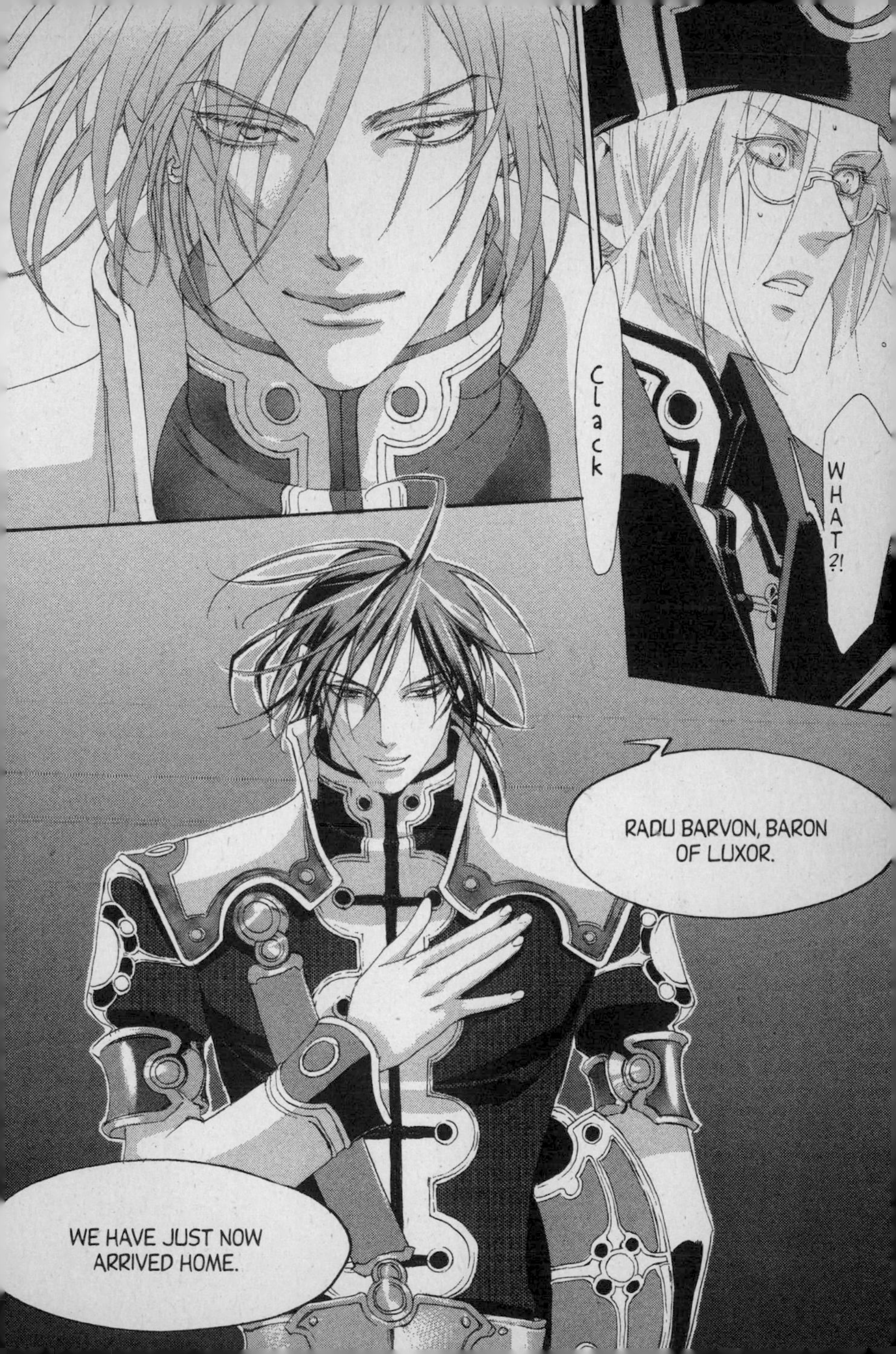
WHAT?!
Clack
RADU BARVON, BARON OF LUXOR.
WE HAVE JUST NOW ARRIVED HOME.

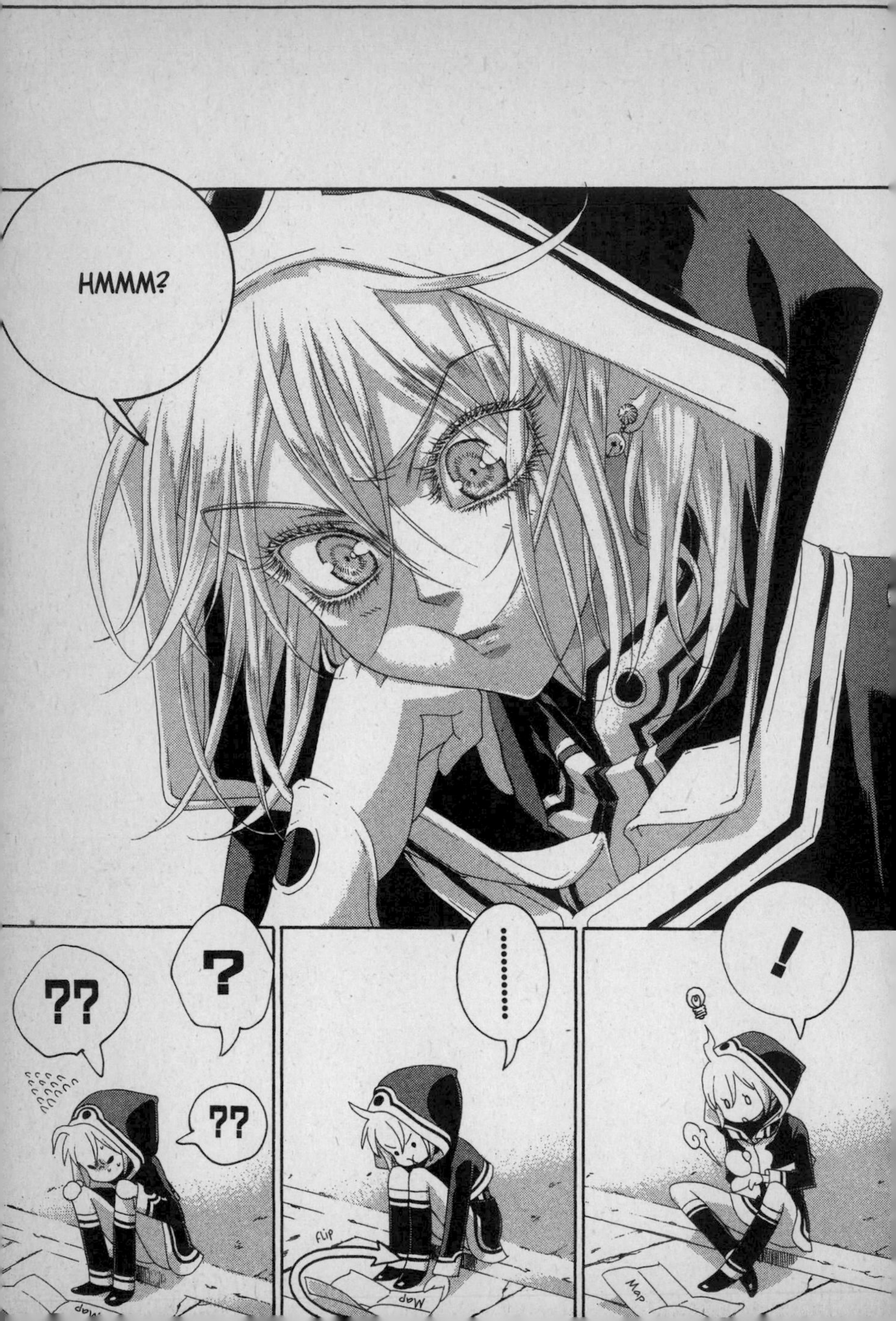
HMMM?
!
Map
……
flip
Map
?
??
??
Map

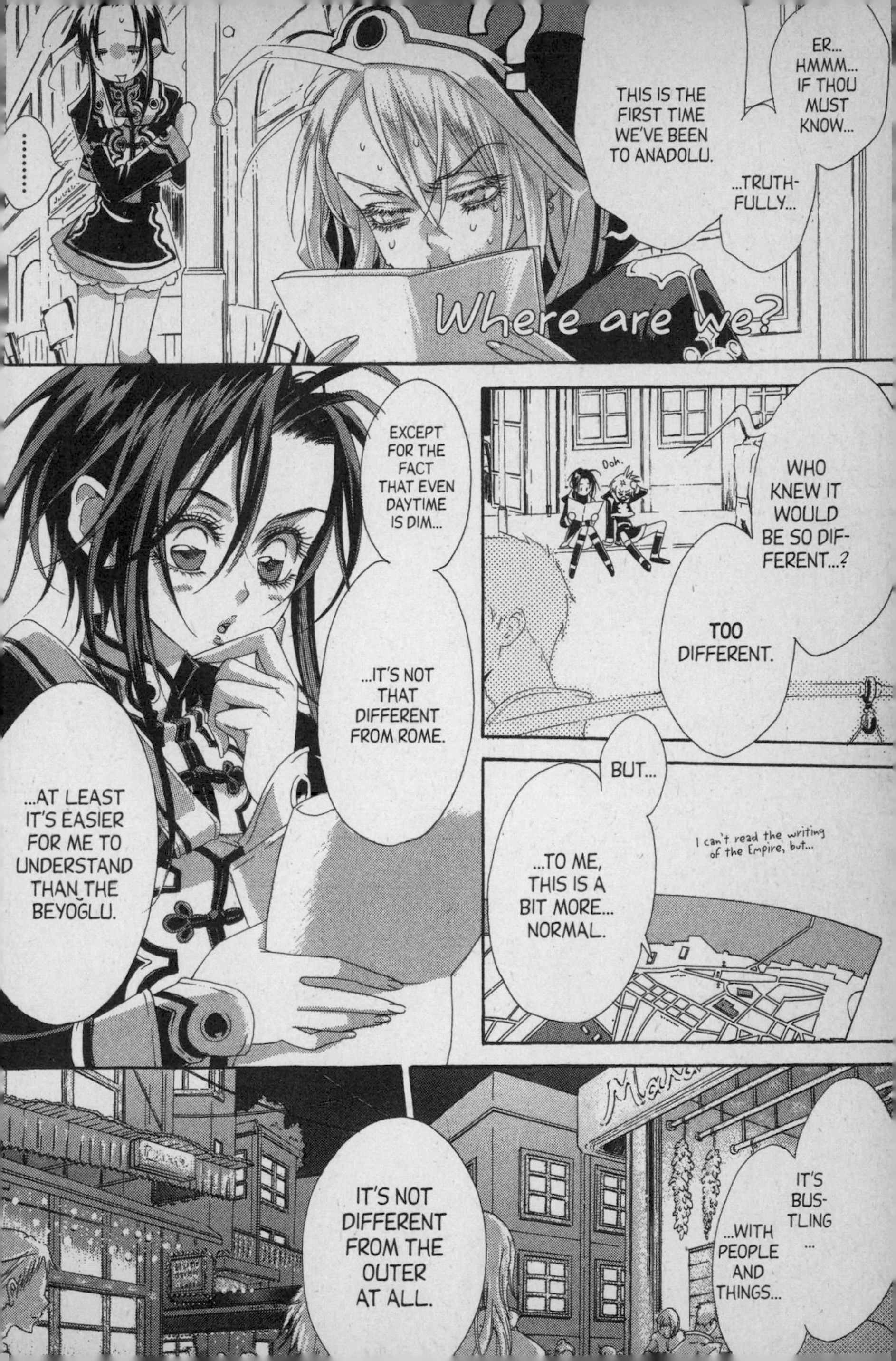
ER... HMMM... IF THOU MUST KNOW...
...TRUTH-FULLY...
THIS IS THE FIRST TIME WE'VE BEEN TO ANADOLU.
Where are we?
......
WHO KNEW IT WOULD BE SO DIF-FERENT...?
TOO DIFFERENT.
Ooh.
EXCEPT FOR THE FACT THAT EVEN DAYTIME IS DIM...
...IT'S NOT THAT DIFFERENT FROM ROME.
BUT...
...TO ME, THIS IS A BIT MORE... NORMAL.
I can't read the writing of the Empire, but...
...AT LEAST IT'S EASIER FOR ME TO UNDERSTAND THAN THE BEYOĞLU.
IT'S BUS-TLING ...
...WITH PEOPLE AND THINGS...
IT'S NOT DIFFERENT FROM THE OUTER AT ALL.

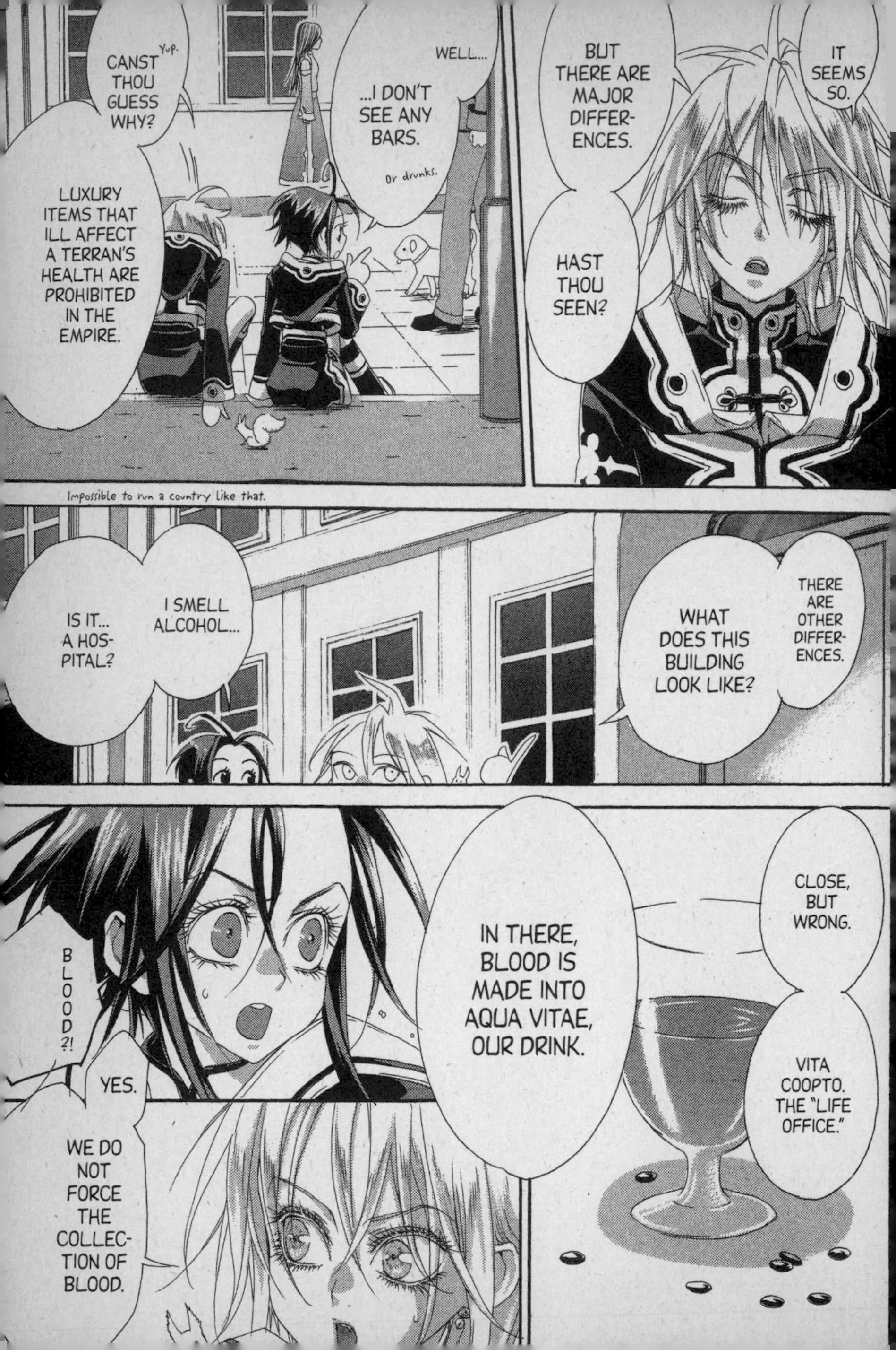
IT SEEMS SO.
BUT THERE ARE MAJOR DIFFERENCES.
HAST THOU SEEN?
WELL...
...I DON'T SEE ANY BARS.
Or drunks.
CANST THOU GUESS WHY?
Yup.
LUXURY ITEMS THAT ILL AFFECT A TERRAN'S HEALTH ARE PROHIBITED IN THE EMPIRE.
Impossible to run a country like that.
THERE ARE OTHER DIFFERENCES.
WHAT DOES THIS BUILDING LOOK LIKE?
I SMELL ALCOHOL...
IS IT... A HOSPITAL?
CLOSE, BUT WRONG.
VITA COOPTO. THE "LIFE OFFICE."
IN THERE, BLOOD IS MADE INTO AQUA VITAE, OUR DRINK.
BLOOD?!
YES.
WE DO NOT FORCE THE COLLECTION OF BLOOD.

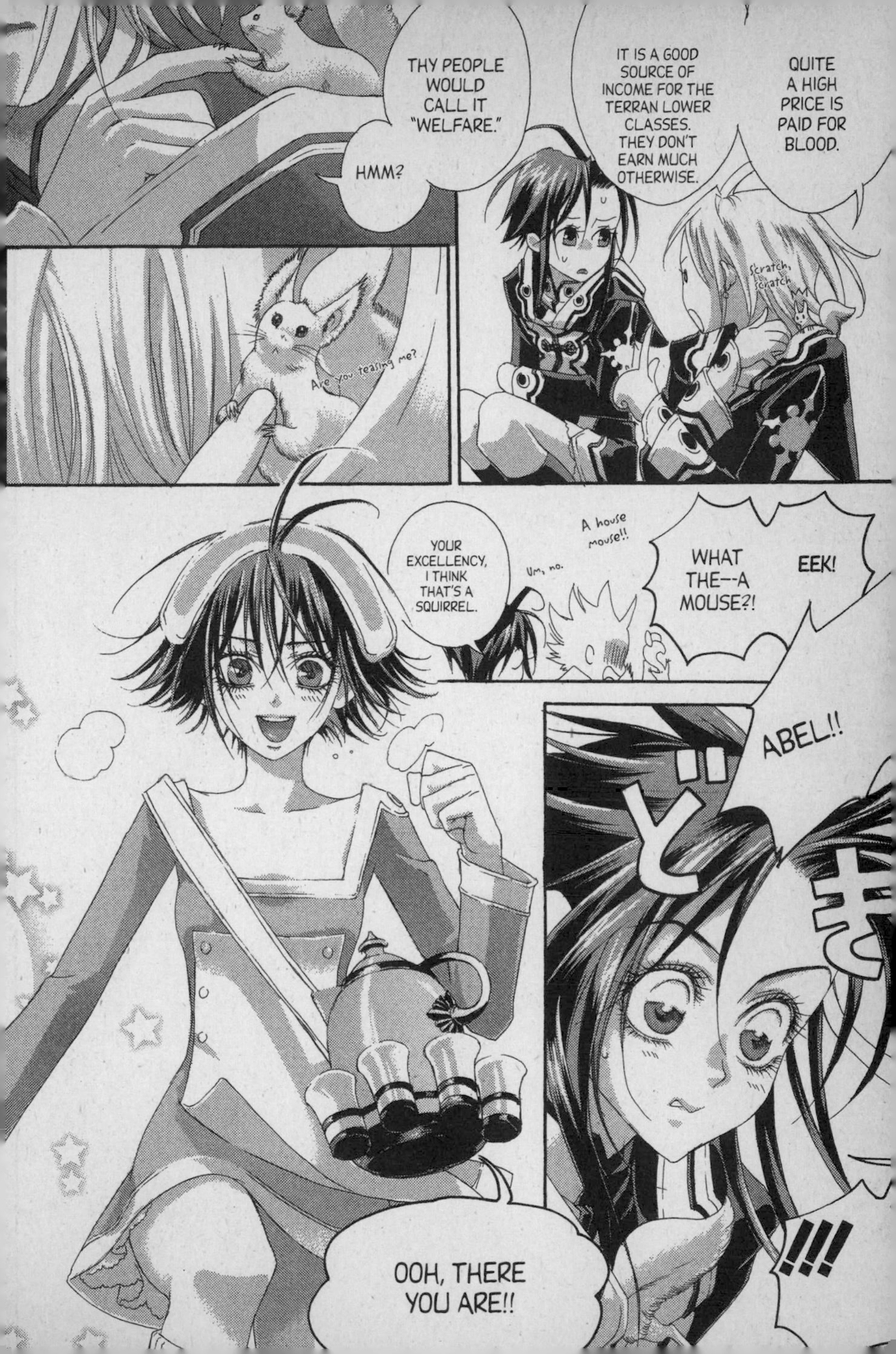
QUITE A HIGH PRICE IS PAID FOR BLOOD.
IT IS A GOOD SOURCE OF INCOME FOR THE TERRAN LOWER CLASSES. THEY DON'T EARN MUCH OTHERWISE.
THY PEOPLE WOULD CALL IT "WELFARE."
HMM?
Scratch, scratch
Are you teasing me?
EEK!
WHAT THE--A MOUSE?!
A house mouse!!
Um, no.
YOUR EXCELLENCY, I THINK THAT'S A SQUIRREL.
ABEL!!
!!!
OOH, THERE YOU ARE!!

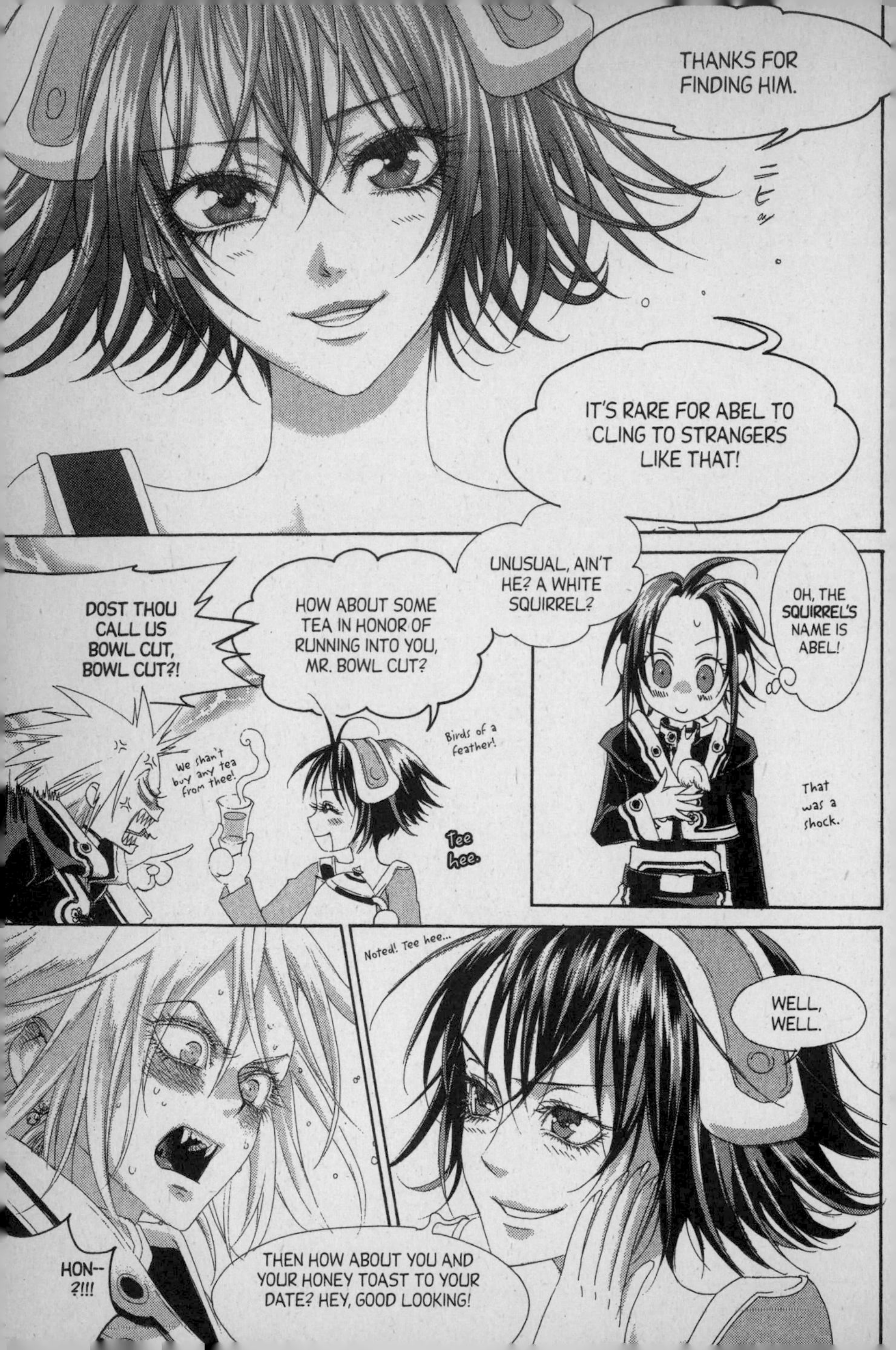
THANKS FOR FINDING HIM.
ニヒッ
IT'S RARE FOR ABEL TO CLING TO STRANGERS LIKE THAT!
UNUSUAL, AIN'T HE? A WHITE SQUIRREL?
OH, THE SQUIRREL'S NAME IS ABEL!
That was a shock.
HOW ABOUT SOME TEA IN HONOR OF RUNNING INTO YOU, MR. BOWL CUT?
Birds of a feather!
DOST THOU CALL US BOWL CUT, BOWL CUT?!
We shan't buy any tea from thee!
Tee hee.
WELL, WELL.
THEN HOW ABOUT YOU AND YOUR HONEY TOAST TO YOUR DATE? HEY, GOOD LOOKING!
Noted! Tee hee...
HON--?!!!

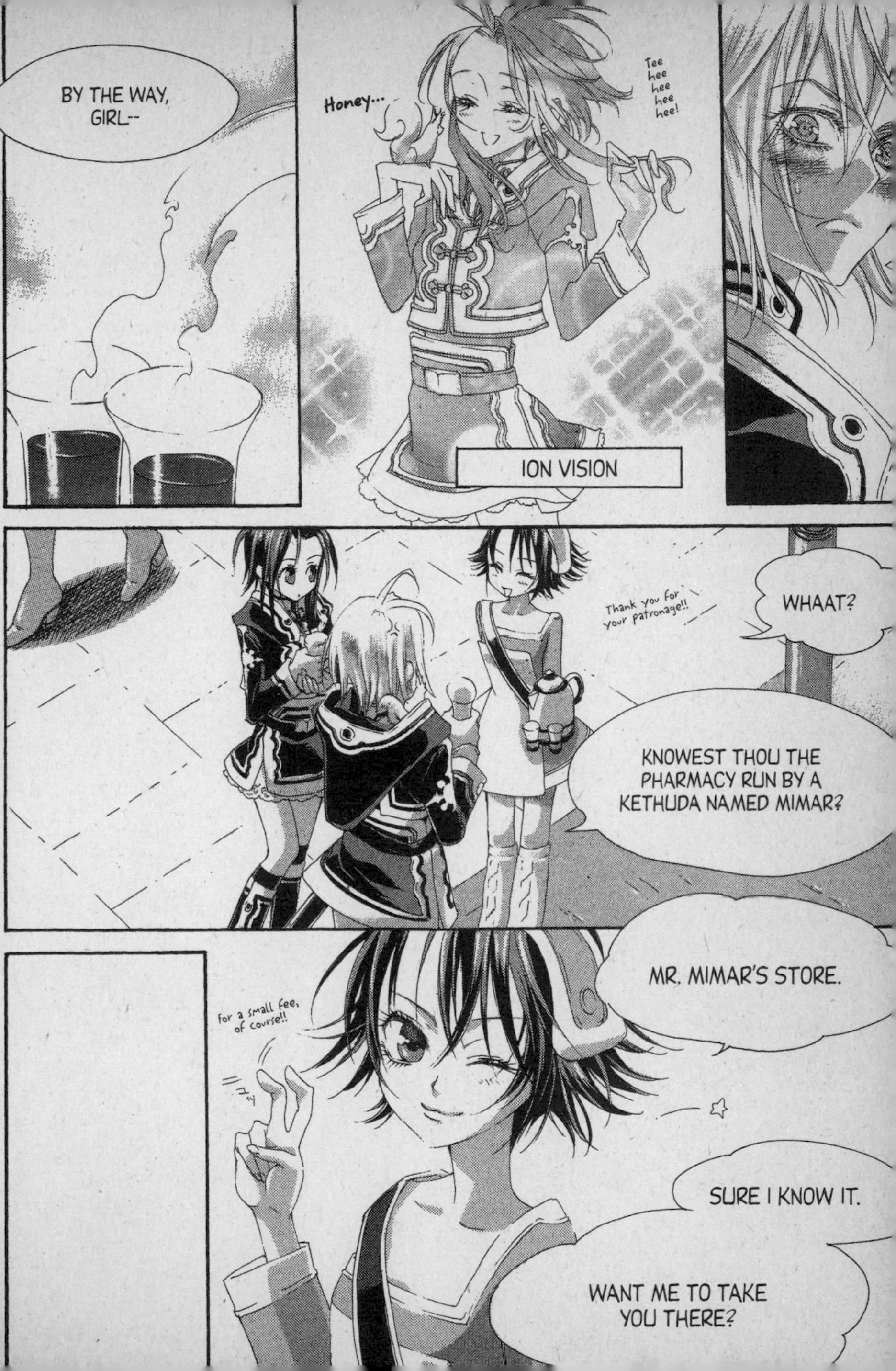
Honey...
Tee hee hee hee hee!
ION VISION
BY THE WAY, GIRL--
WHAAT?
Thank you for your patronage!!
KNOWEST THOU THE PHARMACY RUN BY A KETHUDA NAMED MIMAR?
MR. MIMAR'S STORE.
For a small fee, of course!!
SURE I KNOW IT.
WANT ME TO TAKE YOU THERE?

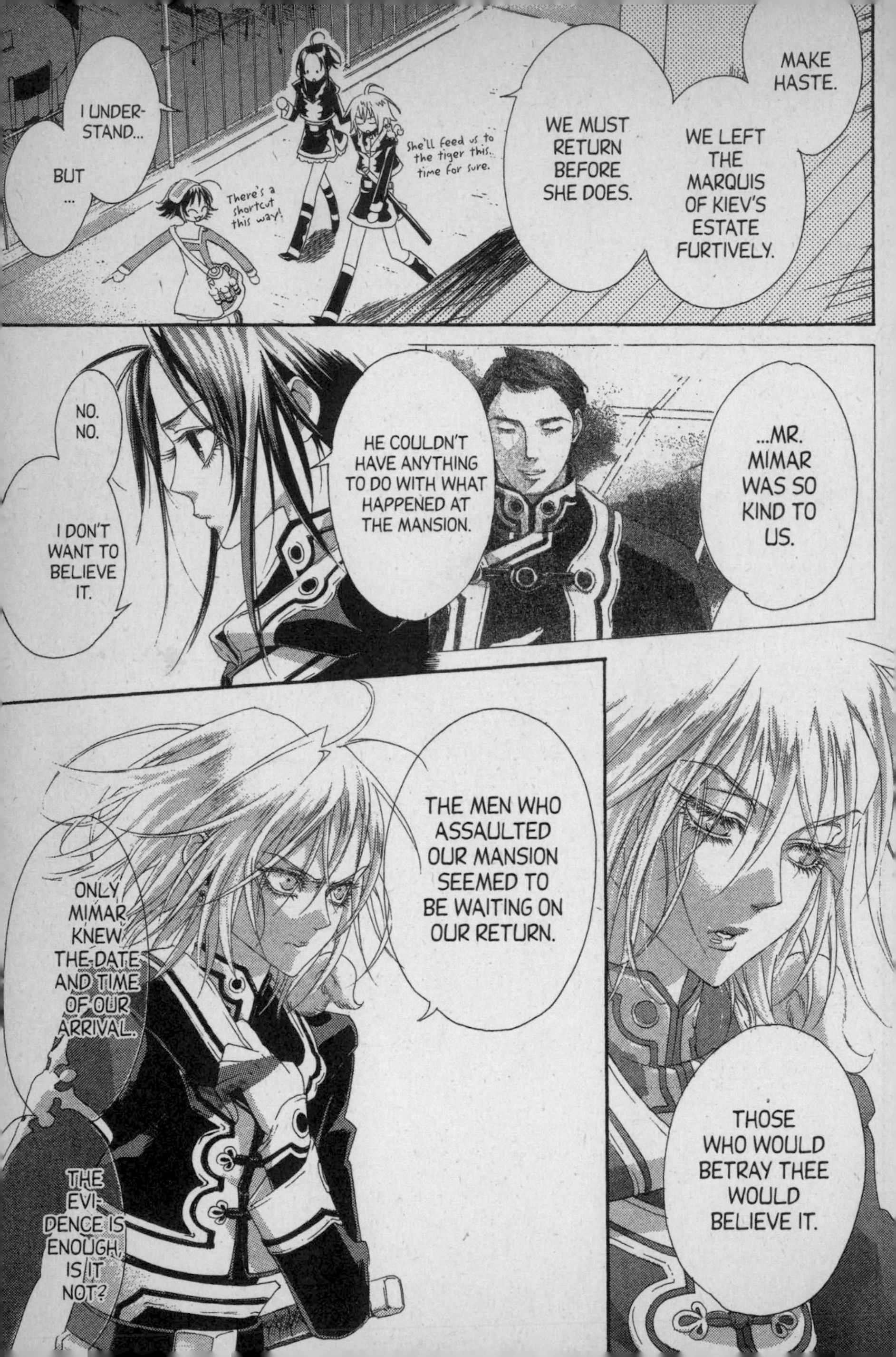
MAKE HASTE.
WE LEFT THE MARQUIS OF KIEV'S ESTATE FURTIVELY.
WE MUST RETURN BEFORE SHE DOES.
She'll feed us to the tiger this time for sure.
There's a shortcut this way!
I UNDERSTAND...
BUT ...
...MR. MIMAR WAS SO KIND TO US.
HE COULDN'T HAVE ANYTHING TO DO WITH WHAT HAPPENED AT THE MANSION.
NO. NO.
I DON'T WANT TO BELIEVE IT.
THOSE WHO WOULD BETRAY THEE WOULD BELIEVE IT.
THE MEN WHO ASSAULTED OUR MANSION SEEMED TO BE WAITING ON OUR RETURN.
ONLY MIMAR KNEW THE DATE AND TIME OF OUR ARRIVAL.
THE EVIDENCE IS ENOUGH, IS IT NOT?

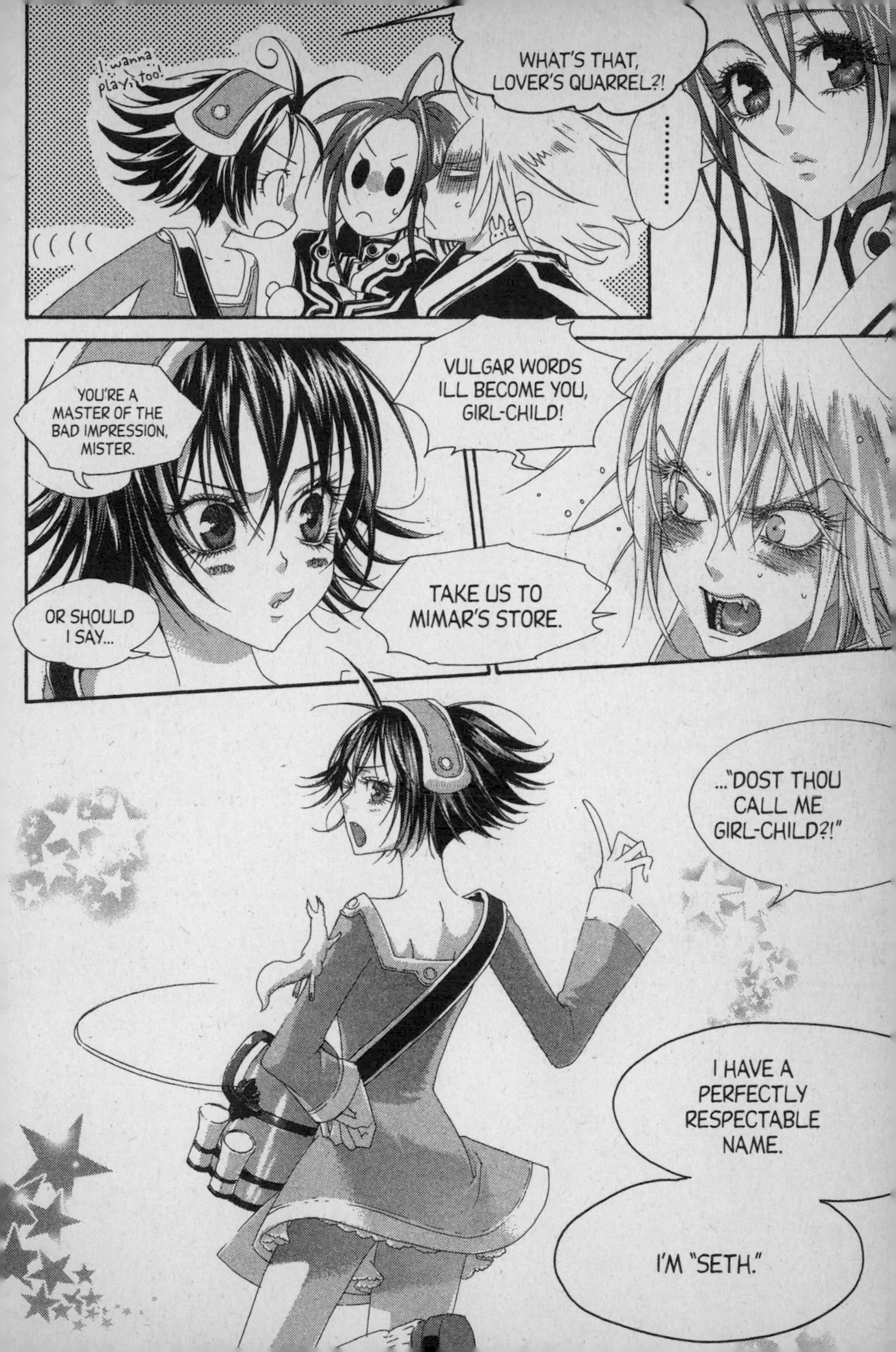
I wanna play, too!
WHAT'S THAT, LOVER'S QUARREL?!
......
YOU'RE A MASTER OF THE BAD IMPRESSION, MISTER.
VULGAR WORDS ILL BECOME YOU, GIRL-CHILD!
OR SHOULD I SAY...
TAKE US TO MIMAR'S STORE.
..."DOST THOU CALL ME GIRL-CHILD?!"
I HAVE A PERFECTLY RESPECTABLE NAME.
I'M "SETH."

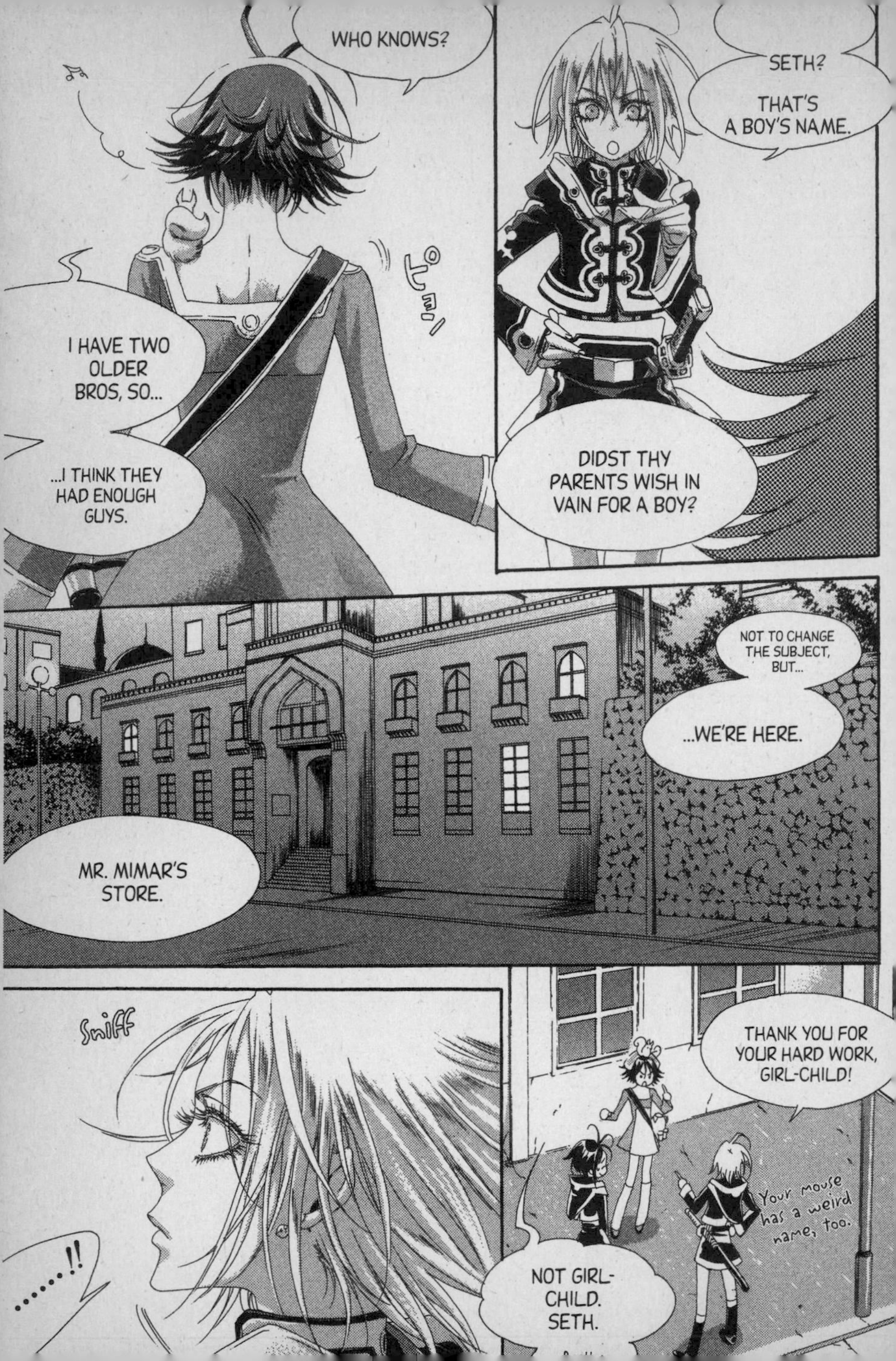
SETH?
THAT'S A BOY'S NAME.
DIDST THY PARENTS WISH IN VAIN FOR A BOY?
WHO KNOWS?
I HAVE TWO OLDER BROS, SO...
...I THINK THEY HAD ENOUGH GUYS.
NOT TO CHANGE THE SUBJECT, BUT...
...WE'RE HERE.
MR. MIMAR'S STORE.
THANK YOU FOR YOUR HARD WORK, GIRL-CHILD!
Your mouse has a weird name, too.
NOT GIRL-CHILD. SETH.
Sniff
......!!

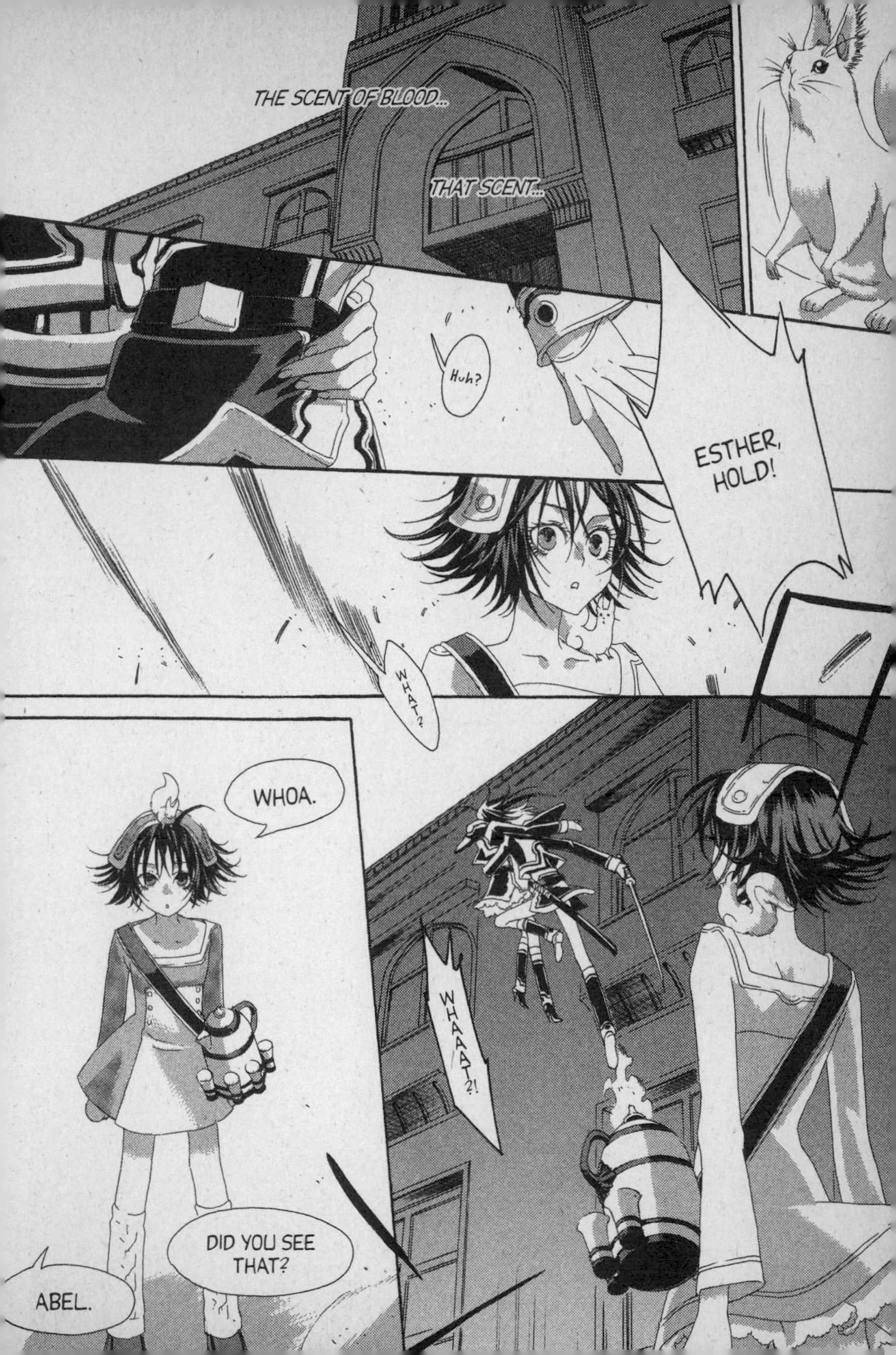

THE SCENT OF BLOOD...
THAT SCENT...
Huh?
ESTHER, HOLD!
WHAT?
WHOA.
WHAAAAT?!
DID YOU SEE THAT?
ABEL.

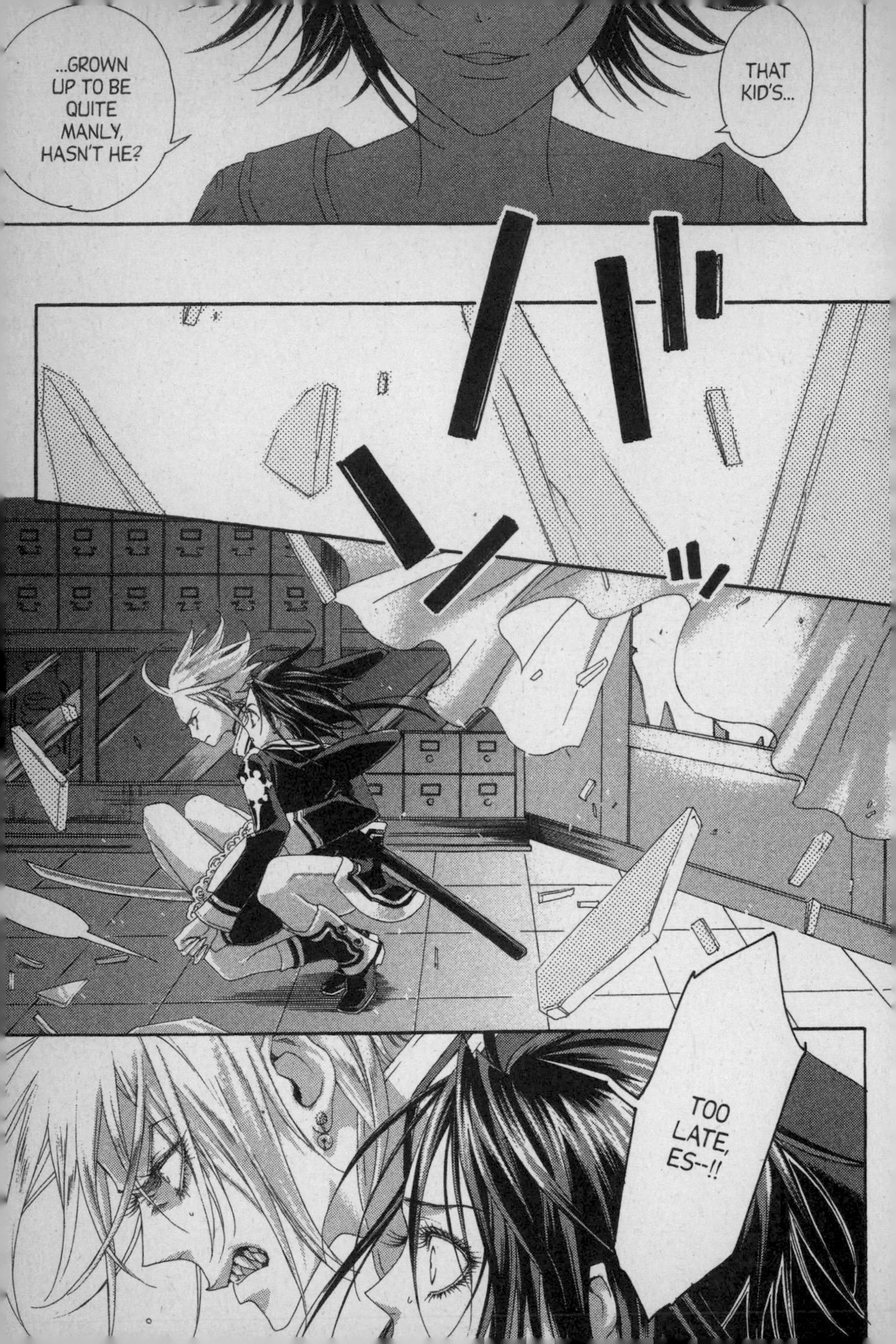
THAT KID'S...
...GROWN UP TO BE QUITE MANLY, HASN'T HE?
TOO LATE, ES--!!

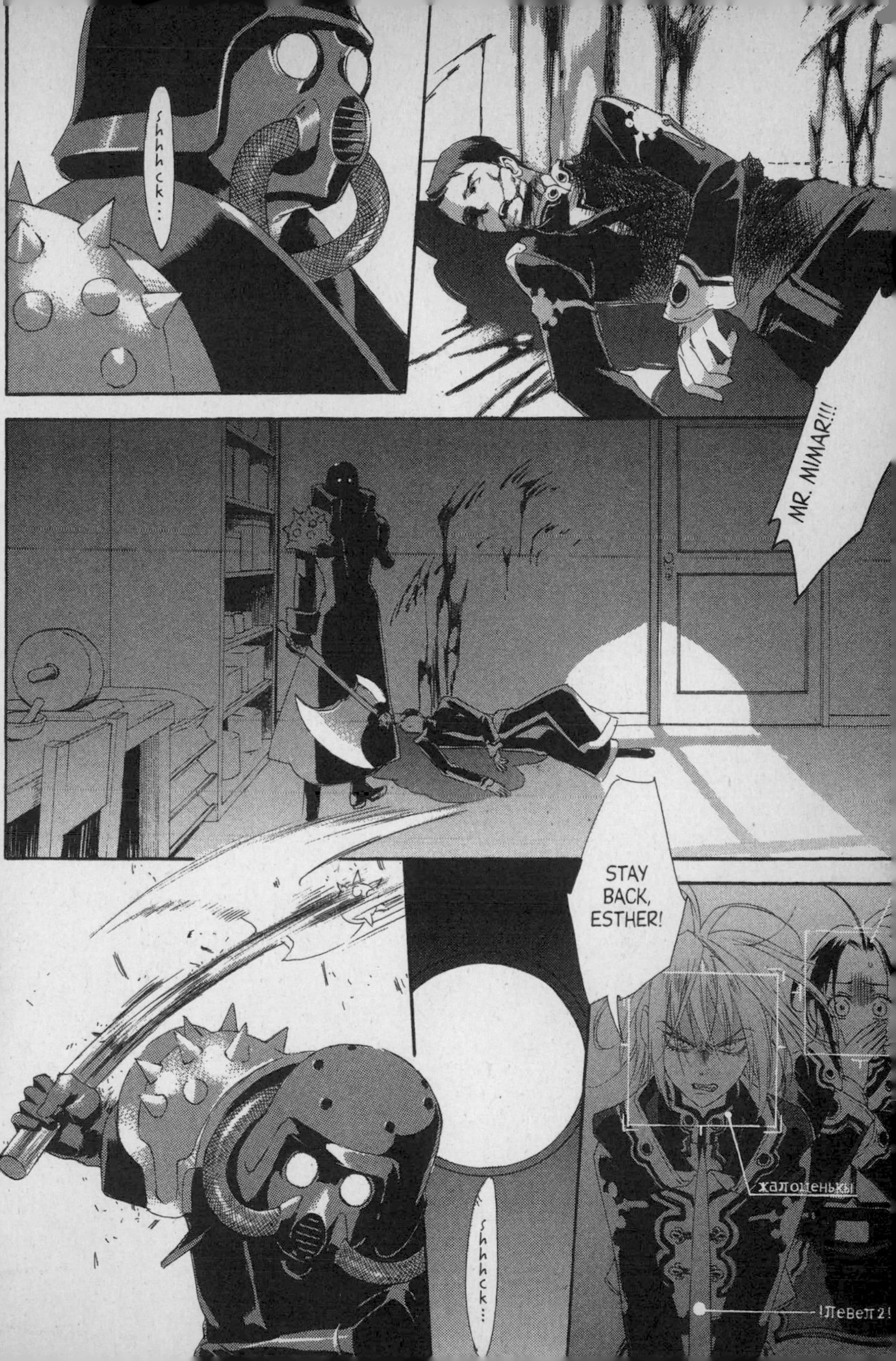
shhhck...
MR. MIMAR!!!
STAY BACK, ESTHER!
shhhck...

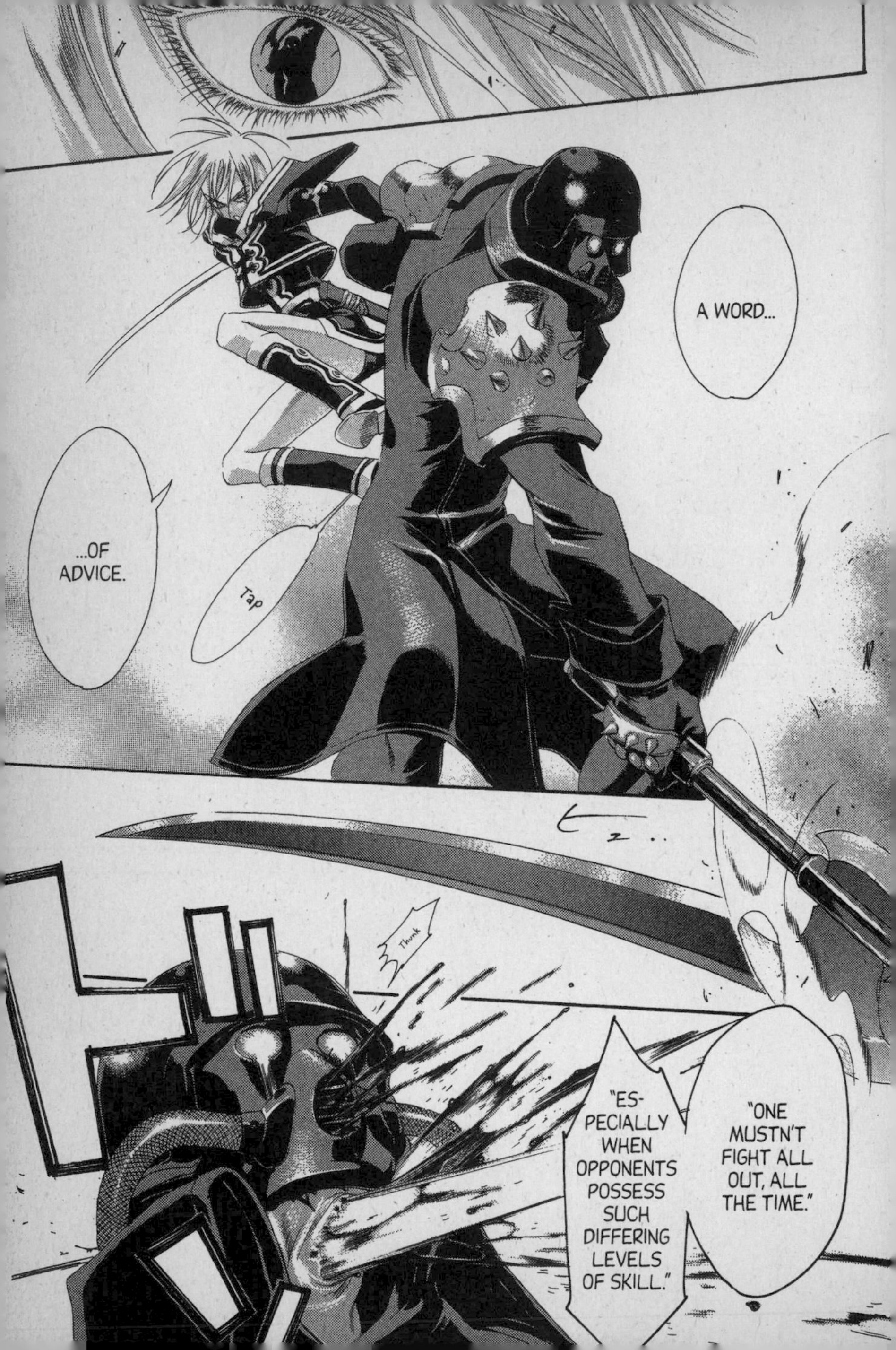
A WORD...
...OF ADVICE.
Tap
Thunk
"ONE MUSTN'T FIGHT ALL OUT, ALL THE TIME."
"ES-PECIALLY WHEN OPPONENTS POSSESS SUCH DIFFERING LEVELS OF SKILL."

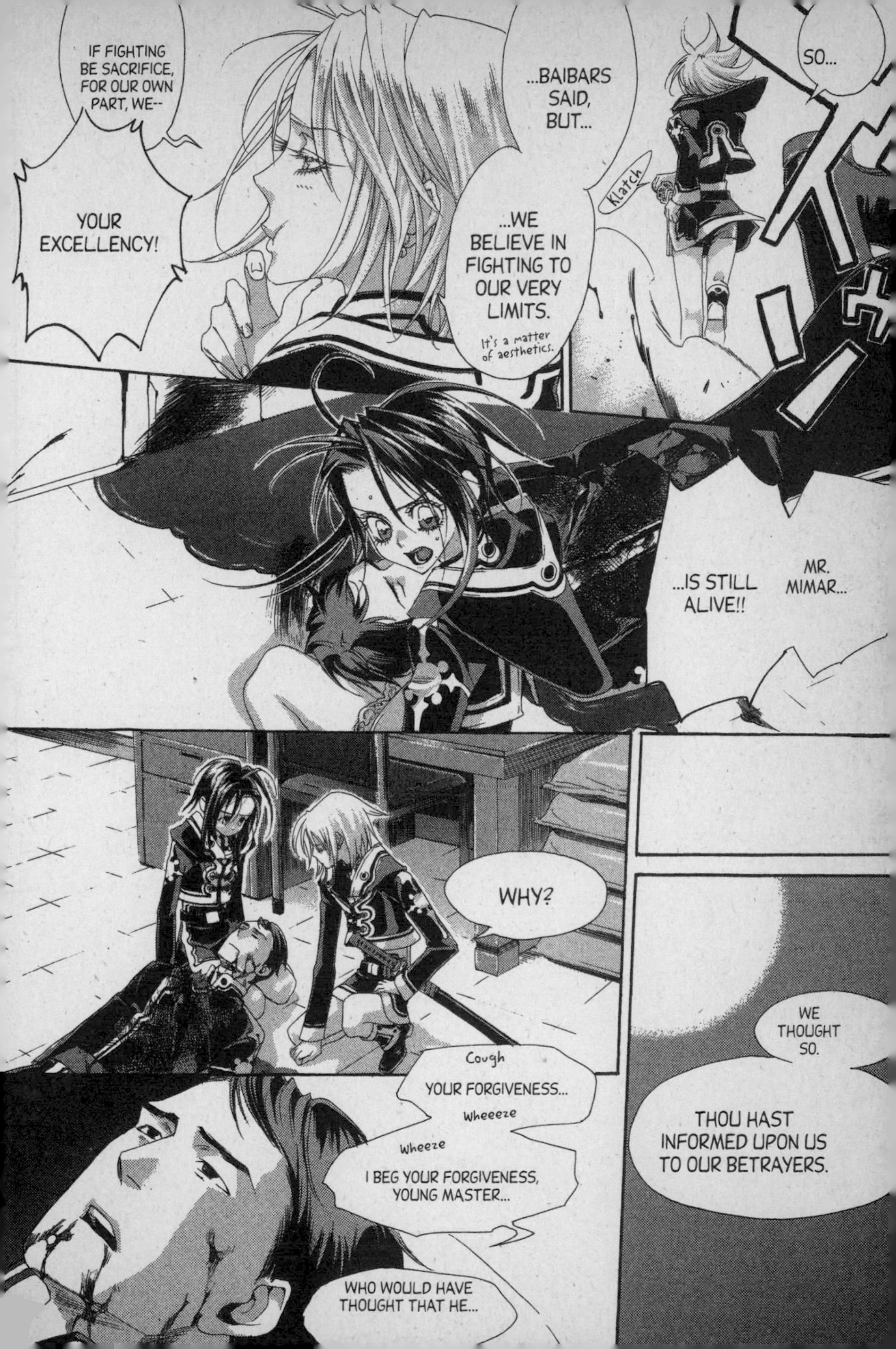
SO...
Klatch
...BAIBARS SAID, BUT...
...WE BELIEVE IN FIGHTING TO OUR VERY LIMITS.
It's a matter of aesthetics.
IF FIGHTING BE SACRIFICE, FOR OUR OWN PART, WE--
YOUR EXCELLENCY!
MR. MIMAR...
...IS STILL ALIVE!!
WHY?
Cough
YOUR FORGIVENESS...
Wheeeze
Wheeze
I BEG YOUR FORGIVENESS, YOUNG MASTER...
WHO WOULD HAVE THOUGHT THAT HE...
WE THOUGHT SO.
THOU HAST INFORMED UPON US TO OUR BETRAYERS.

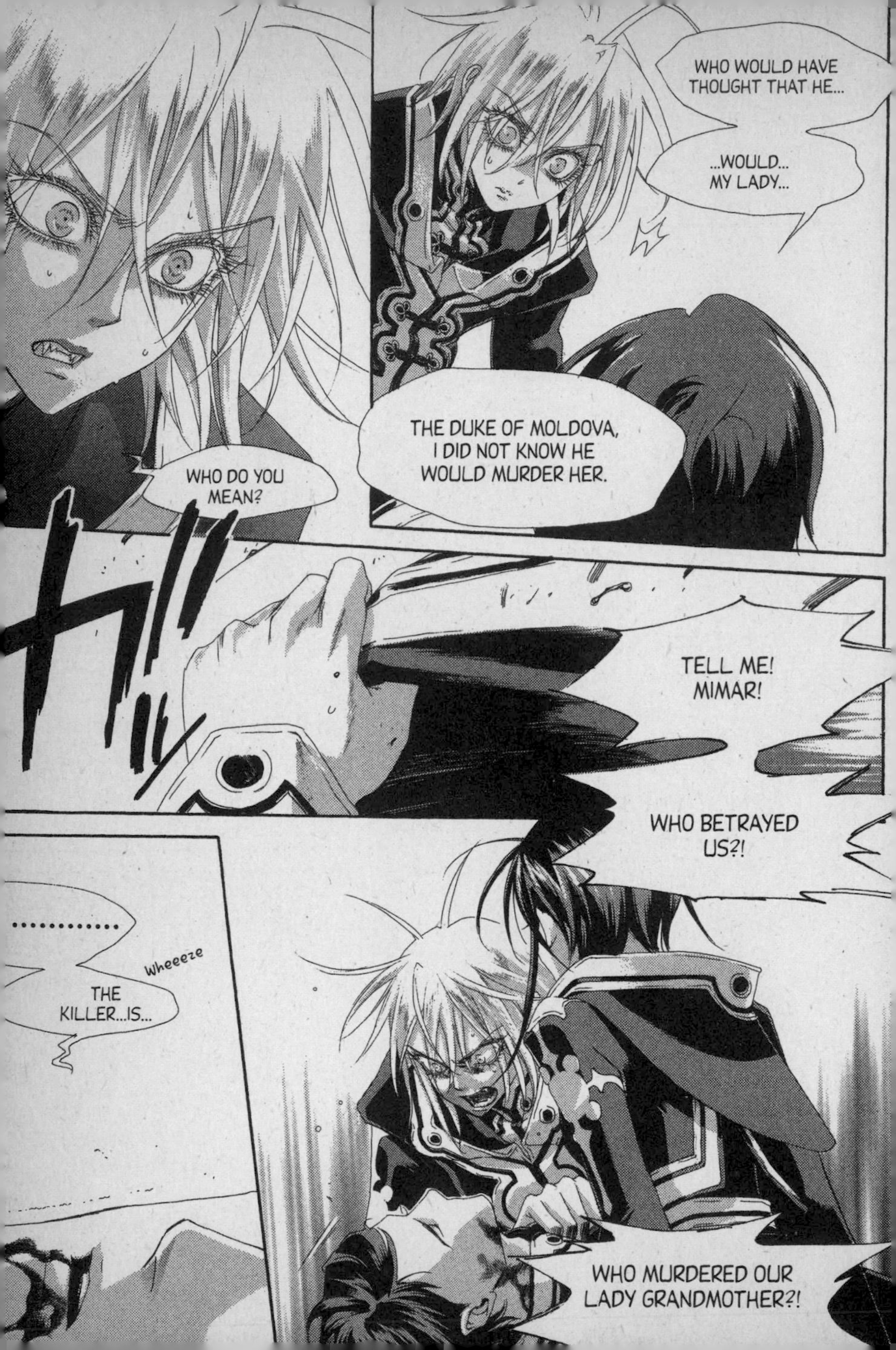
WHO WOULD HAVE THOUGHT THAT HE...
...WOULD... MY LADY...
THE DUKE OF MOLDOVA, I DID NOT KNOW HE WOULD MURDER HER.
WHO DO YOU MEAN?
TELL ME! MIMAR!
WHO BETRAYED US?!
WHO MURDERED OUR LADY GRANDMOTHER?!
.............
Wheeeze
THE KILLER...IS...

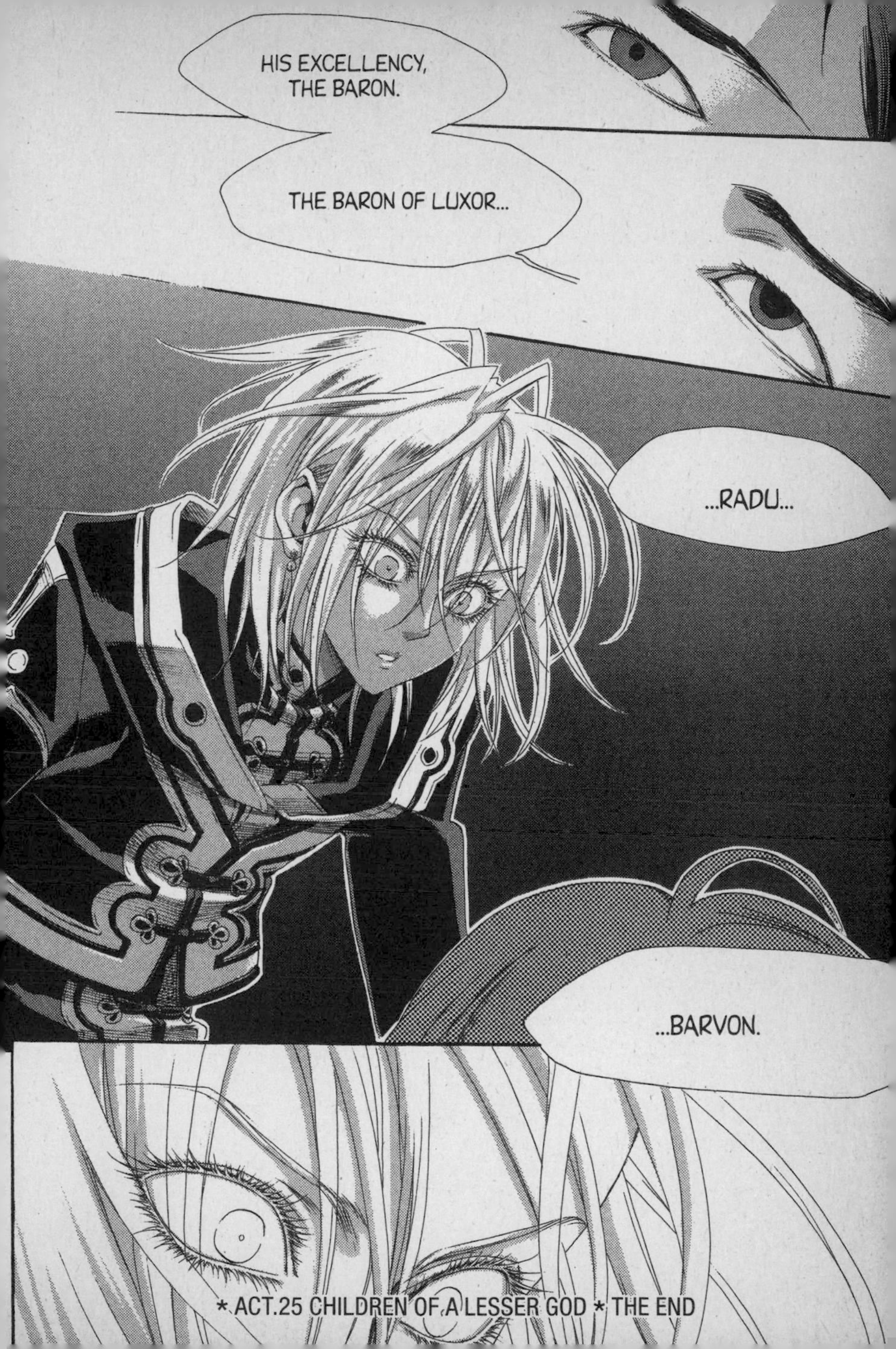
HIS EXCELLENCY, THE BARON.
THE BARON OF LUXOR...
...RADU...
...BARVON.

* ACT.25 CHILDREN OF A LESSER GOD * THE END

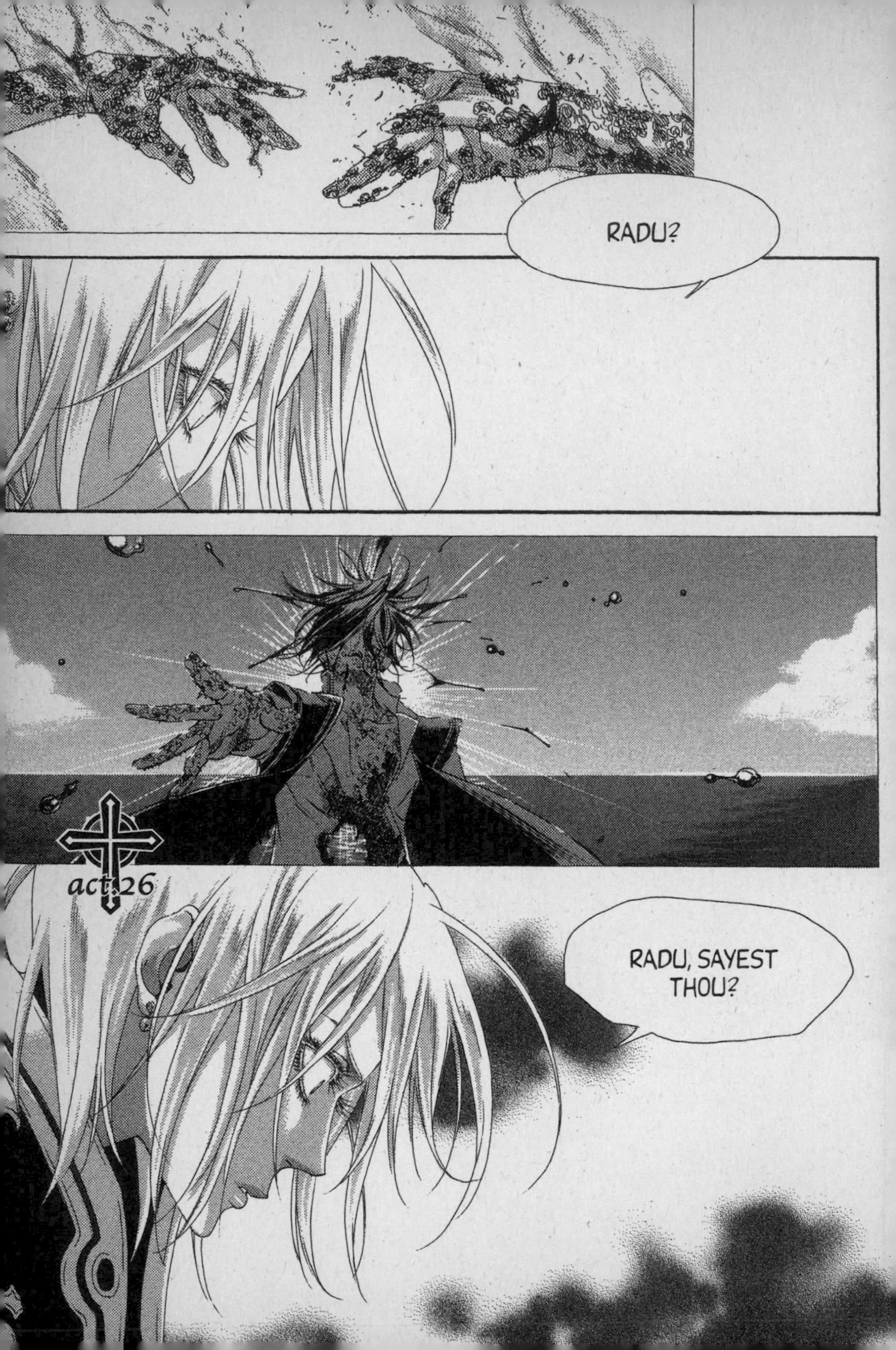
RADU?
act.26
RADU, SAYEST
THOU?

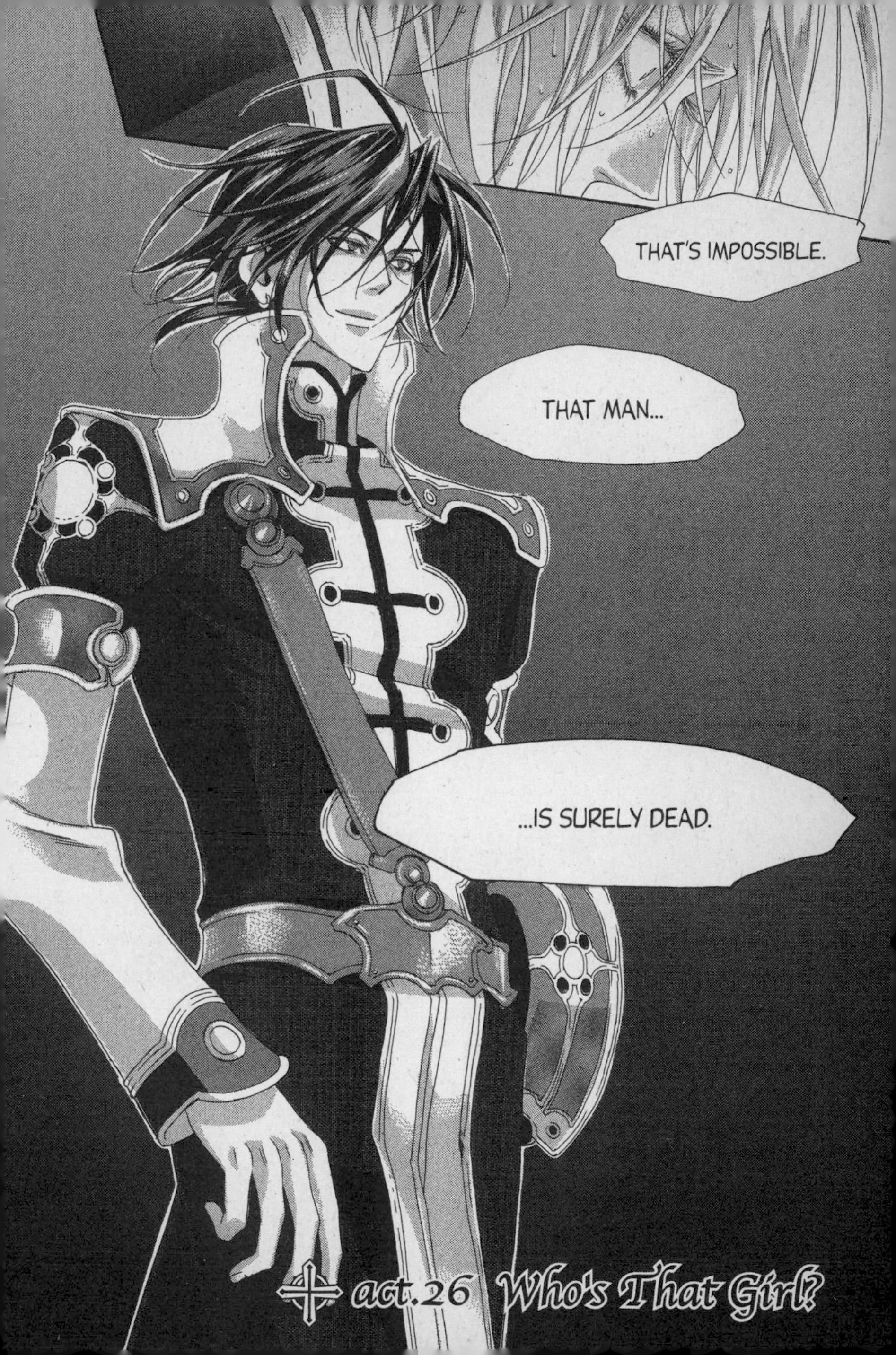
THAT'S IMPOSSIBLE.
THAT MAN...
...IS SURELY DEAD.
act.26 Who's That Girl?

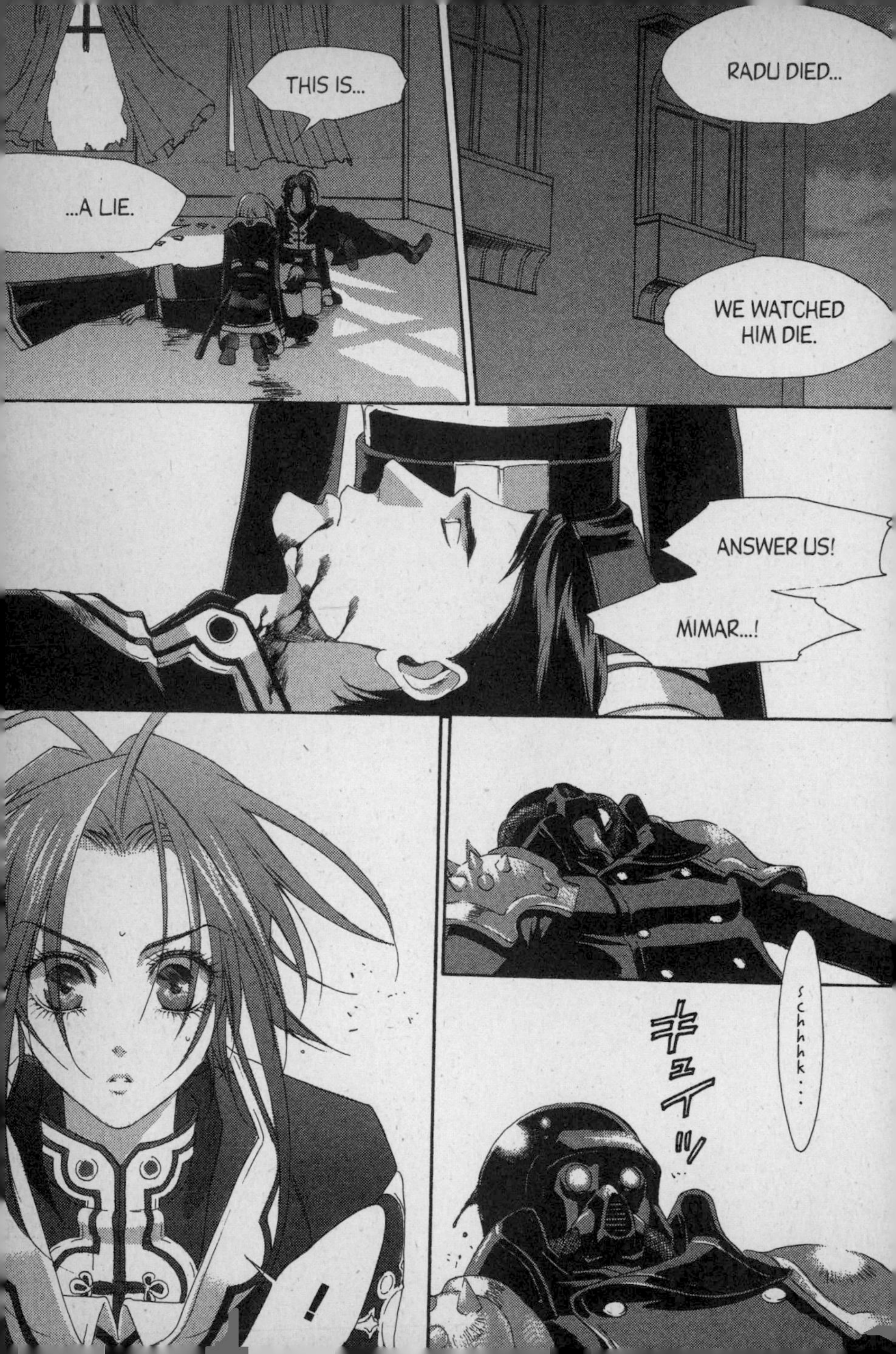
RADU DIED...
WE WATCHED HIM DIE.
THIS IS...
...A LIE.
ANSWER US!
MIMAR...!
Schhhk...
キュイッ
!

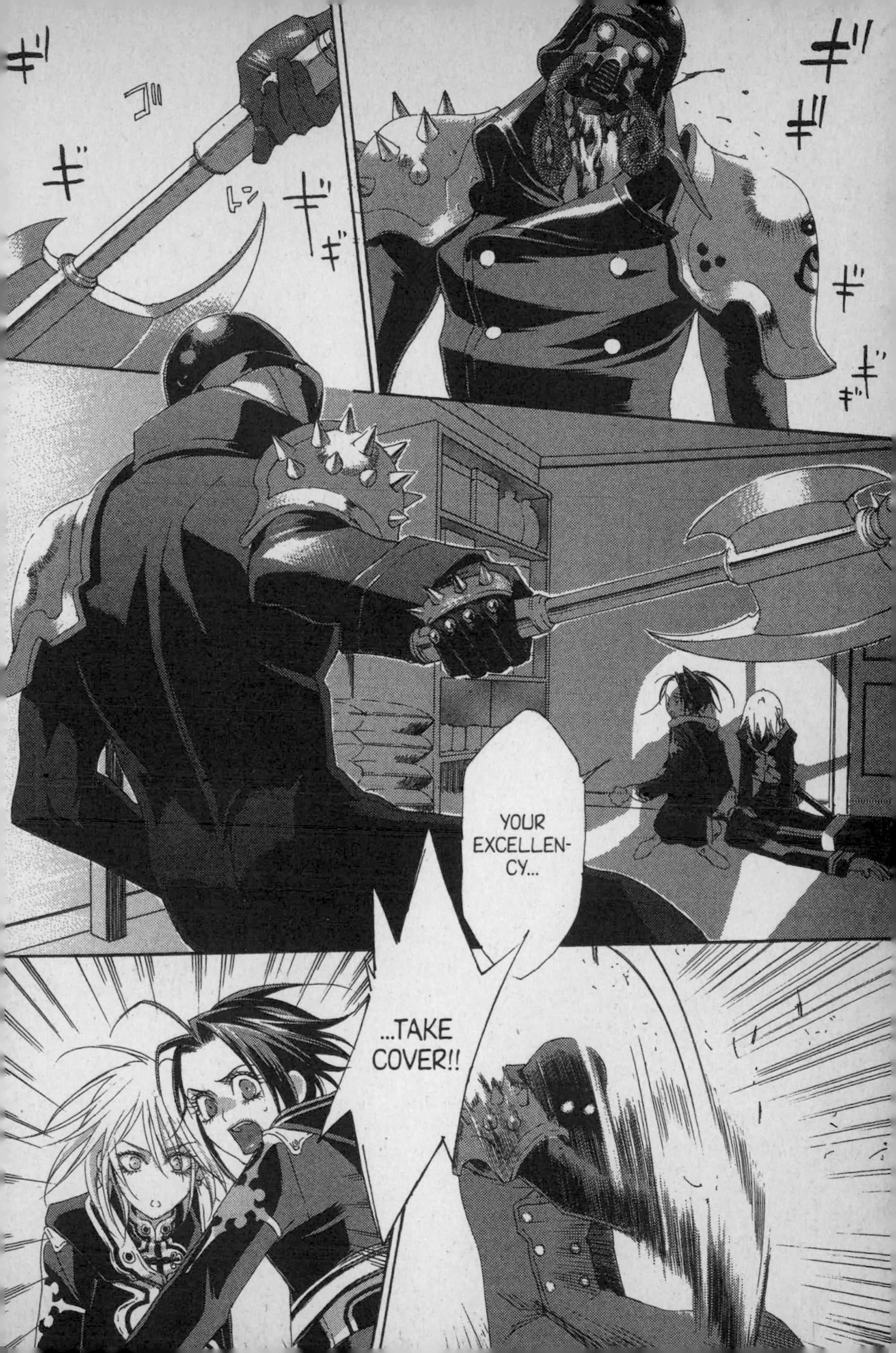
ギ
ゴ
ギ
ドン
ギ
ギ
ギ
ギ
ギ
ギ
ギ
YOUR EXCELLENCY...
...TAKE COVER!!

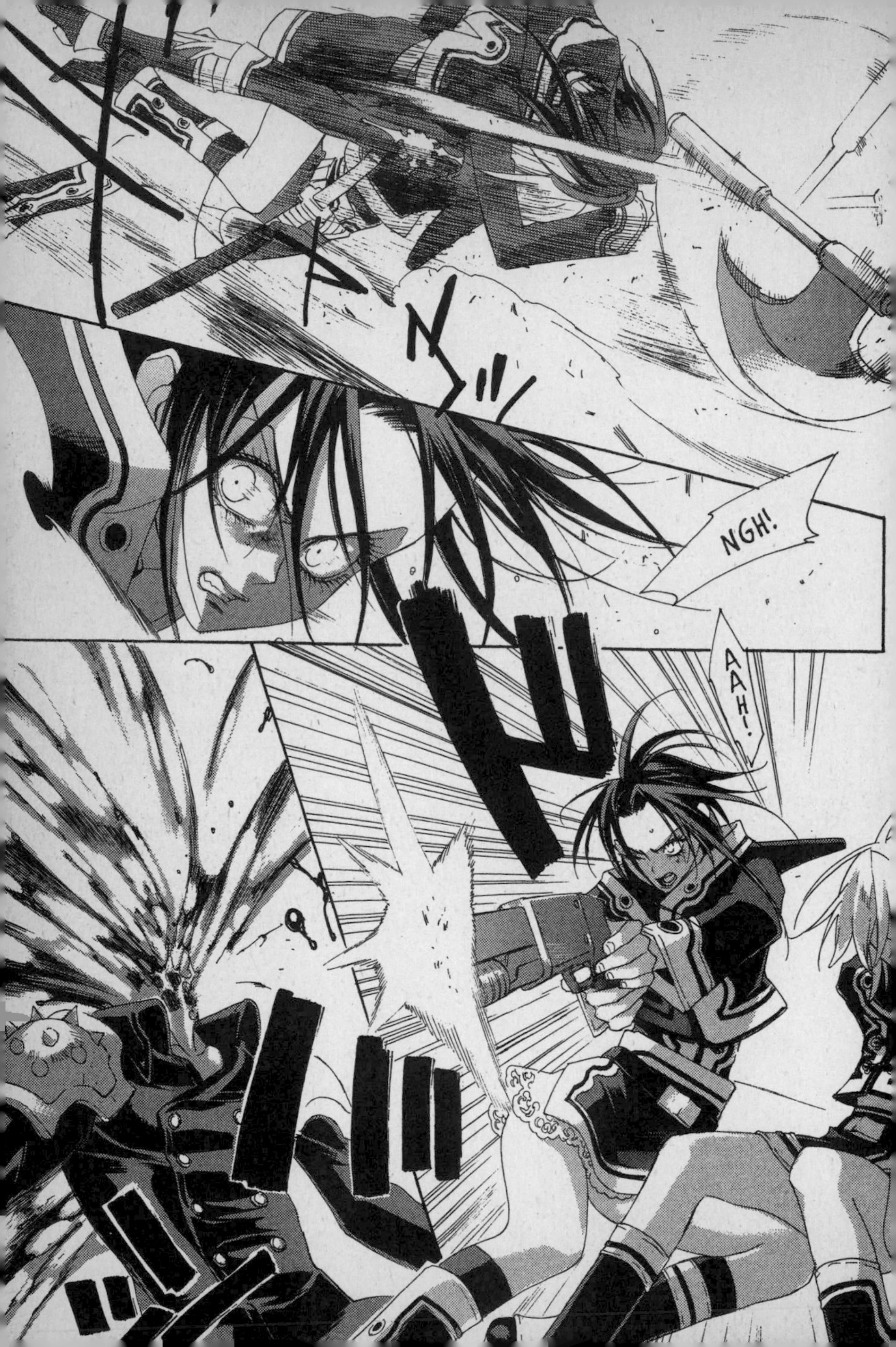
NGH!
AAH!

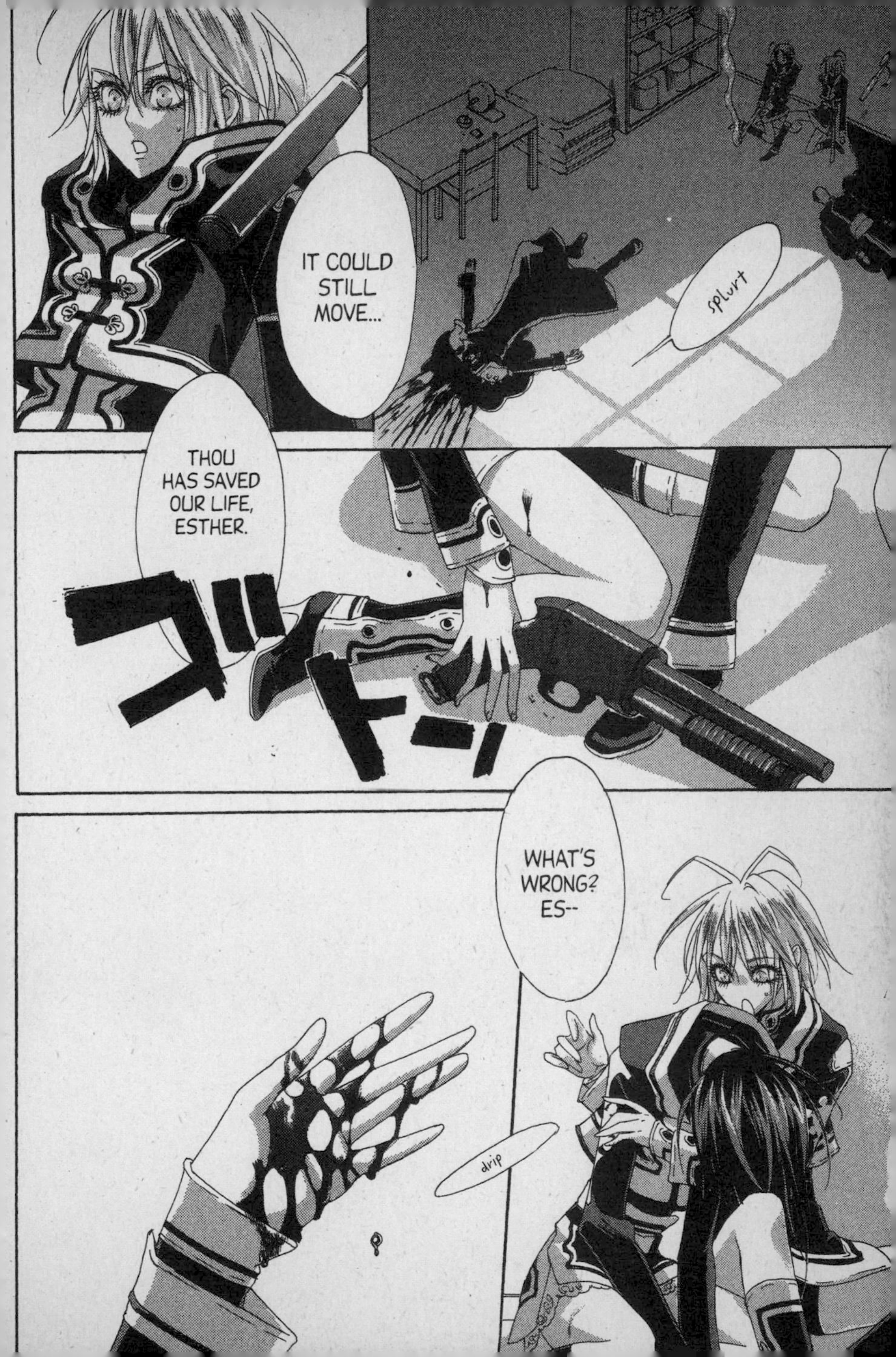
splurt
IT COULD STILL MOVE...
THOU HAS SAVED OUR LIFE, ESTHER.
ゴトッ
WHAT'S WRONG? ES--
drip

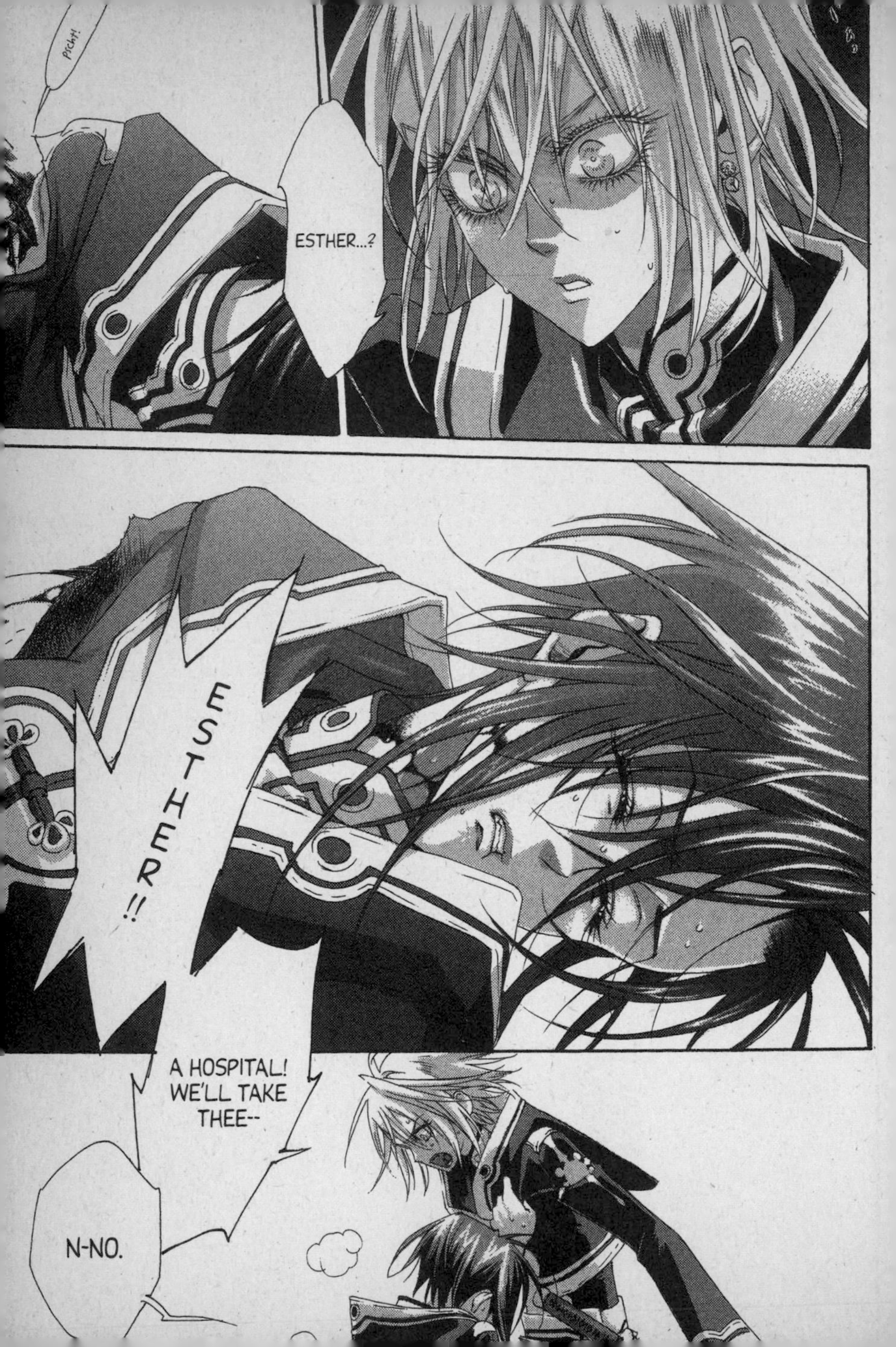
pscht!
ESTHER...?
ESTHER!!
A HOSPITAL! WE'LL TAKE THEE--
N-NO.

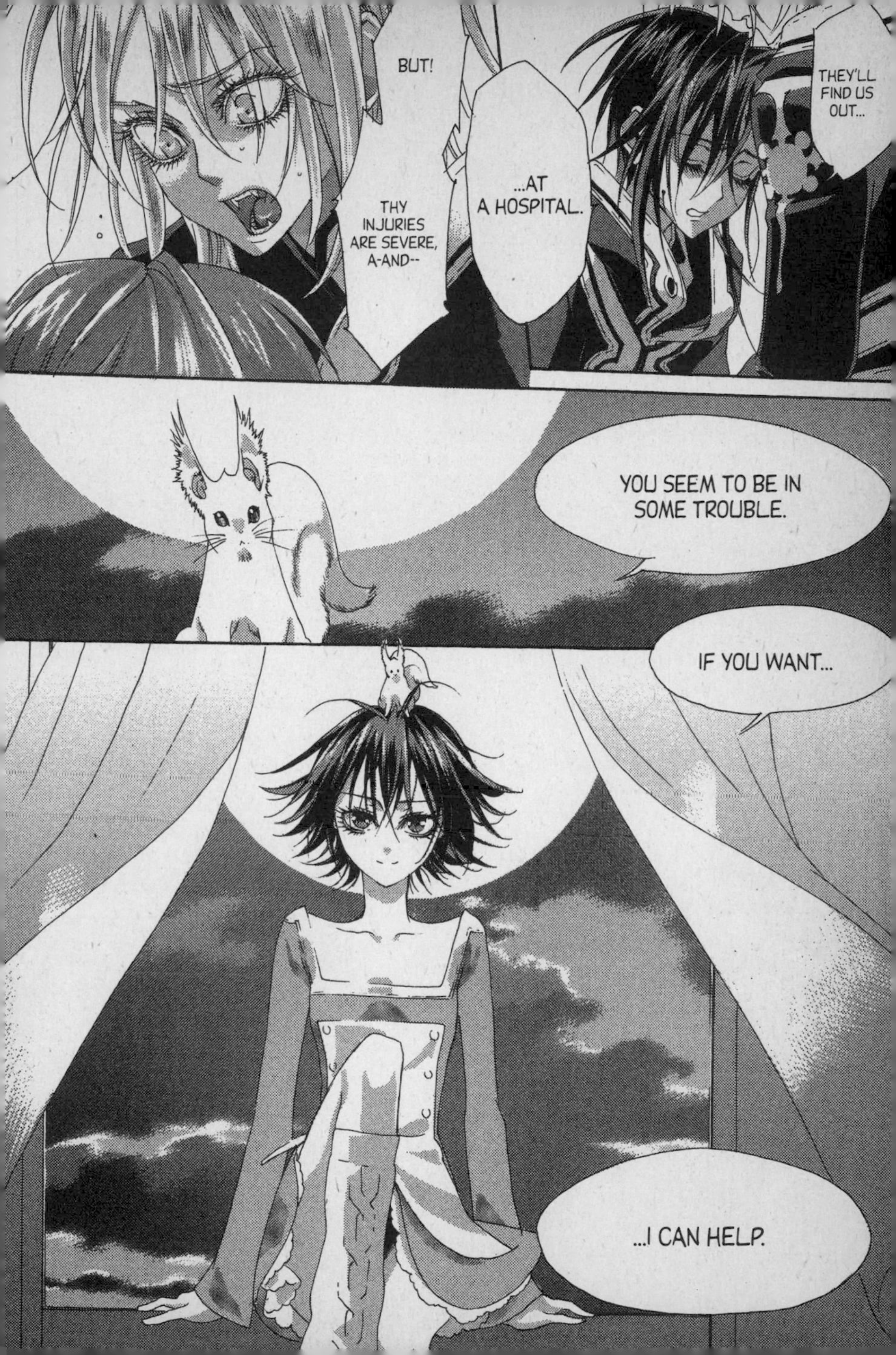
THEY'LL FIND US OUT...
...AT A HOSPITAL.
BUT!
THY INJURIES ARE SEVERE, A-AND--
YOU SEEM TO BE IN SOME TROUBLE.
IF YOU WANT...
...I CAN HELP.

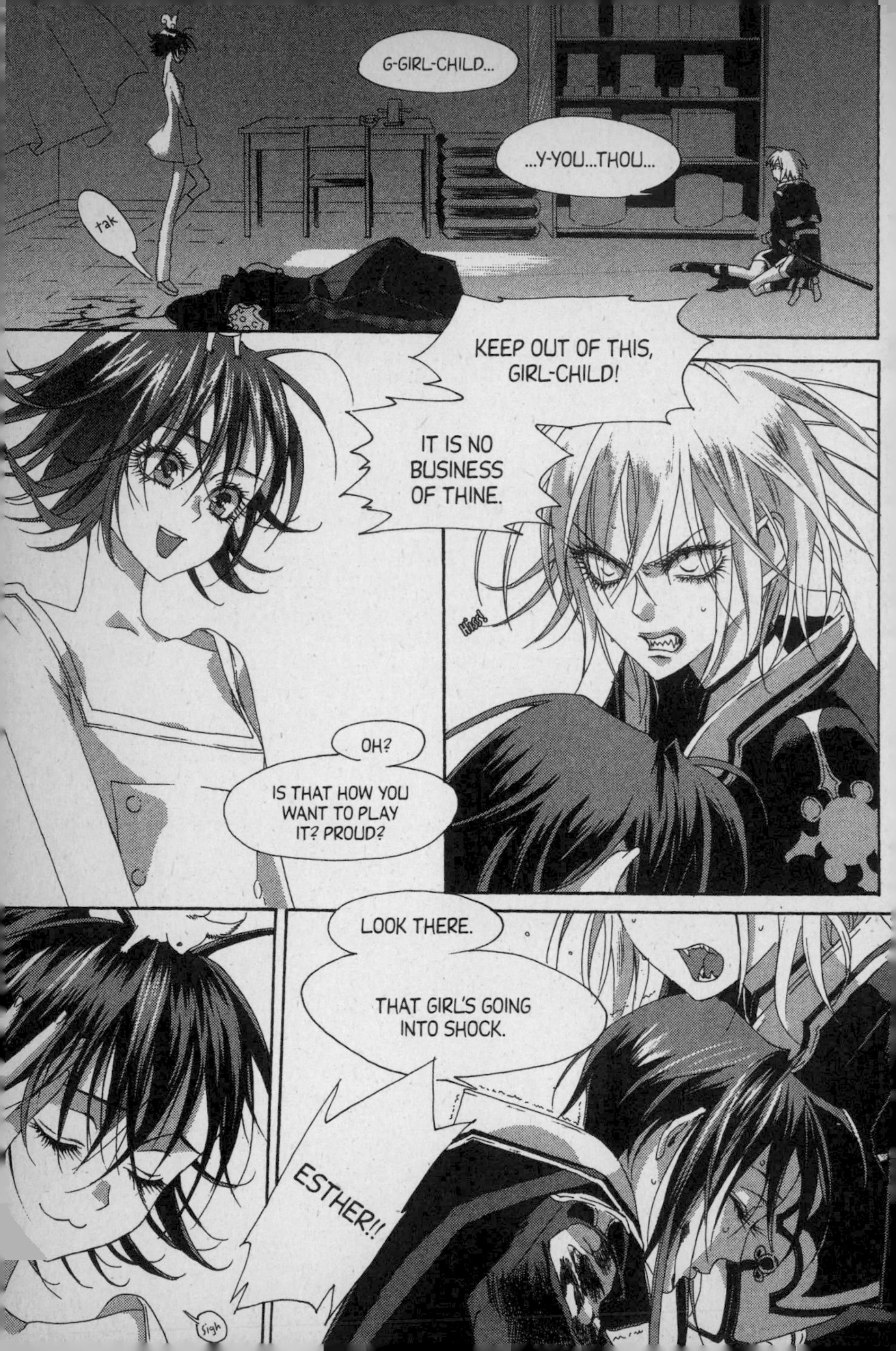
G-GIRL-CHILD...
...Y-YOU...THOU...
tak
KEEP OUT OF THIS, GIRL-CHILD!
IT IS NO BUSINESS OF THINE.
Hiss!
OH?
IS THAT HOW YOU WANT TO PLAY IT? PROUD?
LOOK THERE.
THAT GIRL'S GOING INTO SHOCK.
ESTHER!!
Sigh

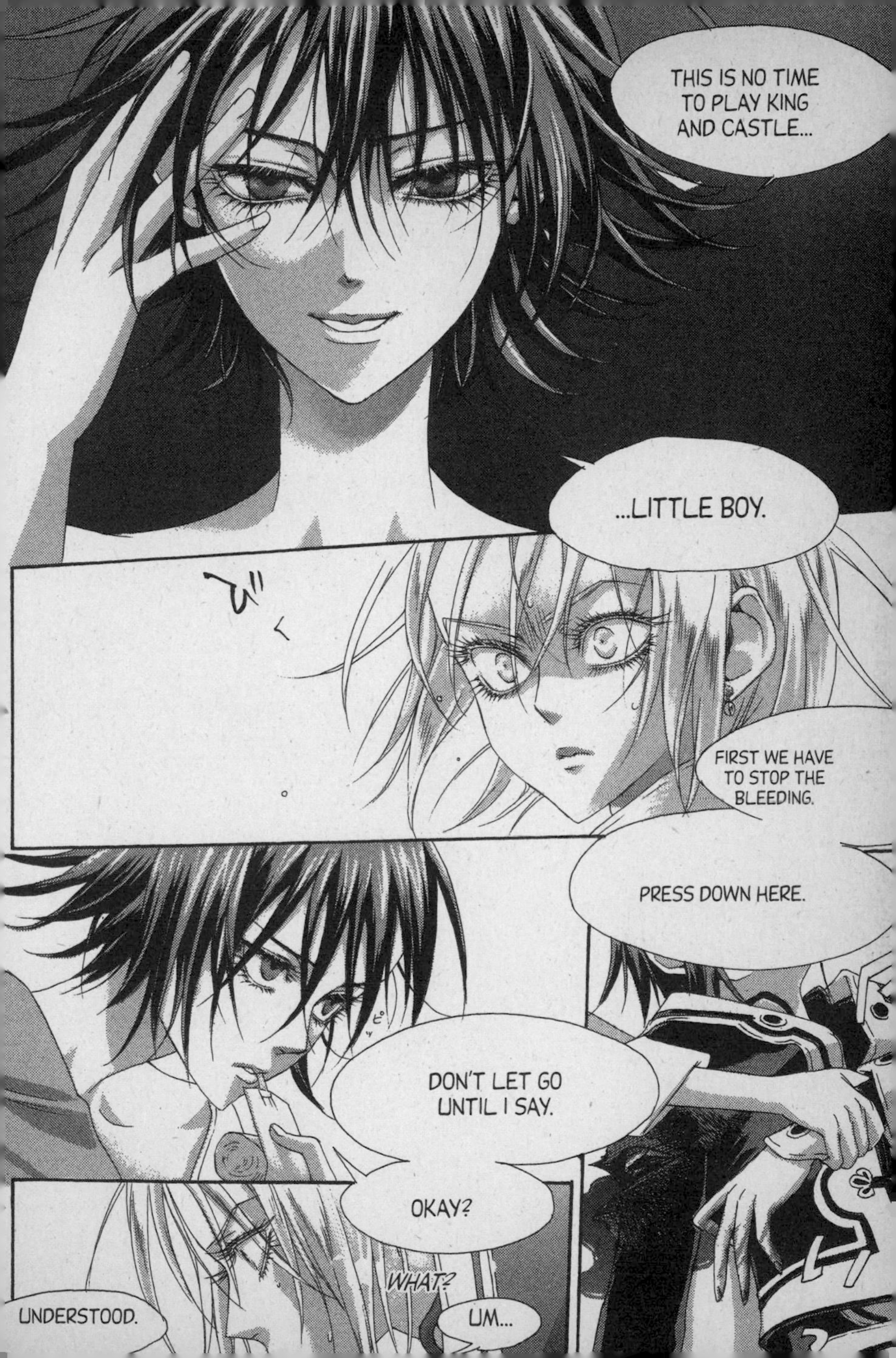
THIS IS NO TIME TO PLAY KING AND CASTLE...
...LITTLE BOY.
びく
FIRST WE HAVE TO STOP THE BLEEDING.
PRESS DOWN HERE.
DON'T LET GO UNTIL I SAY.
OKAY?
UM...
WHAT?
UNDERSTOOD.

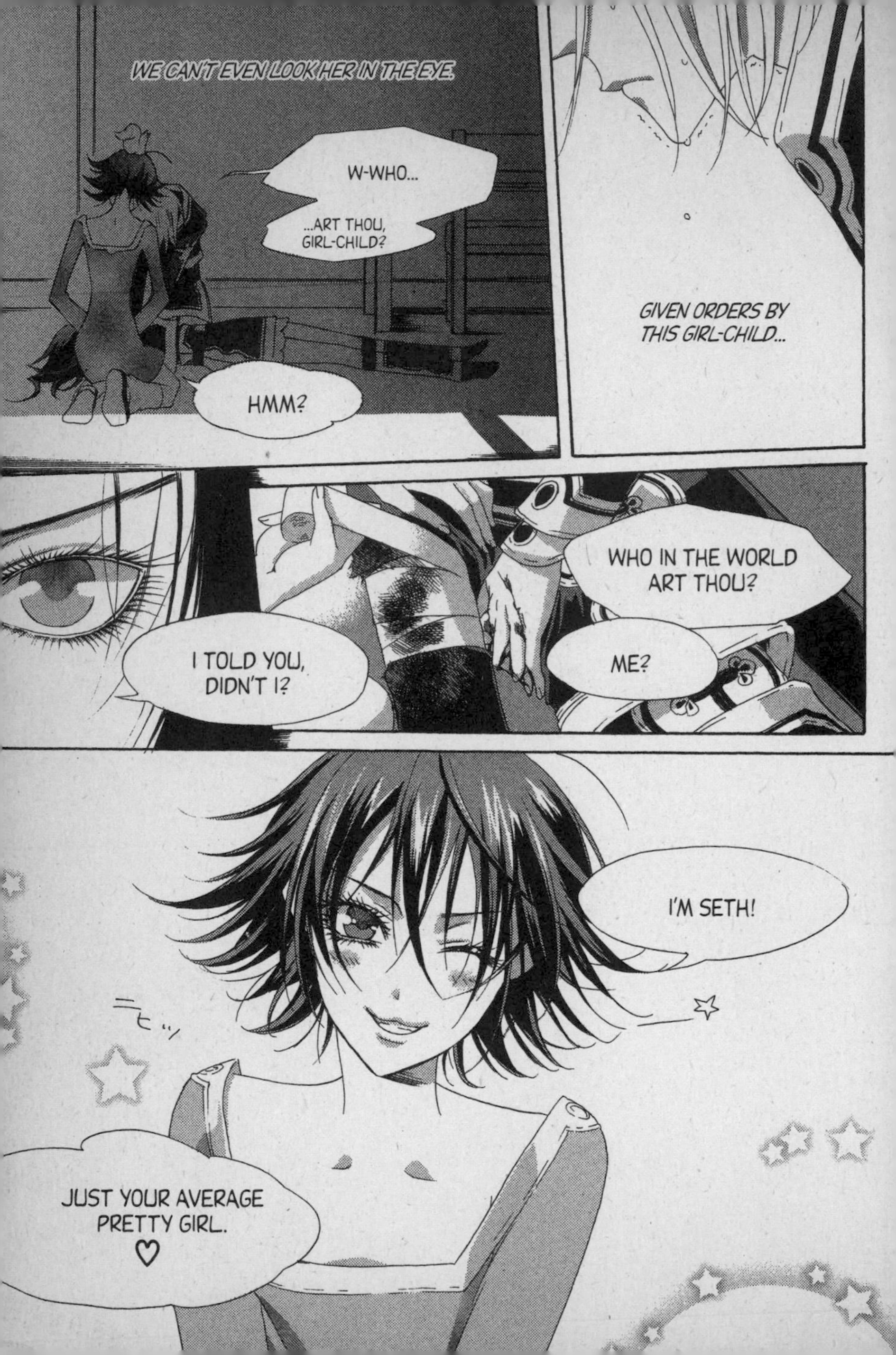
GIVEN ORDERS BY THIS GIRL-CHILD...
WE CAN'T EVEN LOOK HER IN THE EYE.
W-WHO...
...ART THOU, GIRL-CHILD?
HMM?
WHO IN THE WORLD ART THOU?
ME?
I TOLD YOU, DIDN'T I?
I'M SETH!
ニヒッ
JUST YOUR AVERAGE PRETTY GIRL. ♡

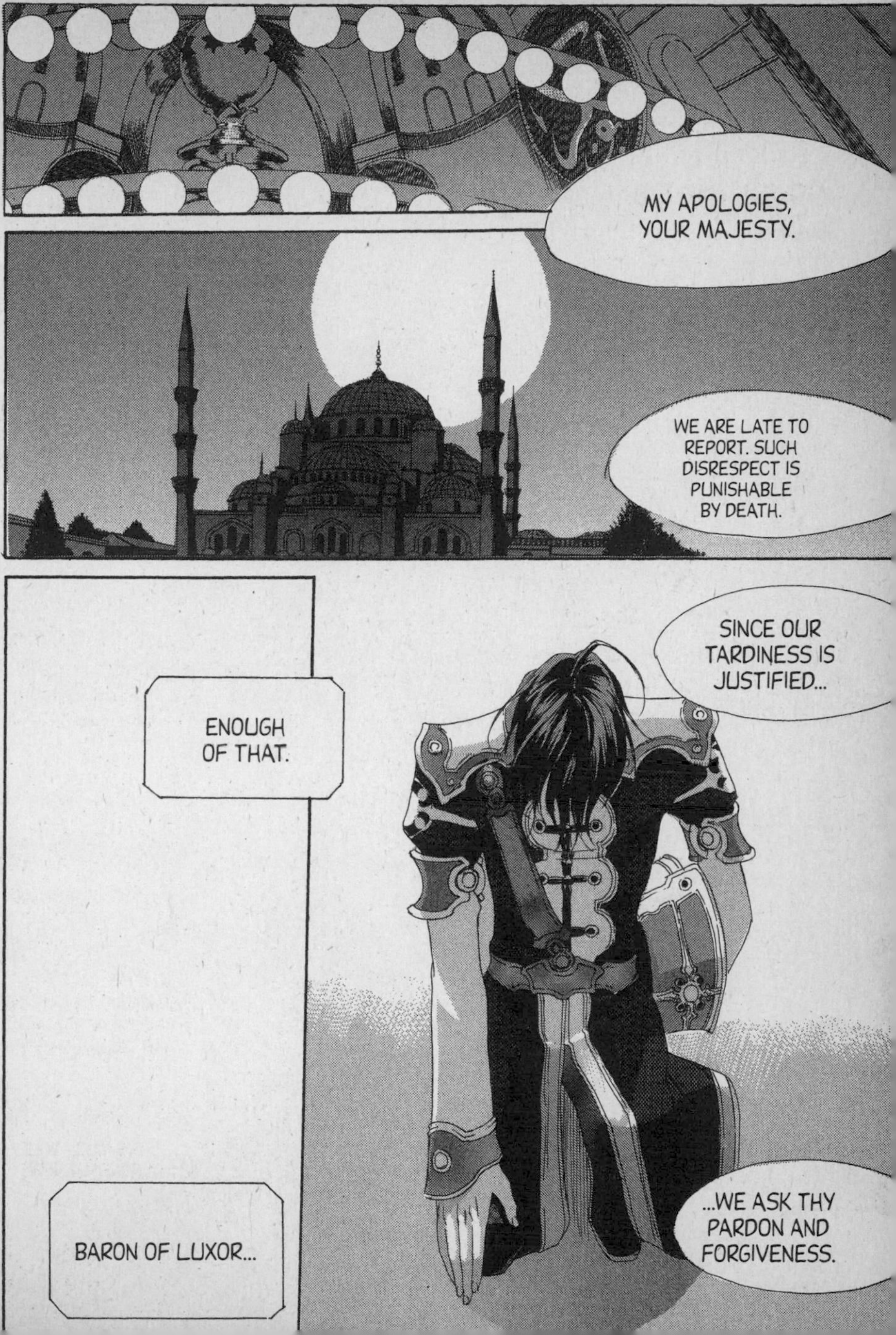

MY APOLOGIES, YOUR MAJESTY.
WE ARE LATE TO REPORT. SUCH DISRESPECT IS PUNISHABLE BY DEATH.
SINCE OUR TARDINESS IS JUSTIFIED...
...WE ASK THY PARDON AND FORGIVENESS.
ENOUGH OF THAT.
BARON OF LUXOR...

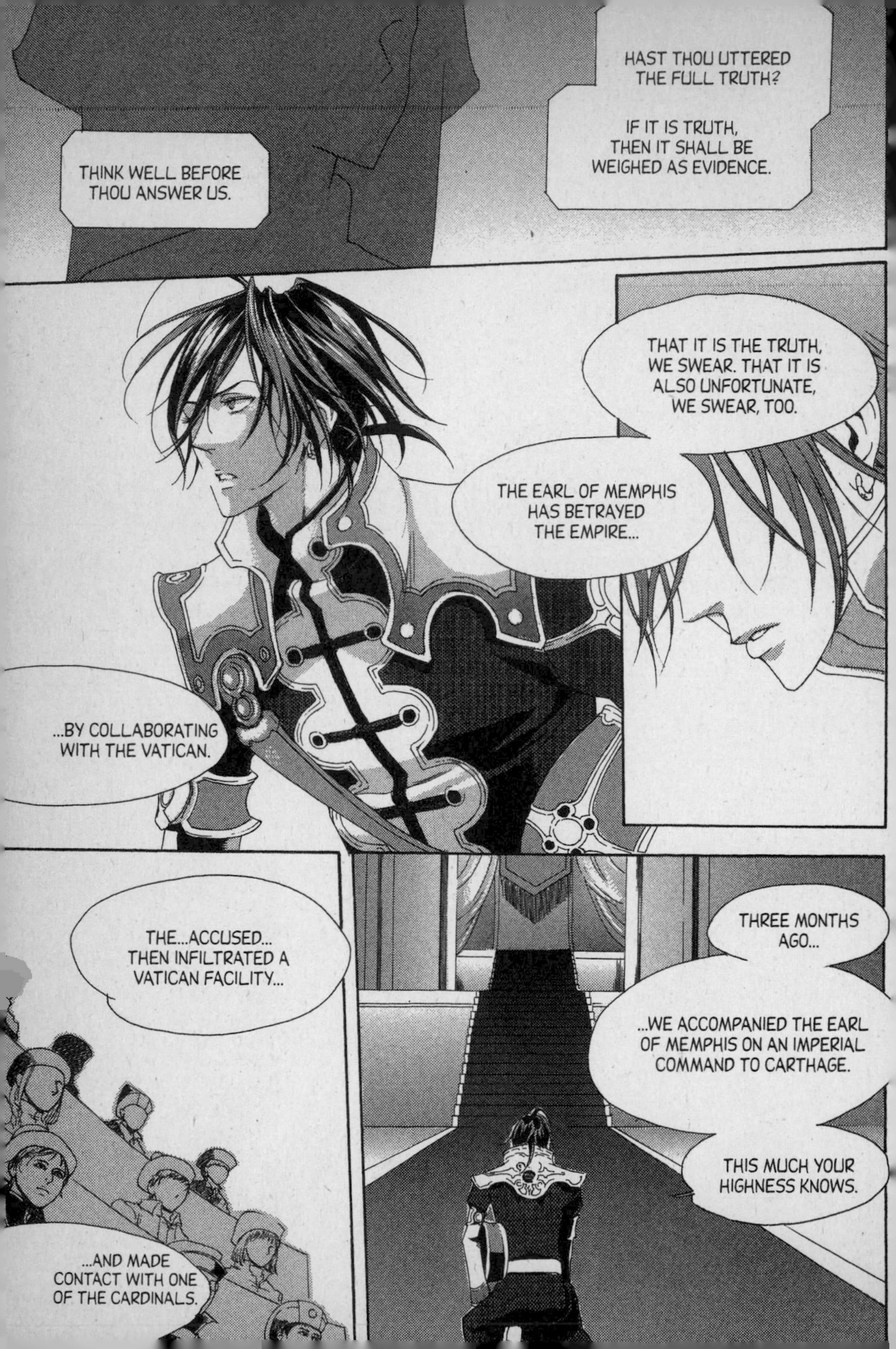
THINK WELL BEFORE THOU ANSWER US.
HAST THOU UTTERED THE FULL TRUTH?
IF IT IS TRUTH, THEN IT SHALL BE WEIGHED AS EVIDENCE.
THAT IT IS THE TRUTH, WE SWEAR. THAT IT IS ALSO UNFORTUNATE, WE SWEAR, TOO.
THE EARL OF MEMPHIS HAS BETRAYED THE EMPIRE...
...BY COLLABORATING WITH THE VATICAN.
THREE MONTHS AGO...
...WE ACCOMPANIED THE EARL OF MEMPHIS ON AN IMPERIAL COMMAND TO CARTHAGE.
THIS MUCH YOUR HIGHNESS KNOWS.
THE...ACCUSED... THEN INFILTRATED A VATICAN FACILITY...
...AND MADE CONTACT WITH ONE OF THE CARDINALS.

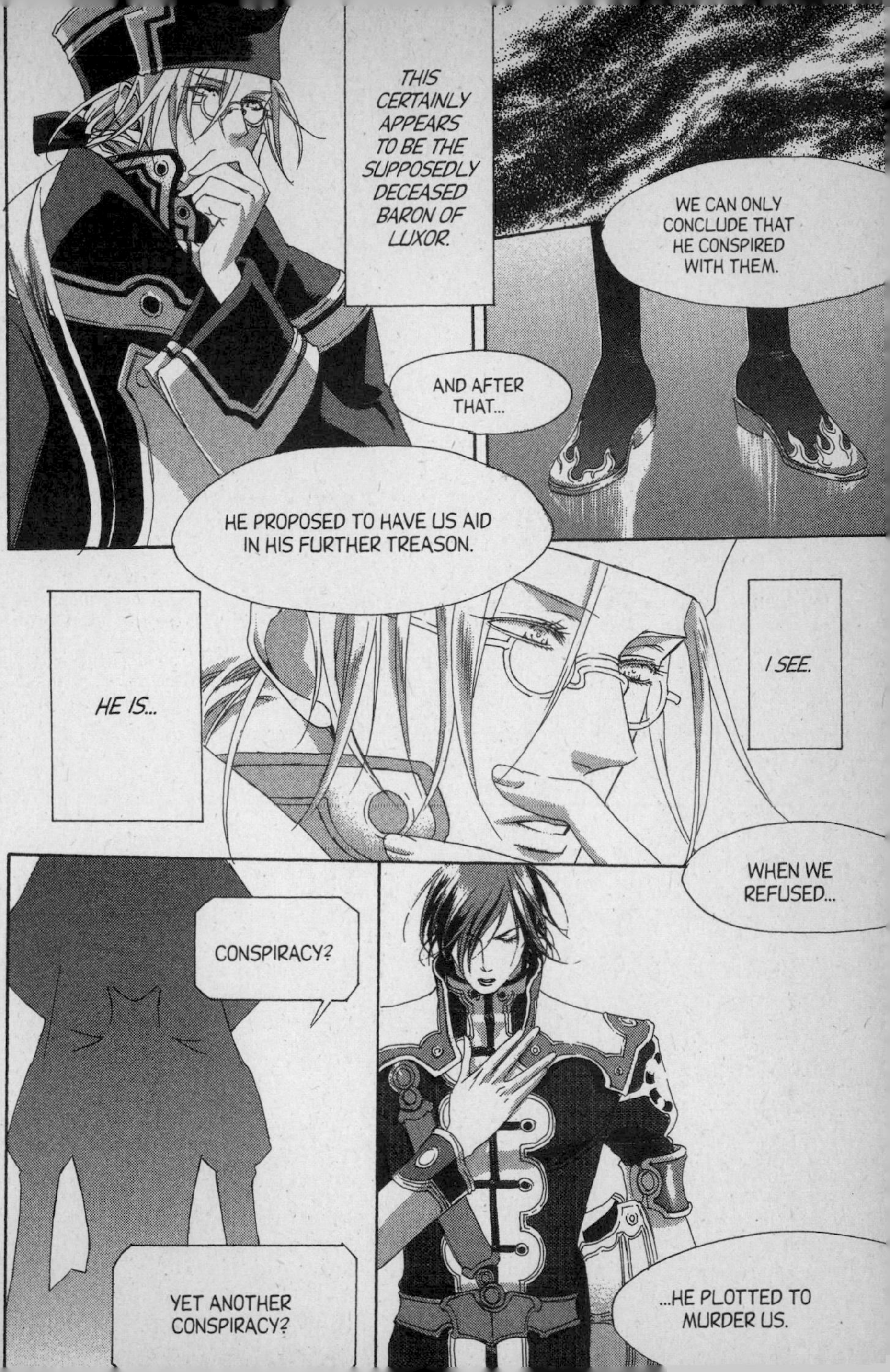
WE CAN ONLY CONCLUDE THAT HE CONSPIRED WITH THEM.
THIS CERTAINLY APPEARS TO BE THE SUPPOSEDLY DECEASED BARON OF LUXOR.
AND AFTER THAT...
HE PROPOSED TO HAVE US AID IN HIS FURTHER TREASON.
I SEE.
HE IS...
WHEN WE REFUSED...
...HE PLOTTED TO MURDER US.
CONSPIRACY?
YET ANOTHER CONSPIRACY?

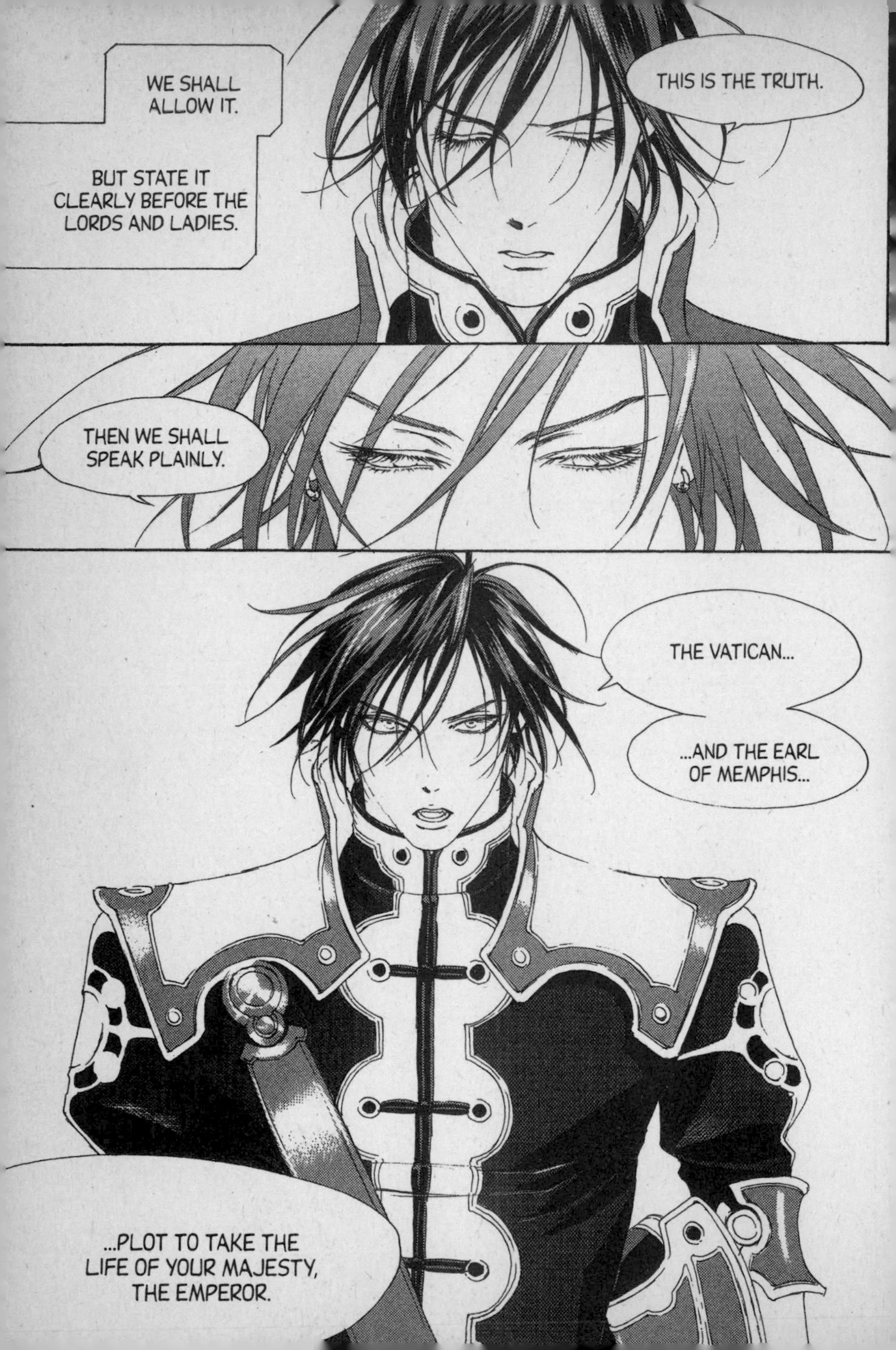
THIS IS THE TRUTH.
WE SHALL ALLOW IT.
BUT STATE IT CLEARLY BEFORE THE LORDS AND LADIES.
THEN WE SHALL SPEAK PLAINLY.
THE VATICAN...
...AND THE EARL OF MEMPHIS...
...PLOT TO TAKE THE LIFE OF YOUR MAJESTY, THE EMPEROR.

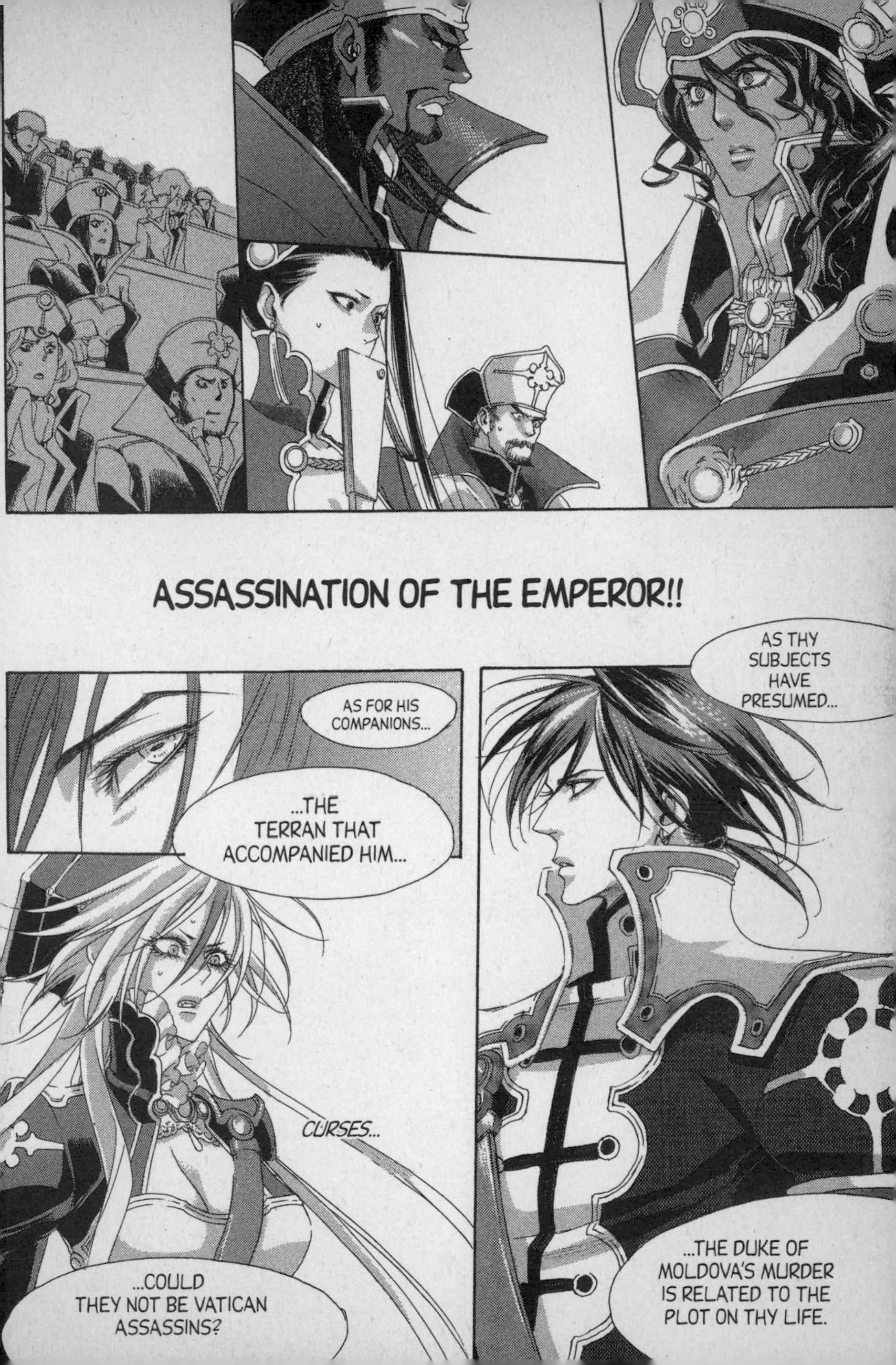
ASSASSINATION OF THE EMPEROR!!
AS THY SUBJECTS HAVE PRESUMED...
...THE DUKE OF MOLDOVA'S MURDER IS RELATED TO THE PLOT ON THY LIFE.
AS FOR HIS COMPANIONS...
...THE TERRAN THAT ACCOMPANIED HIM...
CURSES...
...COULD THEY NOT BE VATICAN ASSASSINS?

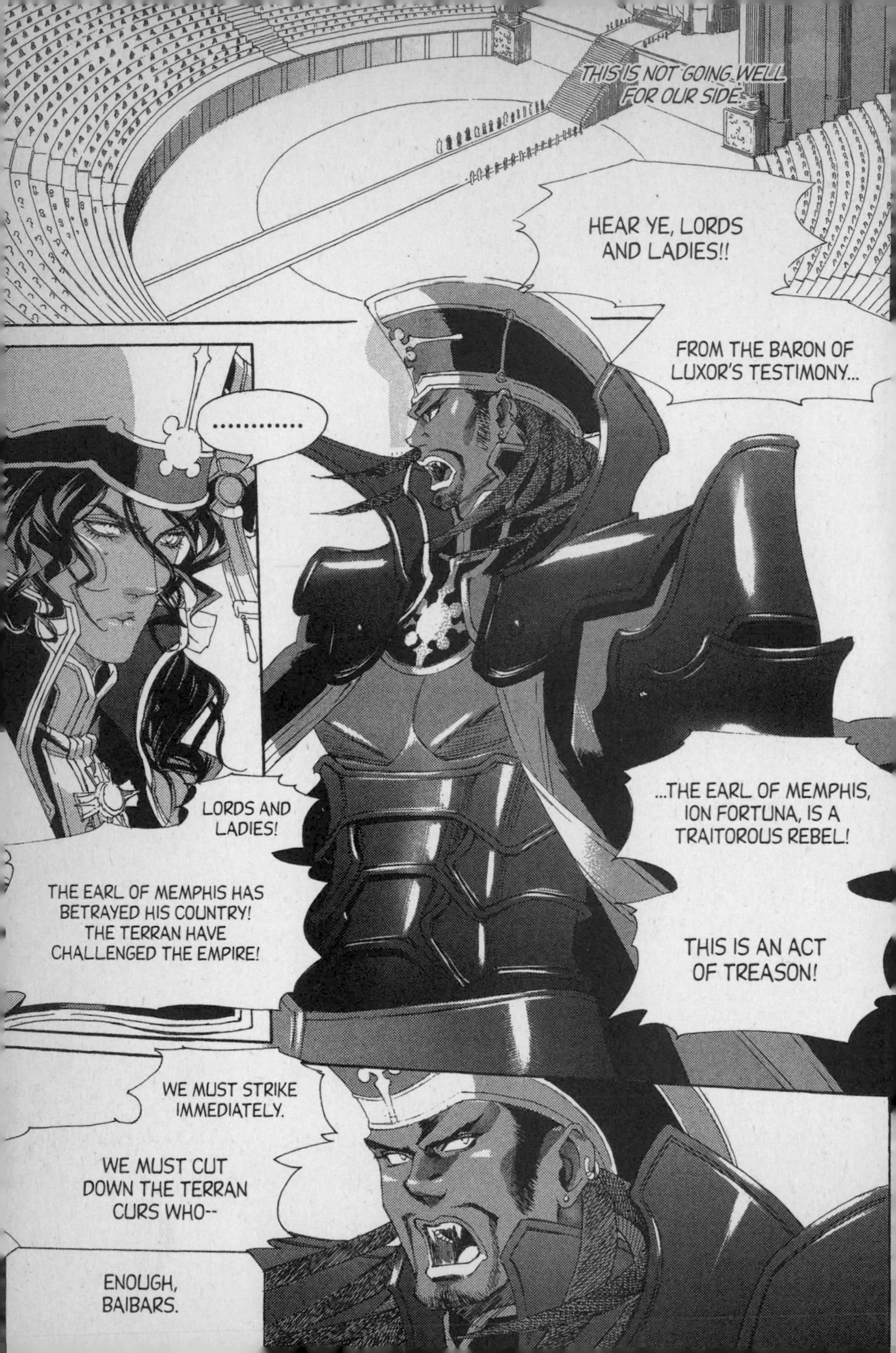
THIS IS NOT GOING WELL FOR OUR SIDE.
HEAR YE, LORDS AND LADIES!!
FROM THE BARON OF LUXOR'S TESTIMONY...
.............
...THE EARL OF MEMPHIS, ION FORTUNA, IS A TRAITOROUS REBEL!
LORDS AND LADIES!
THE EARL OF MEMPHIS HAS BETRAYED HIS COUNTRY! THE TERRAN HAVE CHALLENGED THE EMPIRE!
THIS IS AN ACT OF TREASON!
WE MUST STRIKE IMMEDIATELY.
WE MUST CUT DOWN THE TERRAN CURS WHO--
ENOUGH, BAIBARS.

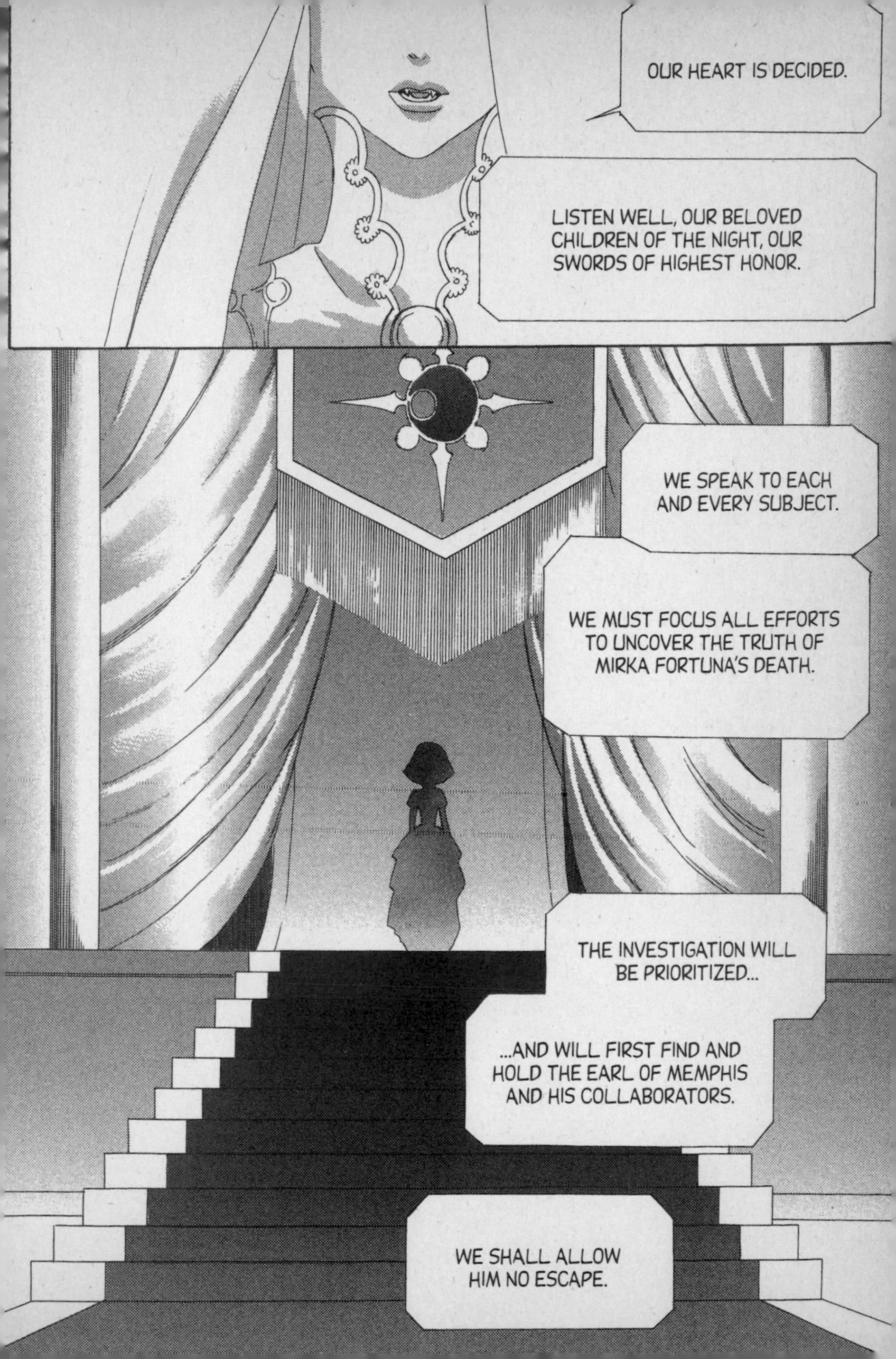
OUR HEART IS DECIDED.
LISTEN WELL, OUR BELOVED CHILDREN OF THE NIGHT, OUR SWORDS OF HIGHEST HONOR.
WE SPEAK TO EACH AND EVERY SUBJECT.
WE MUST FOCUS ALL EFFORTS TO UNCOVER THE TRUTH OF MIRKA FORTUNA'S DEATH.
THE INVESTIGATION WILL BE PRIORITIZED...
...AND WILL FIRST FIND AND HOLD THE EARL OF MEMPHIS AND HIS COLLABORATORS.
WE SHALL ALLOW HIM NO ESCAPE.

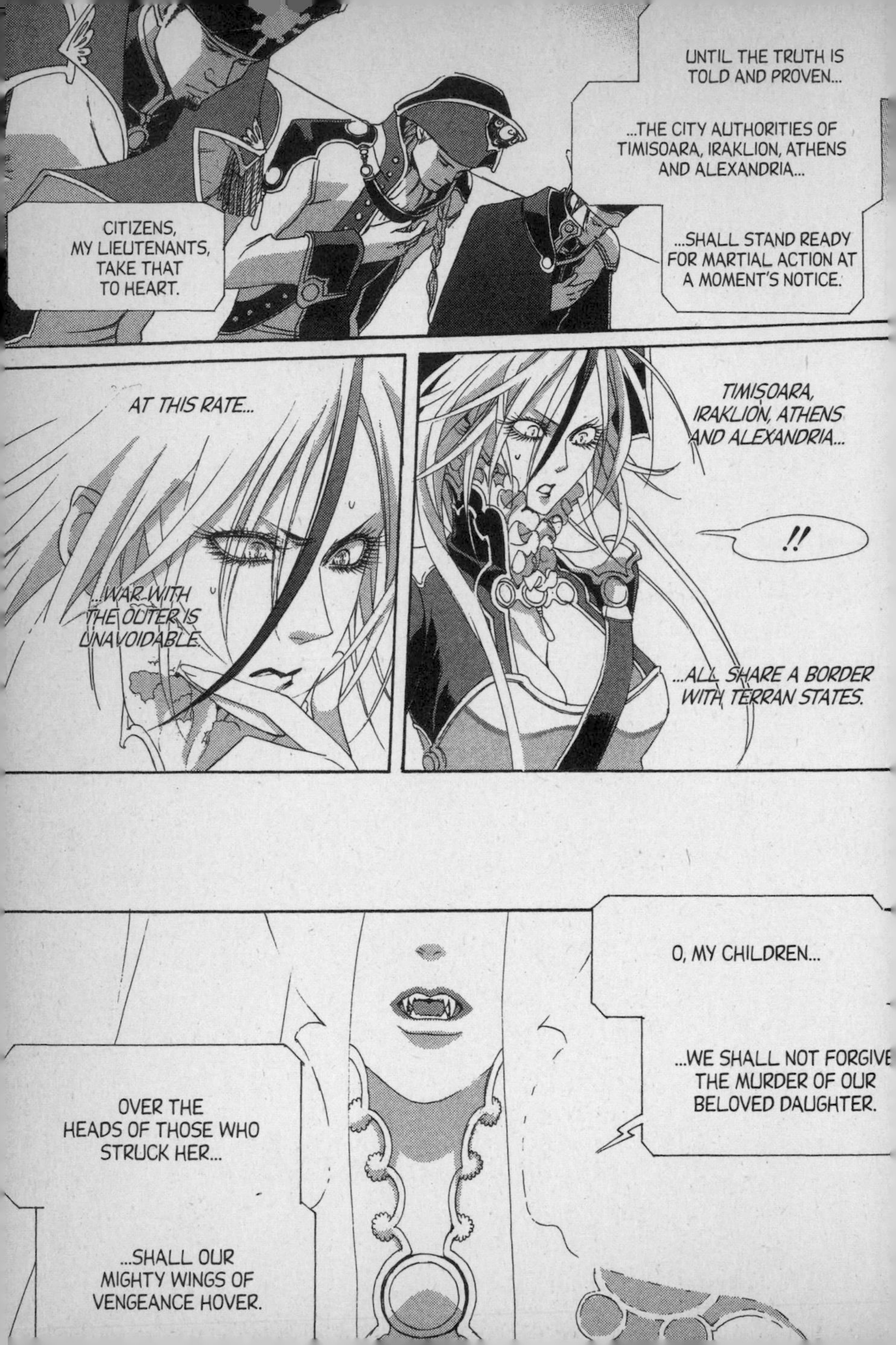
UNTIL THE TRUTH IS TOLD AND PROVEN...
...THE CITY AUTHORITIES OF TIMISOARA, IRAKLION, ATHENS AND ALEXANDRIA...
...SHALL STAND READY FOR MARTIAL ACTION AT A MOMENT'S NOTICE.
CITIZENS, MY LIEUTENANTS, TAKE THAT TO HEART.
TIMIȘOARA, IRAKLION, ATHENS AND ALEXANDRIA...
!!
...ALL SHARE A BORDER WITH TERRAN STATES.
AT THIS RATE...
...WAR WITH THE OUTER IS UNAVOIDABLE.
O, MY CHILDREN...
...WE SHALL NOT FORGIVE THE MURDER OF OUR BELOVED DAUGHTER.
OVER THE HEADS OF THOSE WHO STRUCK HER...
...SHALL OUR MIGHTY WINGS OF VENGEANCE HOVER.

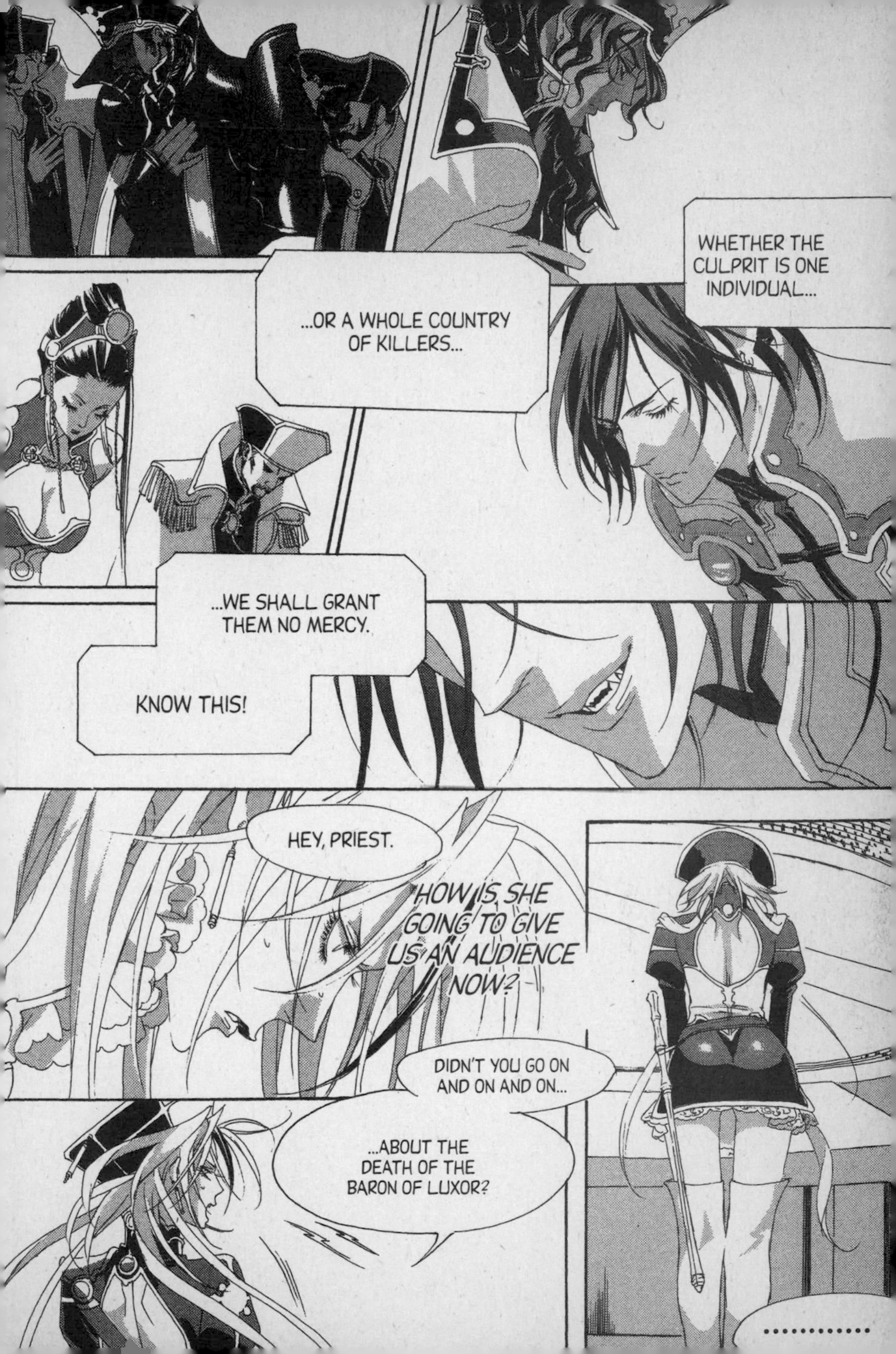

WHETHER THE CULPRIT IS ONE INDIVIDUAL...
...OR A WHOLE COUNTRY OF KILLERS...
KNOW THIS!
...WE SHALL GRANT THEM NO MERCY.
HEY, PRIEST.
HOW IS SHE GOING TO GIVE US AN AUDIENCE NOW?
DIDN'T YOU GO ON AND ON AND ON...
...ABOUT THE DEATH OF THE BARON OF LUXOR?
........

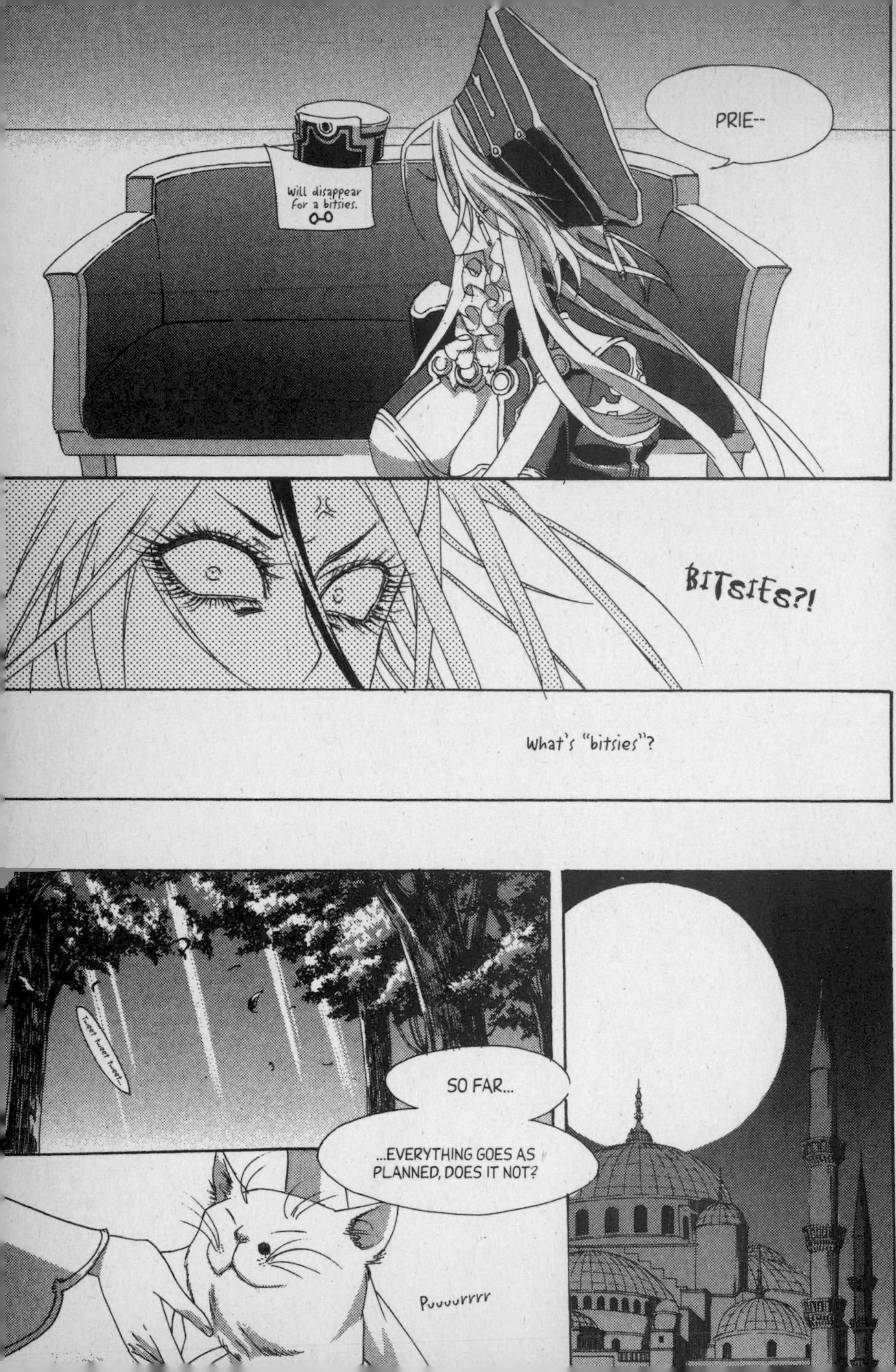
PRIE--
Will disappear for a bitsies.
BITSIES?!
What's "bitsies"?
Tweet tweet tweet...
SO FAR...
...EVERYTHING GOES AS PLANNED, DOES IT NOT?
Puuuurrrr

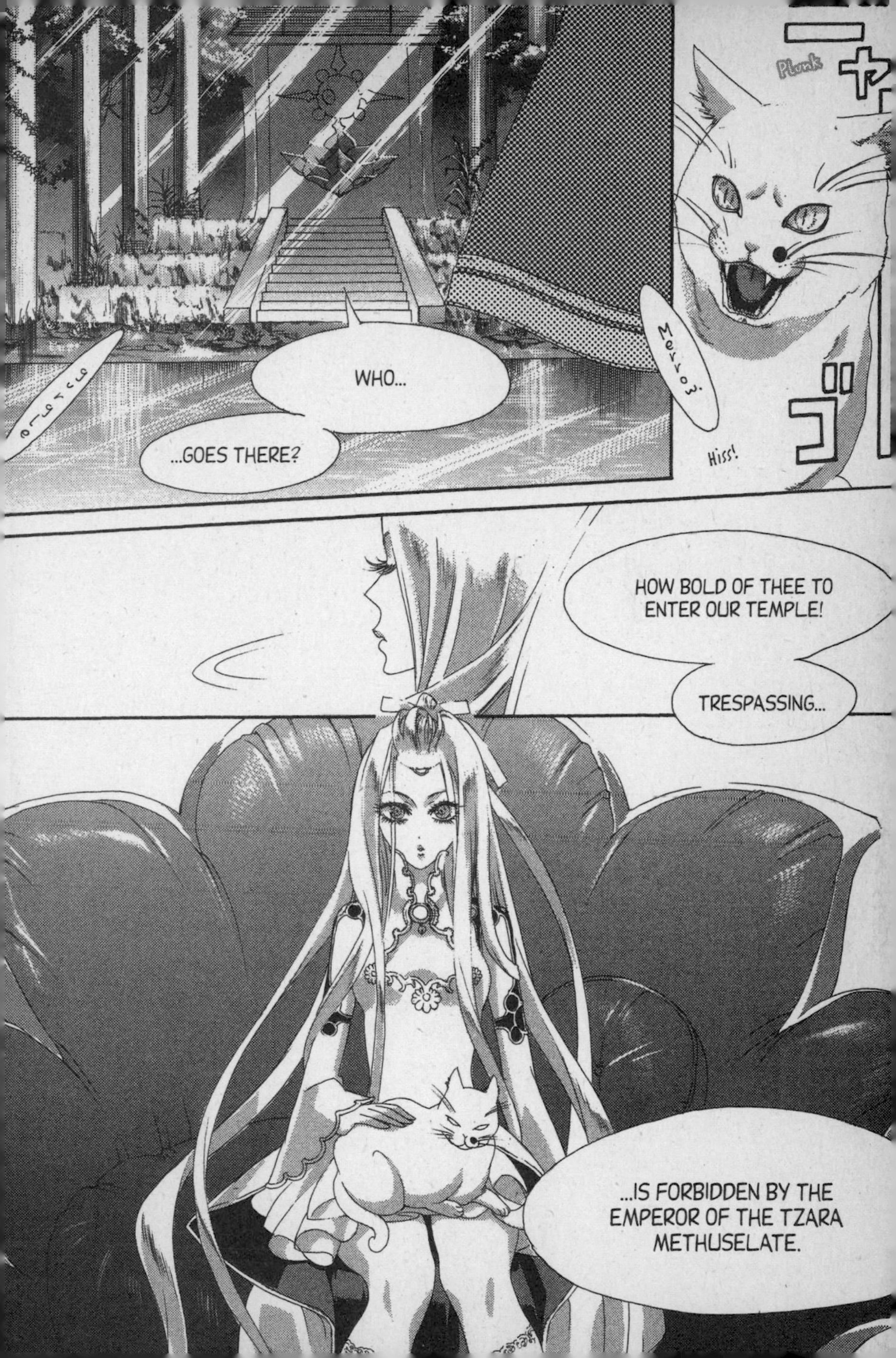

ニャ
Plonk
Merrow!
ゴ
Hiss!
WHO...
...GOES THERE?
HOW BOLD OF THEE TO ENTER OUR TEMPLE!
TRESPASSING...
...IS FORBIDDEN BY THE EMPEROR OF THE TZARA METHUSELATE.

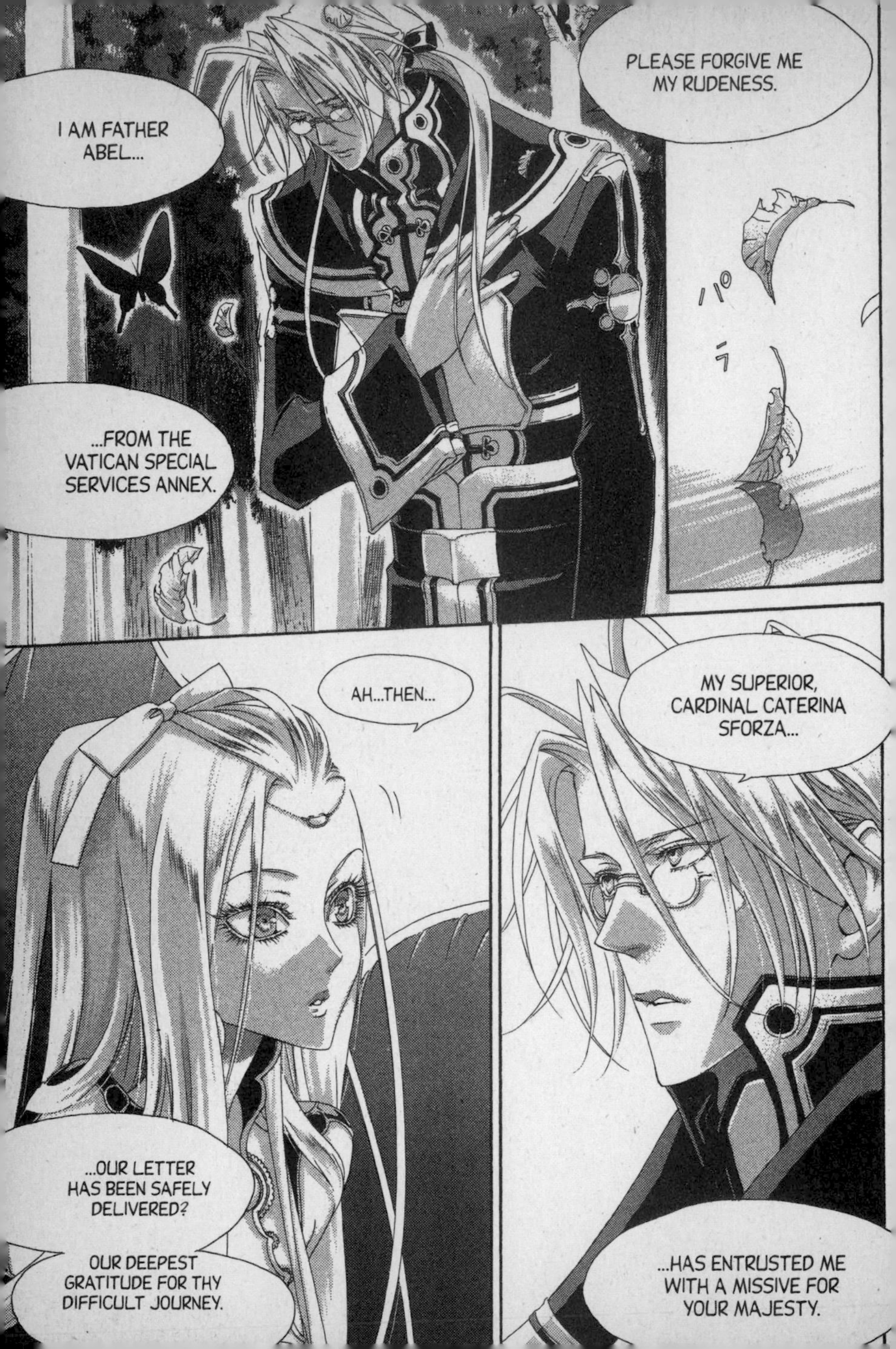
PLEASE FORGIVE ME MY RUDENESS.
I AM FATHER ABEL...
...FROM THE VATICAN SPECIAL SERVICES ANNEX.
MY SUPERIOR, CARDINAL CATERINA SFORZA...
...HAS ENTRUSTED ME WITH A MISSIVE FOR YOUR MAJESTY.
AH...THEN...
...OUR LETTER HAS BEEN SAFELY DELIVERED?
OUR DEEPEST GRATITUDE FOR THY DIFFICULT JOURNEY.

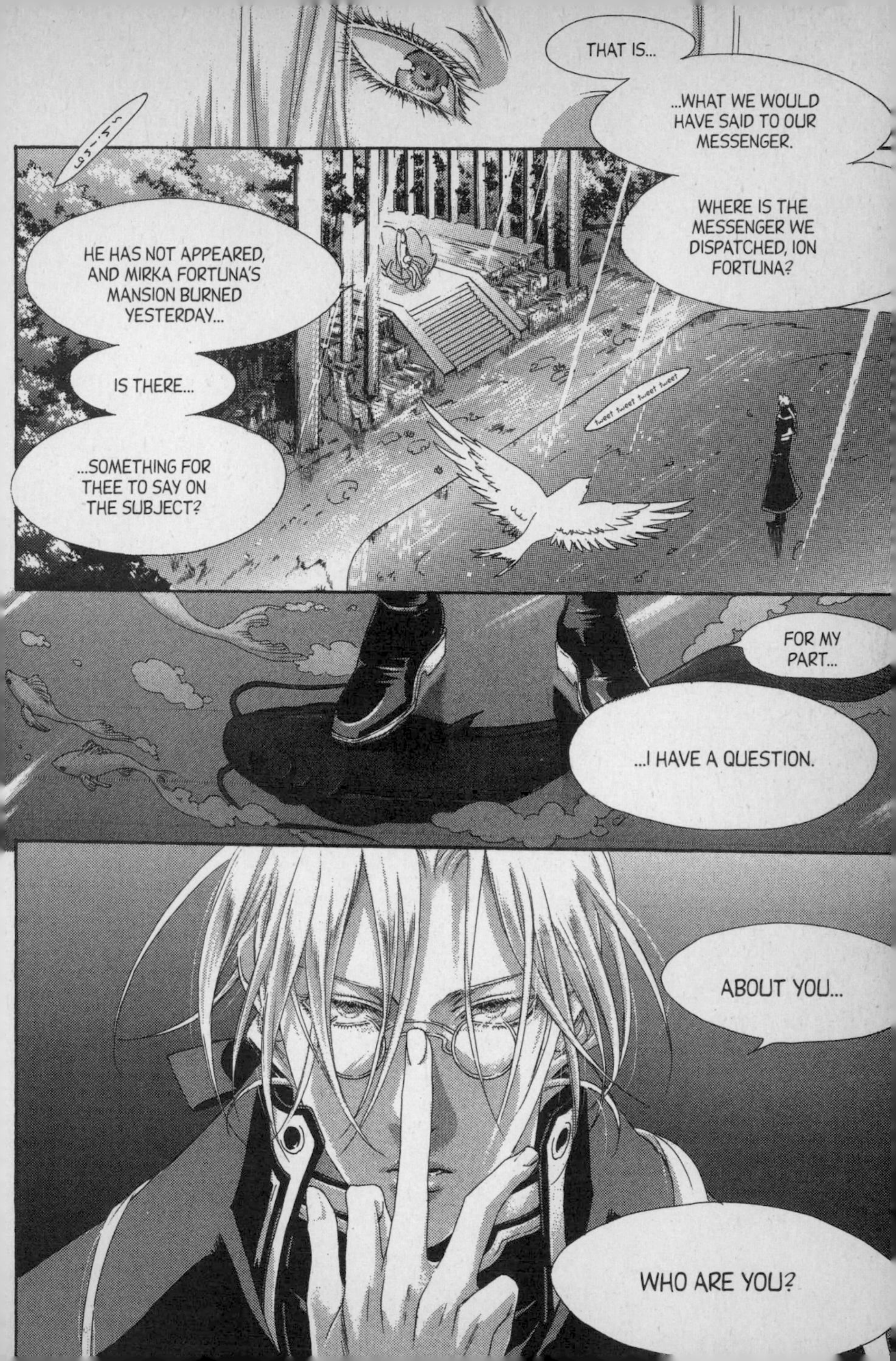
THAT IS...
...WHAT WE WOULD HAVE SAID TO OUR MESSENGER.
WHERE IS THE MESSENGER WE DISPATCHED, ION FORTUNA?
HE HAS NOT APPEARED, AND MIRKA FORTUNA'S MANSION BURNED YESTERDAY...
IS THERE...
...SOMETHING FOR THEE TO SAY ON THE SUBJECT?
tweet tweet tweet tweet
FOR MY PART...
...I HAVE A QUESTION.
ABOUT YOU...
WHO ARE YOU?

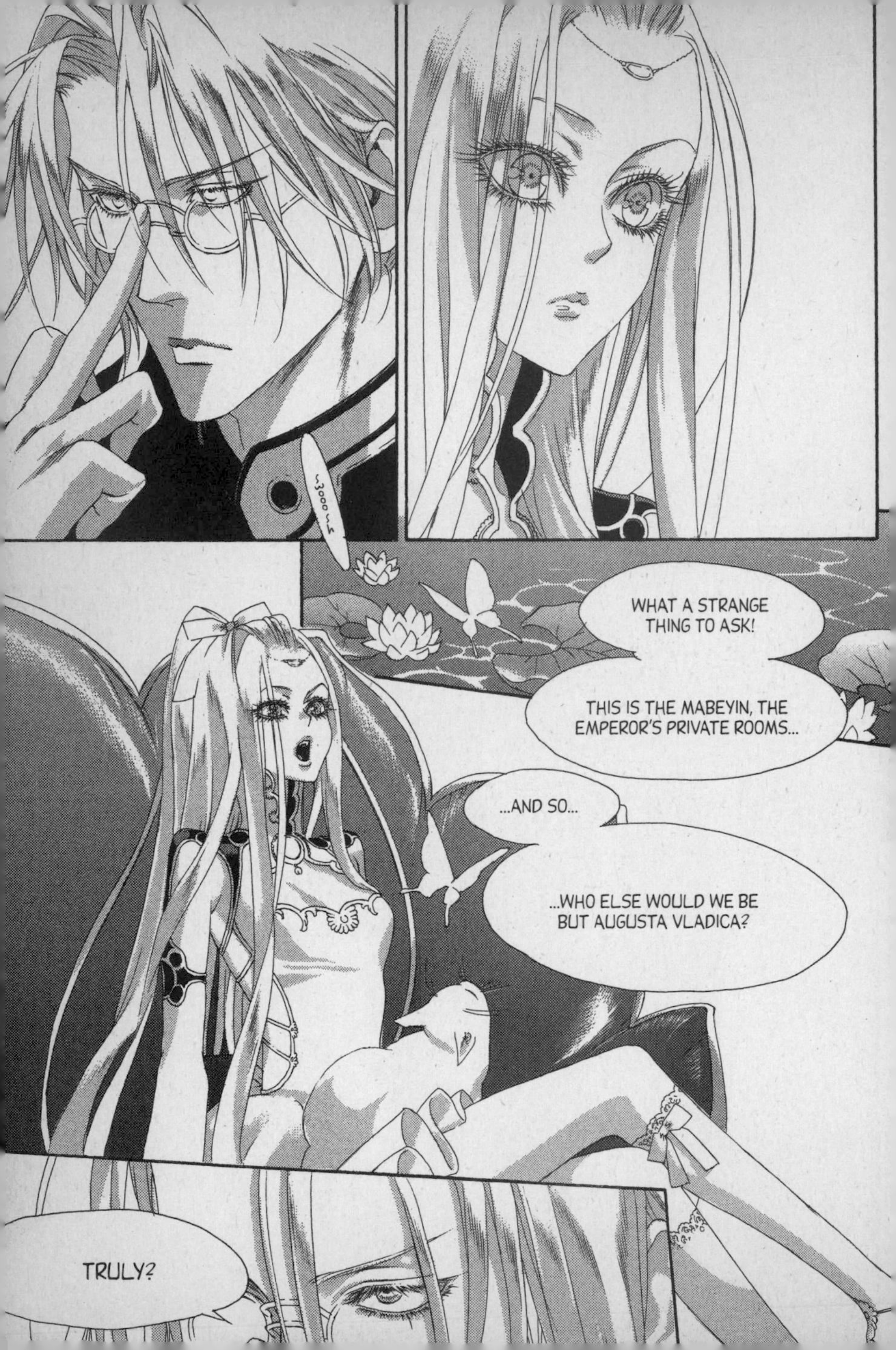
WHAT A STRANGE THING TO ASK!
THIS IS THE MABEYIN, THE EMPEROR'S PRIVATE ROOMS...
...AND SO...
...WHO ELSE WOULD WE BE BUT AUGUSTA VLADICA?
TRULY?

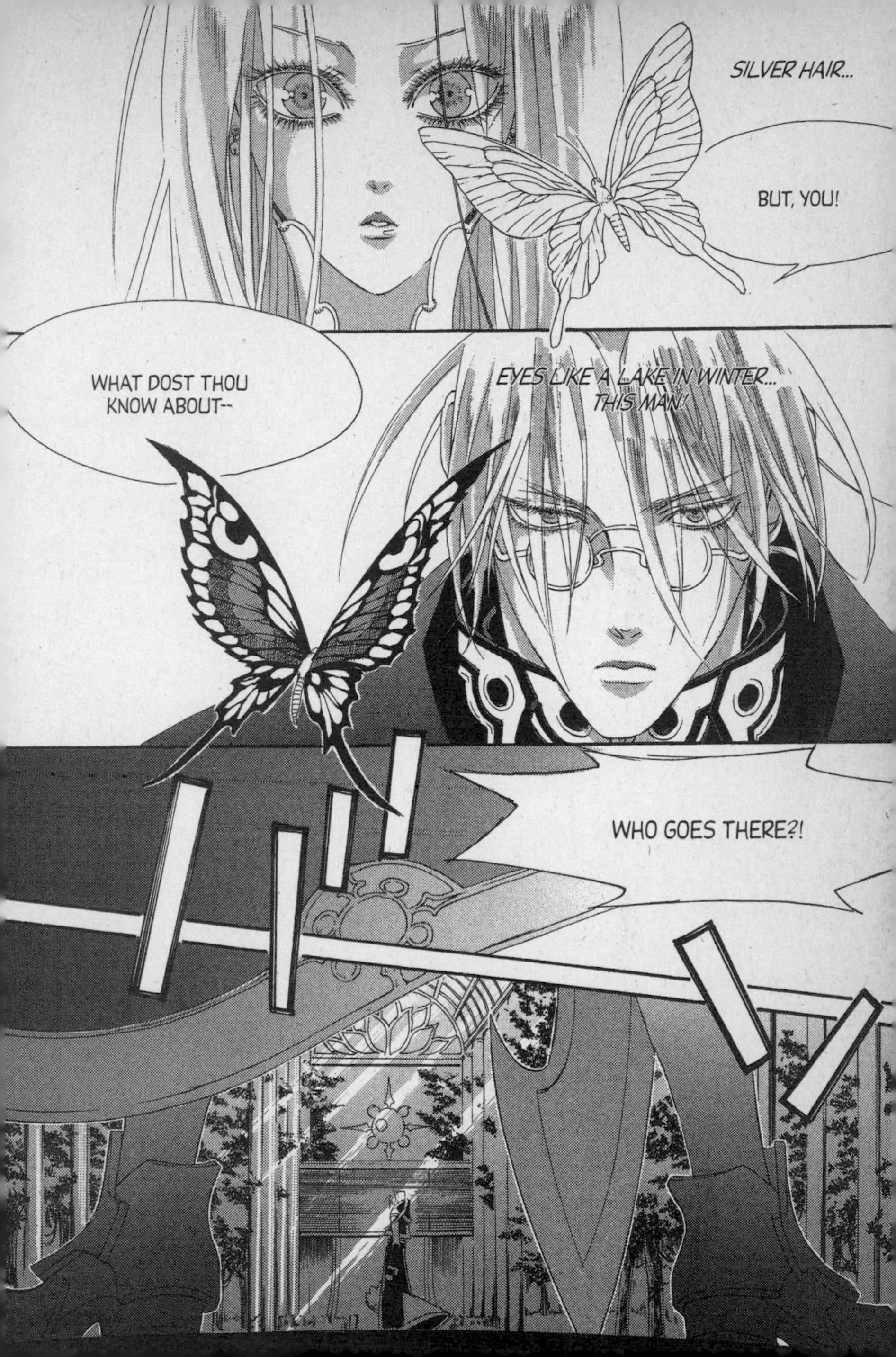
SILVER HAIR...
BUT, YOU!
EYES LIKE A LAKE IN WINTER... THIS MAN!
WHAT DOST THOU KNOW ABOUT--
WHO GOES THERE?!

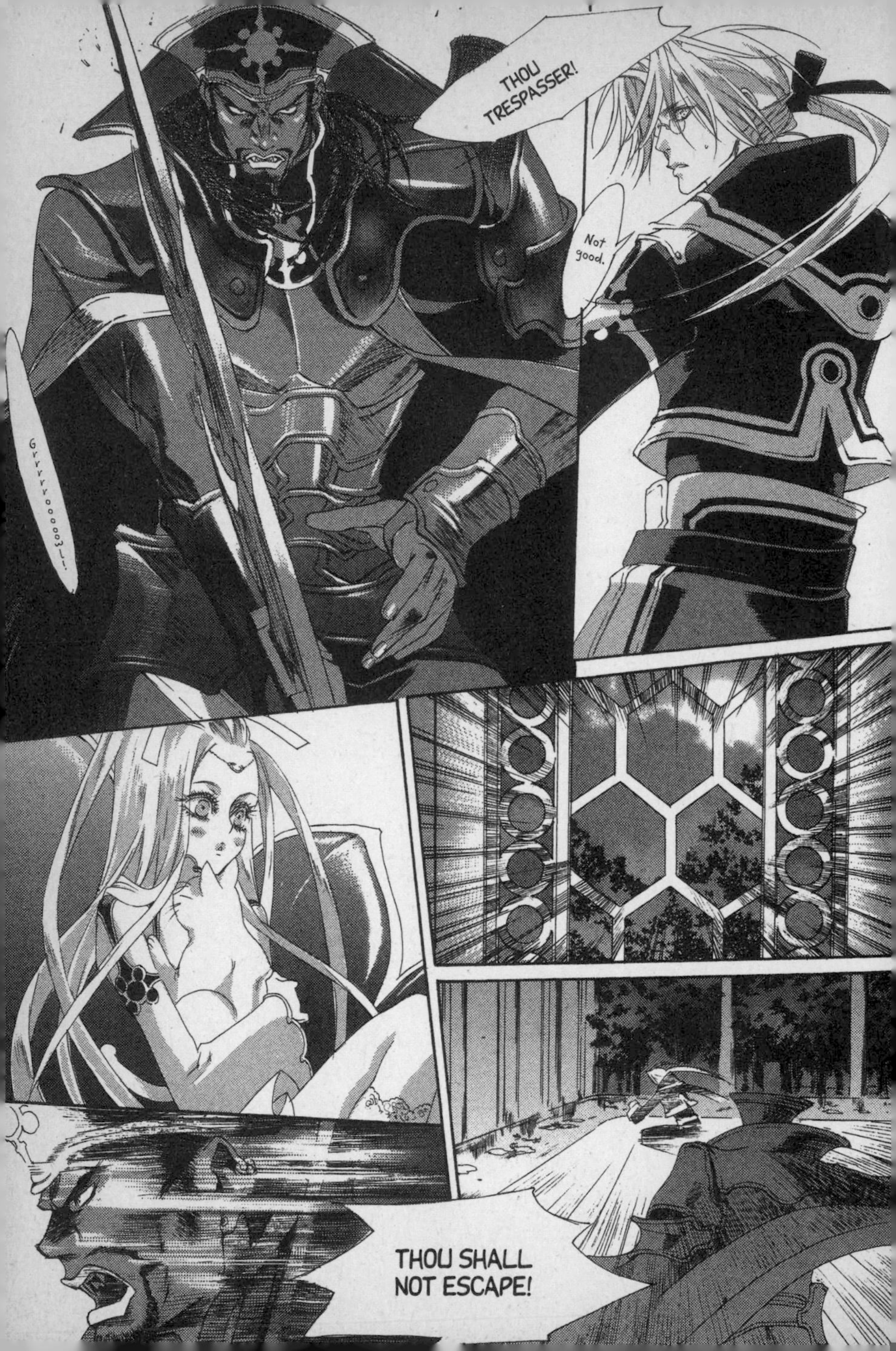
THOU TRESPASSER!
Not good.
Grrrrroooowl!
THOU SHALL NOT ESCAPE!

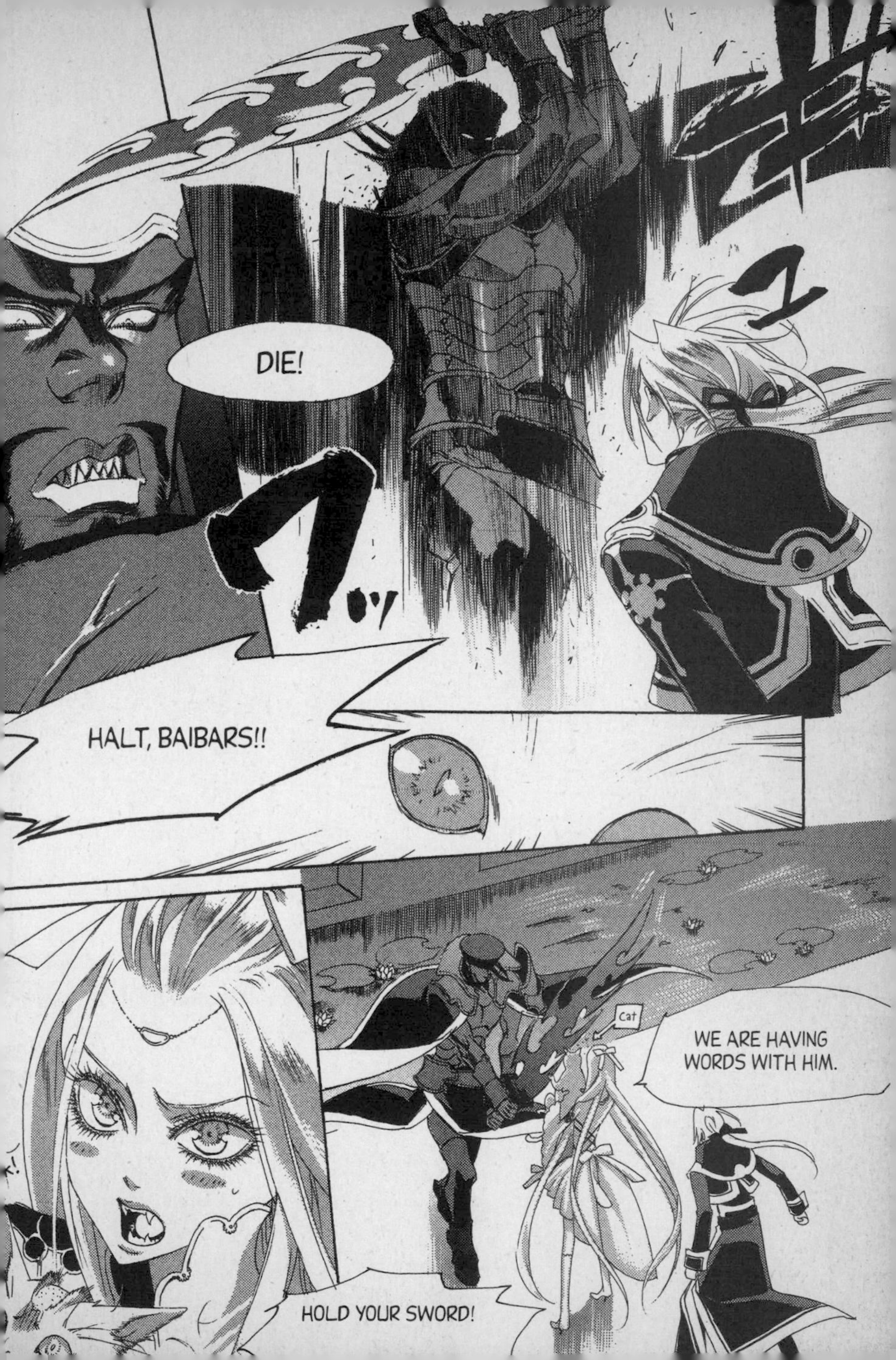
DIE!
HALT, BAIBARS!!
Cat
WE ARE HAVING WORDS WITH HIM.
HOLD YOUR SWORD!

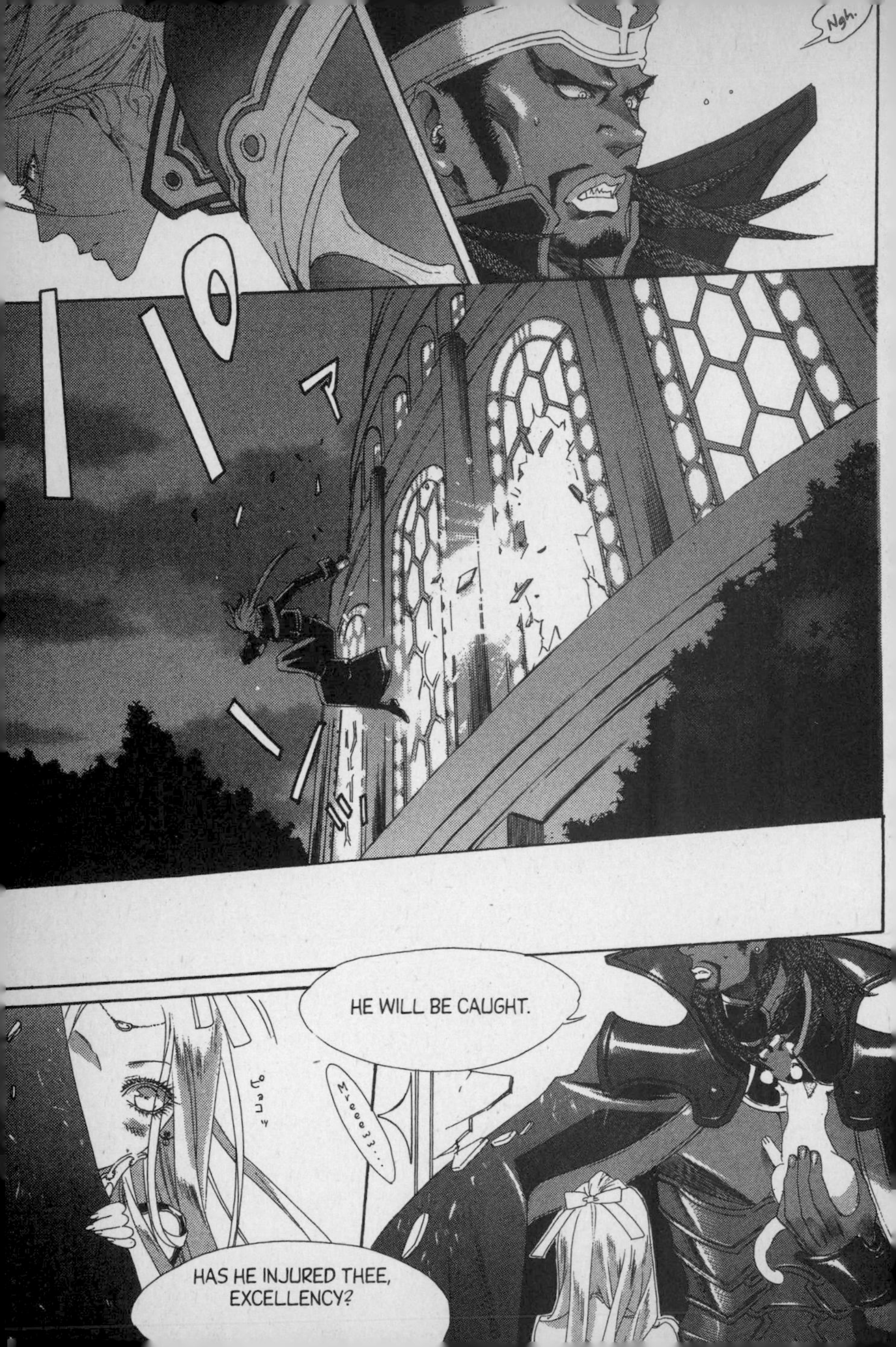

Ngh.
HE WILL BE CAUGHT.
Mreeeww...
HAS HE INJURED THEE, EXCELLENCY?

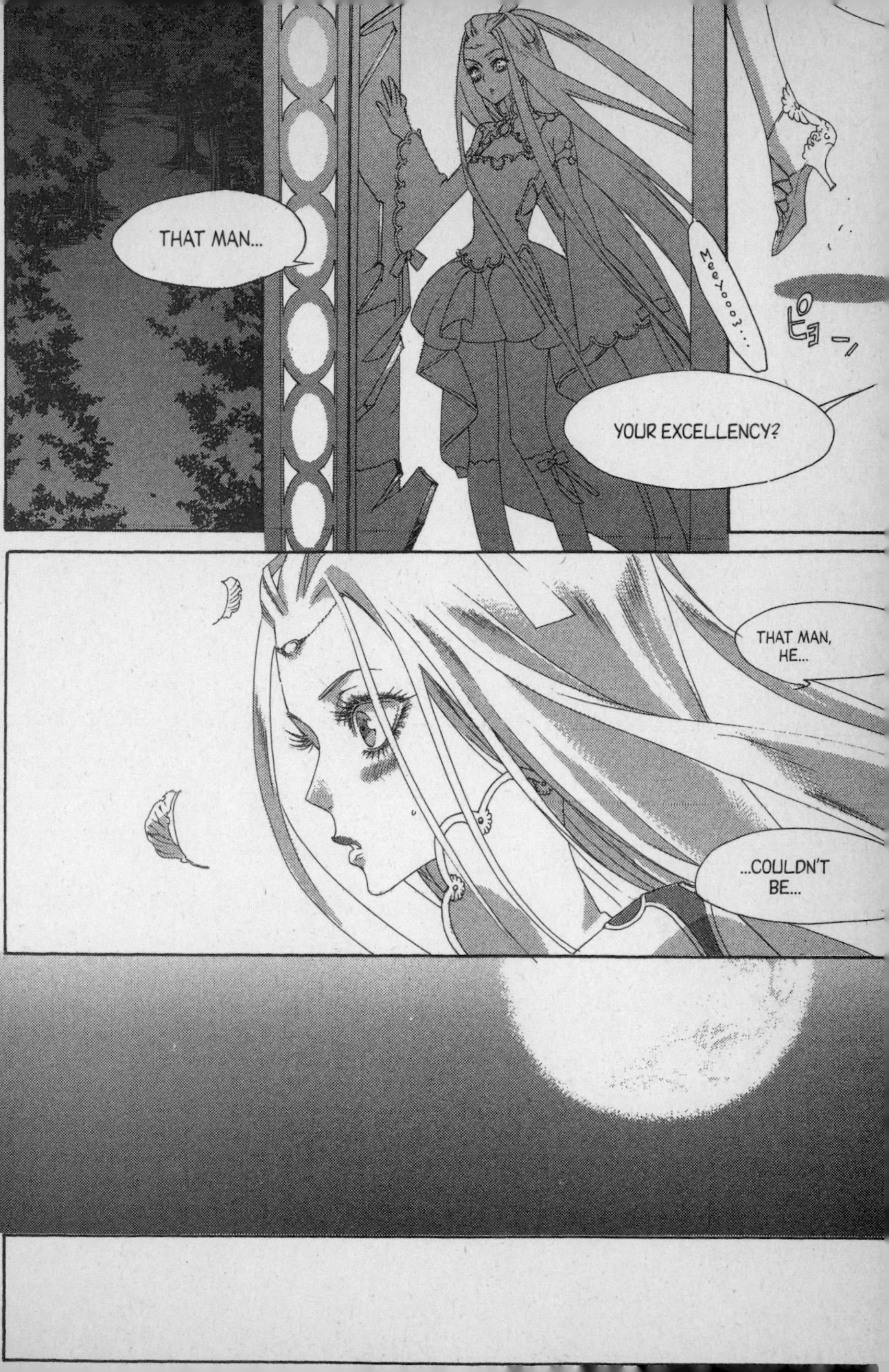
Meeyooo...
YOUR EXCELLENCY?
THAT MAN...
THAT MAN, HE...
...COULDN'T BE...

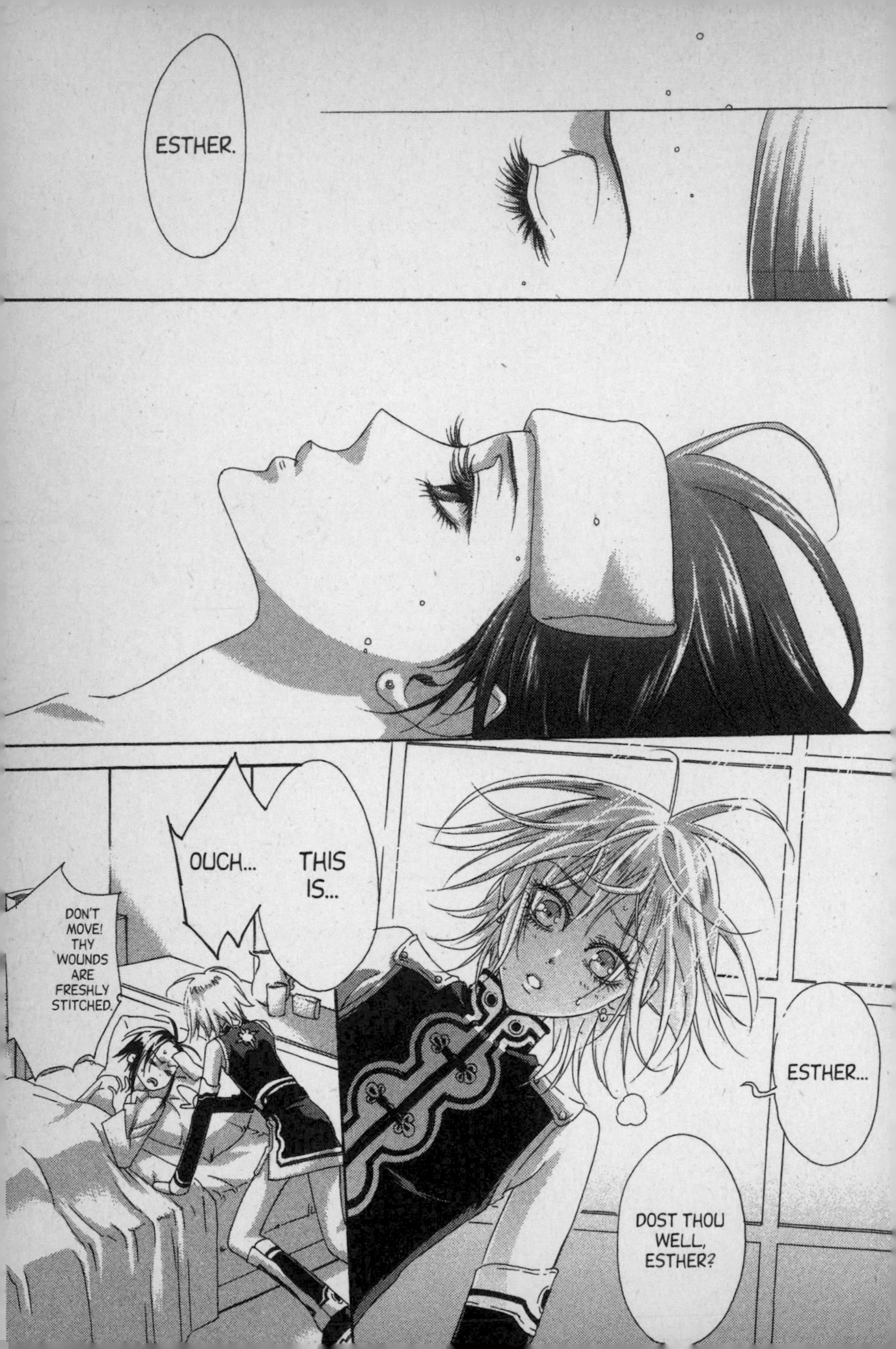
ESTHER.
ESTHER...
DOST THOU WELL, ESTHER?
THIS IS...
OUCH...
DON'T MOVE! THY WOUNDS ARE FRESHLY STITCHED.

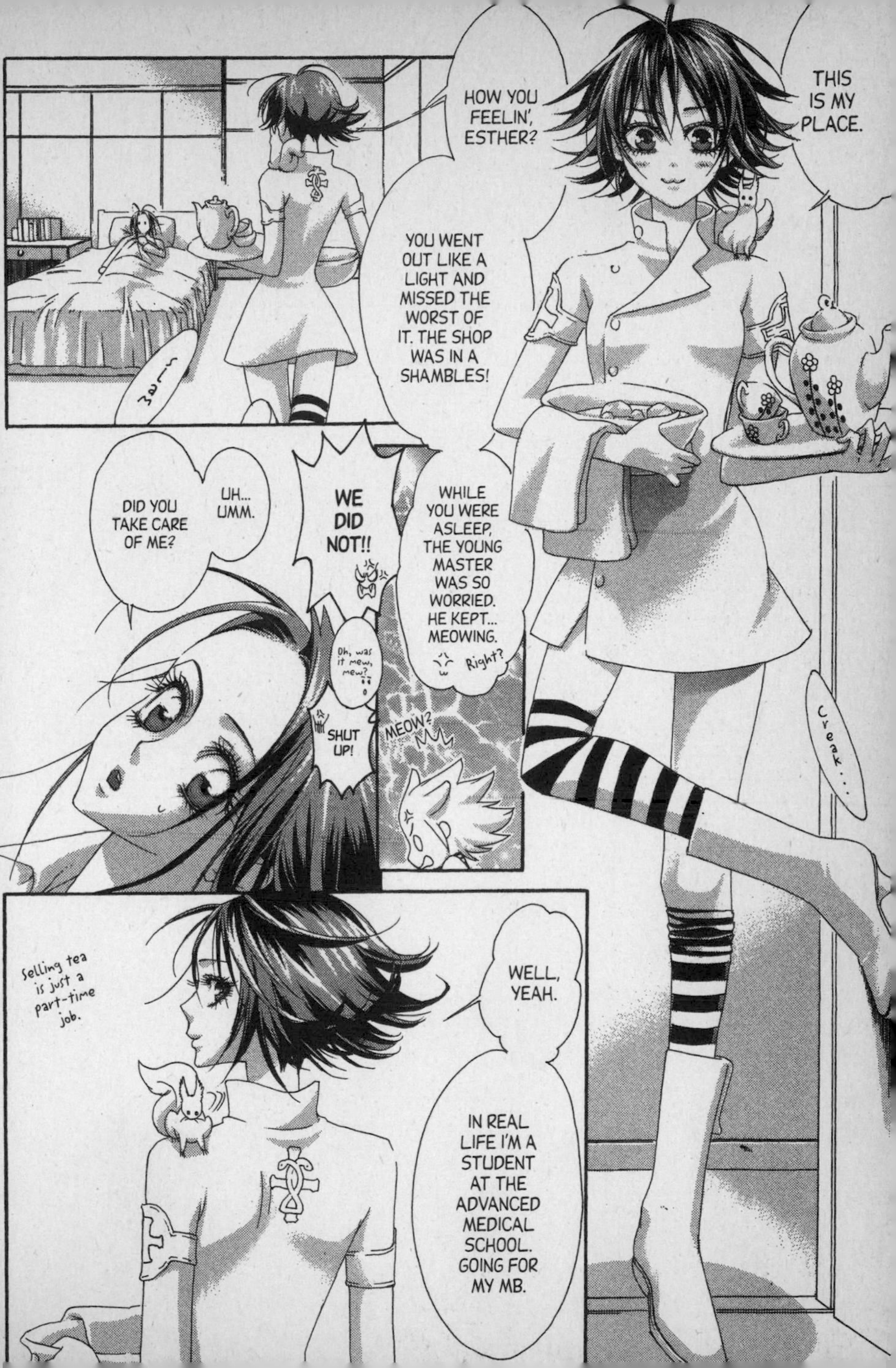
THIS IS MY PLACE.
HOW YOU FEELIN', ESTHER?
YOU WENT OUT LIKE A LIGHT AND MISSED THE WORST OF IT. THE SHOP WAS IN A SHAMBLES!
Creak...
WHILE YOU WERE ASLEEP, THE YOUNG MASTER WAS SO WORRIED. HE KEPT... MEOWING.
Right?
WE DID NOT!!
MEOW?
Oh, was it mew, mew?
SHUT UP!
UH... UMM.
DID YOU TAKE CARE OF ME?
WELL, YEAH.
IN REAL LIFE I'M A STUDENT AT THE ADVANCED MEDICAL SCHOOL. GOING FOR MY MB.
Selling tea is just a part-time job.

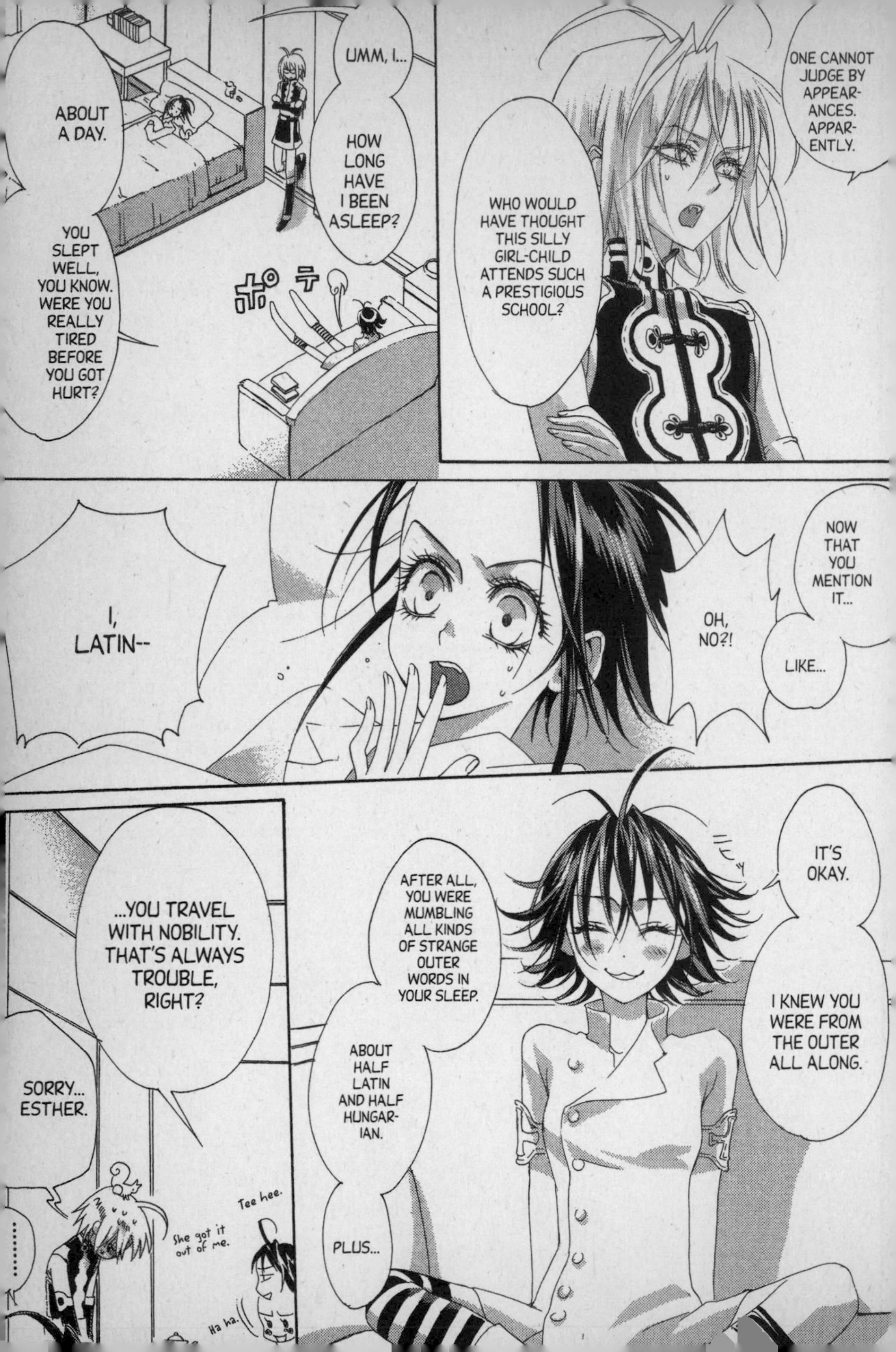
ONE CANNOT JUDGE BY APPEARANCES. APPARENTLY.
WHO WOULD HAVE THOUGHT THIS SILLY GIRL-CHILD ATTENDS SUCH A PRESTIGIOUS SCHOOL?
UMM, I...
HOW LONG HAVE I BEEN ASLEEP?
ポテ
ABOUT A DAY.
YOU SLEPT WELL, YOU KNOW. WERE YOU REALLY TIRED BEFORE YOU GOT HURT?
NOW THAT YOU MENTION IT...
LIKE...
OH, NO?!
I, LATIN--
IT'S OKAY.
I KNEW YOU WERE FROM THE OUTER ALL ALONG.
AFTER ALL, YOU WERE MUMBLING ALL KINDS OF STRANGE OUTER WORDS IN YOUR SLEEP.
ABOUT HALF LATIN AND HALF HUNGARIAN.
PLUS...
...YOU TRAVEL WITH NOBILITY. THAT'S ALWAYS TROUBLE, RIGHT?
SORRY... ESTHER.
......
Tee hee.
She got it out of me.
Ha ha.

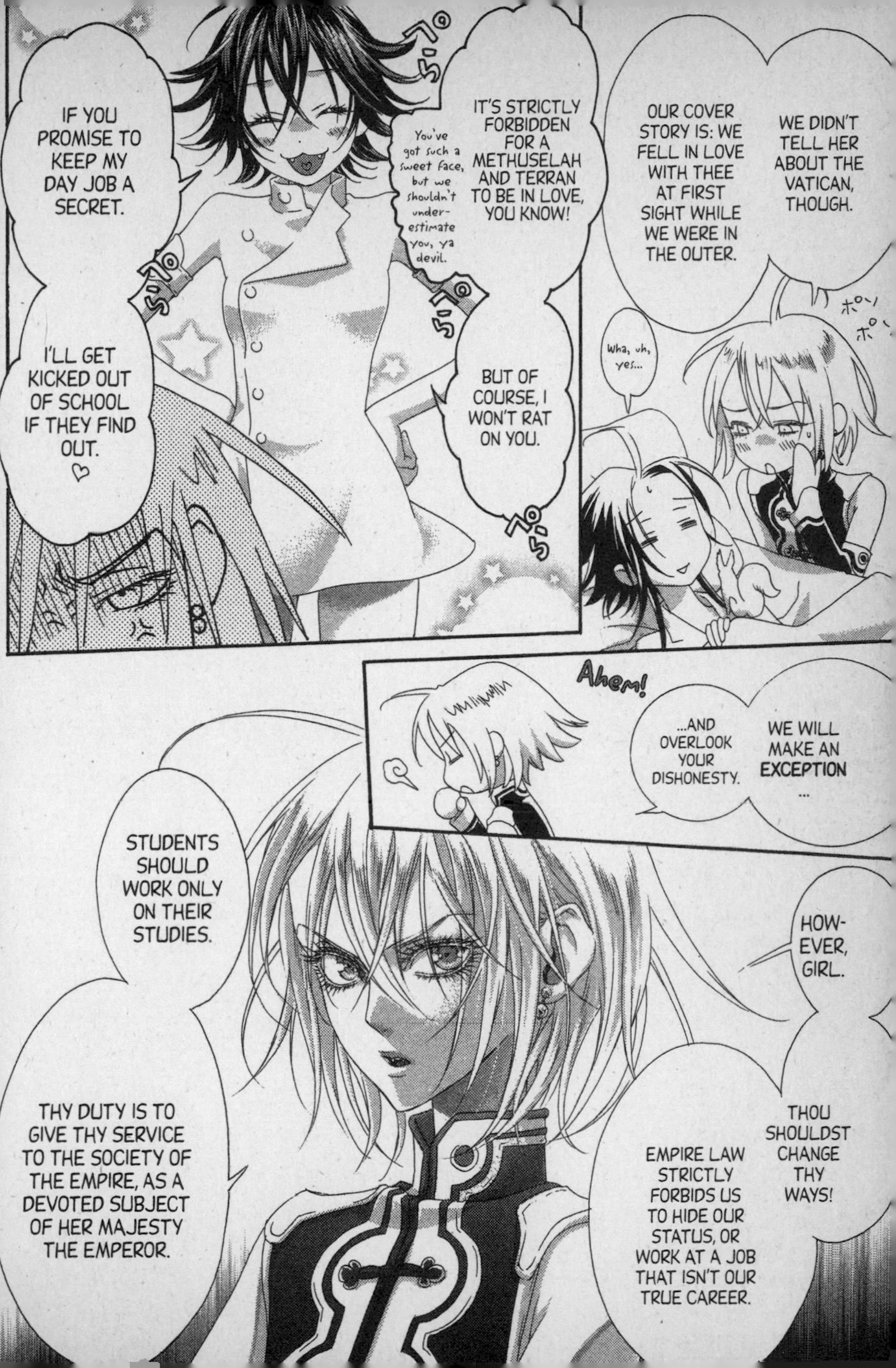
WE DIDN'T TELL HER ABOUT THE VATICAN, THOUGH.
OUR COVER STORY IS: WE FELL IN LOVE WITH THEE AT FIRST SIGHT WHILE WE WERE IN THE OUTER.
Wha, uh, yes...
IT'S STRICTLY FORBIDDEN FOR A METHUSELAH AND TERRAN TO BE IN LOVE, YOU KNOW!
You've got such a sweet face, but we shouldn't under-estimate you, ya devil.
BUT OF COURSE, I WON'T RAT ON YOU.
IF YOU PROMISE TO KEEP MY DAY JOB A SECRET.
I'LL GET KICKED OUT OF SCHOOL IF THEY FIND OUT. ♡
Ahem!
WE WILL MAKE AN **EXCEPTION**...
...AND OVERLOOK YOUR DISHONESTY.
HOW-EVER, GIRL.
THOU SHOULDST CHANGE THY WAYS!
EMPIRE LAW STRICTLY FORBIDS US TO HIDE OUR STATUS, OR WORK AT A JOB THAT ISN'T OUR TRUE CAREER.
STUDENTS SHOULD WORK ONLY ON THEIR STUDIES.
THY DUTY IS TO GIVE THY SERVICE TO THE SOCIETY OF THE EMPIRE, AS A DEVOTED SUBJECT OF HER MAJESTY THE EMPEROR.

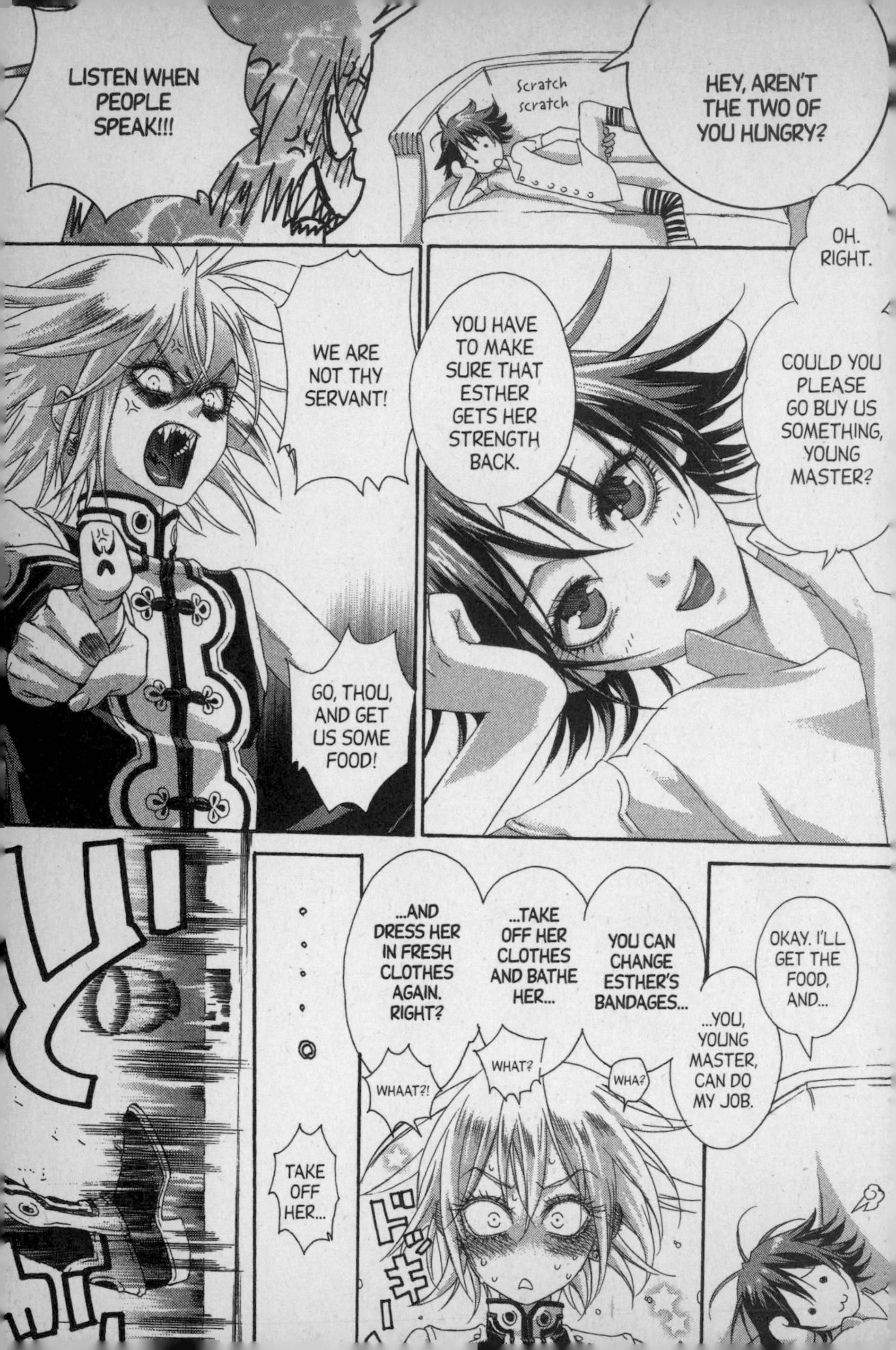
HEY, AREN'T THE TWO OF YOU HUNGRY?
Scratch scratch
LISTEN WHEN PEOPLE SPEAK!!!
OH. RIGHT.
COULD YOU PLEASE GO BUY US SOMETHING, YOUNG MASTER?
YOU HAVE TO MAKE SURE THAT ESTHER GETS HER STRENGTH BACK.
WE ARE NOT THY SERVANT!
GO, THOU, AND GET US SOME FOOD!
OKAY. I'LL GET THE FOOD, AND...
...YOU, YOUNG MASTER, CAN DO MY JOB.
WHA?
YOU CAN CHANGE ESTHER'S BANDAGES...
WHAT?
...TAKE OFF HER CLOTHES AND BATHE HER...
WHAAT?!
...AND DRESS HER IN FRESH CLOTHES AGAIN. RIGHT?
TAKE OFF HER...

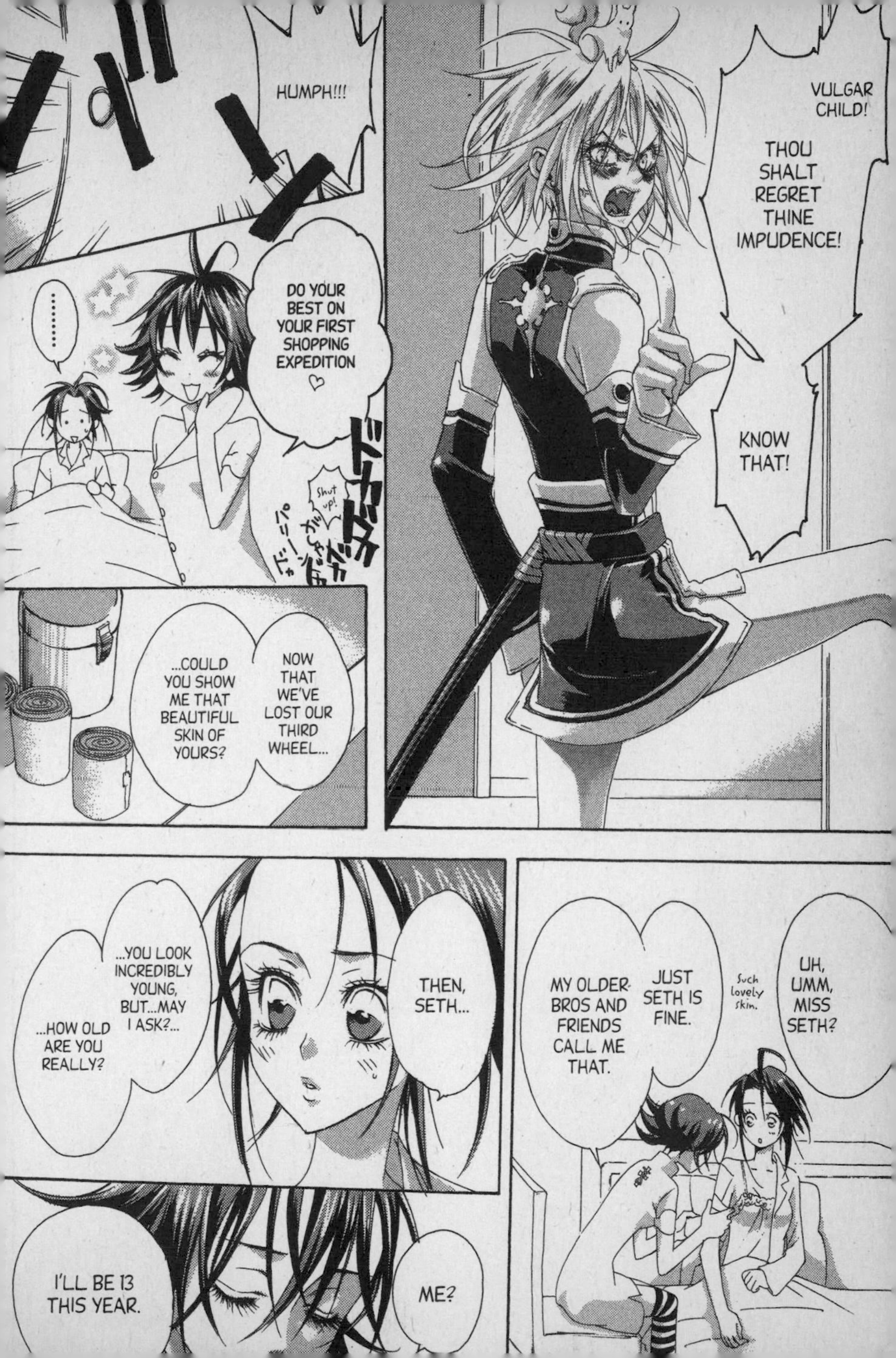
VULGAR CHILD!
THOU SHALT REGRET THINE IMPUDENCE!
KNOW THAT!
HUMPH!!!
DO YOUR BEST ON YOUR FIRST SHOPPING EXPEDITION ♡
......
Shut up!
NOW THAT WE'VE LOST OUR THIRD WHEEL...
...COULD YOU SHOW ME THAT BEAUTIFUL SKIN OF YOURS?
UH, UMM, MISS SETH?
Such lovely skin.
JUST SETH IS FINE.
MY OLDER BROS AND FRIENDS CALL ME THAT.
THEN, SETH...
...YOU LOOK INCREDIBLY YOUNG, BUT...MAY I ASK?...
...HOW OLD ARE YOU REALLY?
ME?
I'LL BE 13 THIS YEAR.

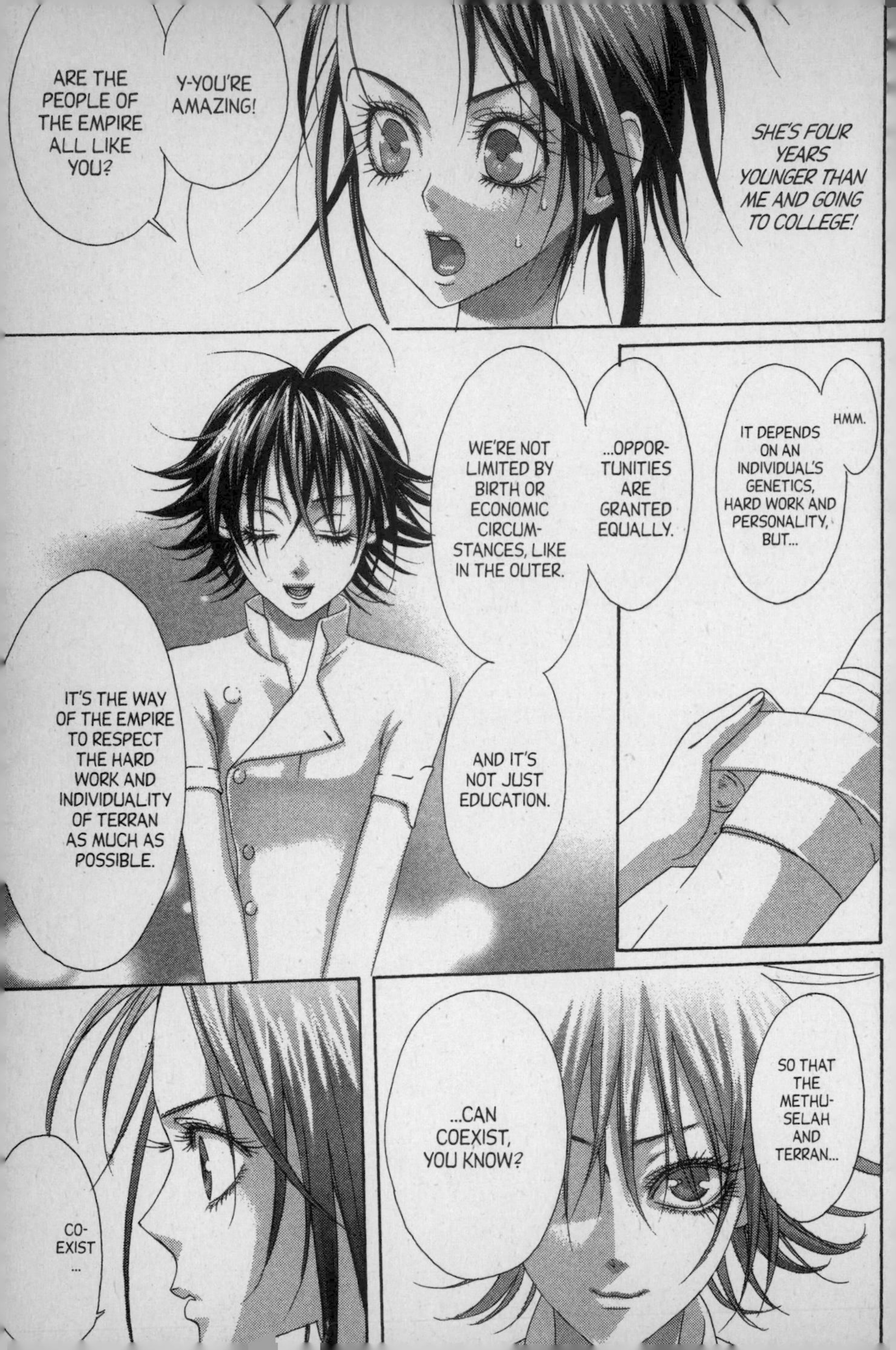
SHE'S FOUR YEARS YOUNGER THAN ME AND GOING TO COLLEGE!
Y-YOU'RE AMAZING!
ARE THE PEOPLE OF THE EMPIRE ALL LIKE YOU?
HMM.
IT DEPENDS ON AN INDIVIDUAL'S GENETICS, HARD WORK AND PERSONALITY, BUT...
...OPPOR-TUNITIES ARE GRANTED EQUALLY.
WE'RE NOT LIMITED BY BIRTH OR ECONOMIC CIRCUM-STANCES, LIKE IN THE OUTER.
AND IT'S NOT JUST EDUCATION.
IT'S THE WAY OF THE EMPIRE TO RESPECT THE HARD WORK AND INDIVIDUALITY OF TERRAN AS MUCH AS POSSIBLE.
SO THAT THE METHU-SELAH AND TERRAN...
...CAN COEXIST, YOU KNOW?
CO-EXIST ...

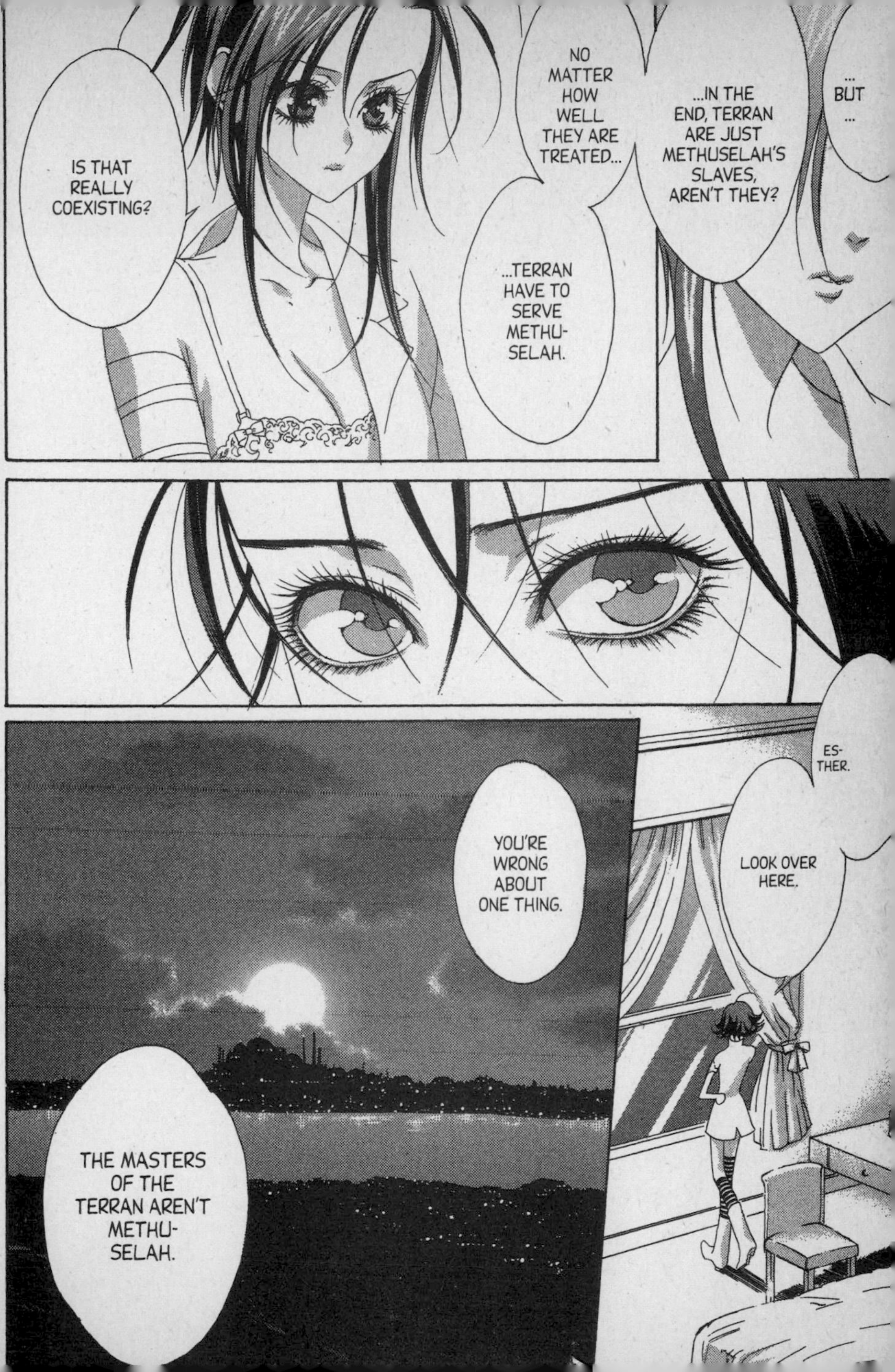

... BUT ...
...IN THE END, TERRAN ARE JUST METHUSELAH'S SLAVES, AREN'T THEY?
NO MATTER HOW WELL THEY ARE TREATED...
...TERRAN HAVE TO SERVE METHUSELAH.
IS THAT REALLY COEXISTING?
ESTHER.
LOOK OVER HERE.
YOU'RE WRONG ABOUT ONE THING.
THE MASTERS OF THE TERRAN AREN'T METHUSELAH.

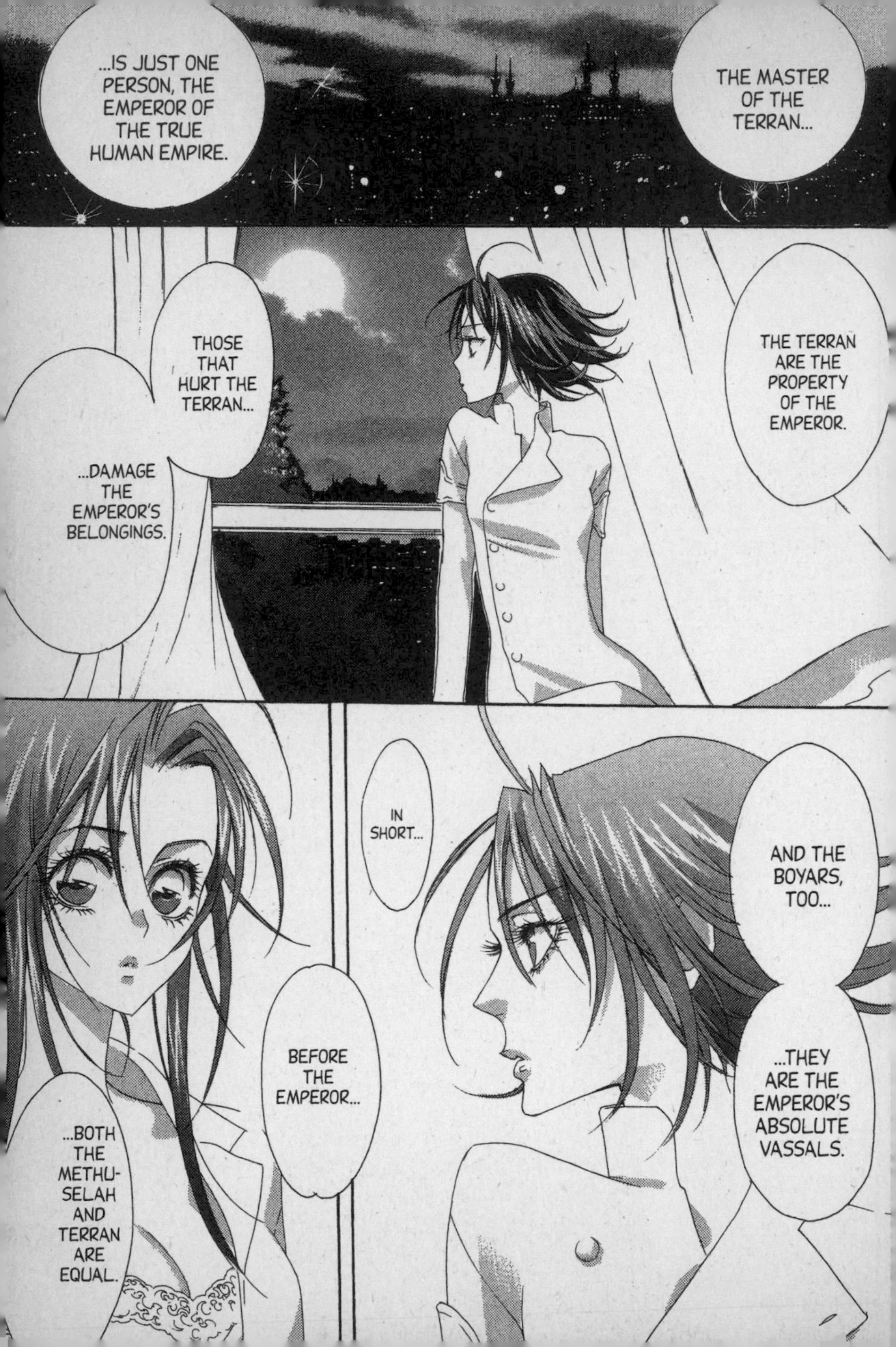
THE MASTER OF THE TERRAN...
...IS JUST ONE PERSON, THE EMPEROR OF THE TRUE HUMAN EMPIRE.
THE TERRAN ARE THE PROPERTY OF THE EMPEROR.
THOSE THAT HURT THE TERRAN...
...DAMAGE THE EMPEROR'S BELONGINGS.
AND THE BOYARS, TOO...
...THEY ARE THE EMPEROR'S ABSOLUTE VASSALS.
IN SHORT...
BEFORE THE EMPEROR...
...BOTH THE METHU-SELAH AND TERRAN ARE EQUAL.

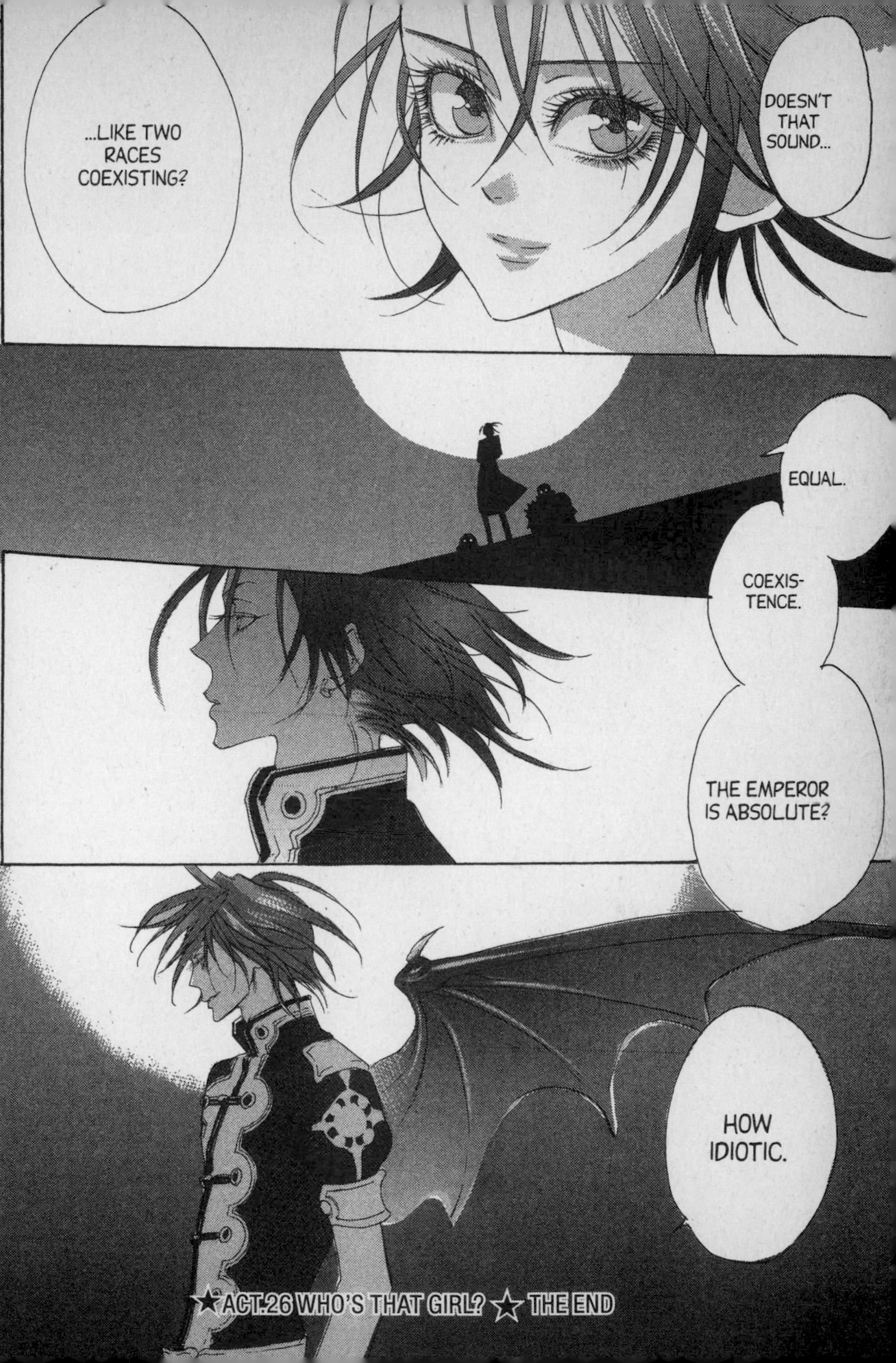
DOESN'T THAT SOUND...
...LIKE TWO RACES COEXISTING?
EQUAL.
COEXIS-TENCE.
THE EMPEROR IS ABSOLUTE?
HOW IDIOTIC.
★ACT.26 WHO'S THAT GIRL?★THE END

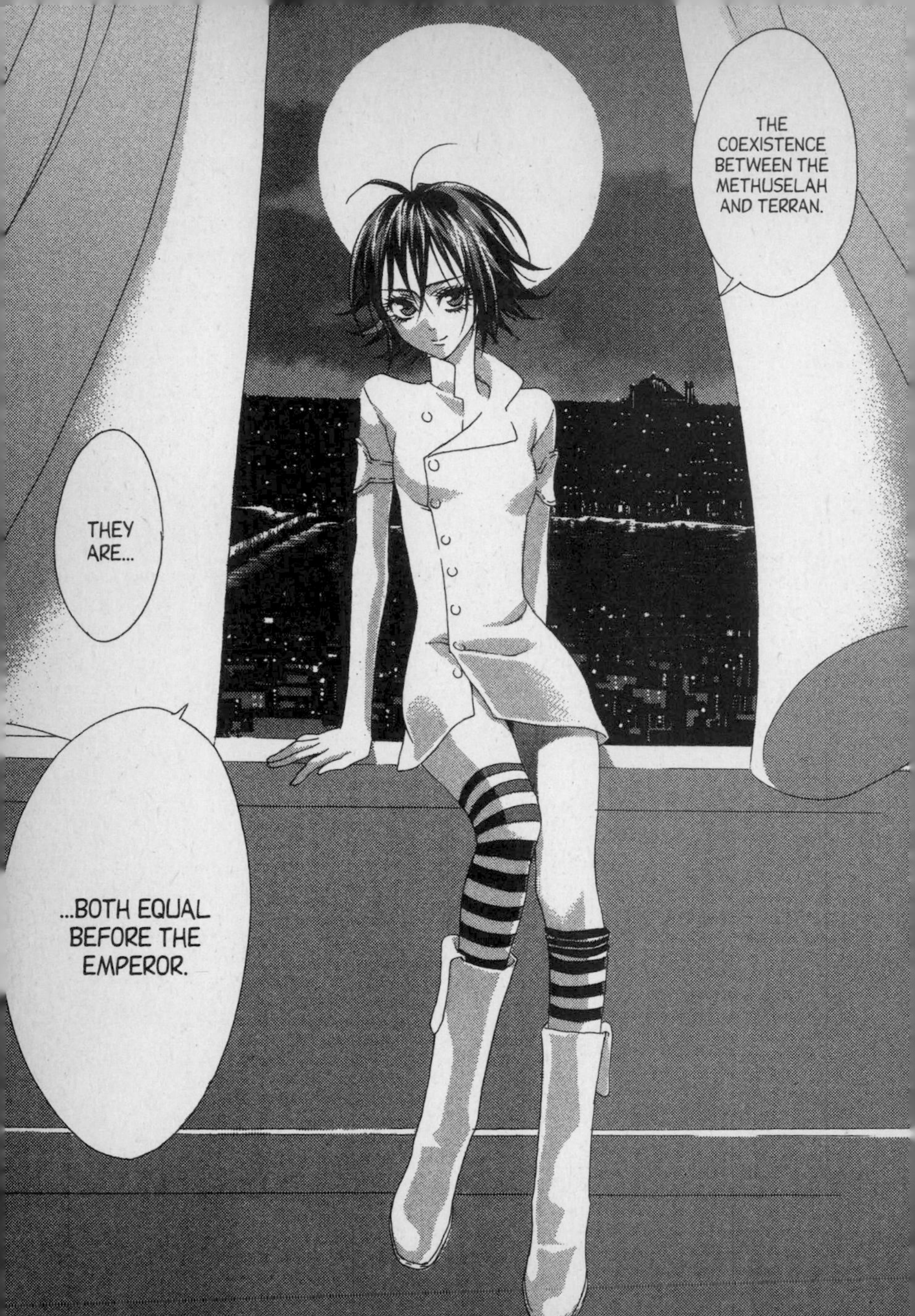
THE COEXISTENCE BETWEEN THE METHUSELAH AND TERRAN.
THEY ARE...
...BOTH EQUAL BEFORE THE EMPEROR.

## act.27 Bright Lights, Big City

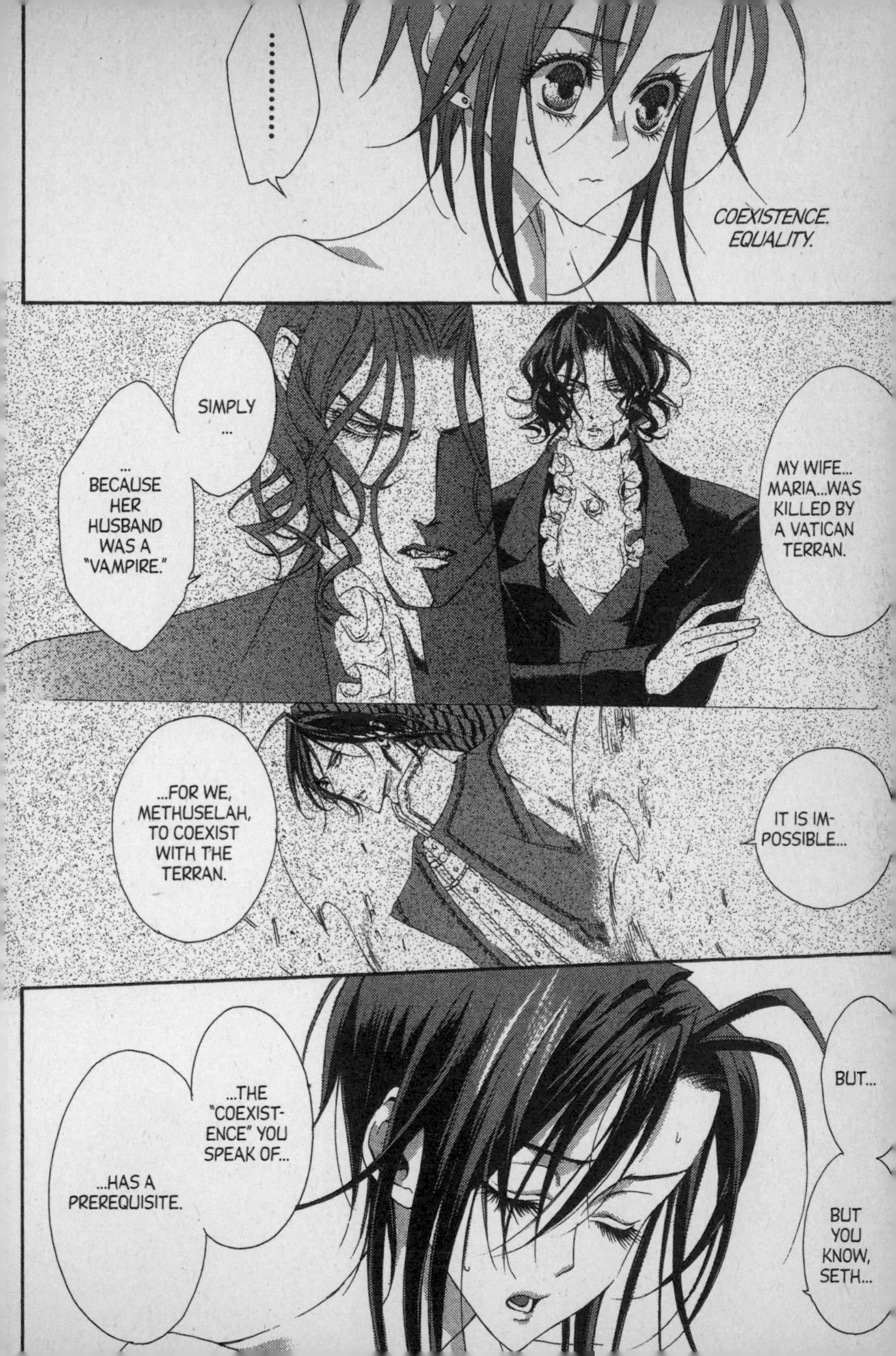

COEXISTENCE. EQUALITY.
......
MY WIFE... MARIA...WAS KILLED BY A VATICAN TERRAN.
SIMPLY ...
... BECAUSE HER HUSBAND WAS A "VAMPIRE."
IT IS IM-POSSIBLE...
...FOR WE, METHUSELAH, TO COEXIST WITH THE TERRAN.
BUT...
BUT YOU KNOW, SETH...
...THE "COEXIST-ENCE" YOU SPEAK OF...
...HAS A PREREQUISITE.

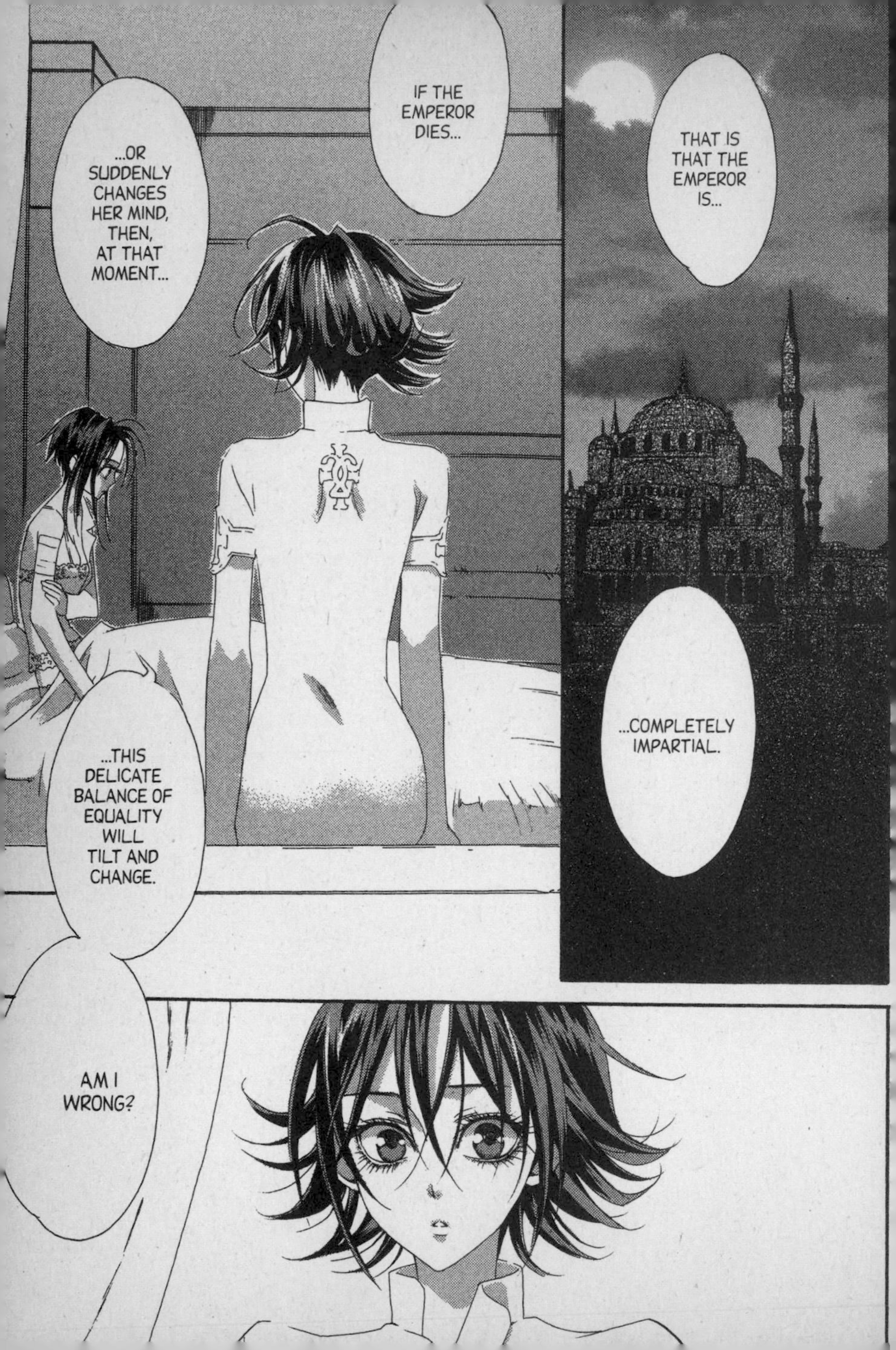
THAT IS THAT THE EMPEROR IS...
...COMPLETELY IMPARTIAL.
IF THE EMPEROR DIES...
...OR SUDDENLY CHANGES HER MIND, THEN, AT THAT MOMENT...
...THIS DELICATE BALANCE OF EQUALITY WILL TILT AND CHANGE.
AM I WRONG?

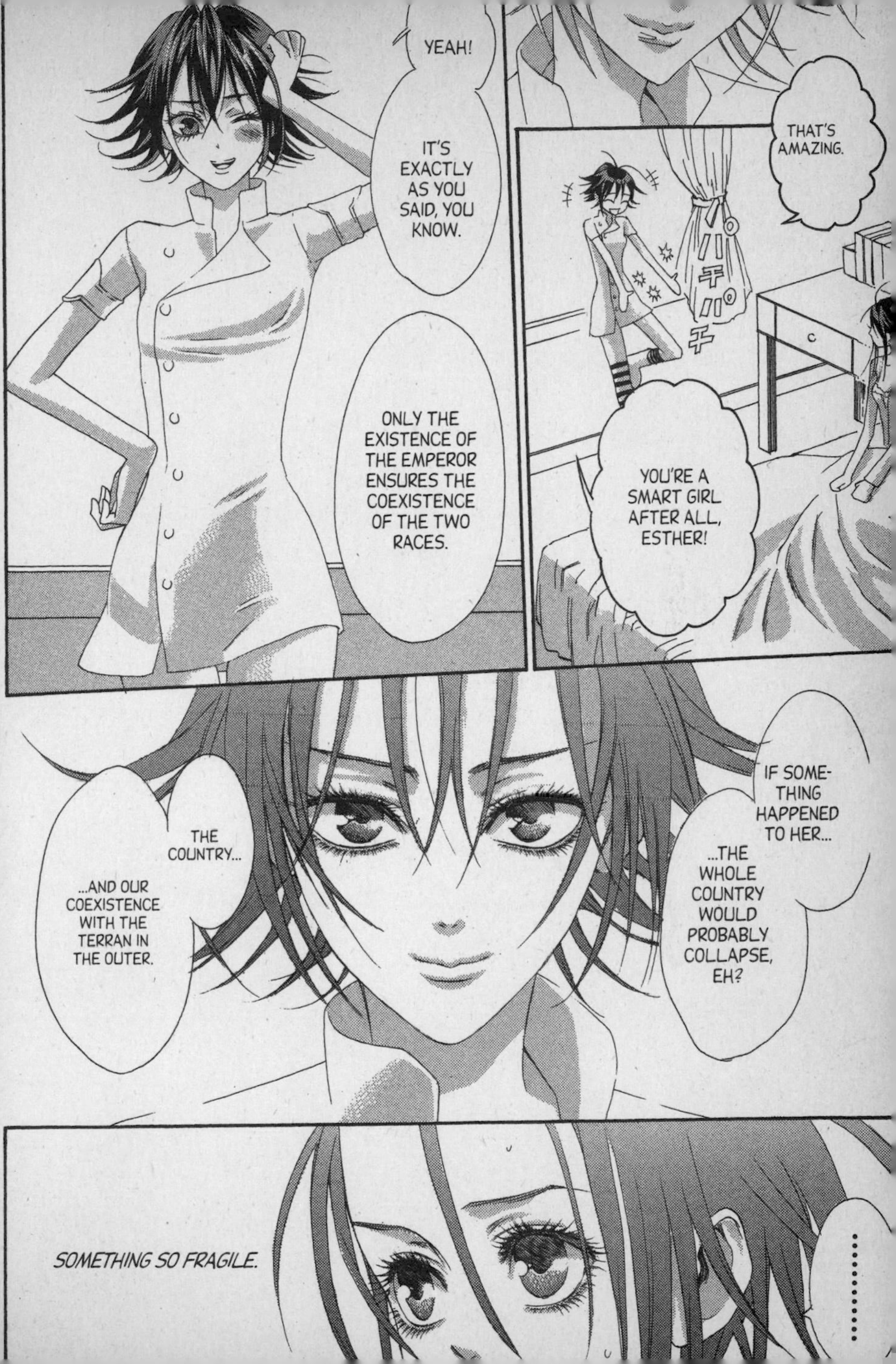
THAT'S AMAZING.
パチパチ
YOU'RE A SMART GIRL AFTER ALL, ESTHER!
YEAH!
IT'S EXACTLY AS YOU SAID, YOU KNOW.
ONLY THE EXISTENCE OF THE EMPEROR ENSURES THE COEXISTENCE OF THE TWO RACES.
IF SOME-THING HAPPENED TO HER...
...THE WHOLE COUNTRY WOULD PROBABLY COLLAPSE, EH?
THE COUNTRY...
...AND OUR COEXISTENCE WITH THE TERRAN IN THE OUTER.
SOMETHING SO FRAGILE.

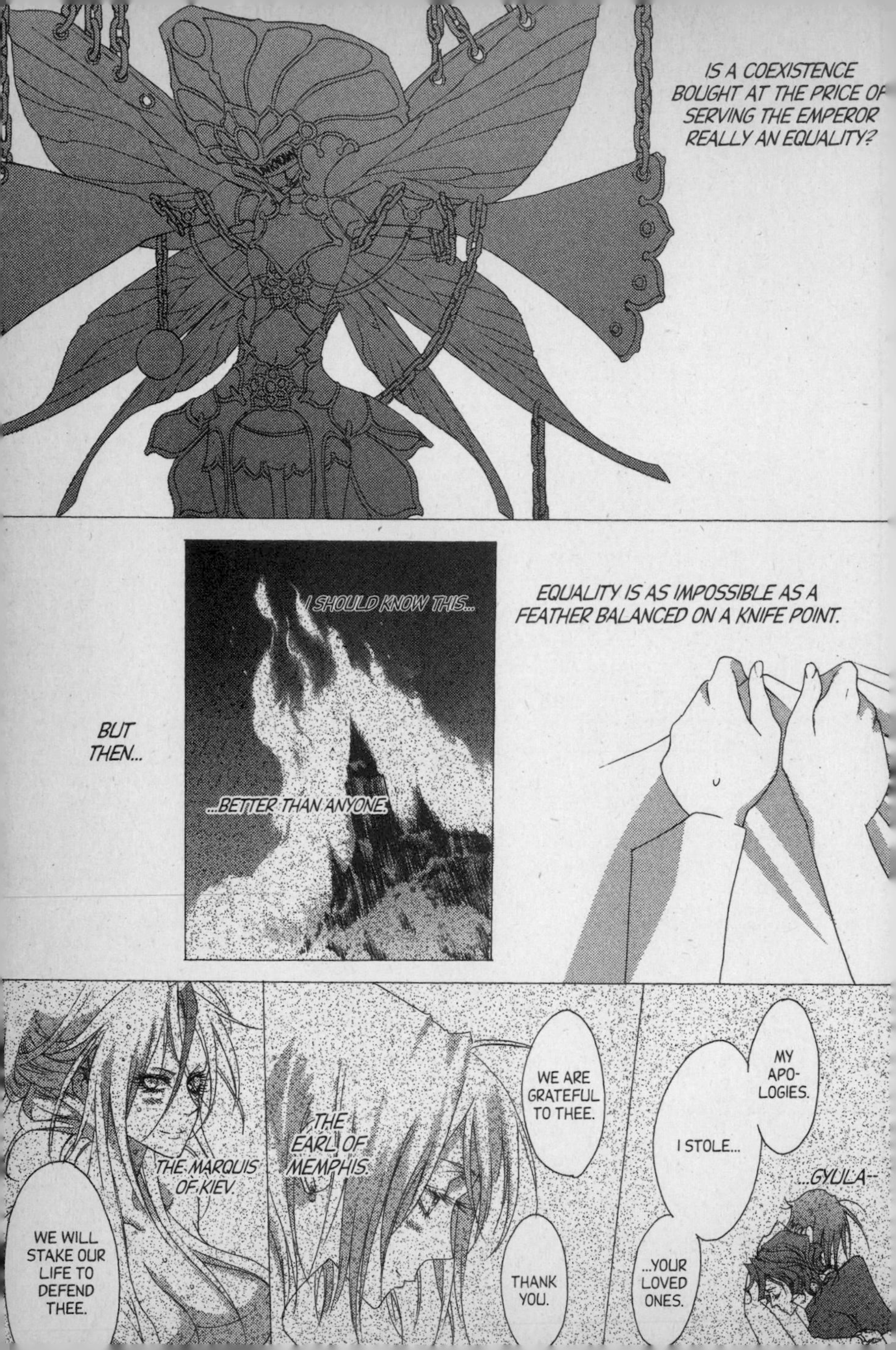
IS A COEXISTENCE BOUGHT AT THE PRICE OF SERVING THE EMPEROR REALLY AN EQUALITY?
EQUALITY IS AS IMPOSSIBLE AS A FEATHER BALANCED ON A KNIFE POINT.
I SHOULD KNOW THIS...
...BETTER THAN ANYONE.
BUT THEN...
...GYULA-
MY APOLOGIES.
I STOLE...
...YOUR LOVED ONES.
WE ARE GRATEFUL TO THEE.
THE EARL OF MEMPHIS.
THANK YOU.
THE MARQUIS OF KIEV.
WE WILL STAKE OUR LIFE TO DEFEND THEE.

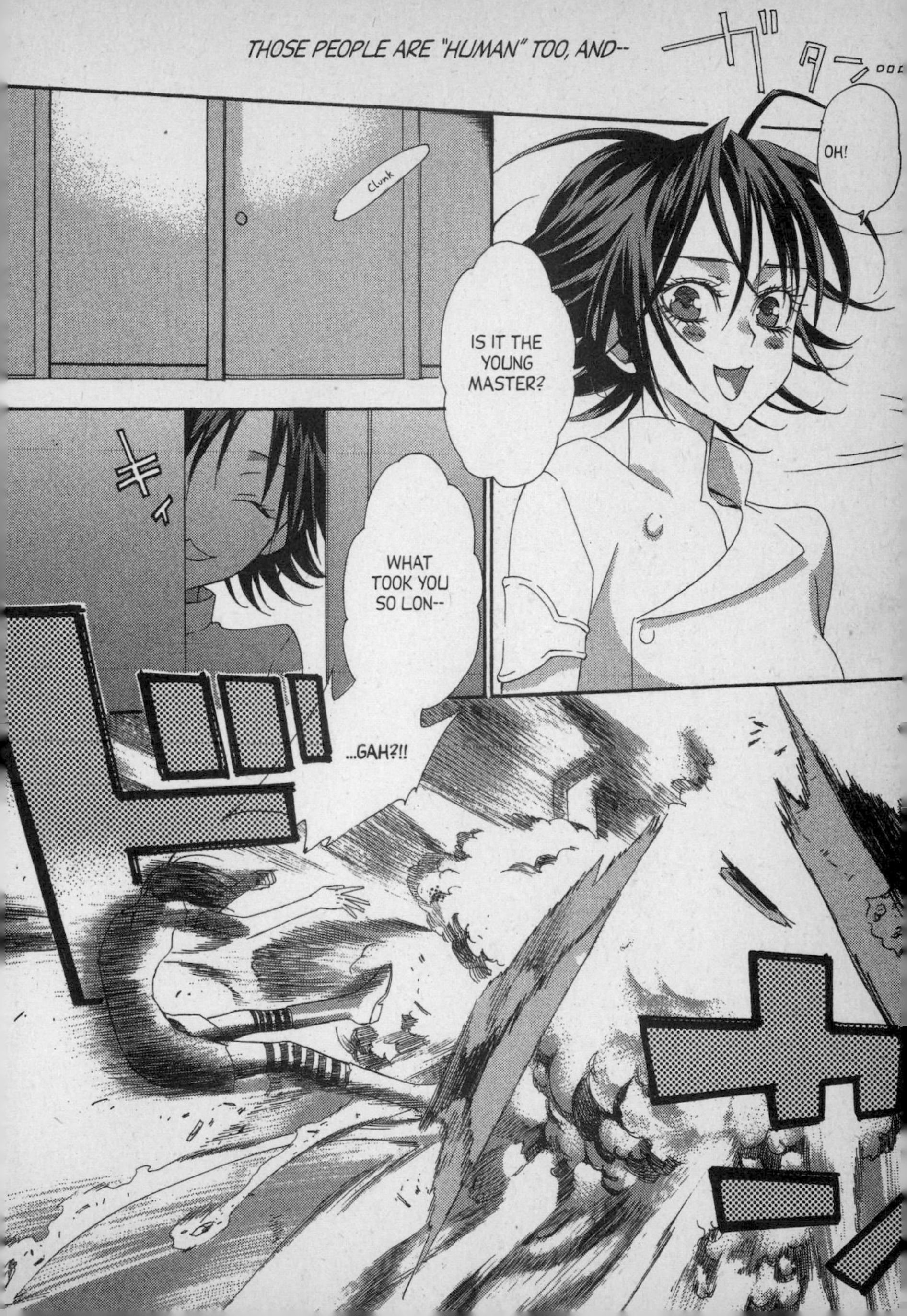
THOSE PEOPLE ARE "HUMAN" TOO, AND--
OH!
Clunk
IS IT THE YOUNG MASTER?
WHAT TOOK YOU SO LON--
...GAH?!!

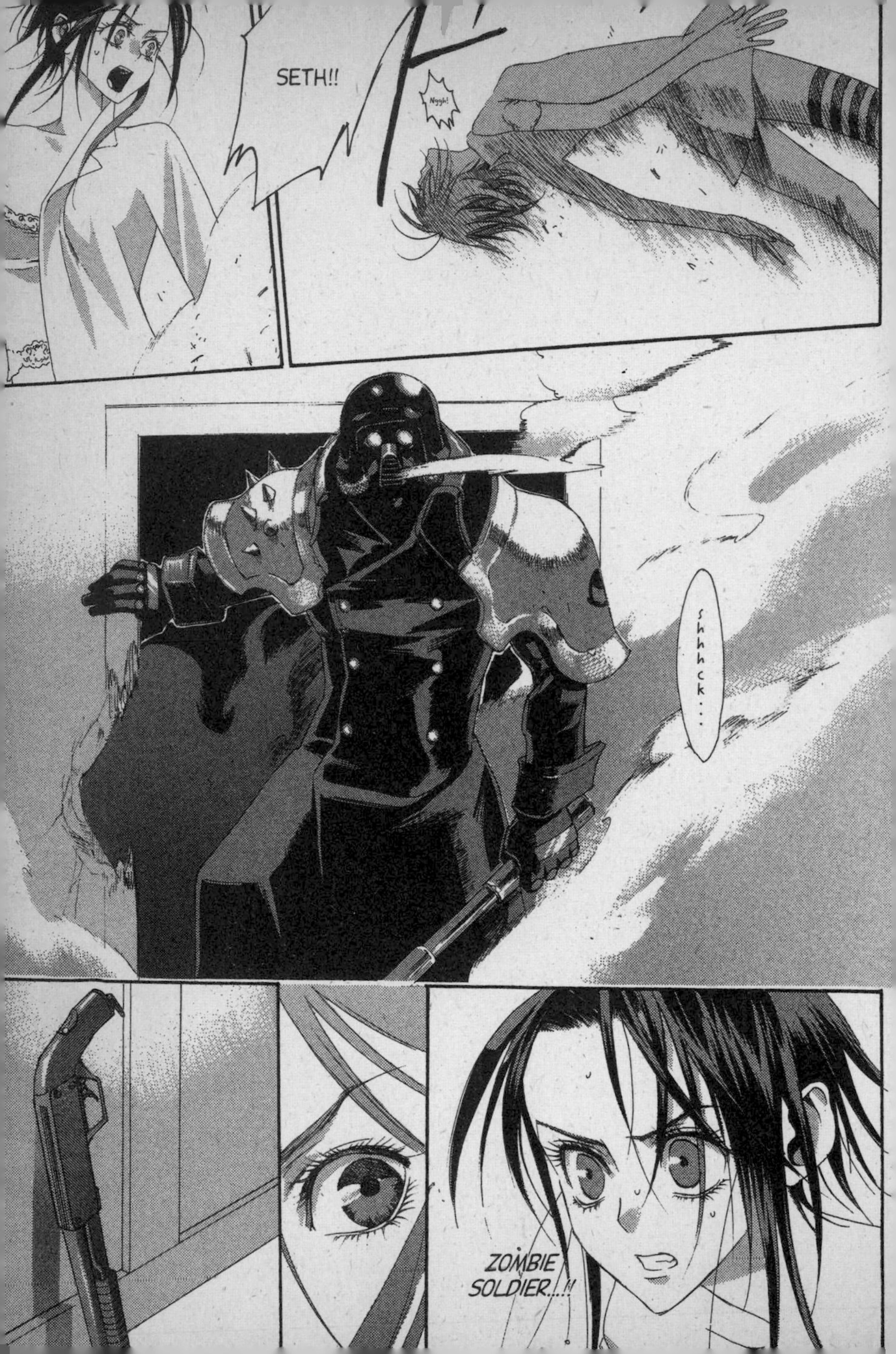
Nggh!
SETH!!
shhhck...
ZOMBIE SOLDIER...!!

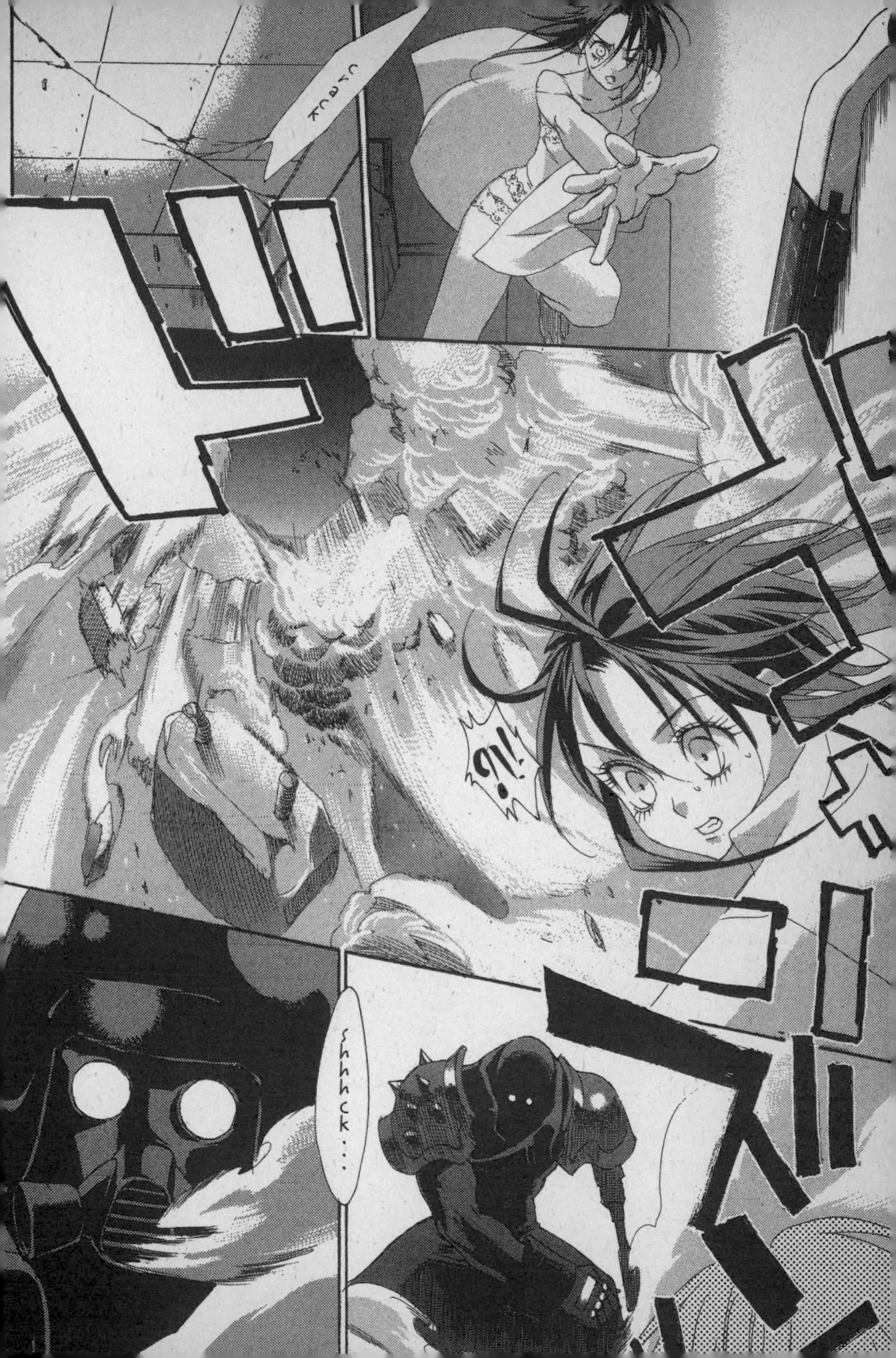
crack
?!
shhhck...

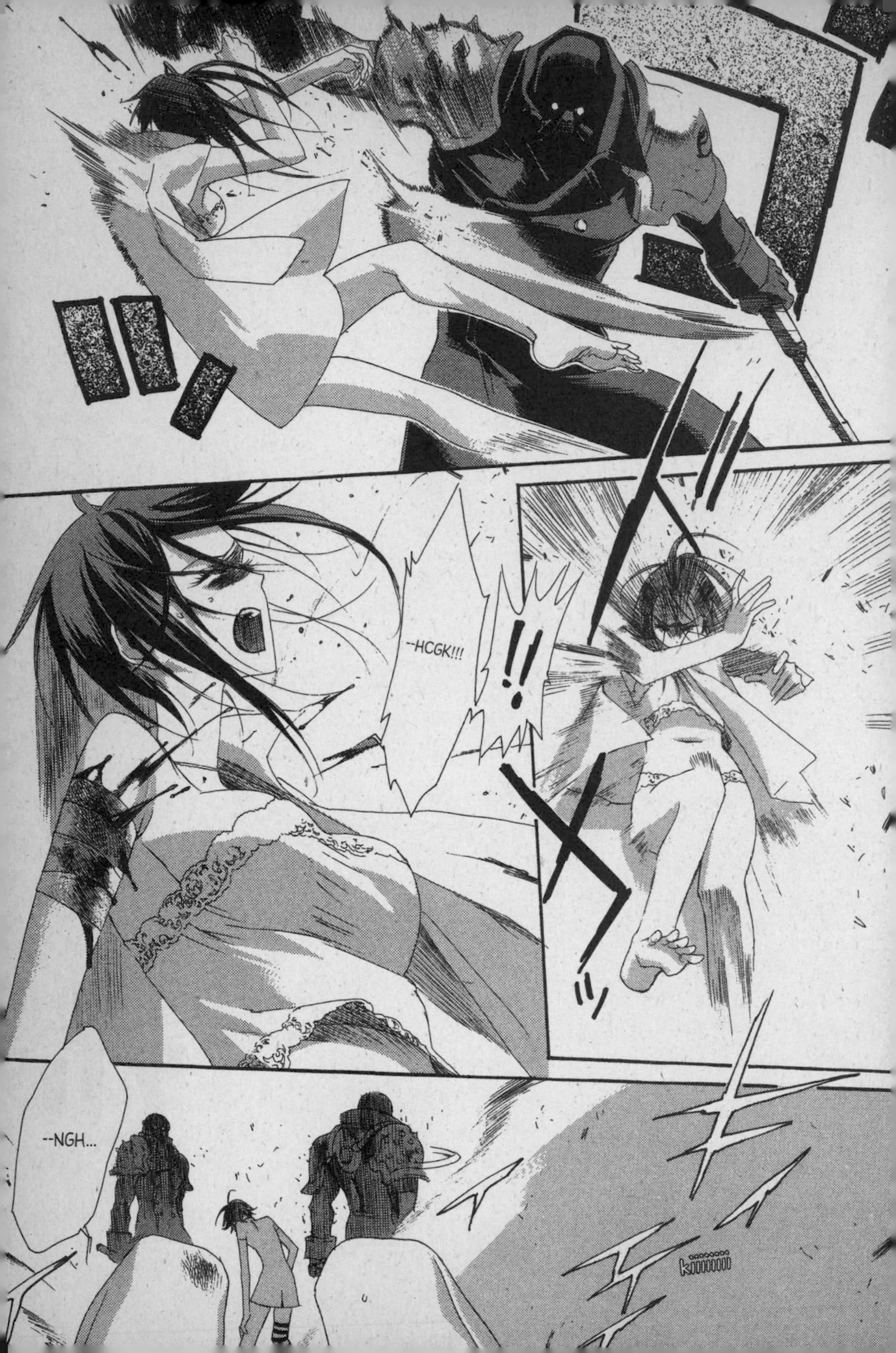
--HCGK!!!
!!
--NGH...
KIIIIIIIII

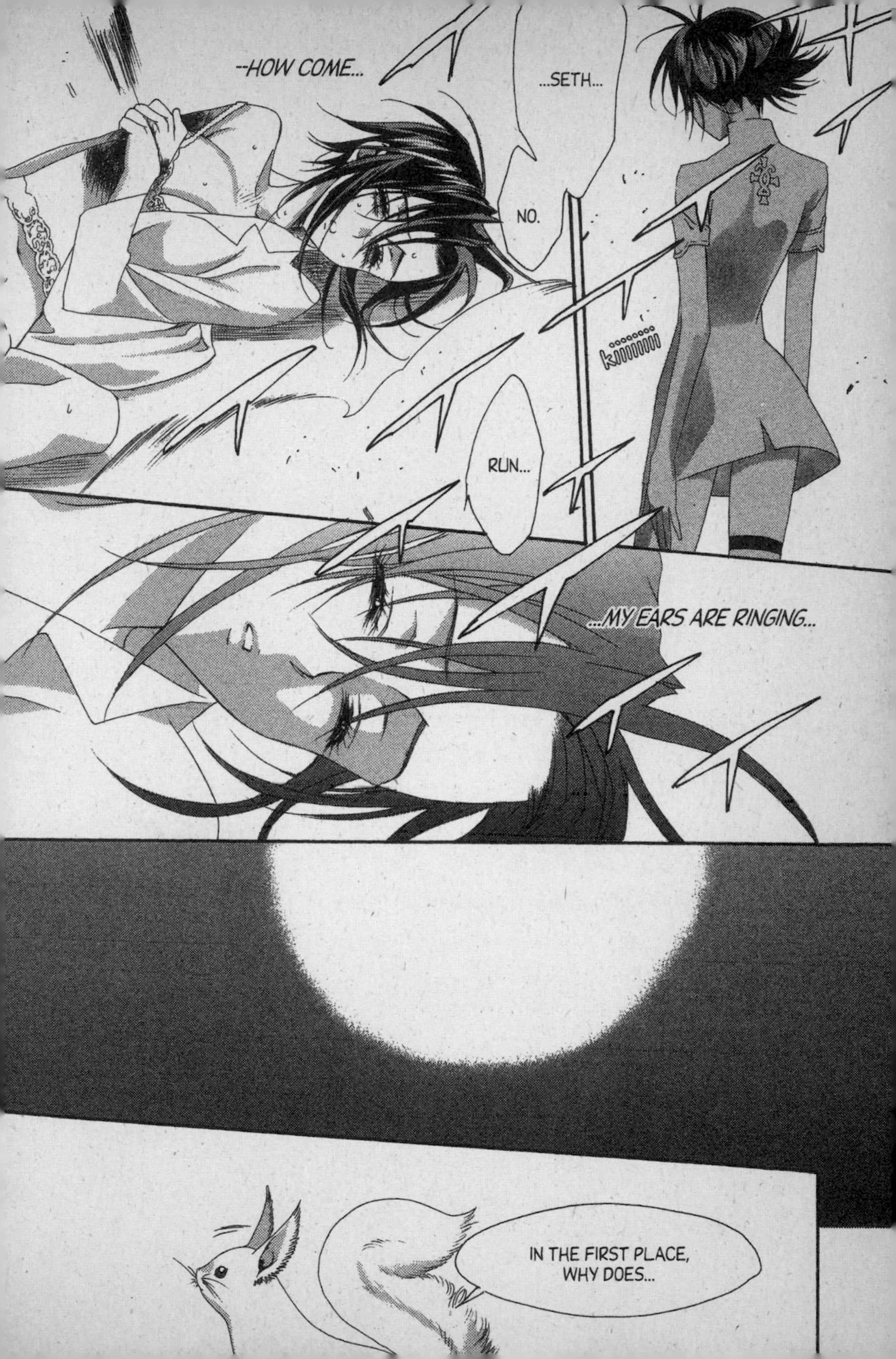

--HOW COME...
...SETH...
NO.
RUN...
KIIIIIIIIII
...MY EARS ARE RINGING...
IN THE FIRST PLACE, WHY DOES...

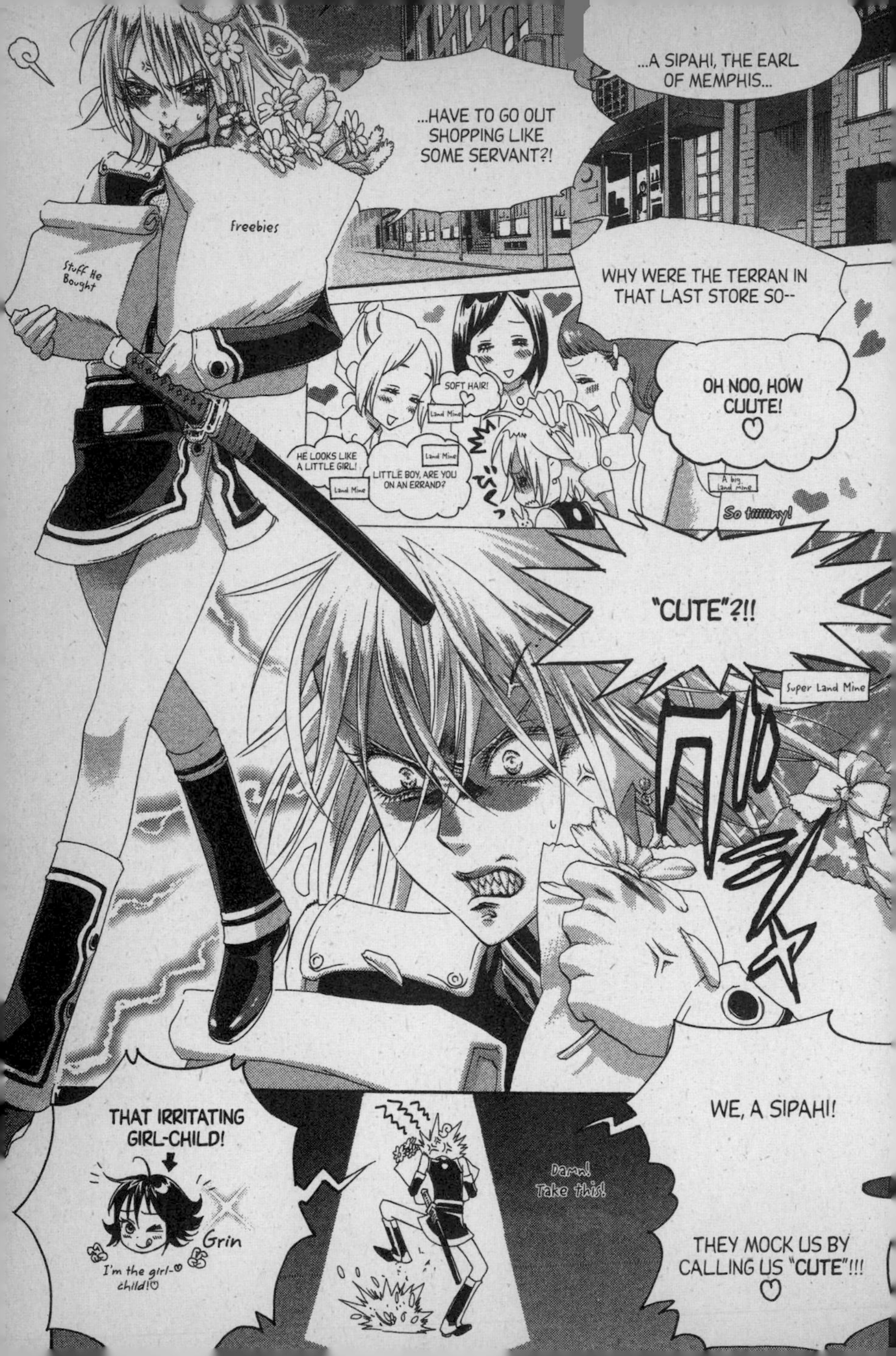

...A SIPAHI, THE EARL OF MEMPHIS...
...HAVE TO GO OUT SHOPPING LIKE SOME SERVANT?!
Freebies
Stuff He Bought
WHY WERE THE TERRAN IN THAT LAST STORE SO--
OH NOO, HOW CUUTE! ♡
A big Land Mine
So tiiiiiny!
SOFT HAIR!
Land Mine
HE LOOKS LIKE A LITTLE GIRL!
Land Mine
LITTLE BOY, ARE YOU ON AN ERRAND?
Land Mine
"CUTE"?!!
Super Land Mine
WE, A SIPAHI!
THEY MOCK US BY CALLING US "CUTE"!!! ♡
Damn! Take this!
THAT IRRITATING GIRL-CHILD!
Grin
I'm the girl-♡ child!♡

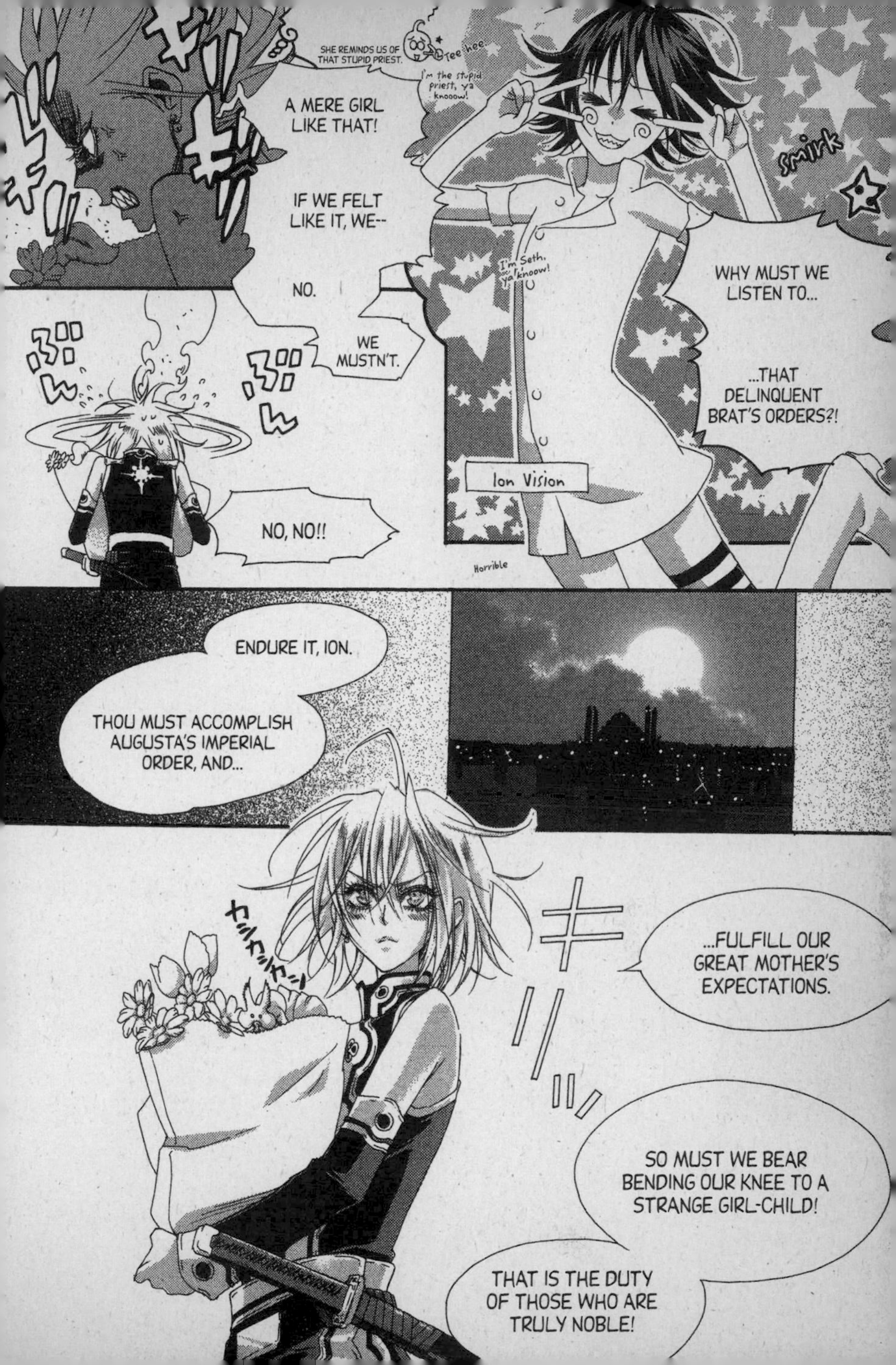
WHY MUST WE LISTEN TO...
...THAT DELINQUENT BRAT'S ORDERS?!
smirk
Tee hee.
I'm the stupid priest, ya knooow!
SHE REMINDS US OF THAT STUPID PRIEST.
A MERE GIRL LIKE THAT!
IF WE FELT LIKE IT, WE--
I'm Seth, ya knoow!
Ion Vision
Horrible
NO.
WE MUSTN'T.
NO, NO!!
ENDURE IT, ION.
THOU MUST ACCOMPLISH AUGUSTA'S IMPERIAL ORDER, AND...
...FULFILL OUR GREAT MOTHER'S EXPECTATIONS.
SO MUST WE BEAR BENDING OUR KNEE TO A STRANGE GIRL-CHILD!
THAT IS THE DUTY OF THOSE WHO ARE TRULY NOBLE!

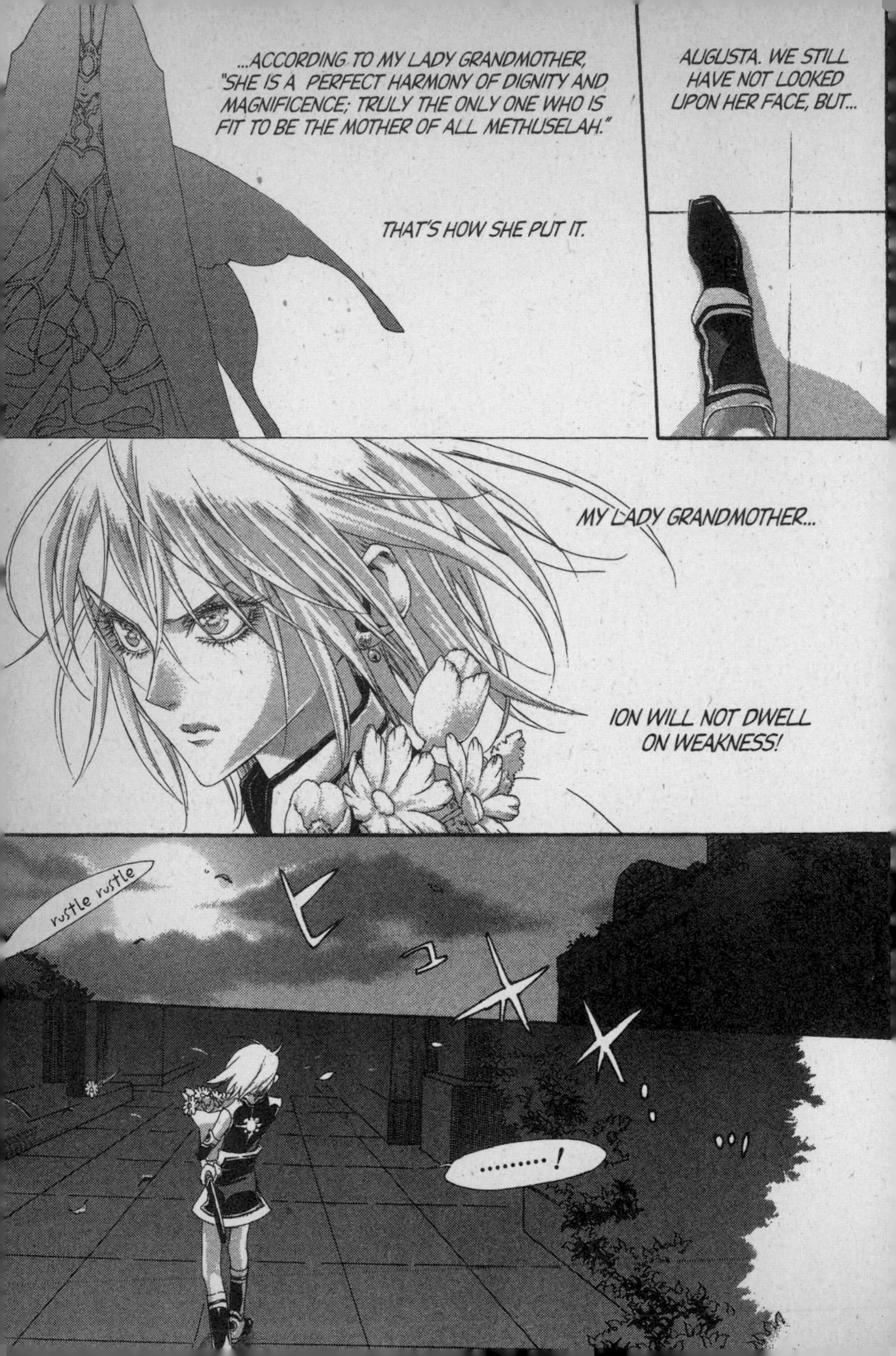
AUGUSTA. WE STILL HAVE NOT LOOKED UPON HER FACE, BUT...
...ACCORDING TO MY LADY GRANDMOTHER, "SHE IS A PERFECT HARMONY OF DIGNITY AND MAGNIFICENCE; TRULY THE ONLY ONE WHO IS FIT TO BE THE MOTHER OF ALL METHUSELAH."
THAT'S HOW SHE PUT IT.
MY LADY GRANDMOTHER...
ION WILL NOT DWELL ON WEAKNESS!
rustle rustle
.........!

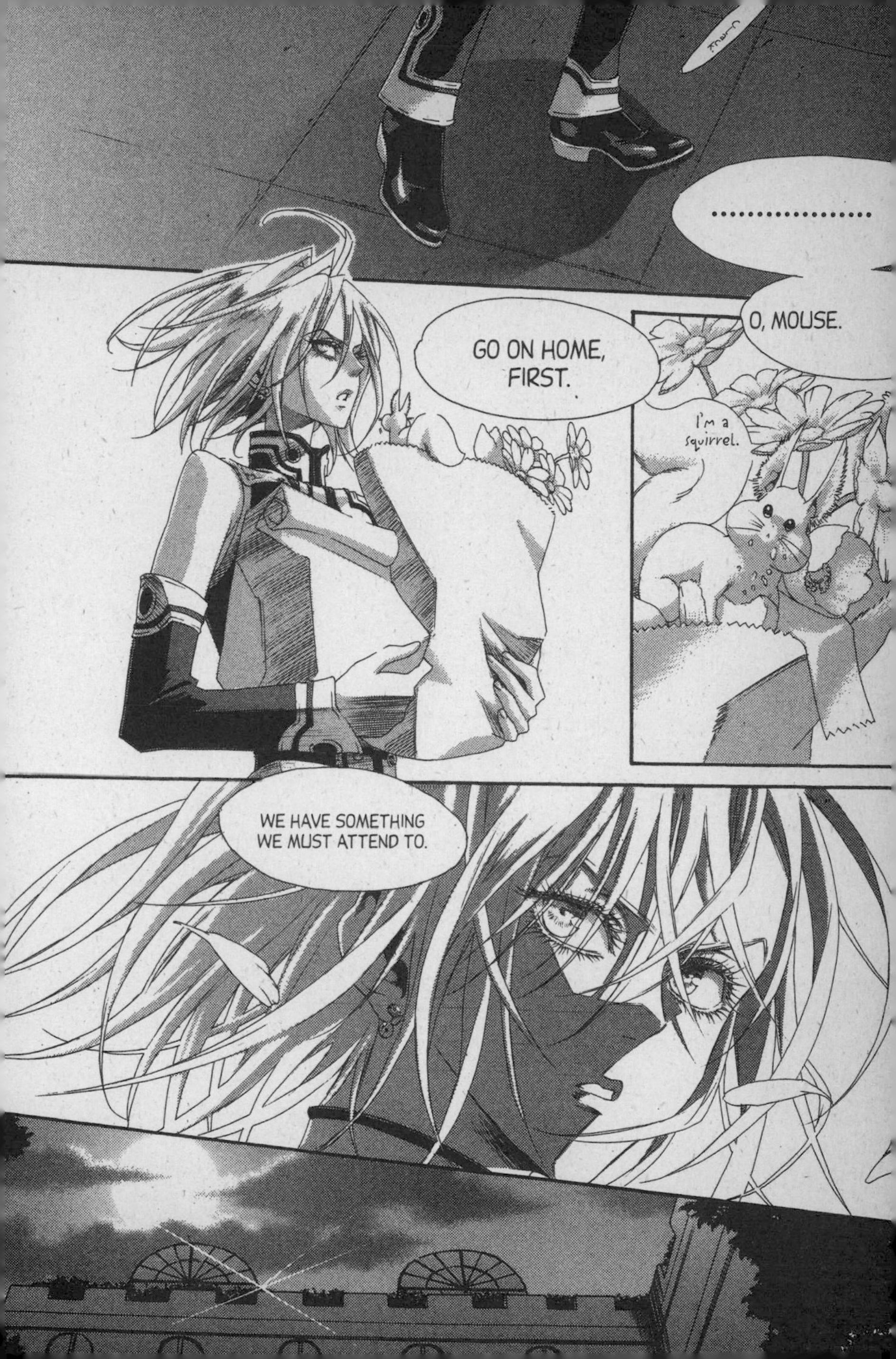

..................
O, MOUSE.
I'm a squirrel.
GO ON HOME, FIRST.
WE HAVE SOMETHING WE MUST ATTEND TO.

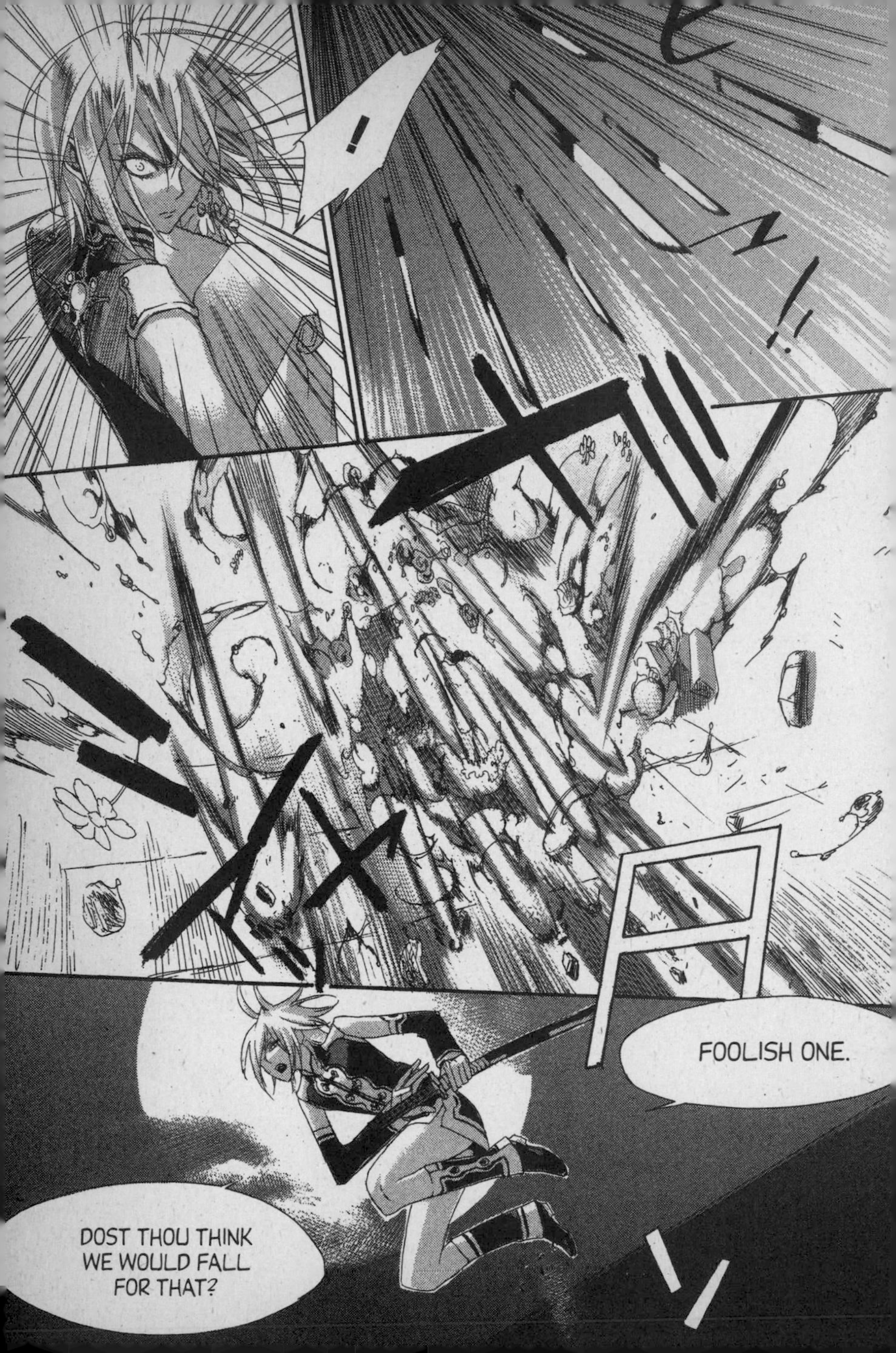
!
FOOLISH ONE.
DOST THOU THINK WE WOULD FALL FOR THAT?

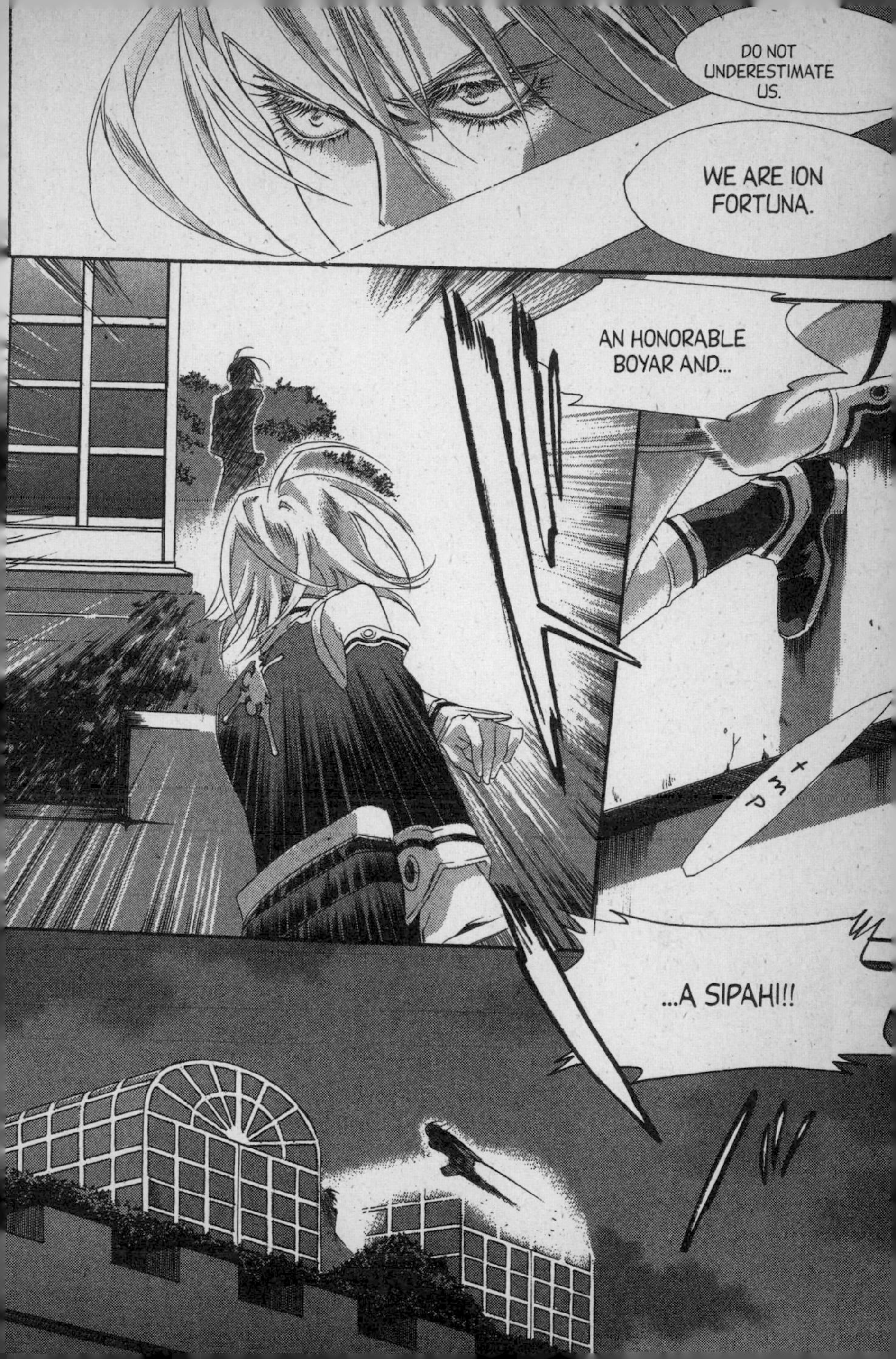
DO NOT UNDERESTIMATE US.
WE ARE ION FORTUNA.
AN HONORABLE BOYAR AND...
...A SIPAHI!!

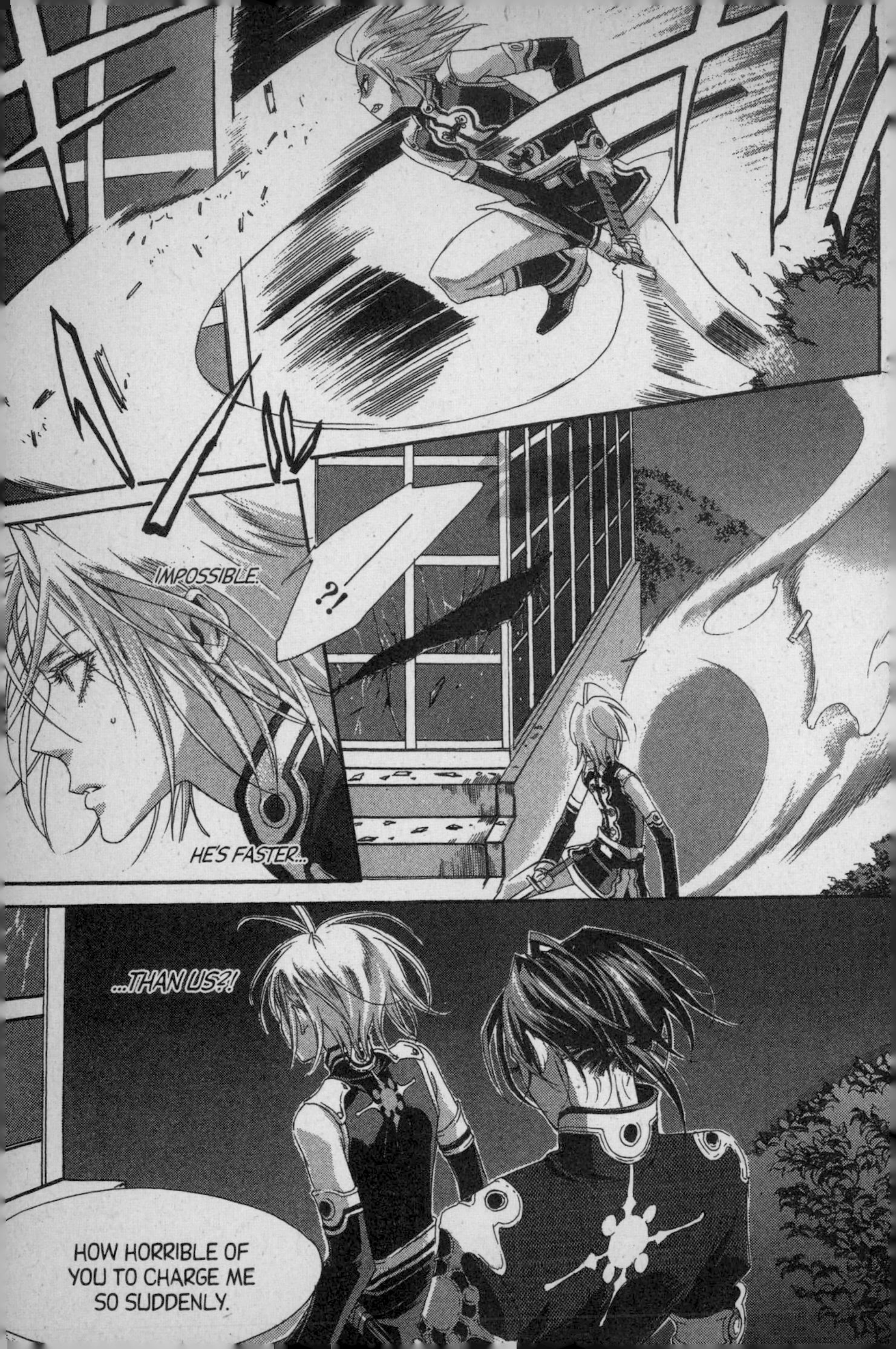
?!
IMPOSSIBLE.
HE'S FASTER...
...THAN US?!
HOW HORRIBLE OF YOU TO CHARGE ME SO SUDDENLY.

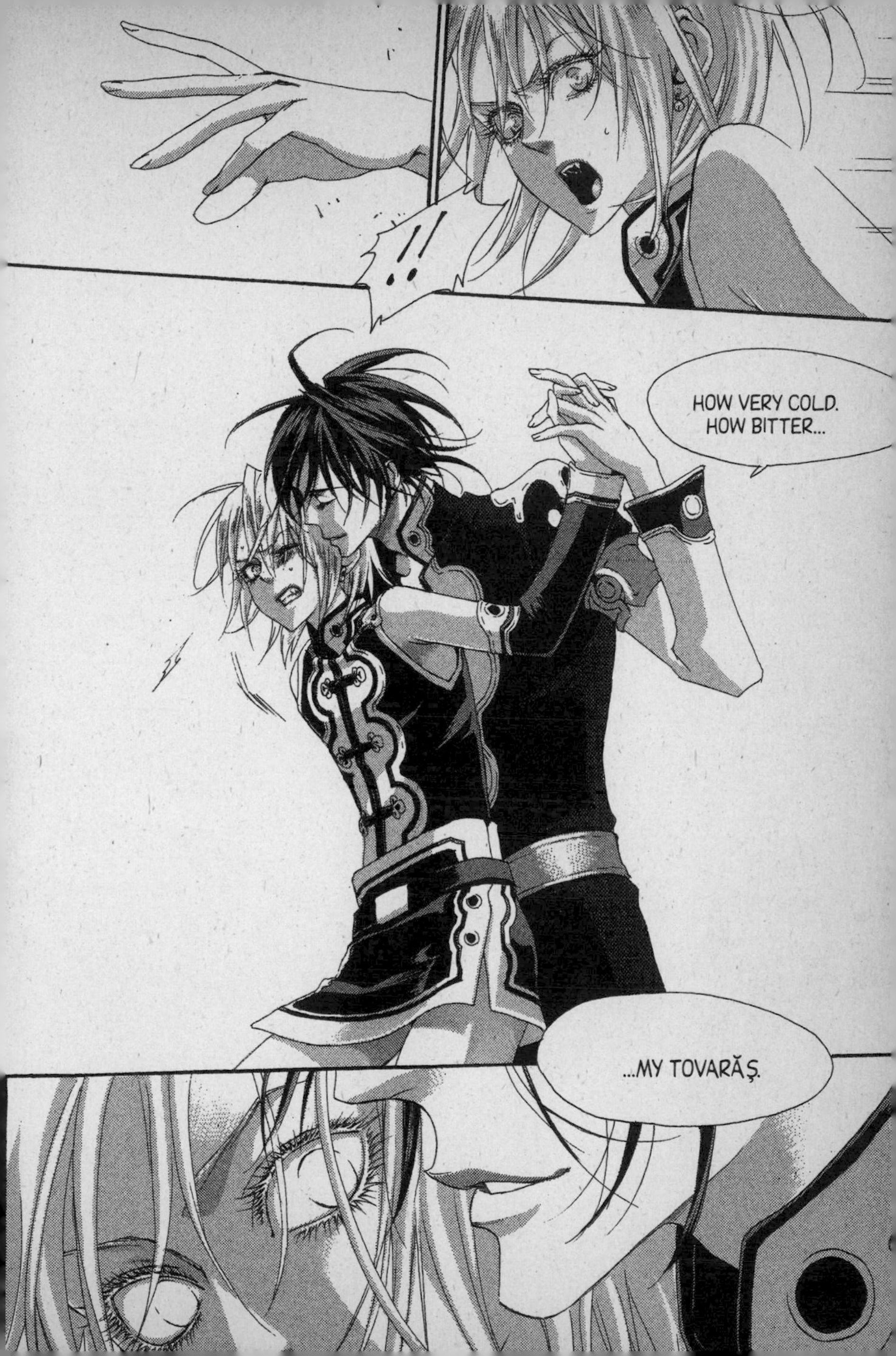
!!
HOW VERY COLD. HOW BITTER...
...MY TOVARĂŞ.

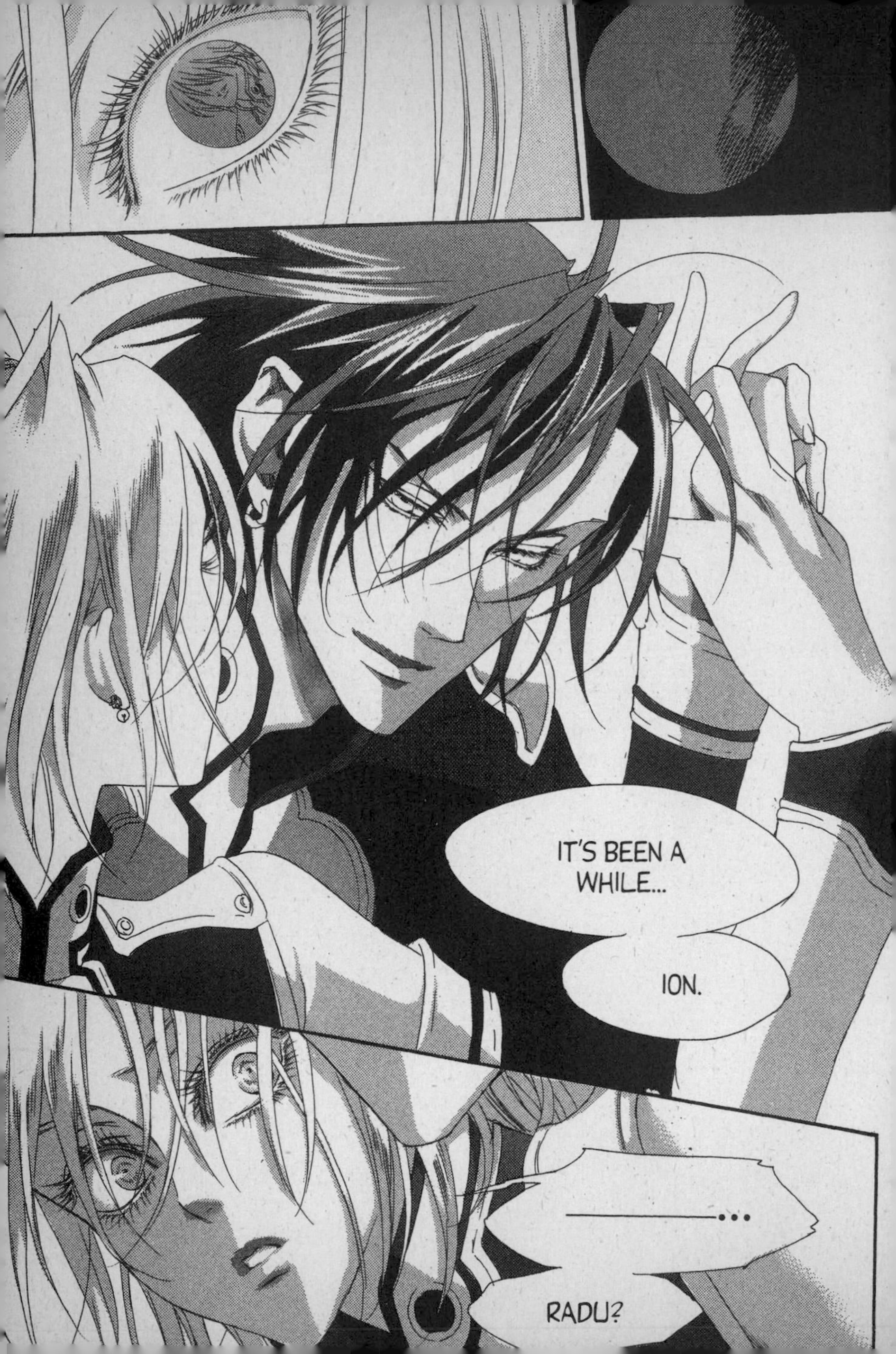
IT'S BEEN A WHILE...
ION.
————————...
RADU?

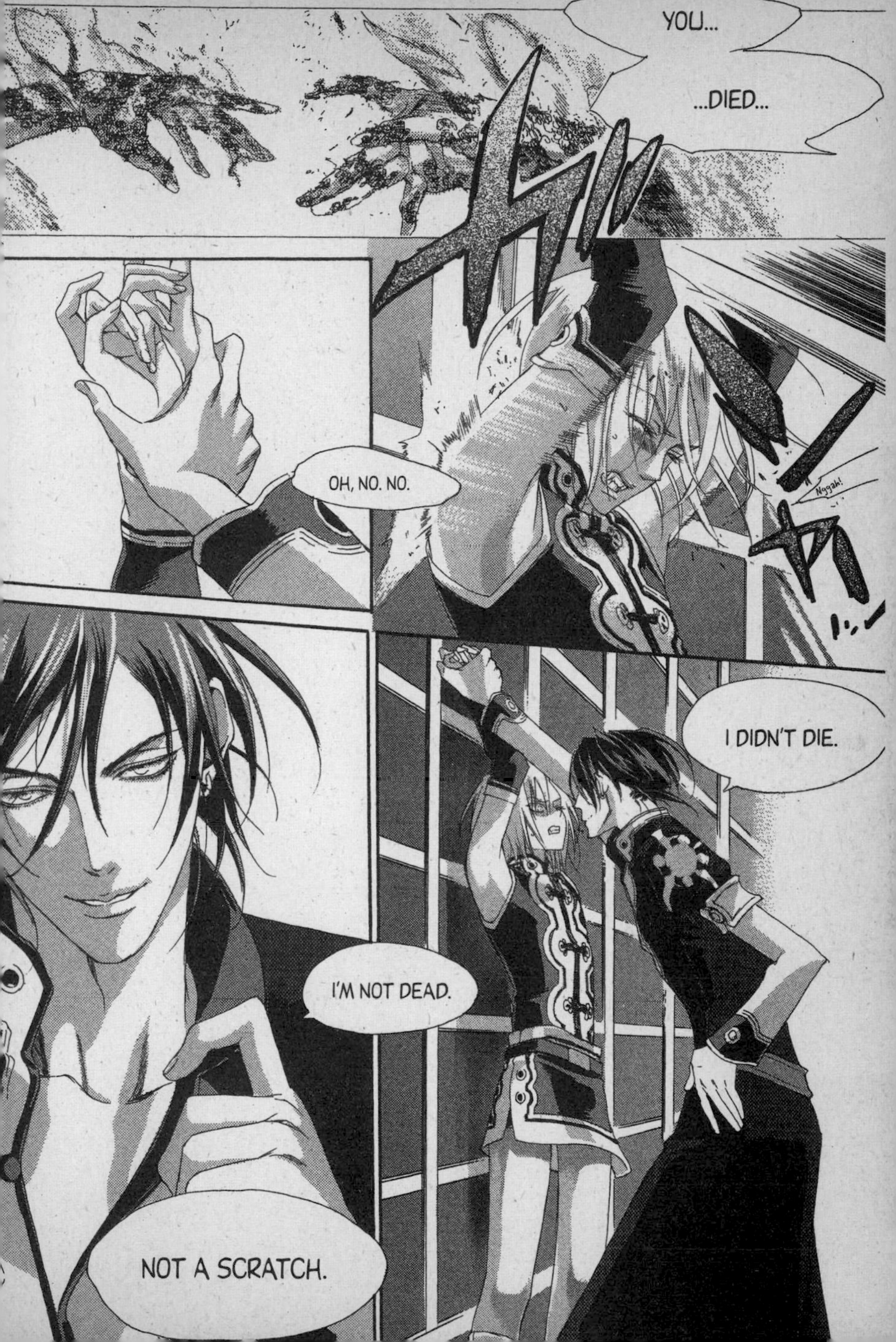
YOU...
...DIED...
Nggah!
OH, NO. NO.
I DIDN'T DIE.
I'M NOT DEAD.
NOT A SCRATCH.

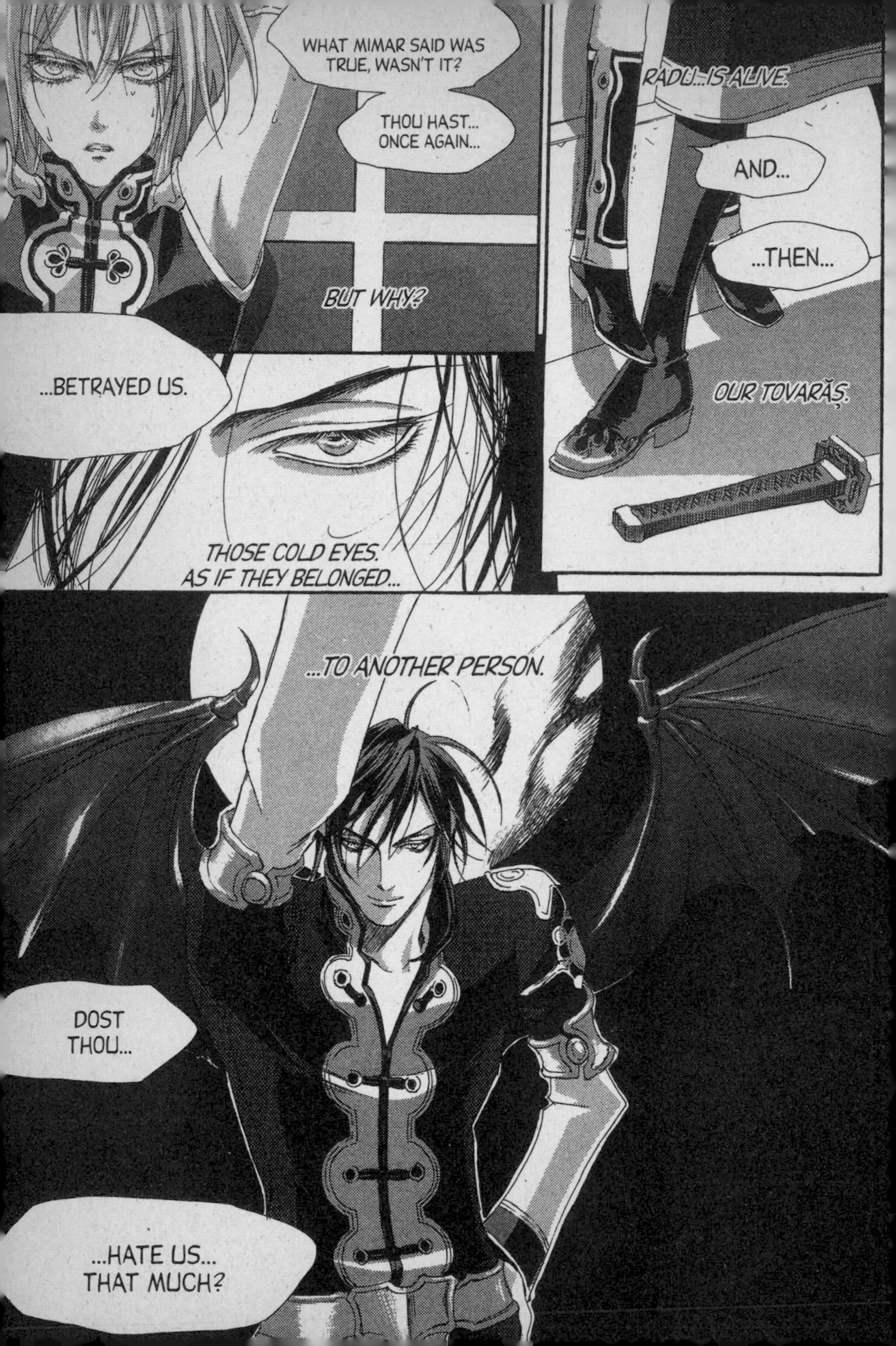

RADU...IS ALIVE.
AND...
...THEN...
OUR TOVARĂȘ.
WHAT MIMAR SAID WAS TRUE, WASN'T IT?
THOU HAST... ONCE AGAIN...
...BETRAYED US.
BUT WHY?
THOSE COLD EYES. AS IF THEY BELONGED...
...TO ANOTHER PERSON.
DOST THOU...
...HATE US... THAT MUCH?

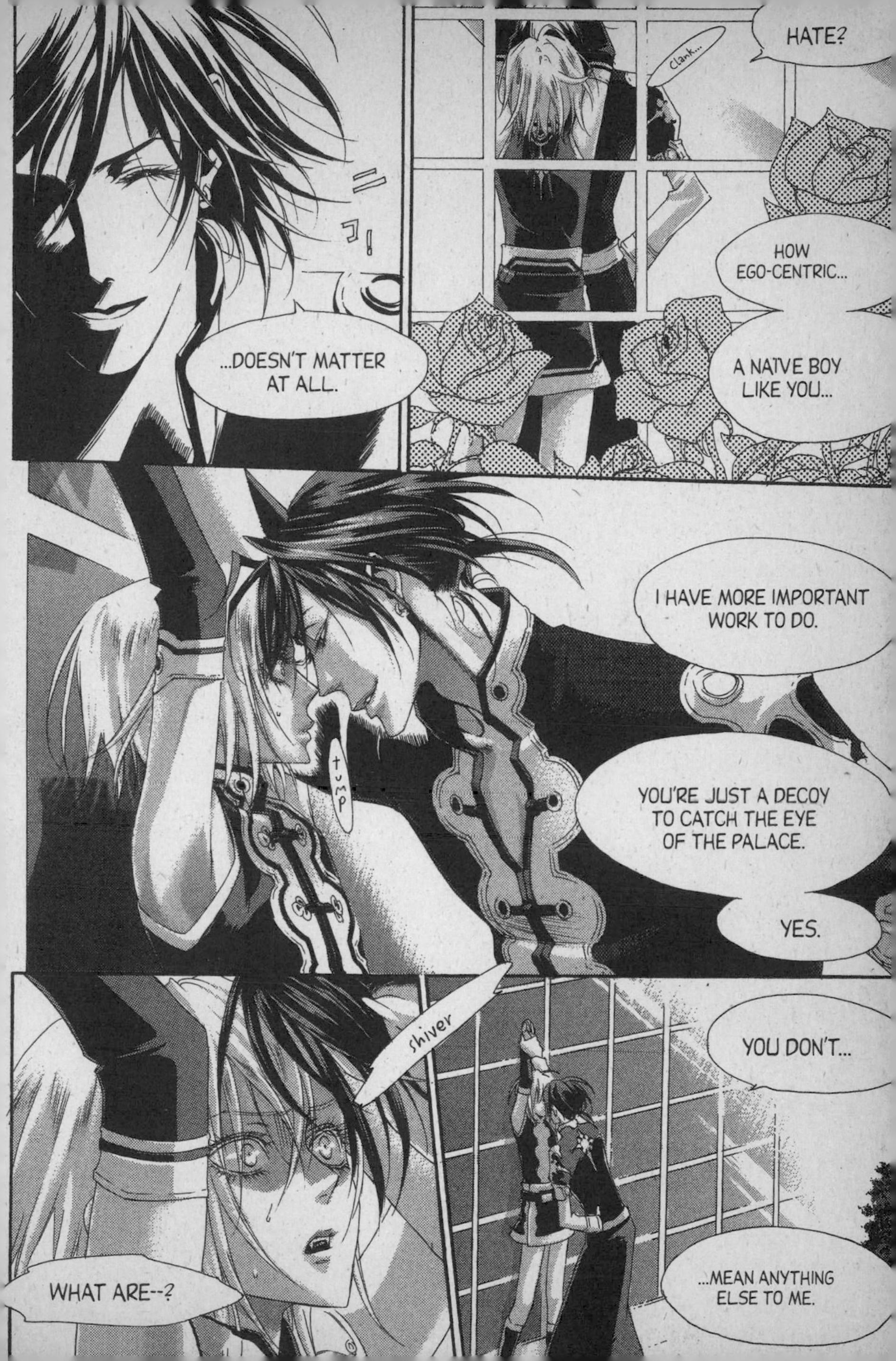

HATE?
Clank...
HOW EGO-CENTRIC...
A NAÏVE BOY LIKE YOU...
...DOESN'T MATTER AT ALL.
I HAVE MORE IMPORTANT WORK TO DO.
tump
YOU'RE JUST A DECOY TO CATCH THE EYE OF THE PALACE.
YES.
YOU DON'T...
...MEAN ANYTHING ELSE TO ME.
shiver
WHAT ARE--?

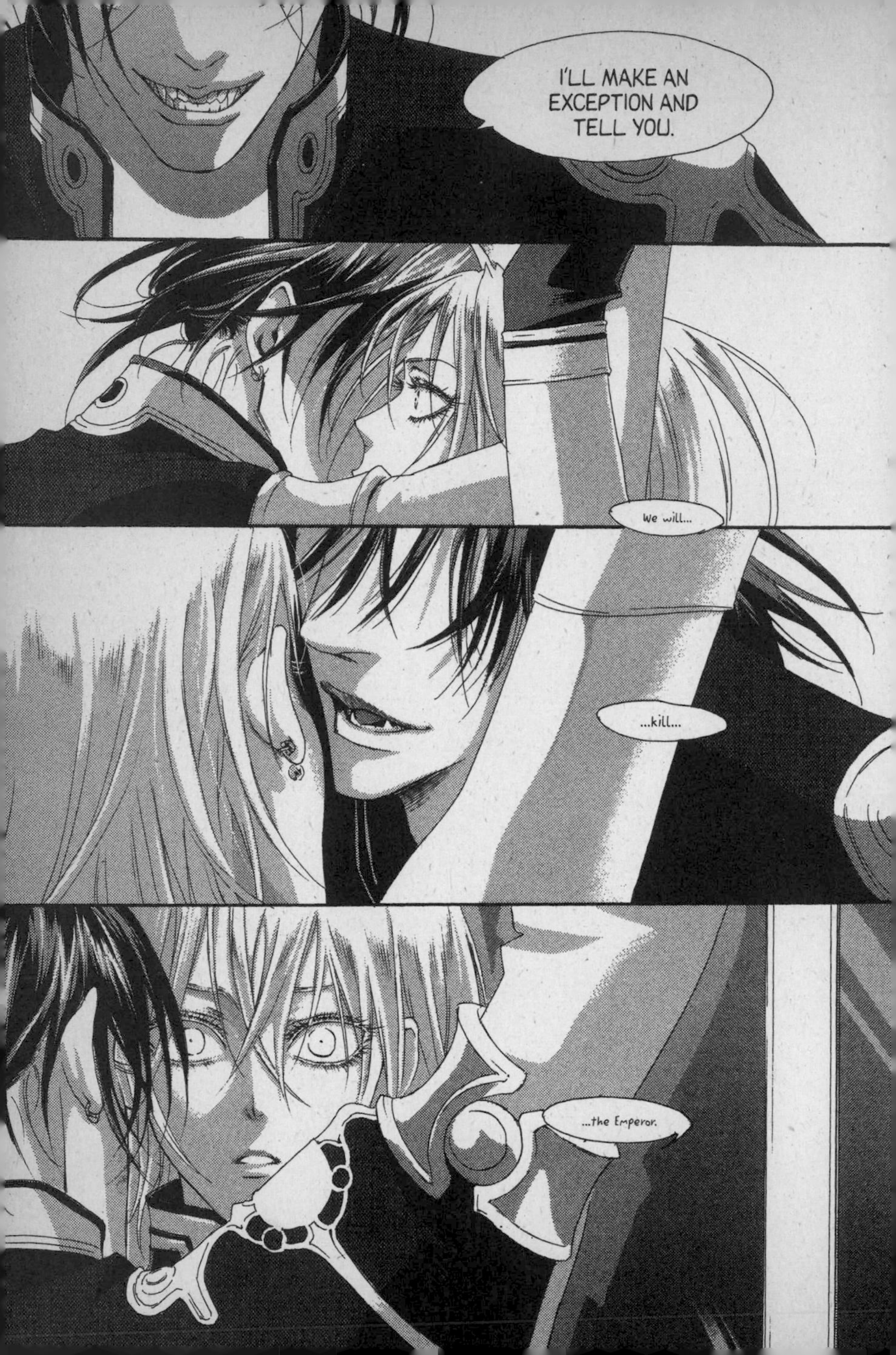
I'LL MAKE AN EXCEPTION AND TELL YOU.
We will...
...kill...
...the Emperor.

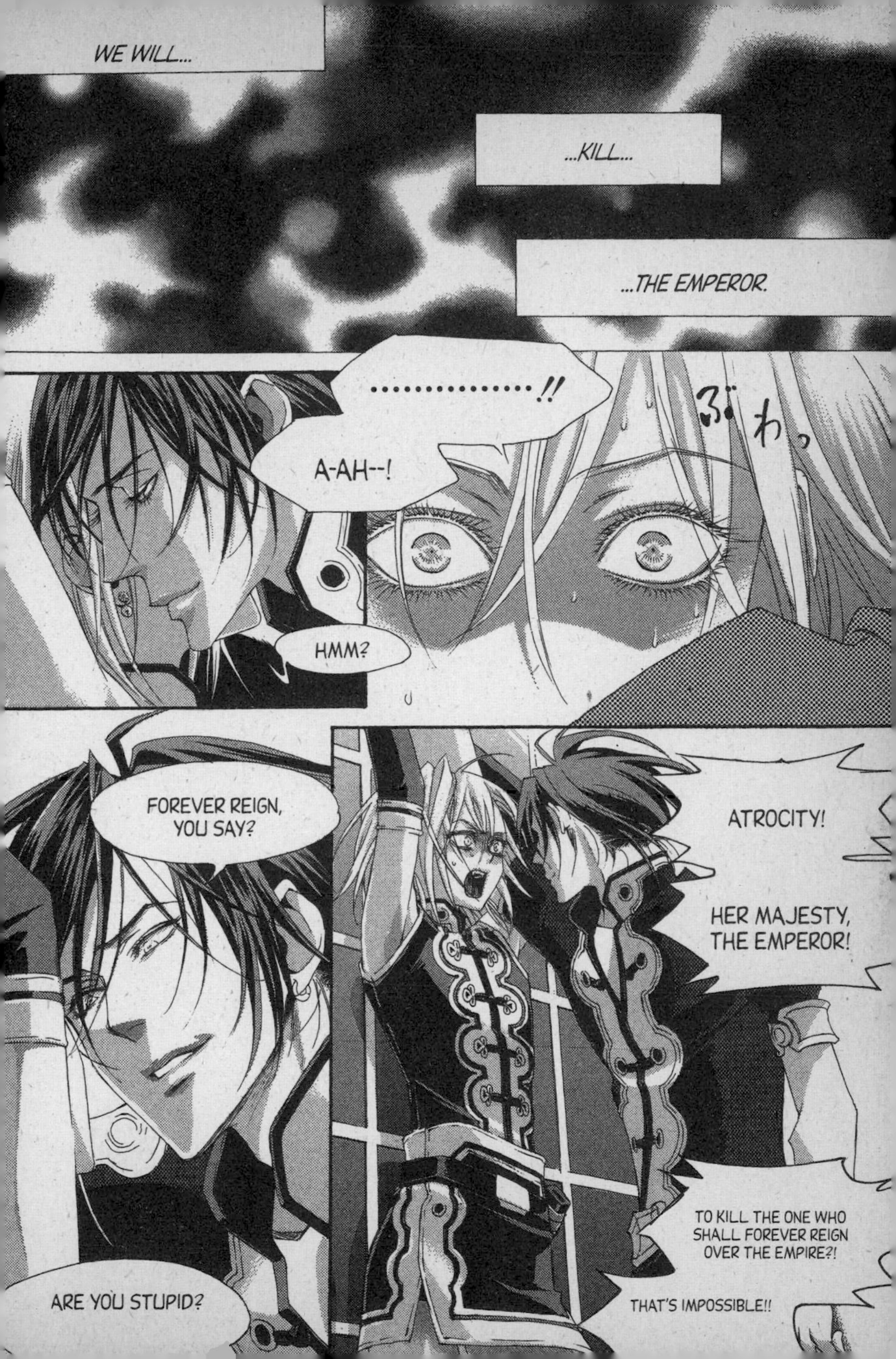

WE WILL...
...KILL...
...THE EMPEROR.
..................!!
ぶわっ
A-AH--!
HMM?
ATROCITY!
HER MAJESTY, THE EMPEROR!
TO KILL THE ONE WHO SHALL FOREVER REIGN OVER THE EMPIRE?!
THAT'S IMPOSSIBLE!!
FOREVER REIGN, YOU SAY?
ARE YOU STUPID?

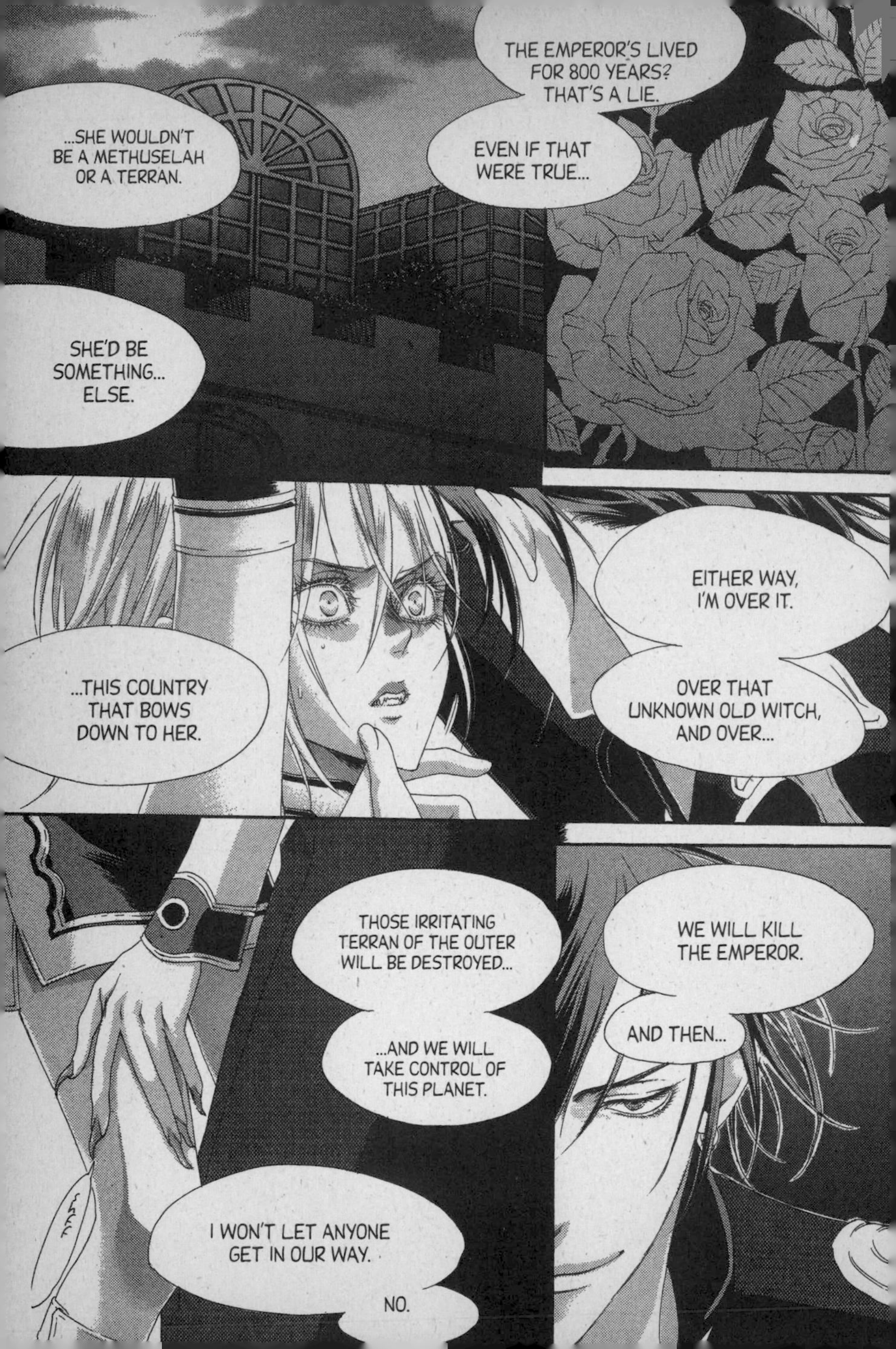
THE EMPEROR'S LIVED FOR 800 YEARS? THAT'S A LIE.
EVEN IF THAT WERE TRUE...
...SHE WOULDN'T BE A METHUSELAH OR A TERRAN.
SHE'D BE SOMETHING... ELSE.
EITHER WAY, I'M OVER IT.
OVER THAT UNKNOWN OLD WITCH, AND OVER...
...THIS COUNTRY THAT BOWS DOWN TO HER.
WE WILL KILL THE EMPEROR.
AND THEN...
THOSE IRRITATING TERRAN OF THE OUTER WILL BE DESTROYED...
...AND WE WILL TAKE CONTROL OF THIS PLANET.
I WON'T LET ANYONE GET IN OUR WAY.
NO.

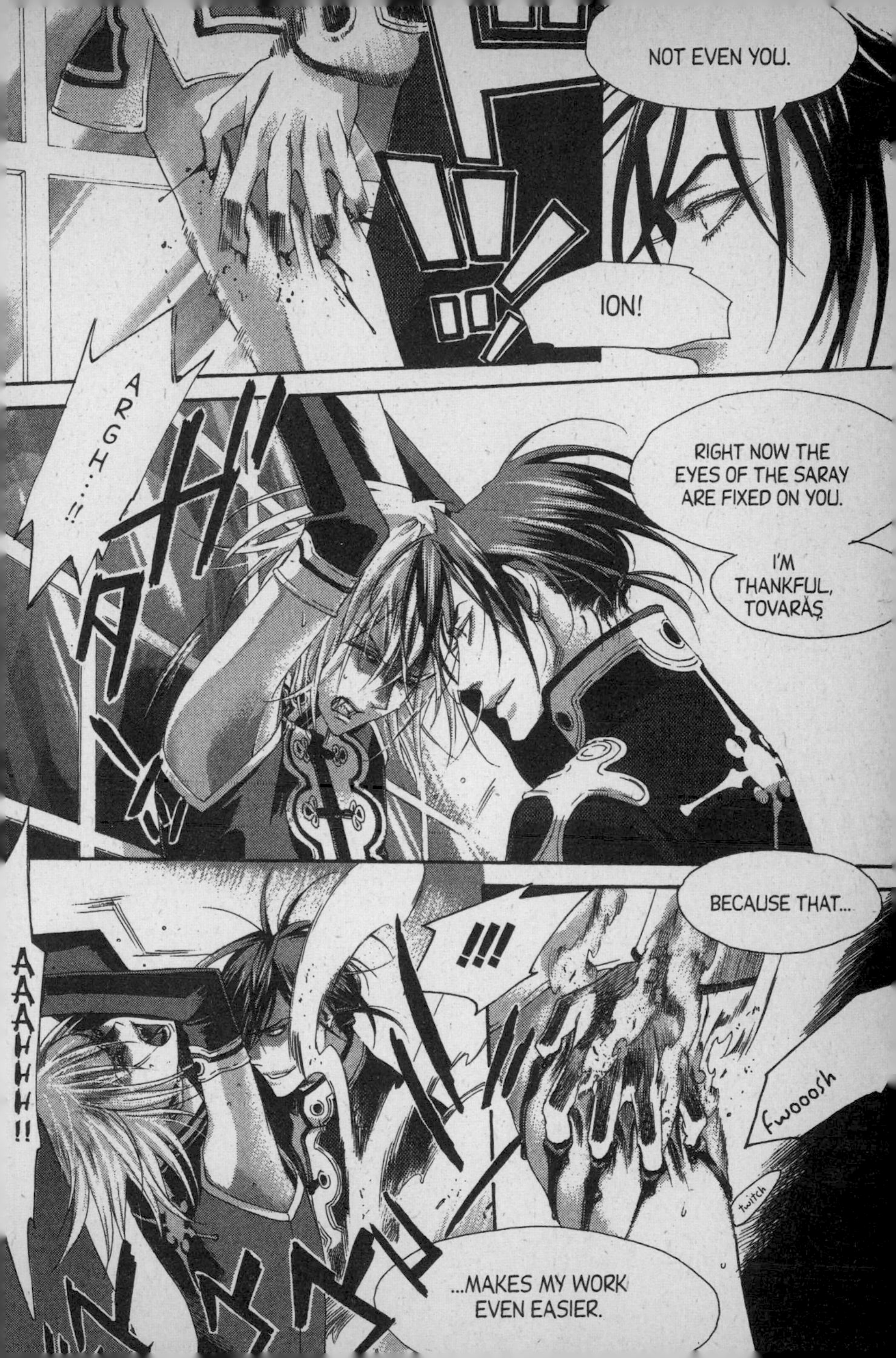

NOT EVEN YOU.
ION!
RIGHT NOW THE EYES OF THE SARAY ARE FIXED ON YOU.
I'M THANKFUL, TOVARĂŞ.
ARGH...!!
BECAUSE THAT...
!!!
fwooosh
twitch
...MAKES MY WORK EVEN EASIER.
AAAHHH!!

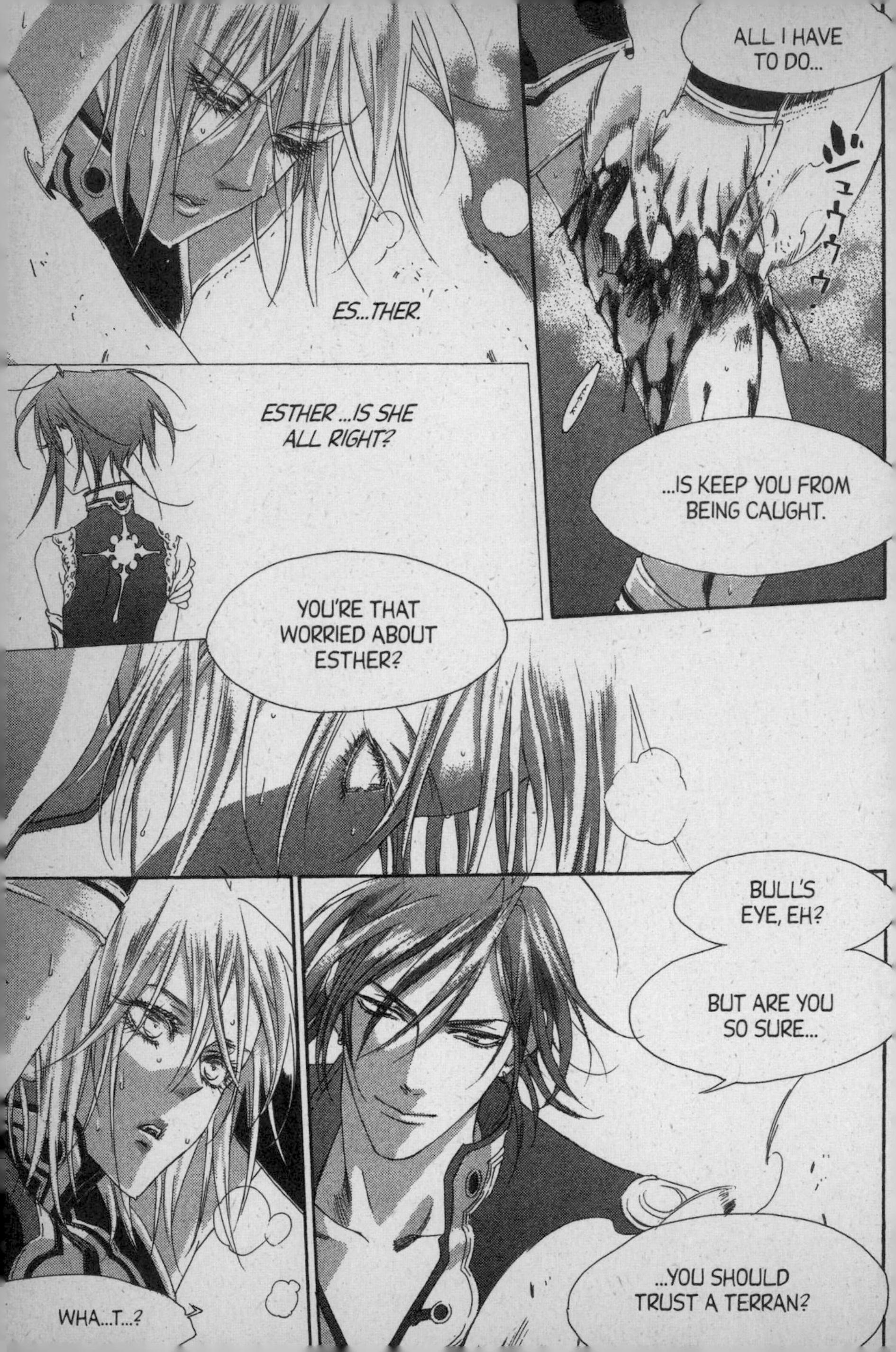
ALL I HAVE TO DO...
ジュウウウウ
...IS KEEP YOU FROM BEING CAUGHT.
ES...THER.
ESTHER ...IS SHE ALL RIGHT?
YOU'RE THAT WORRIED ABOUT ESTHER?
BULL'S EYE, EH?
BUT ARE YOU SO SURE...
...YOU SHOULD TRUST A TERRAN?
WHA...T...?

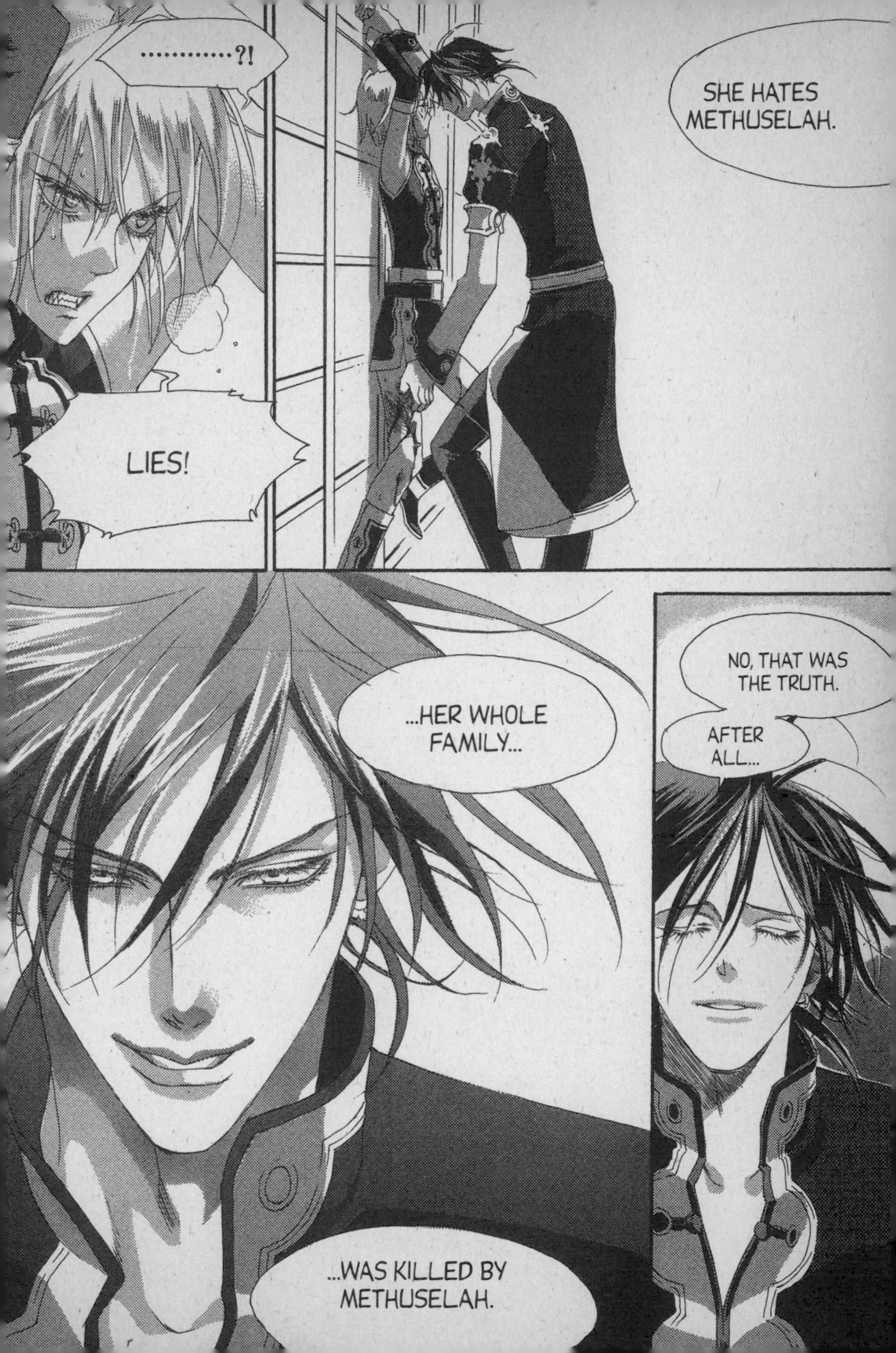
SHE HATES METHUSELAH.
............?!
LIES!
NO, THAT WAS THE TRUTH.
AFTER ALL...
...HER WHOLE FAMILY...
...WAS KILLED BY METHUSELAH.

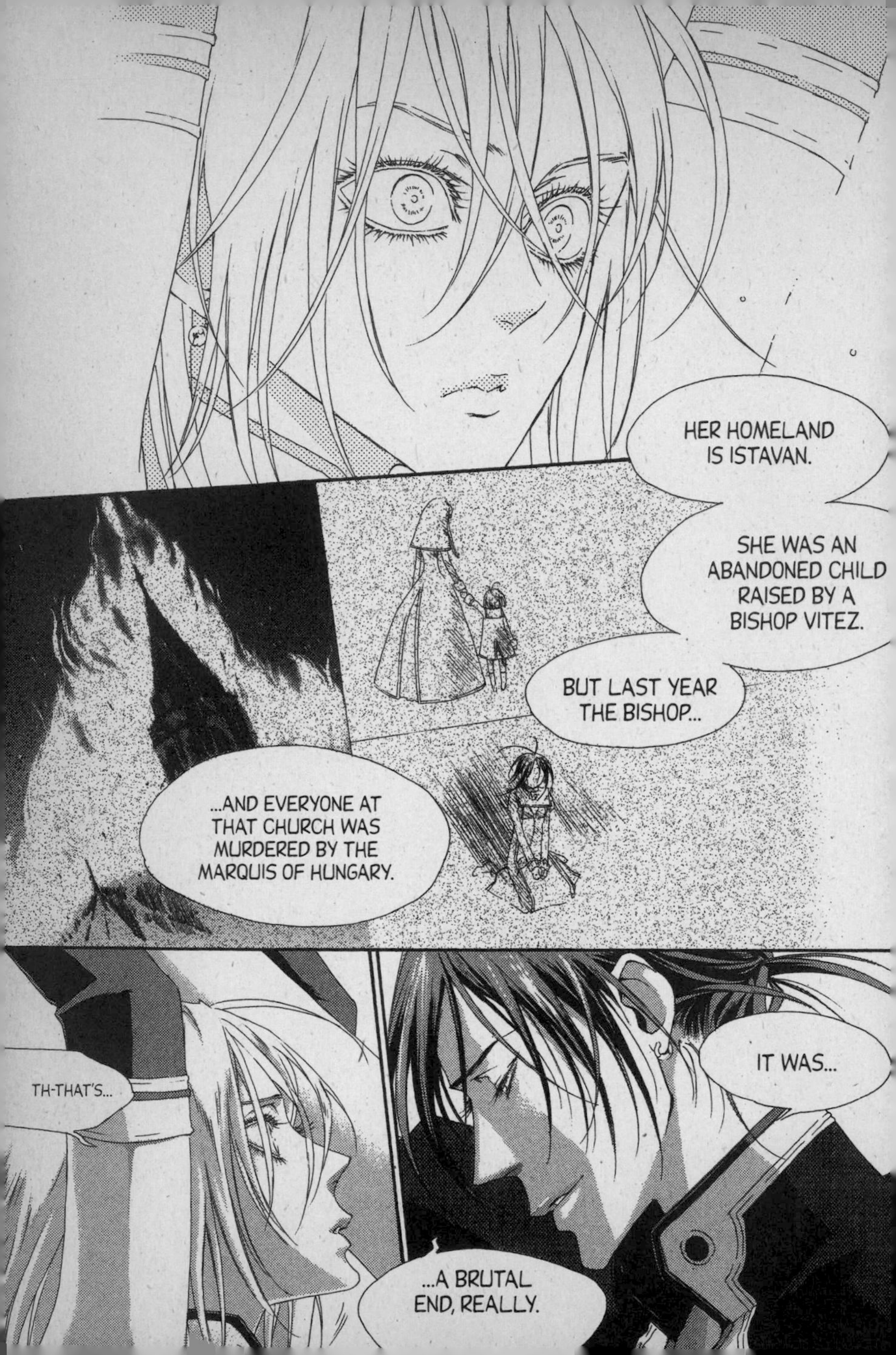
HER HOMELAND IS ISTAVAN.
SHE WAS AN ABANDONED CHILD RAISED BY A BISHOP VITEZ.
BUT LAST YEAR THE BISHOP...
...AND EVERYONE AT THAT CHURCH WAS MURDERED BY THE MARQUIS OF HUNGARY.
IT WAS...
TH-THAT'S...
...A BRUTAL END, REALLY.

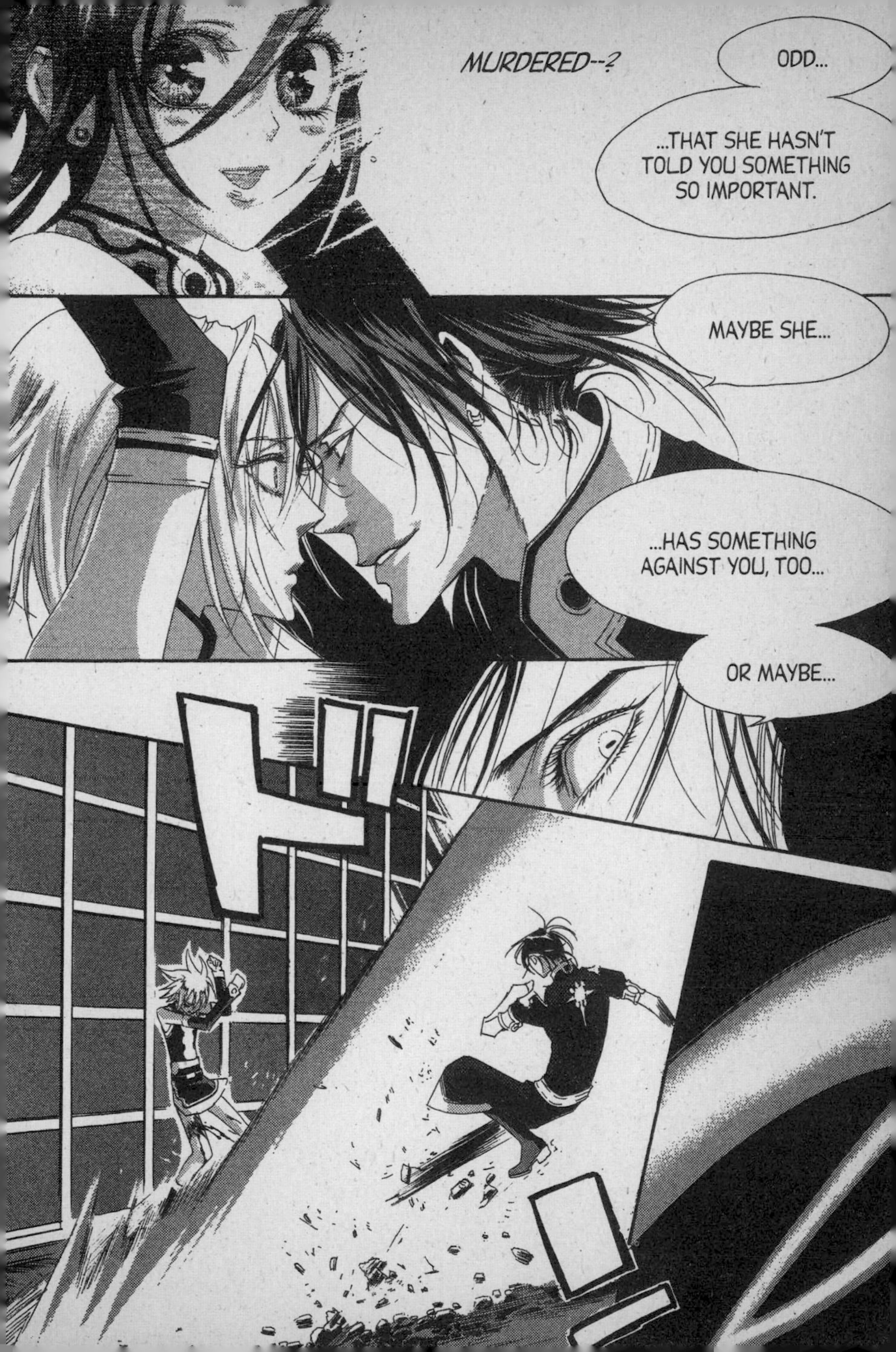
MURDERED--?
ODD...
...THAT SHE HASN'T TOLD YOU SOMETHING SO IMPORTANT.
MAYBE SHE...
...HAS SOMETHING AGAINST YOU, TOO...
OR MAYBE...

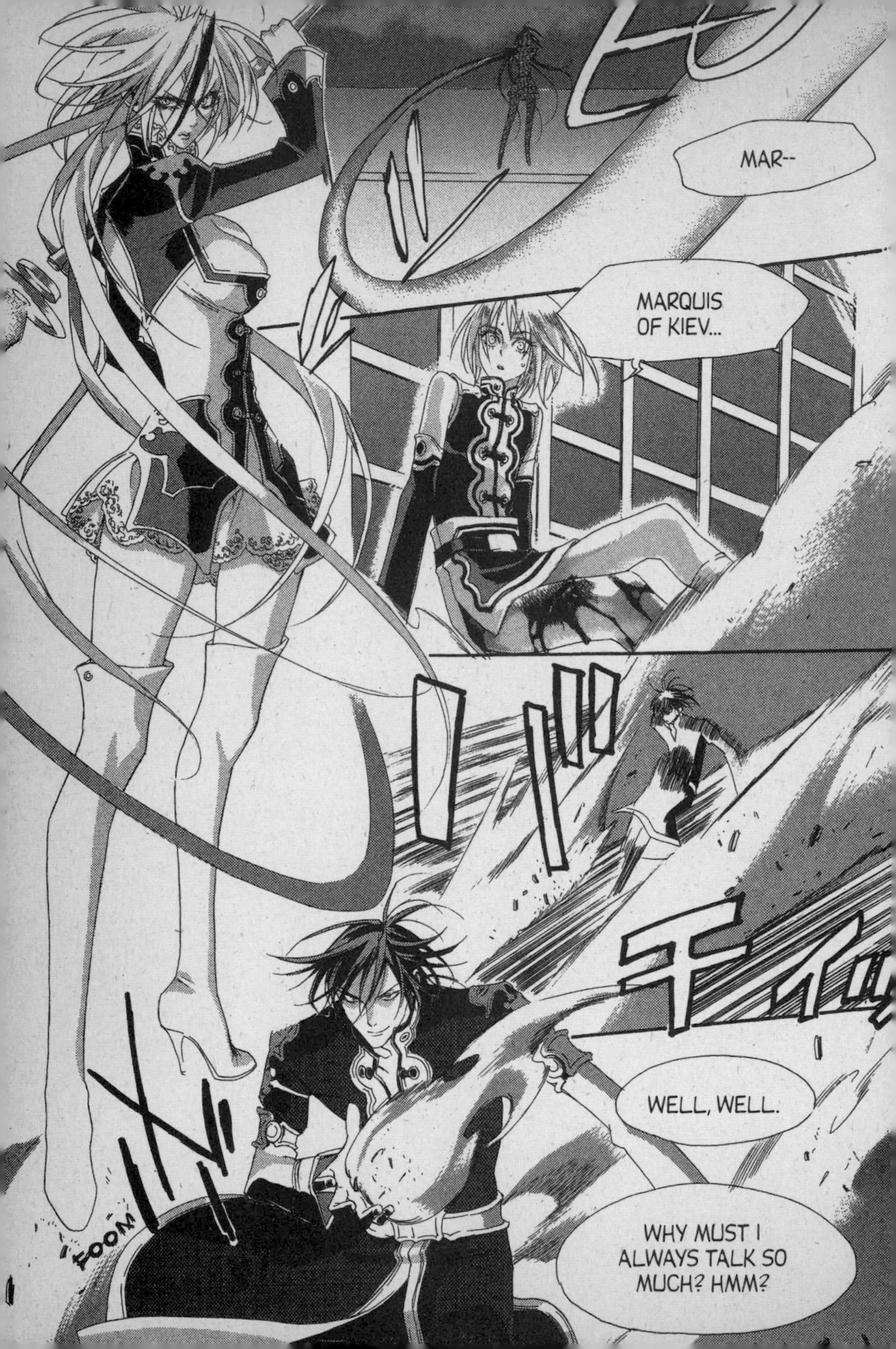
MAR--
MARQUIS OF KIEV...
WELL, WELL.
WHY MUST I ALWAYS TALK SO MUCH? HMM?
FOOM

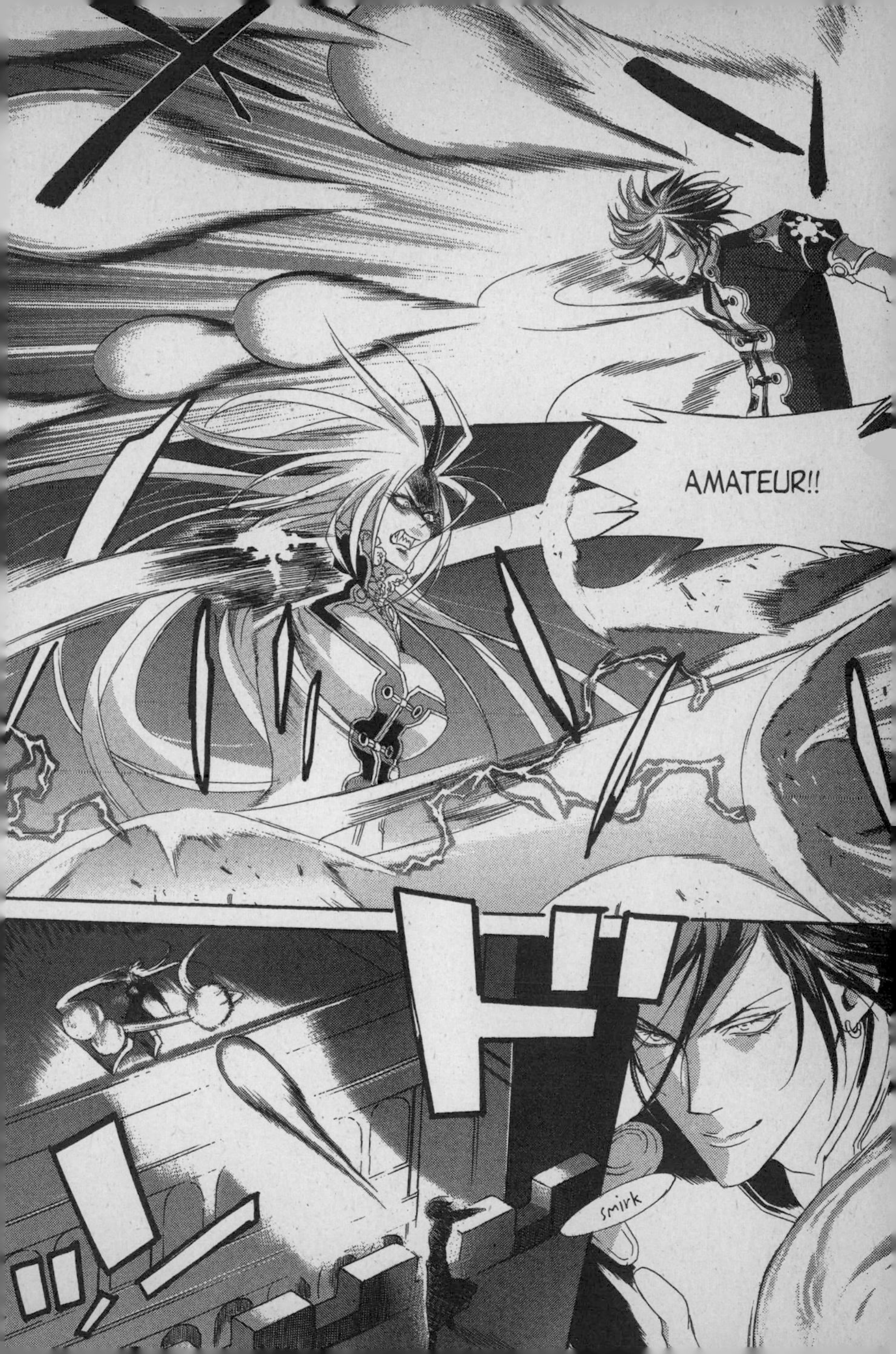
AMATEUR!!
smirk

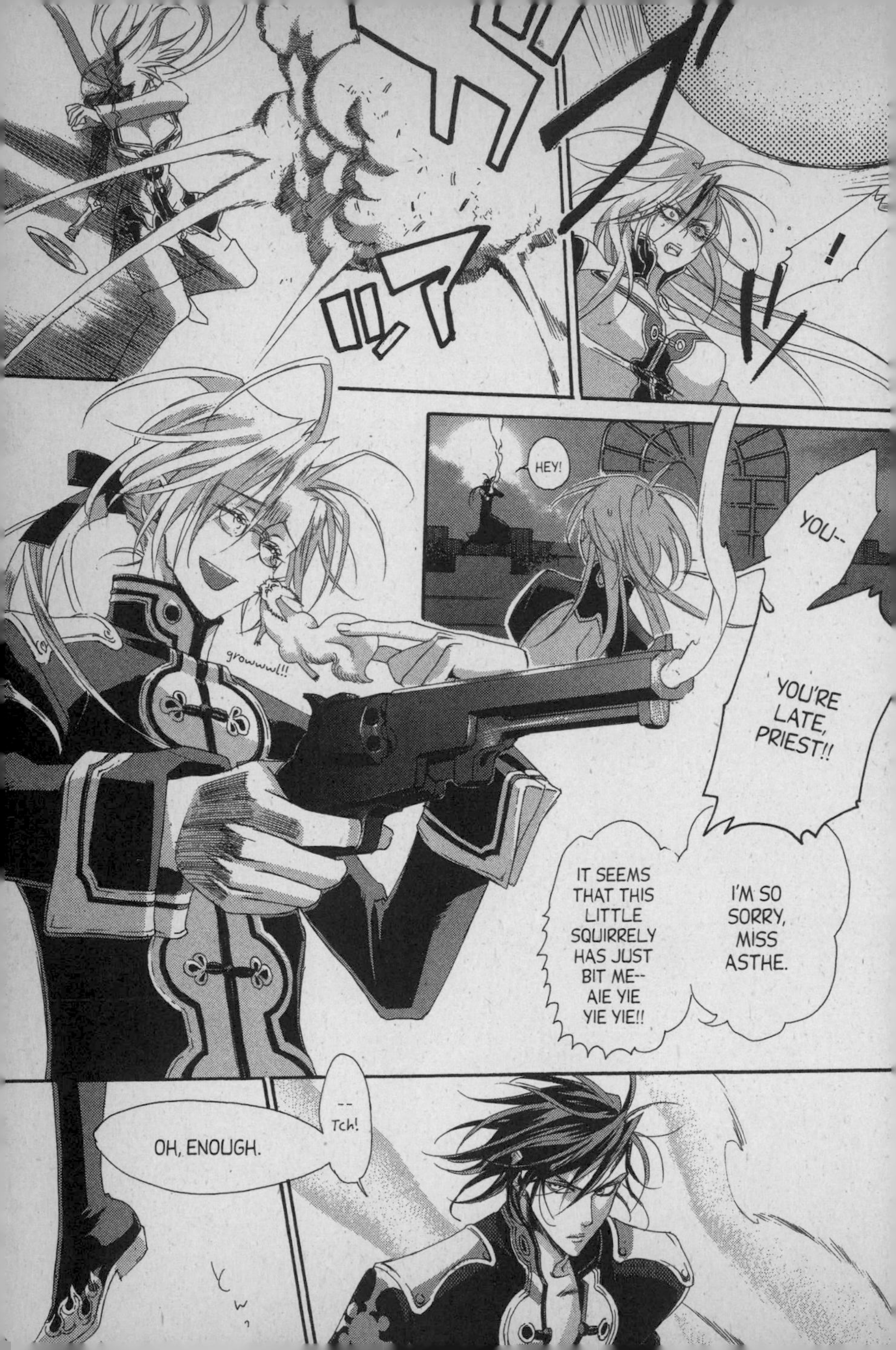
!
HEY!
YOU--
YOU'RE LATE, PRIEST!!
growwwl!!
I'M SO SORRY, MISS ASTHE.
IT SEEMS THAT THIS LITTLE SQUIRRELY HAS JUST BIT ME-- AIE YIE YIE YIE!!
--Tch!
OH, ENOUGH.

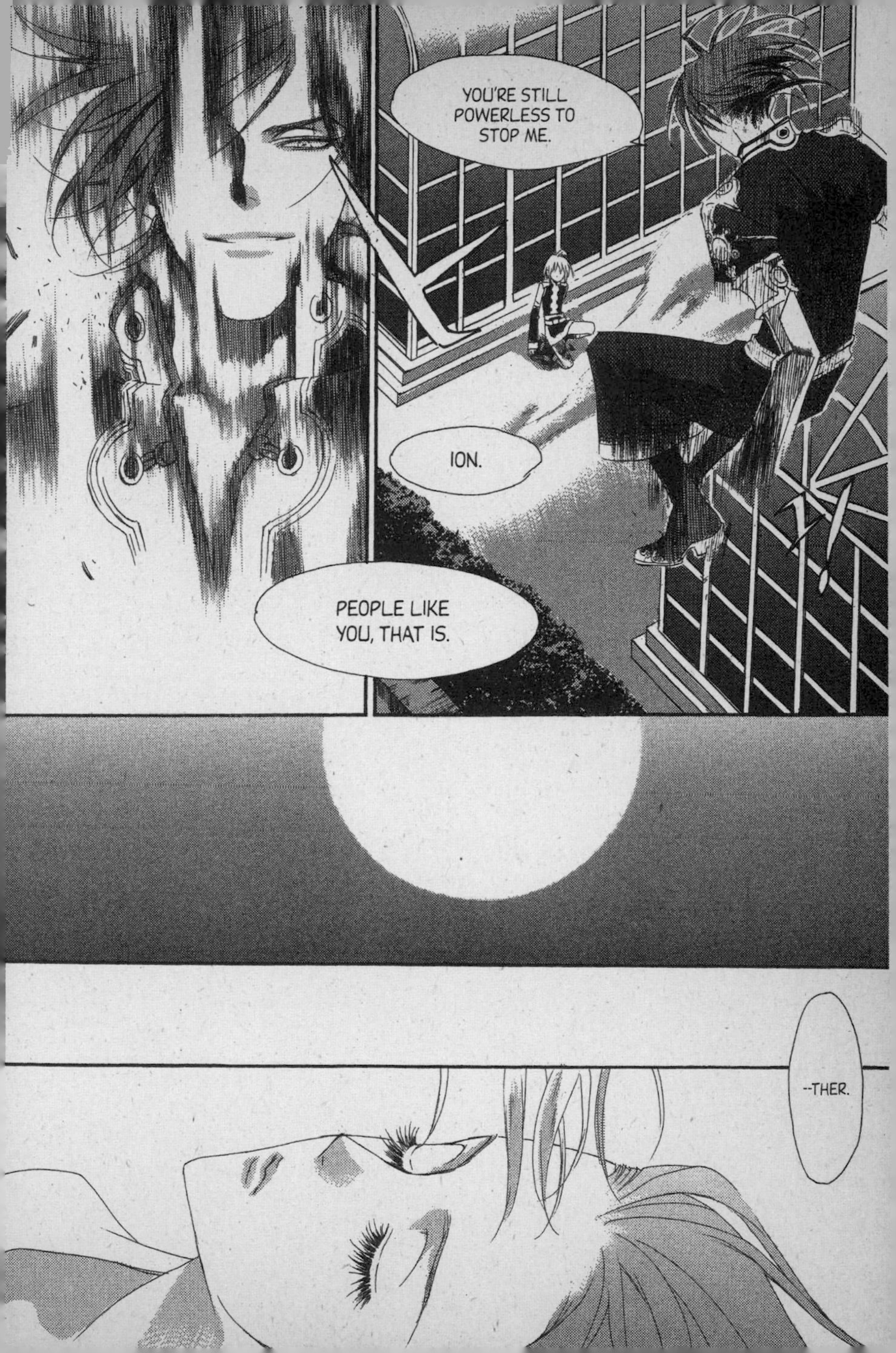
YOU'RE STILL POWERLESS TO STOP ME.
ION.
PEOPLE LIKE YOU, THAT IS.
--THER.

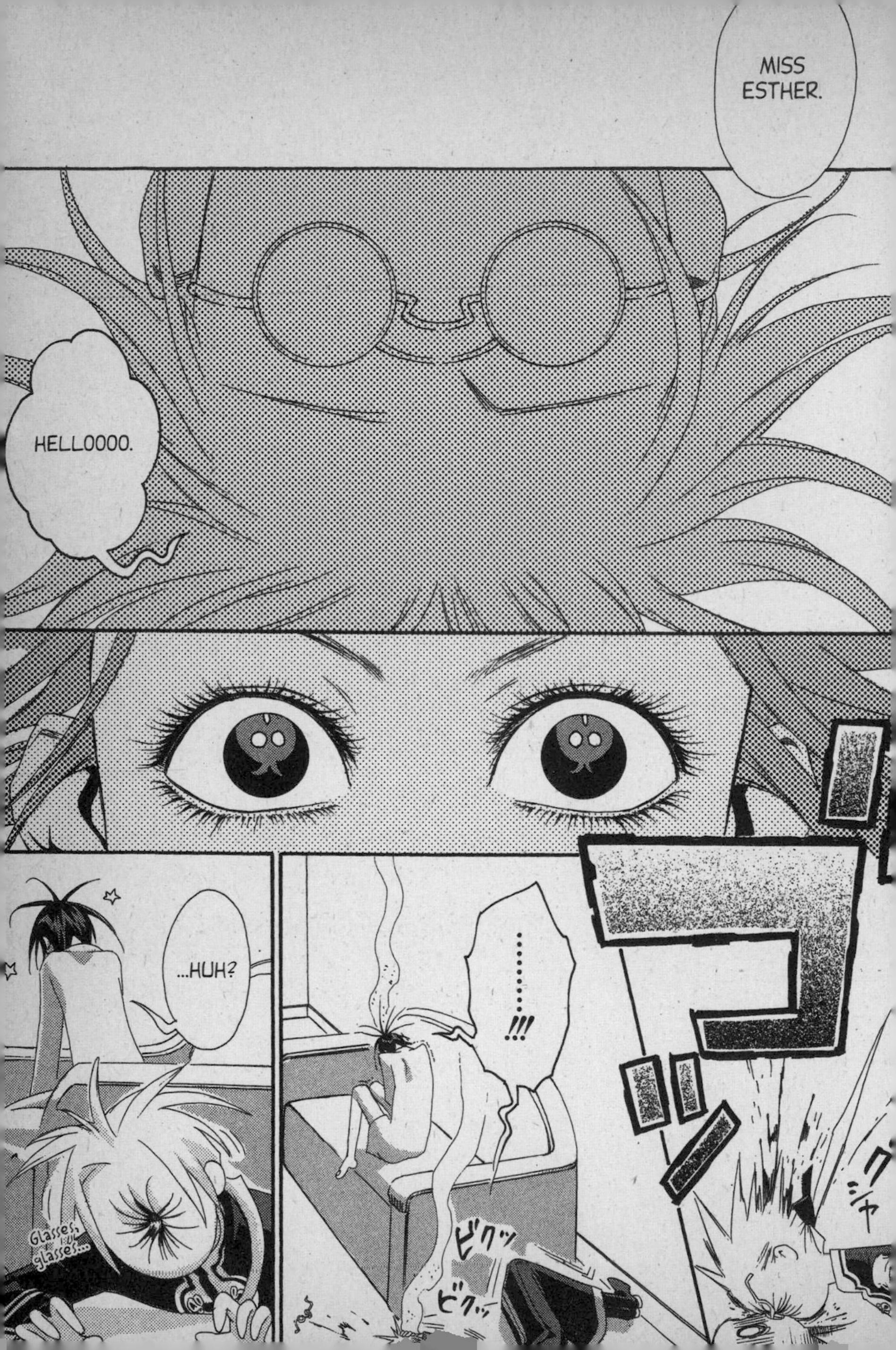
MISS ESTHER.
HELLOOOO.
クシャ
......!!!
ビクッ
ビクッ
...HUH?
Glasses, glasses...

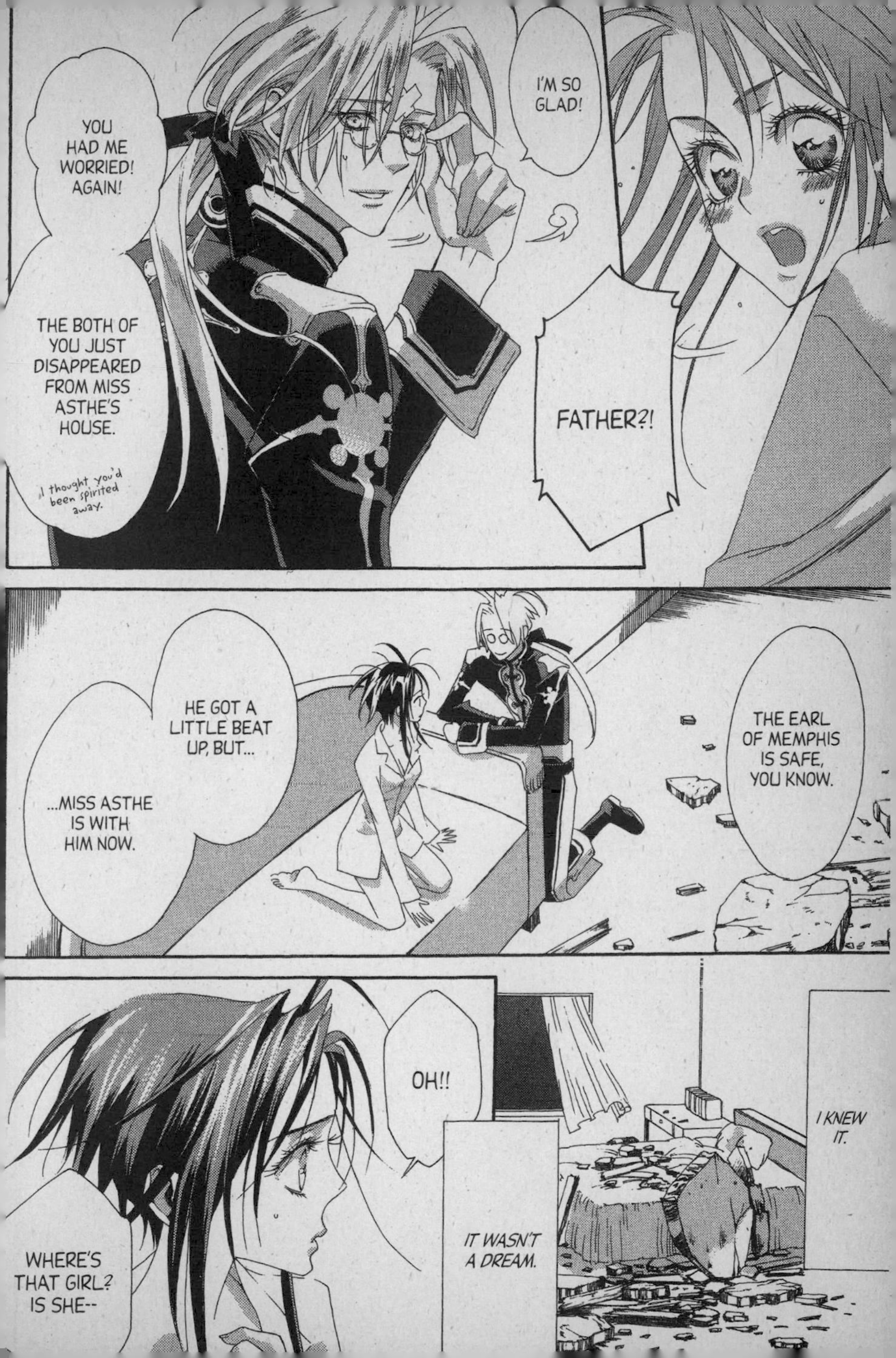
FATHER?!
I'M SO GLAD!
YOU HAD ME WORRIED! AGAIN!
THE BOTH OF YOU JUST DISAPPEARED FROM MISS ASTHE'S HOUSE.
I thought you'd been spirited away.
THE EARL OF MEMPHIS IS SAFE, YOU KNOW.
HE GOT A LITTLE BEAT UP, BUT...
...MISS ASTHE IS WITH HIM NOW.
I KNEW IT.
IT WASN'T A DREAM.
OH!!
WHERE'S THAT GIRL? IS SHE--

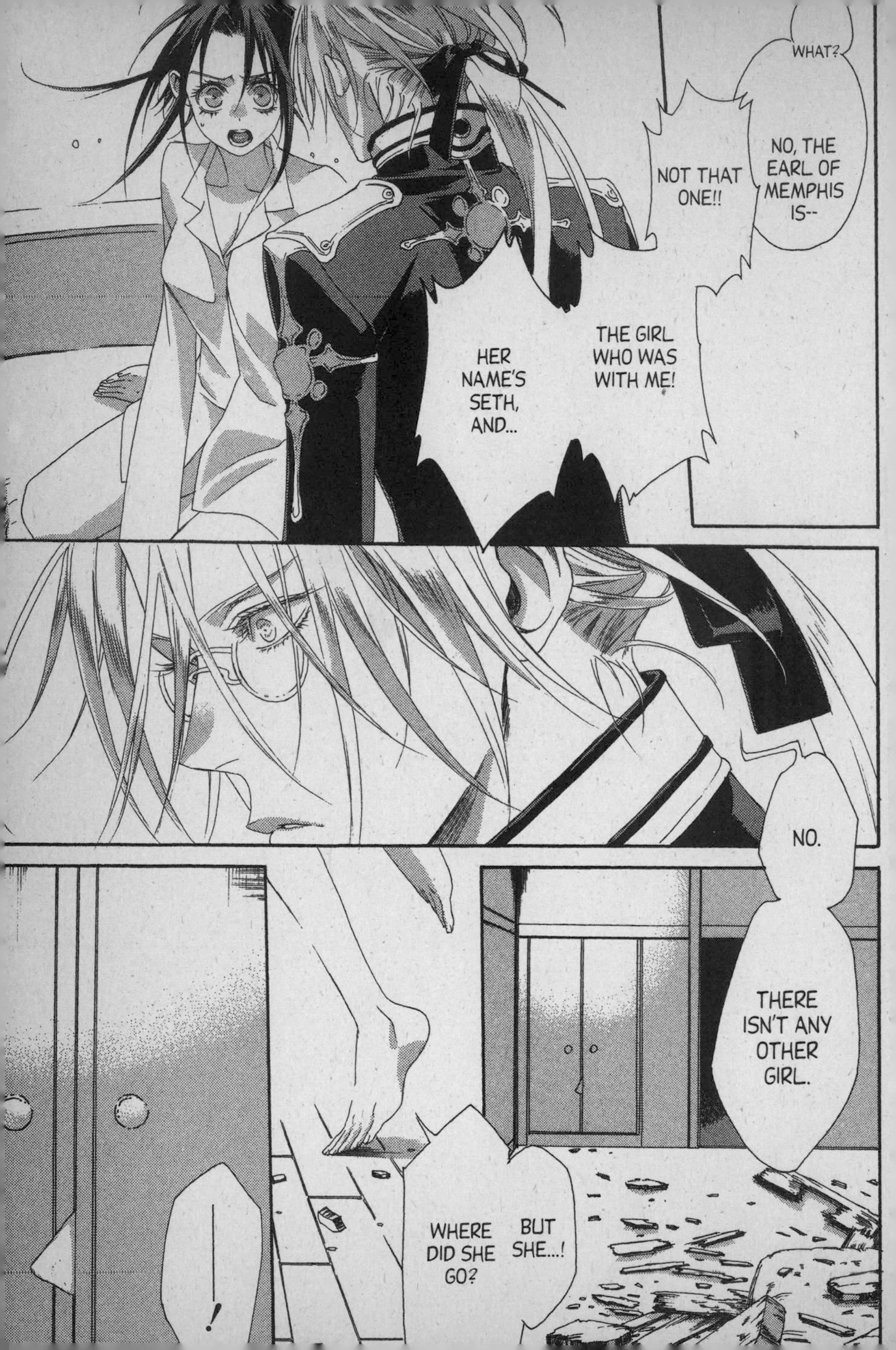
WHAT?
NO, THE EARL OF MEMPHIS IS--
NOT THAT ONE!!
THE GIRL WHO WAS WITH ME!
HER NAME'S SETH, AND...
NO.
THERE ISN'T ANY OTHER GIRL.
BUT SHE...!
WHERE DID SHE GO?
!

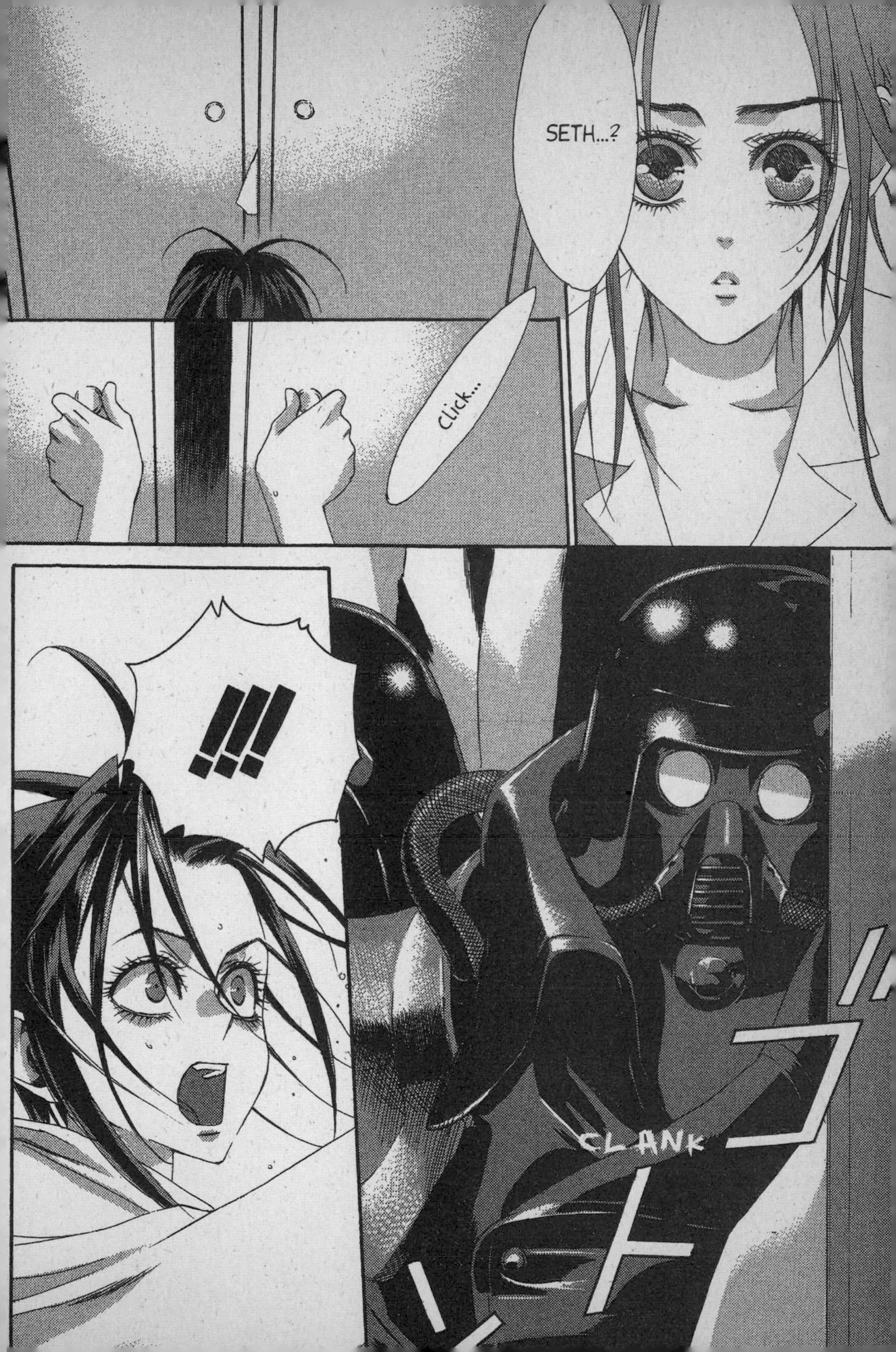
SETH...?
Click...
!!!
CLANK

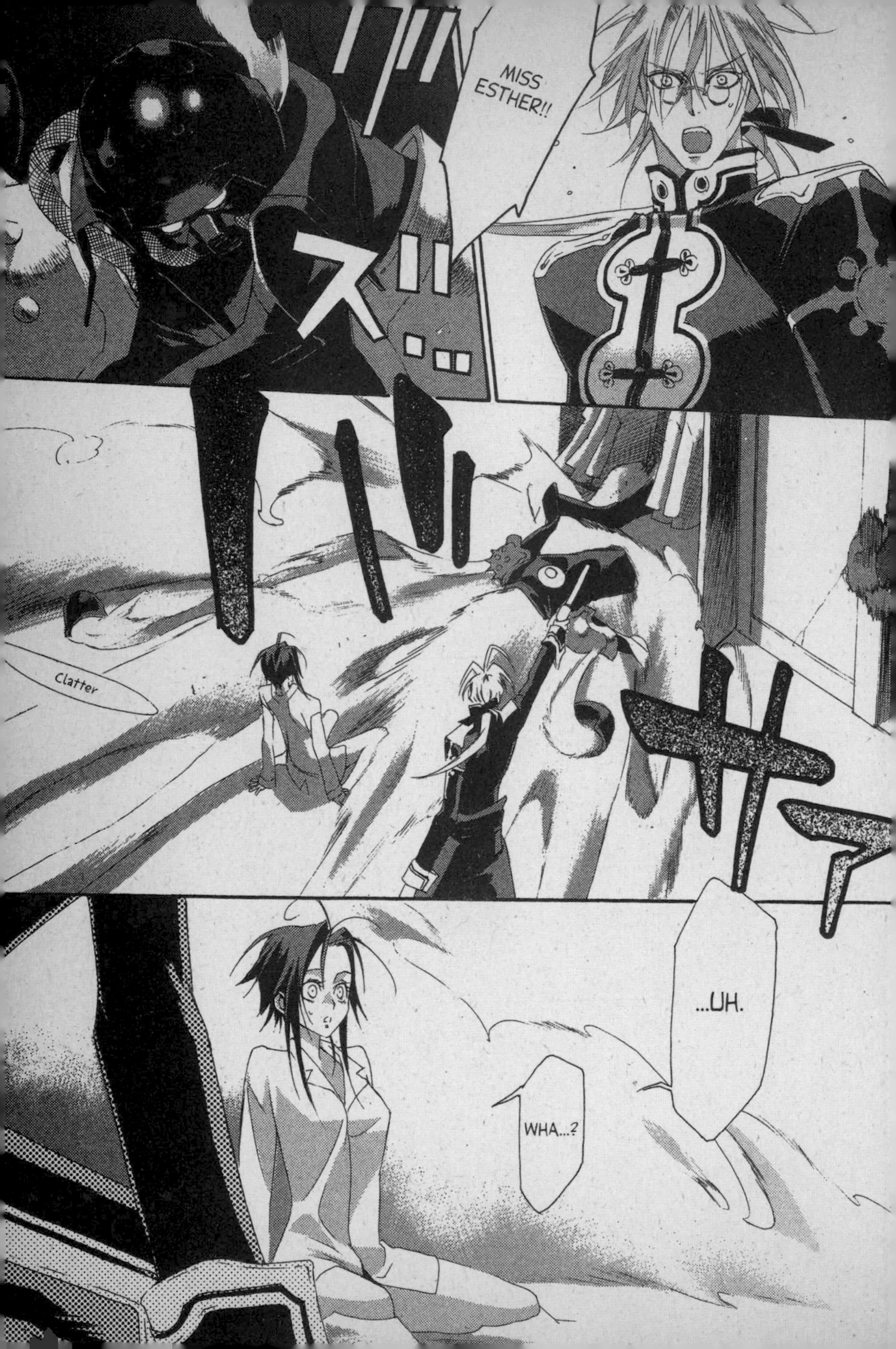
MISS ESTHER!!
Clatter
...UH.
WHA...?

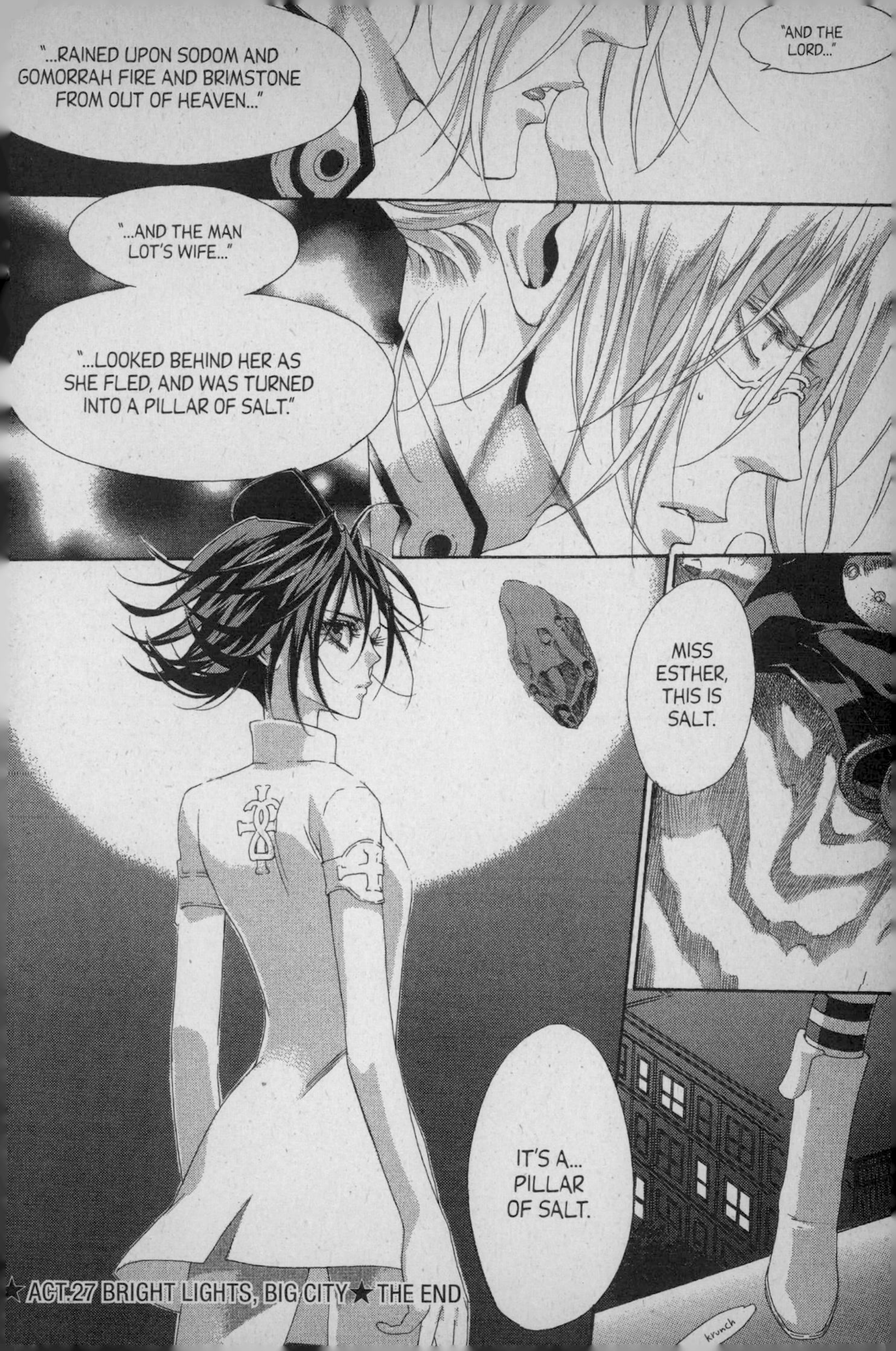
"AND THE LORD..."
"...RAINED UPON SODOM AND GOMORRAH FIRE AND BRIMSTONE FROM OUT OF HEAVEN..."
"...AND THE MAN LOT'S WIFE..."
"...LOOKED BEHIND HER AS SHE FLED, AND WAS TURNED INTO A PILLAR OF SALT."
MISS ESTHER, THIS IS SALT.
IT'S A... PILLAR OF SALT.
krunch
☆ACT.27 BRIGHT LIGHTS, BIG CITY★ THE END

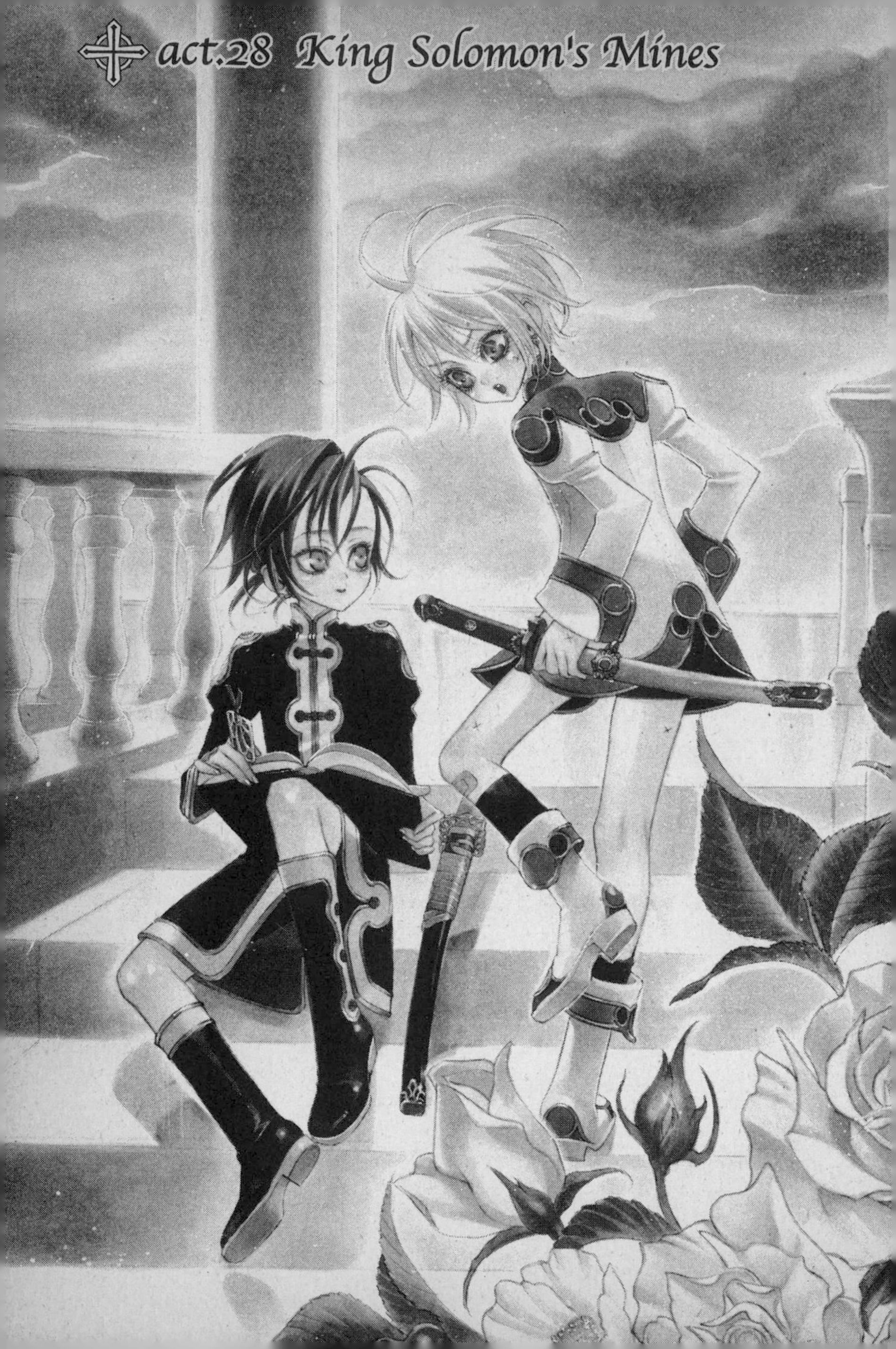
act.28 King Solomon's Mines

TRINITY BLOOD

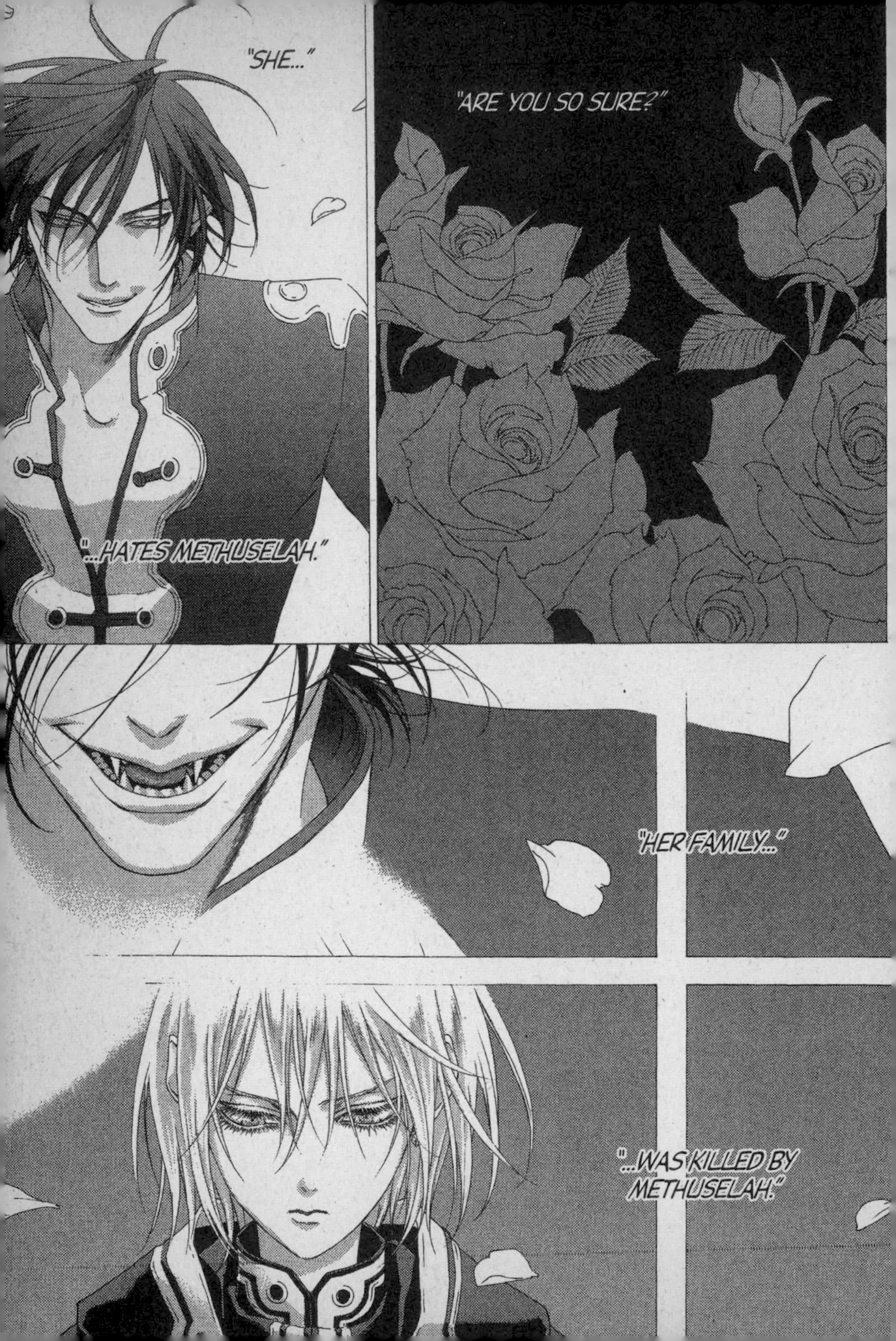
"ARE YOU SO SURE?"
"SHE..."
"...HATES METHUSELAH."
"HER FAMILY..."
"...WAS KILLED BY METHUSELAH."

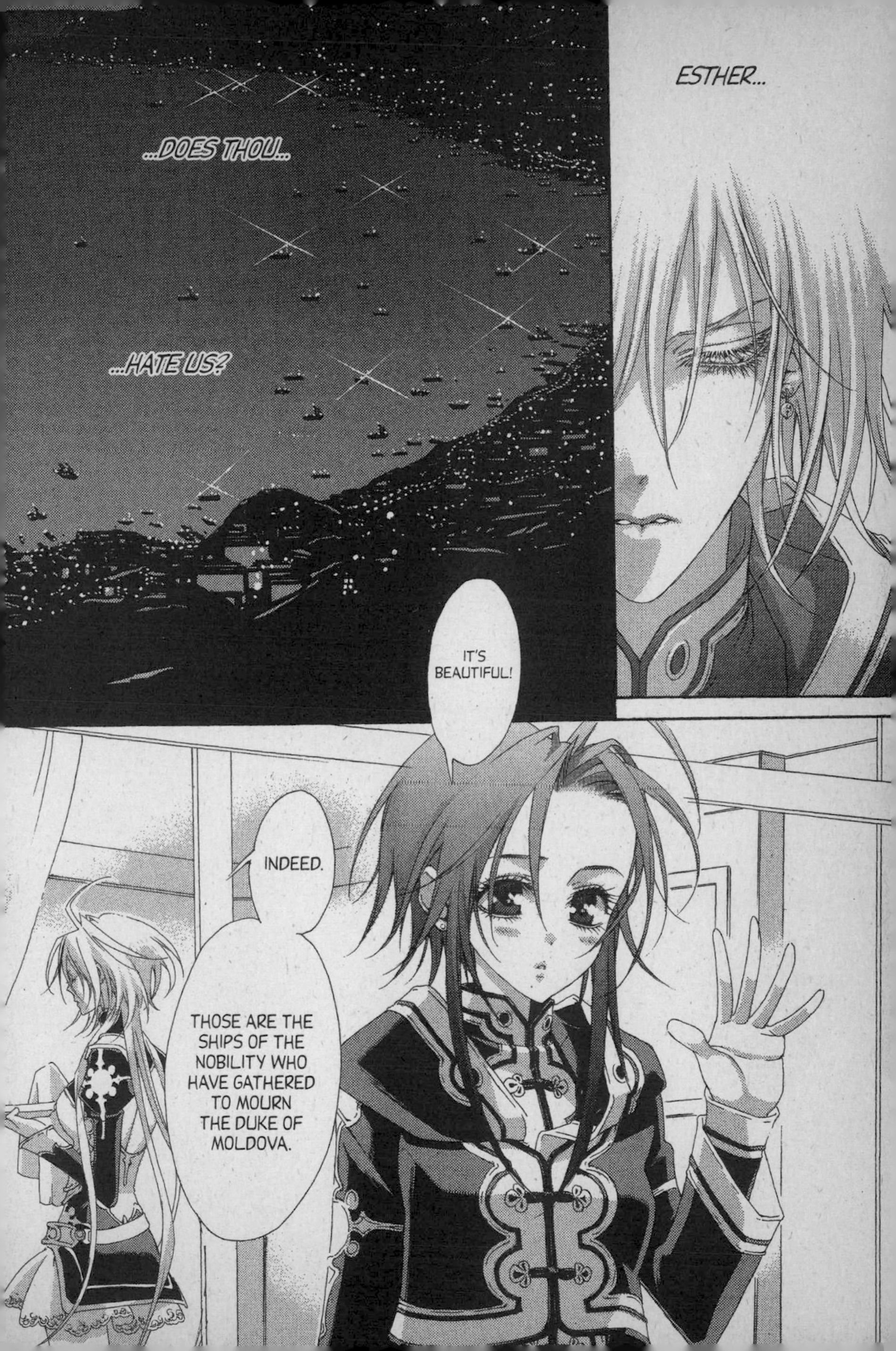
ESTHER...
...DOES THOU...
...HATE US?
IT'S BEAUTIFUL!
INDEED.
THOSE ARE THE SHIPS OF THE NOBILITY WHO HAVE GATHERED TO MOURN THE DUKE OF MOLDOVA.

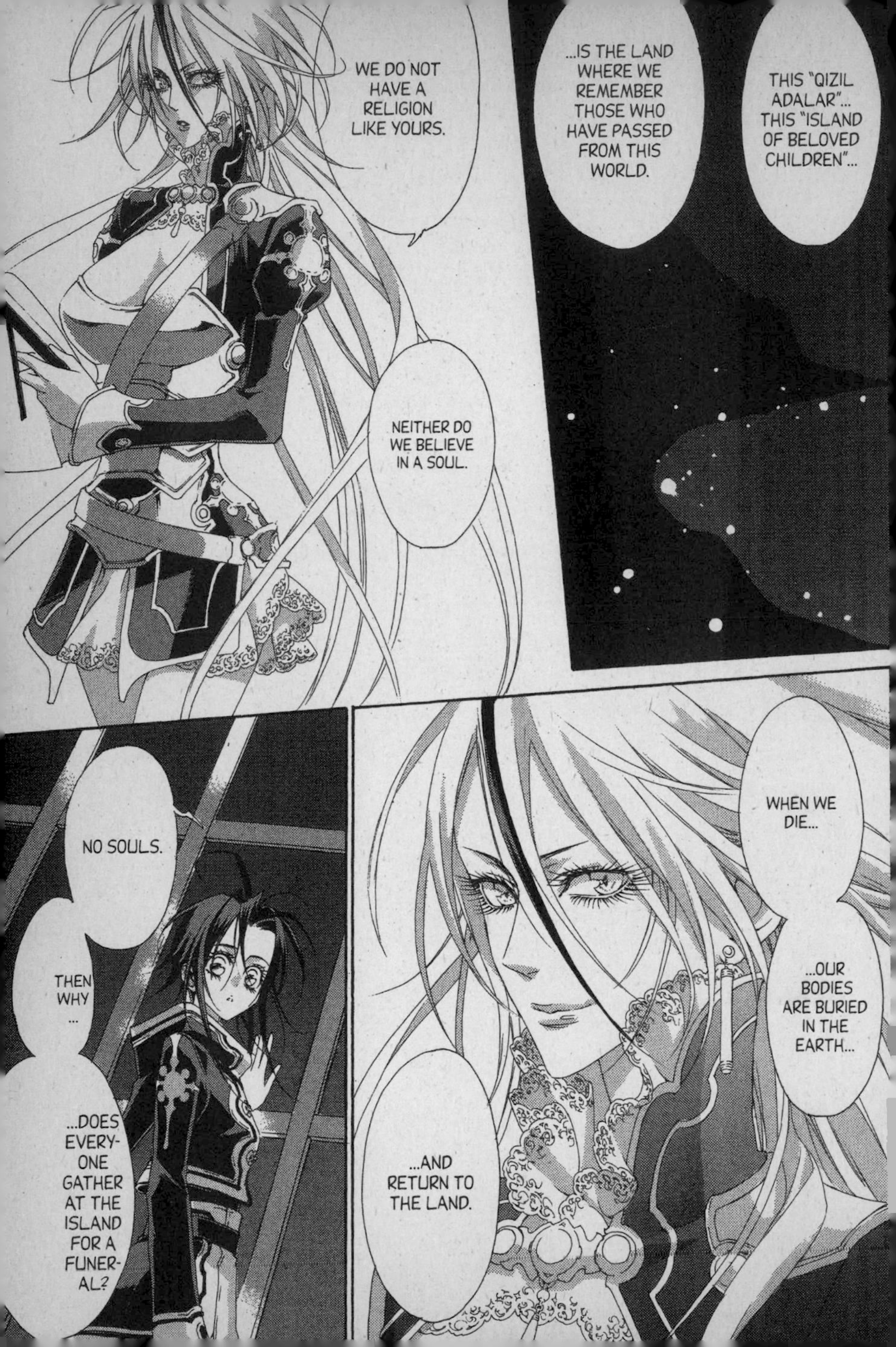
THIS "QIZIL ADALAR"... THIS "ISLAND OF BELOVED CHILDREN"...
...IS THE LAND WHERE WE REMEMBER THOSE WHO HAVE PASSED FROM THIS WORLD.
WE DO NOT HAVE A RELIGION LIKE YOURS.
NEITHER DO WE BELIEVE IN A SOUL.
WHEN WE DIE...
...OUR BODIES ARE BURIED IN THE EARTH...
...AND RETURN TO THE LAND.
NO SOULS.
THEN WHY ...
...DOES EVERY-ONE GATHER AT THE ISLAND FOR A FUNER-AL?

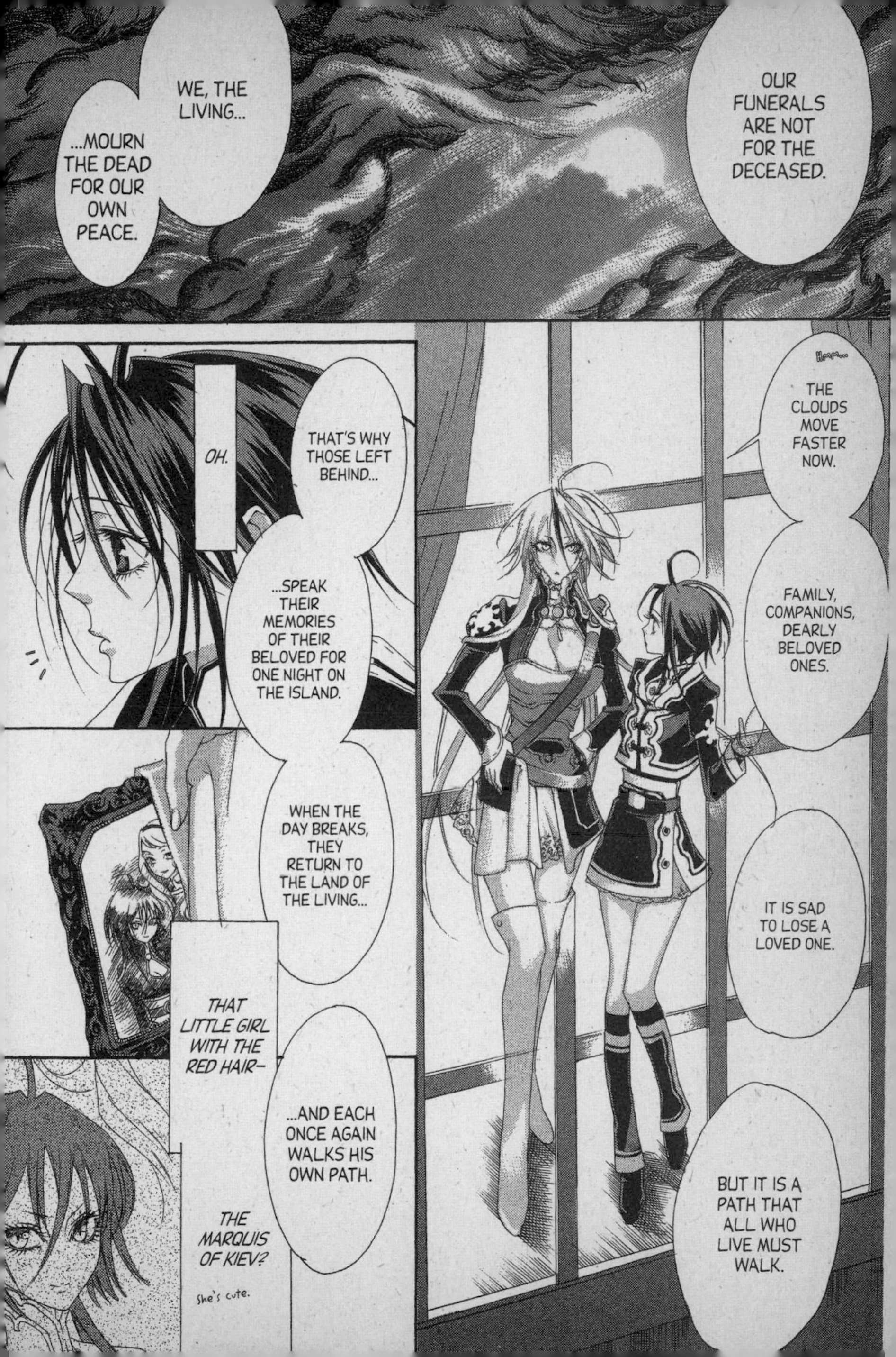
OUR FUNERALS ARE NOT FOR THE DECEASED.
WE, THE LIVING...
...MOURN THE DEAD FOR OUR OWN PEACE.
Hmm...
THE CLOUDS MOVE FASTER NOW.
FAMILY, COMPANIONS, DEARLY BELOVED ONES.
IT IS SAD TO LOSE A LOVED ONE.
BUT IT IS A PATH THAT ALL WHO LIVE MUST WALK.
THAT'S WHY THOSE LEFT BEHIND...
OH.
...SPEAK THEIR MEMORIES OF THEIR BELOVED FOR ONE NIGHT ON THE ISLAND.
WHEN THE DAY BREAKS, THEY RETURN TO THE LAND OF THE LIVING...
THAT LITTLE GIRL WITH THE RED HAIR—
...AND EACH ONCE AGAIN WALKS HIS OWN PATH.
THE MARQUIS OF KIEV?
She's cute.

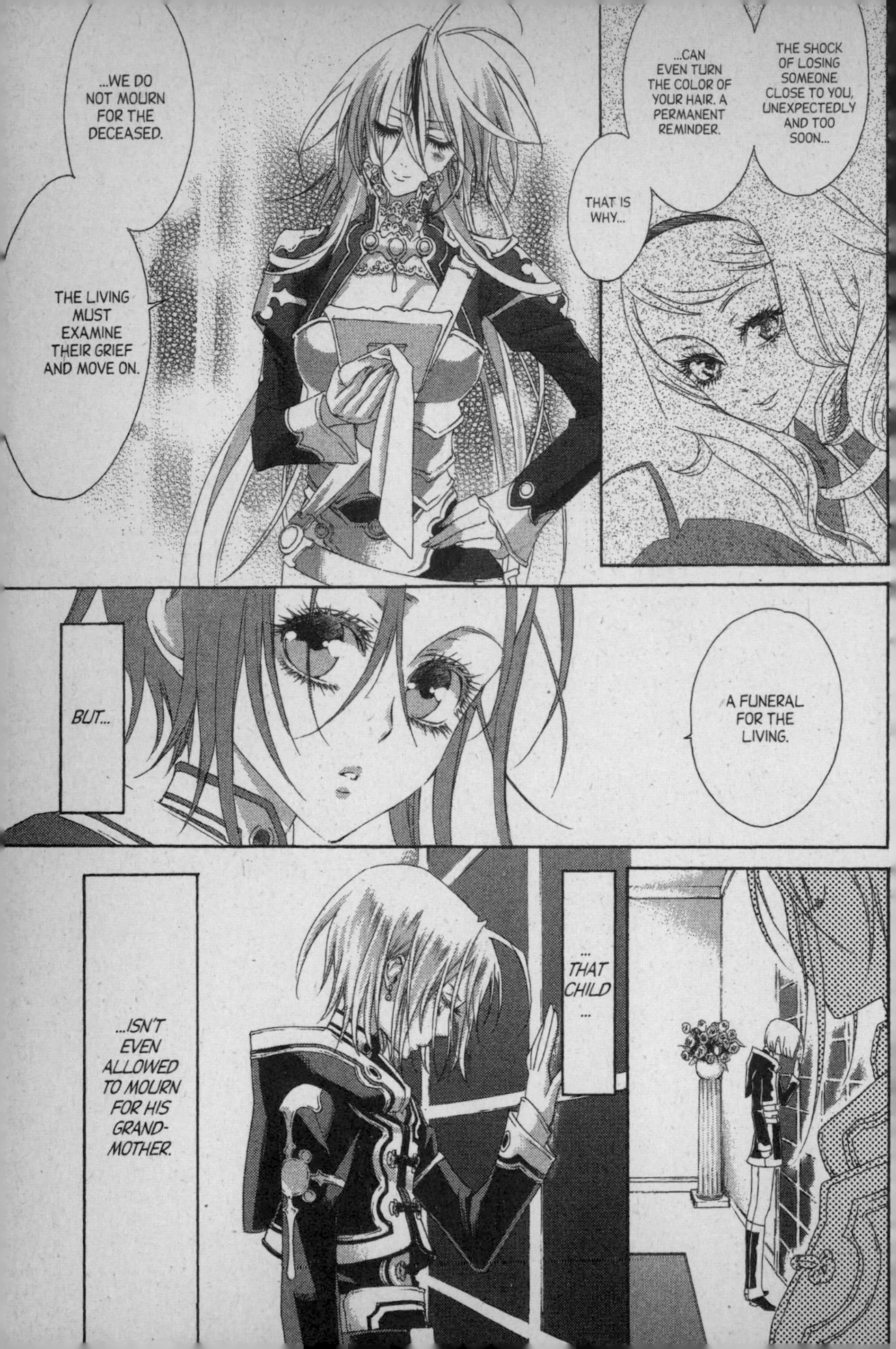
THE SHOCK OF LOSING SOMEONE CLOSE TO YOU, UNEXPECTEDLY AND TOO SOON...
...CAN EVEN TURN THE COLOR OF YOUR HAIR. A PERMANENT REMINDER.
THAT IS WHY...
...WE DO NOT MOURN FOR THE DECEASED.
THE LIVING MUST EXAMINE THEIR GRIEF AND MOVE ON.
A FUNERAL FOR THE LIVING.
BUT...
...THAT CHILD...
...ISN'T EVEN ALLOWED TO MOURN FOR HIS GRANDMOTHER.

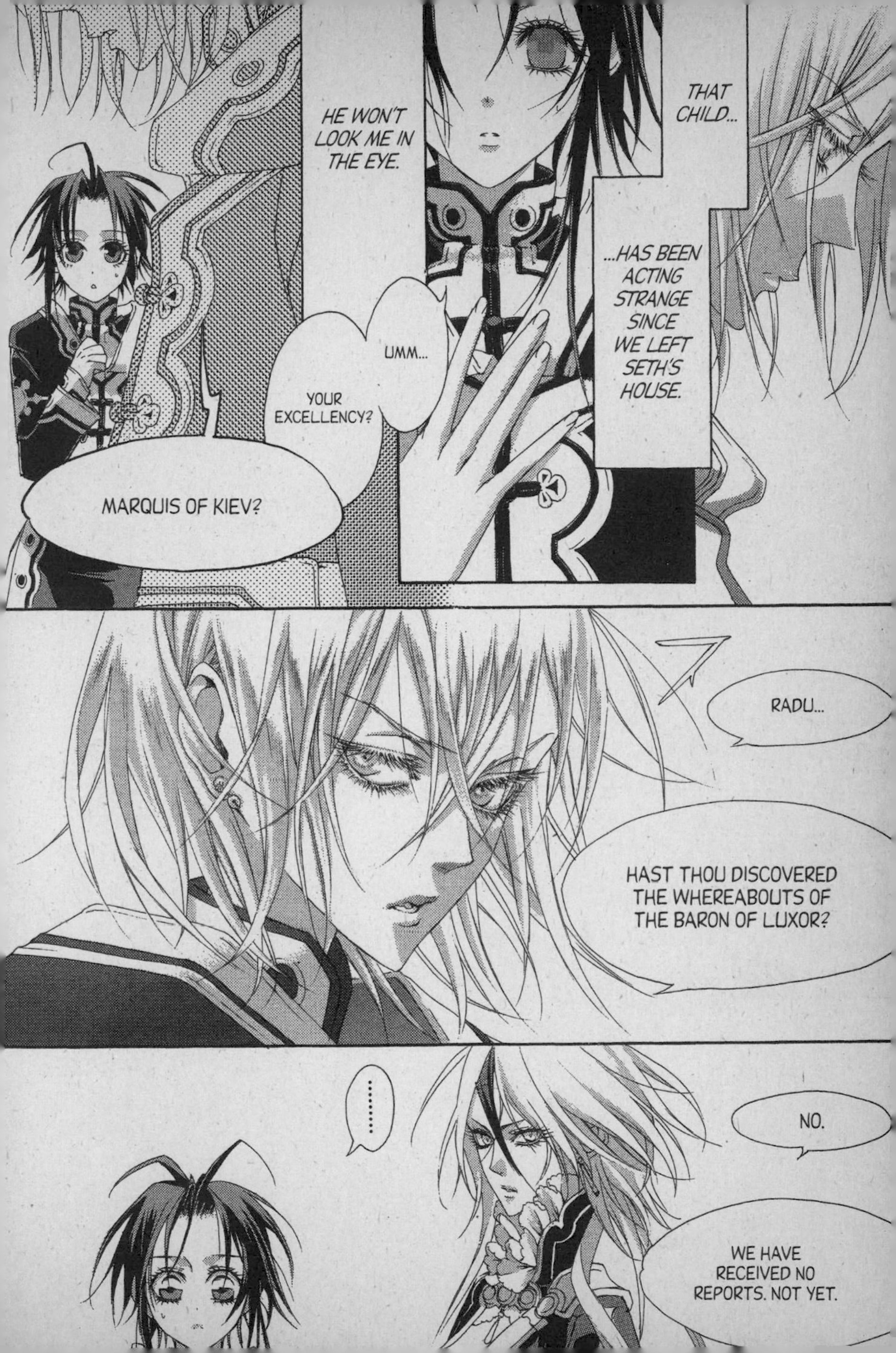
THAT CHILD...
...HAS BEEN ACTING STRANGE SINCE WE LEFT SETH'S HOUSE.
HE WON'T LOOK ME IN THE EYE.
UMM...
YOUR EXCELLENCY?
MARQUIS OF KIEV?
RADU...
HAST THOU DISCOVERED THE WHEREABOUTS OF THE BARON OF LUXOR?
NO.
WE HAVE RECEIVED NO REPORTS. NOT YET.
......

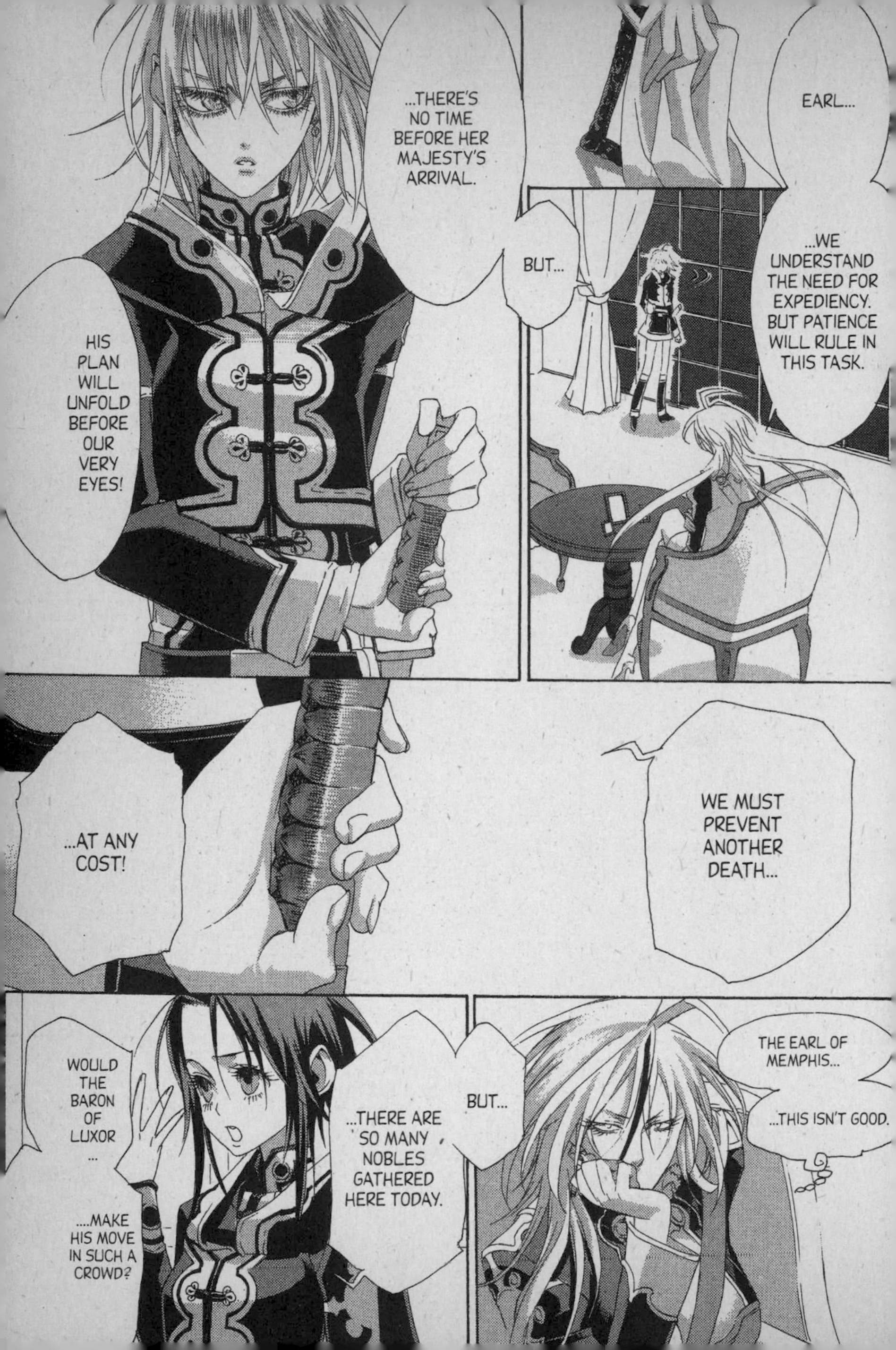

EARL...
...WE UNDERSTAND THE NEED FOR EXPEDIENCY. BUT PATIENCE WILL RULE IN THIS TASK.
BUT...
...THERE'S NO TIME BEFORE HER MAJESTY'S ARRIVAL.
HIS PLAN WILL UNFOLD BEFORE OUR VERY EYES!
WE MUST PREVENT ANOTHER DEATH...
...AT ANY COST!
THE EARL OF MEMPHIS...
...THIS ISN'T GOOD.
BUT...
...THERE ARE SO MANY NOBLES GATHERED HERE TODAY.
WOULD THE BARON OF LUXOR ...
....MAKE HIS MOVE IN SUCH A CROWD?

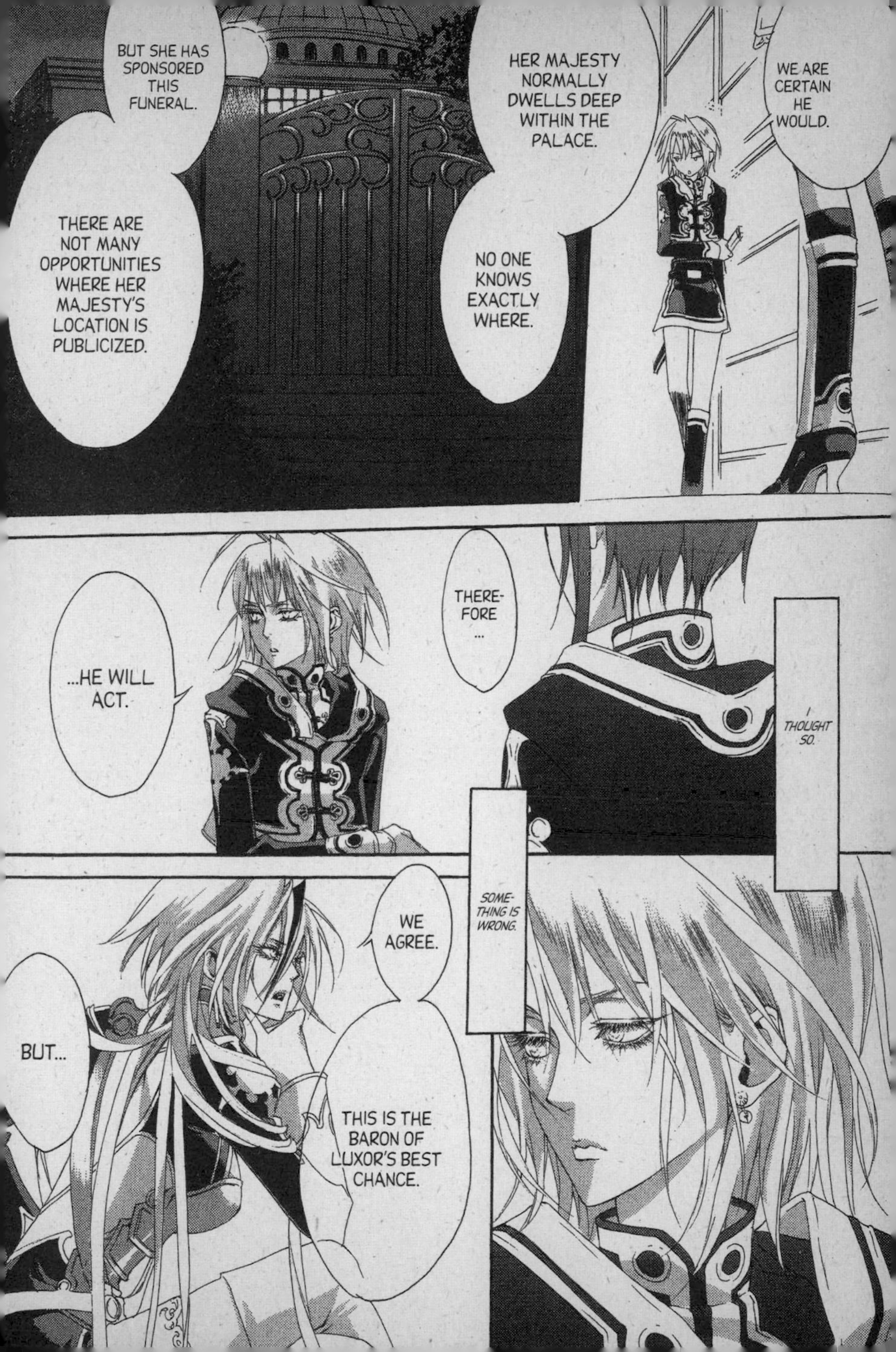
WE ARE CERTAIN HE WOULD.
HER MAJESTY NORMALLY DWELLS DEEP WITHIN THE PALACE.
NO ONE KNOWS EXACTLY WHERE.
BUT SHE HAS SPONSORED THIS FUNERAL.
THERE ARE NOT MANY OPPORTUNITIES WHERE HER MAJESTY'S LOCATION IS PUBLICIZED.
I THOUGHT SO.
THERE-FORE ...
...HE WILL ACT.
SOME-THING IS WRONG.
WE AGREE.
THIS IS THE BARON OF LUXOR'S BEST CHANCE.
BUT...

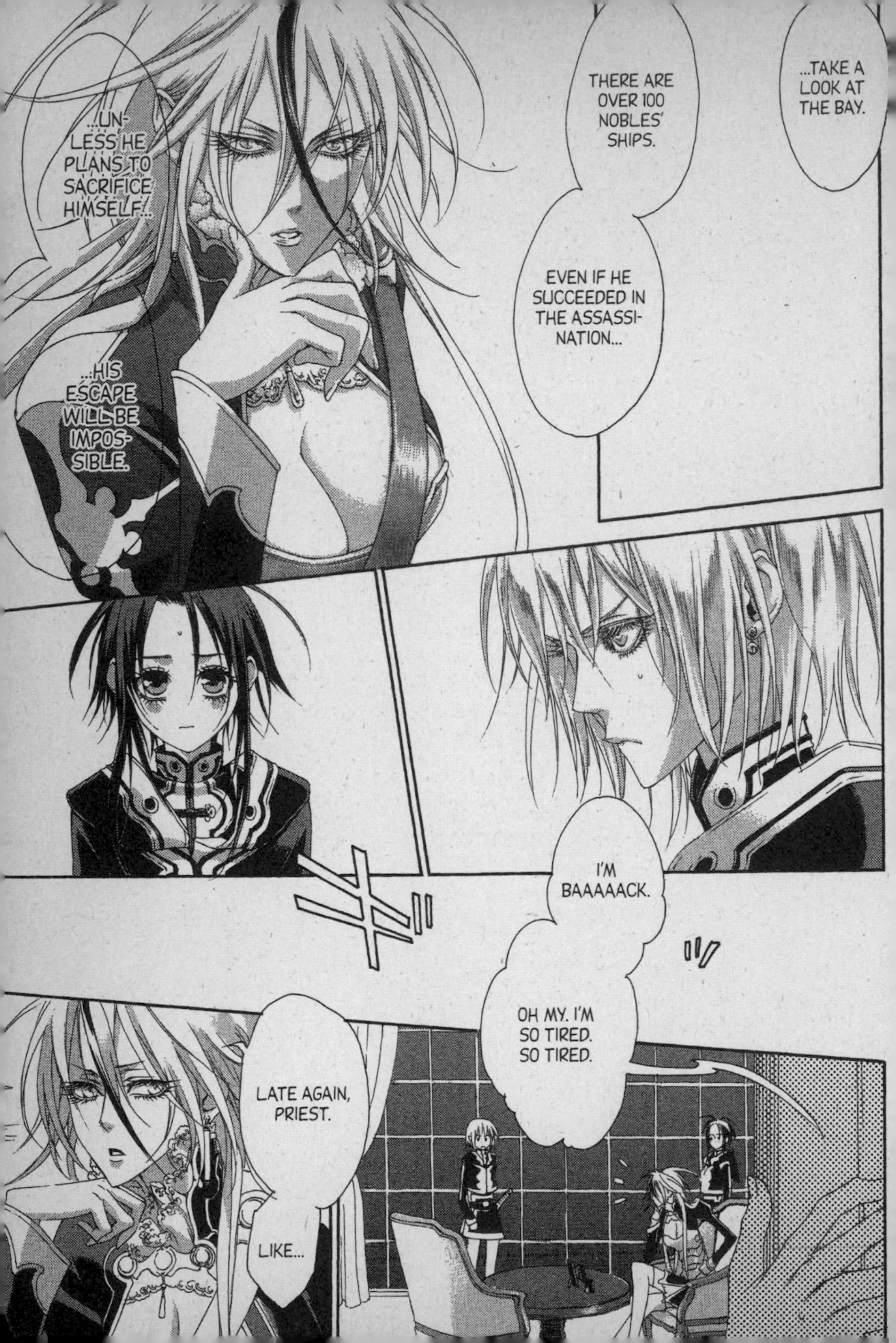
...TAKE A LOOK AT THE BAY.
THERE ARE OVER 100 NOBLES' SHIPS.
EVEN IF HE SUCCEEDED IN THE ASSASSINATION...
...UNLESS HE PLANS TO SACRIFICE HIMSELF...
...HIS ESCAPE WILL BE IMPOSSIBLE.
I'M BAAAAACK.
OH MY. I'M SO TIRED. SO TIRED.
LATE AGAIN, PRIEST.
LIKE...

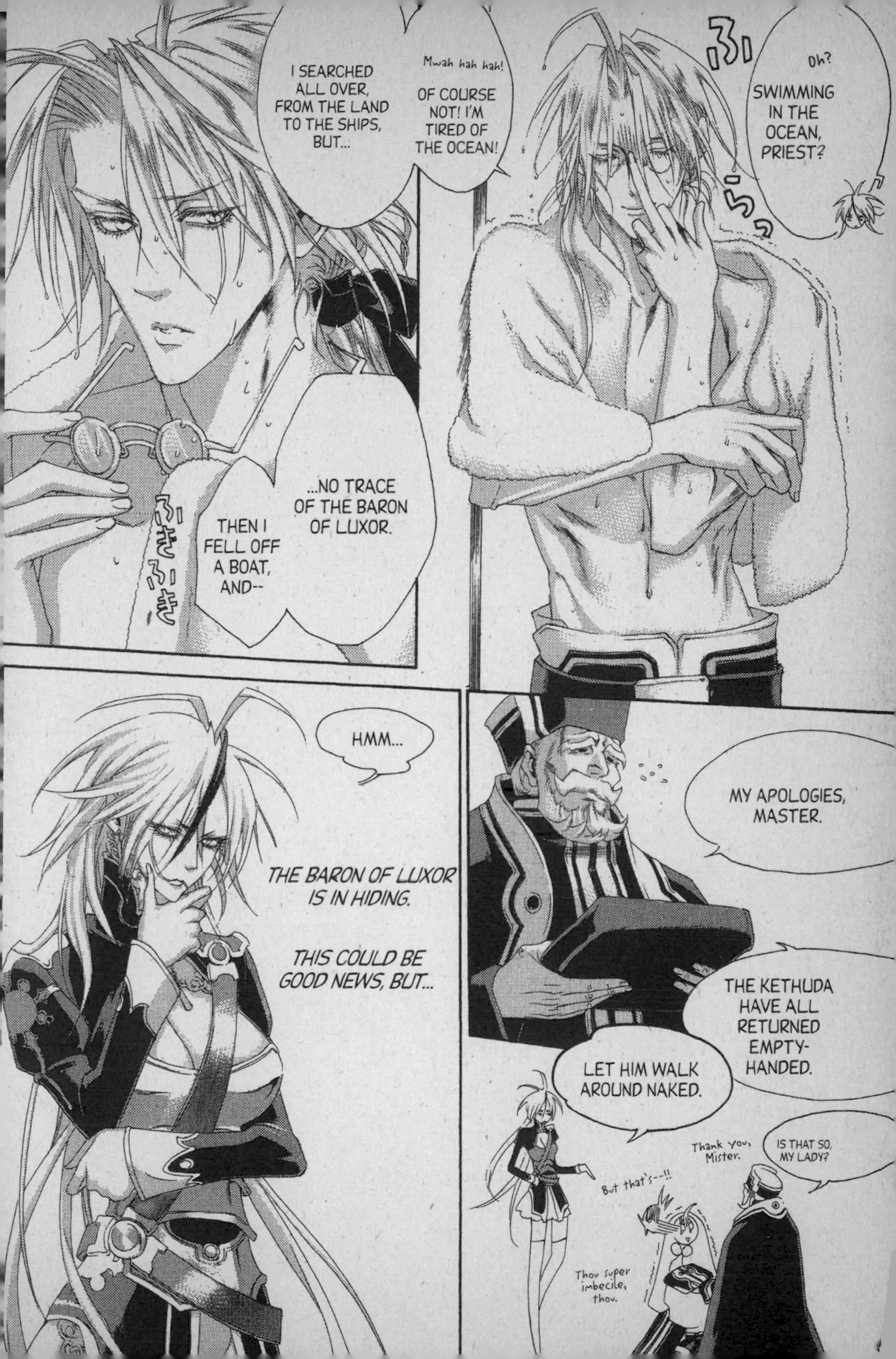
Oh?
SWIMMING IN THE OCEAN, PRIEST?
OF COURSE NOT! I'M TIRED OF THE OCEAN!
Mwah hah hah!
I SEARCHED ALL OVER, FROM THE LAND TO THE SHIPS, BUT...
...NO TRACE OF THE BARON OF LUXOR.
THEN I FELL OFF A BOAT, AND--
ふきふき
MY APOLOGIES, MASTER.
THE KETHUDA HAVE ALL RETURNED EMPTY-HANDED.
LET HIM WALK AROUND NAKED.
IS THAT SO, MY LADY?
Thank you, Mister.
But that's--!!
Thou super imbecile, thou.
HMM...
THE BARON OF LUXOR IS IN HIDING.
THIS COULD BE GOOD NEWS, BUT...

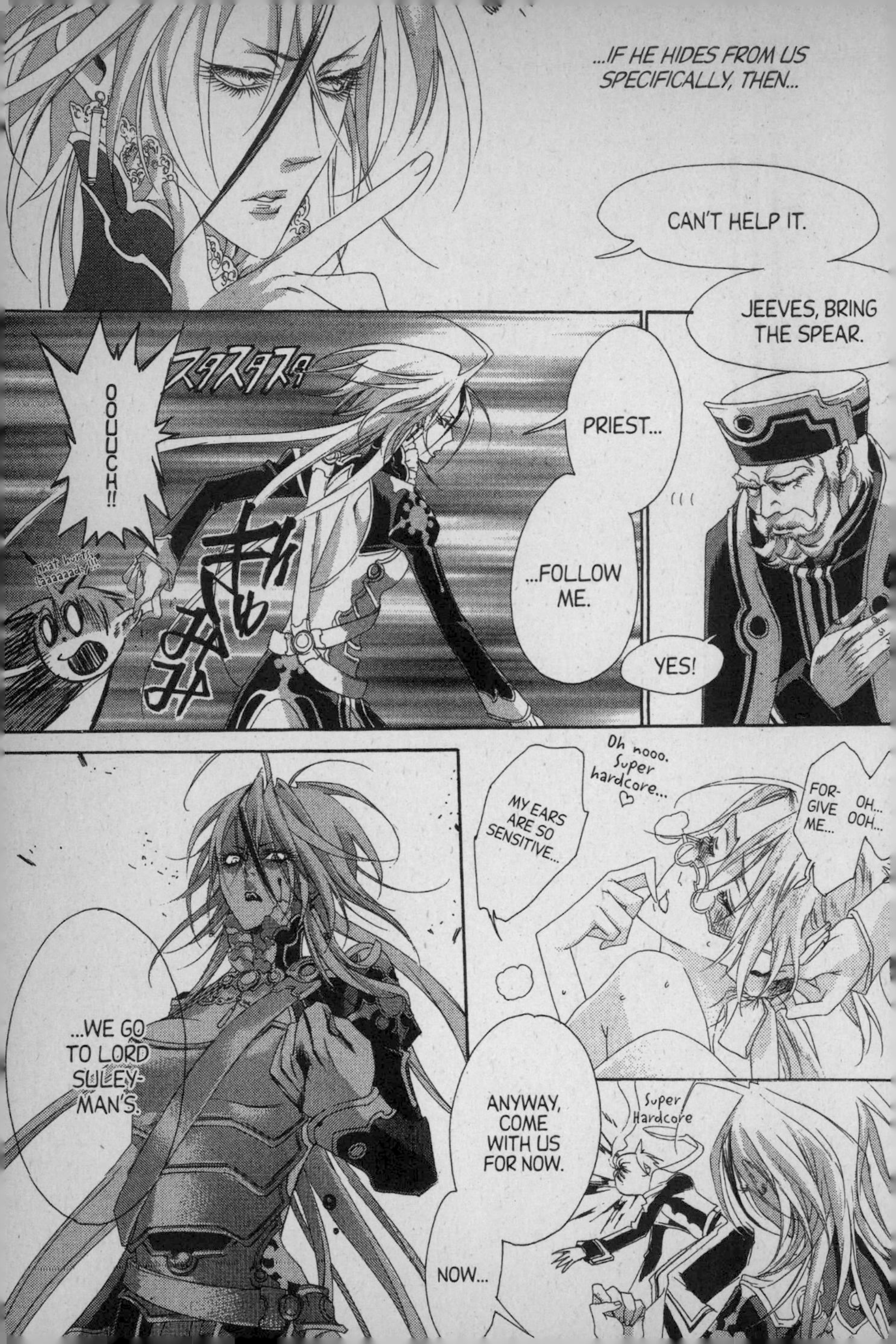
...IF HE HIDES FROM US SPECIFICALLY, THEN...
CAN'T HELP IT.
JEEVES, BRING THE SPEAR.
PRIEST...
...FOLLOW ME.
YES!
OOUUCH!!
That hurts, laaaaaady!!!
FOR-GIVE ME...
OH... OOH...
Oh nooo. Super hardcore...♡
MY EARS ARE SO SENSITIVE...
ANYWAY, COME WITH US FOR NOW.
Super Hardcore
NOW...
...WE GO TO LORD SULEY-MAN'S.

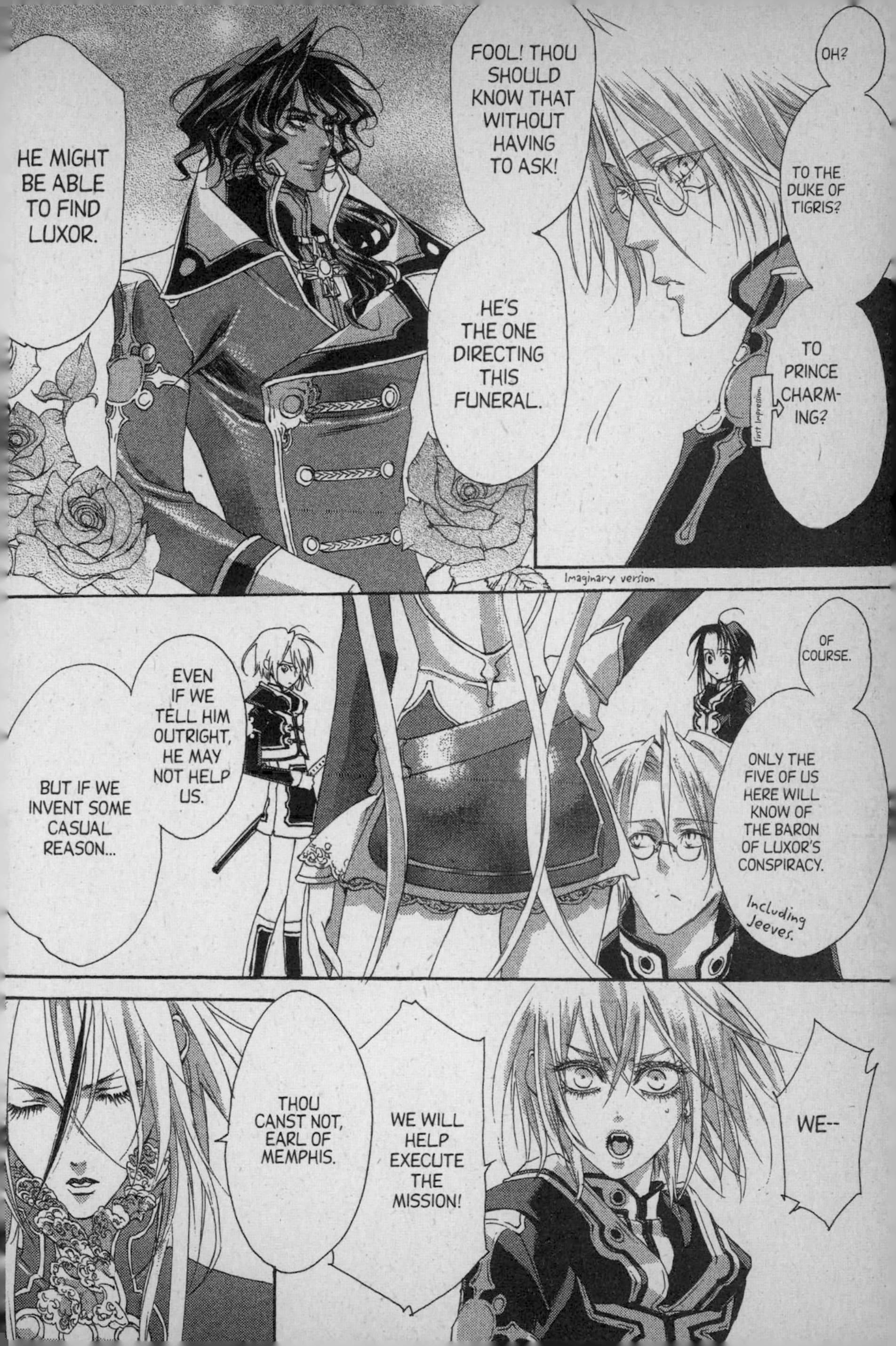

OH?
TO THE DUKE OF TIGRIS?
TO PRINCE CHARMING?
First Impression.
Imaginary version
FOOL! THOU SHOULD KNOW THAT WITHOUT HAVING TO ASK!
HE'S THE ONE DIRECTING THIS FUNERAL.
HE MIGHT BE ABLE TO FIND LUXOR.
OF COURSE.
ONLY THE FIVE OF US HERE WILL KNOW OF THE BARON OF LUXOR'S CONSPIRACY.
Including Jeeves.
EVEN IF WE TELL HIM OUTRIGHT, HE MAY NOT HELP US.
BUT IF WE INVENT SOME CASUAL REASON...
WE--
WE WILL HELP EXECUTE THE MISSION!
THOU CANST NOT, EARL OF MEMPHIS.

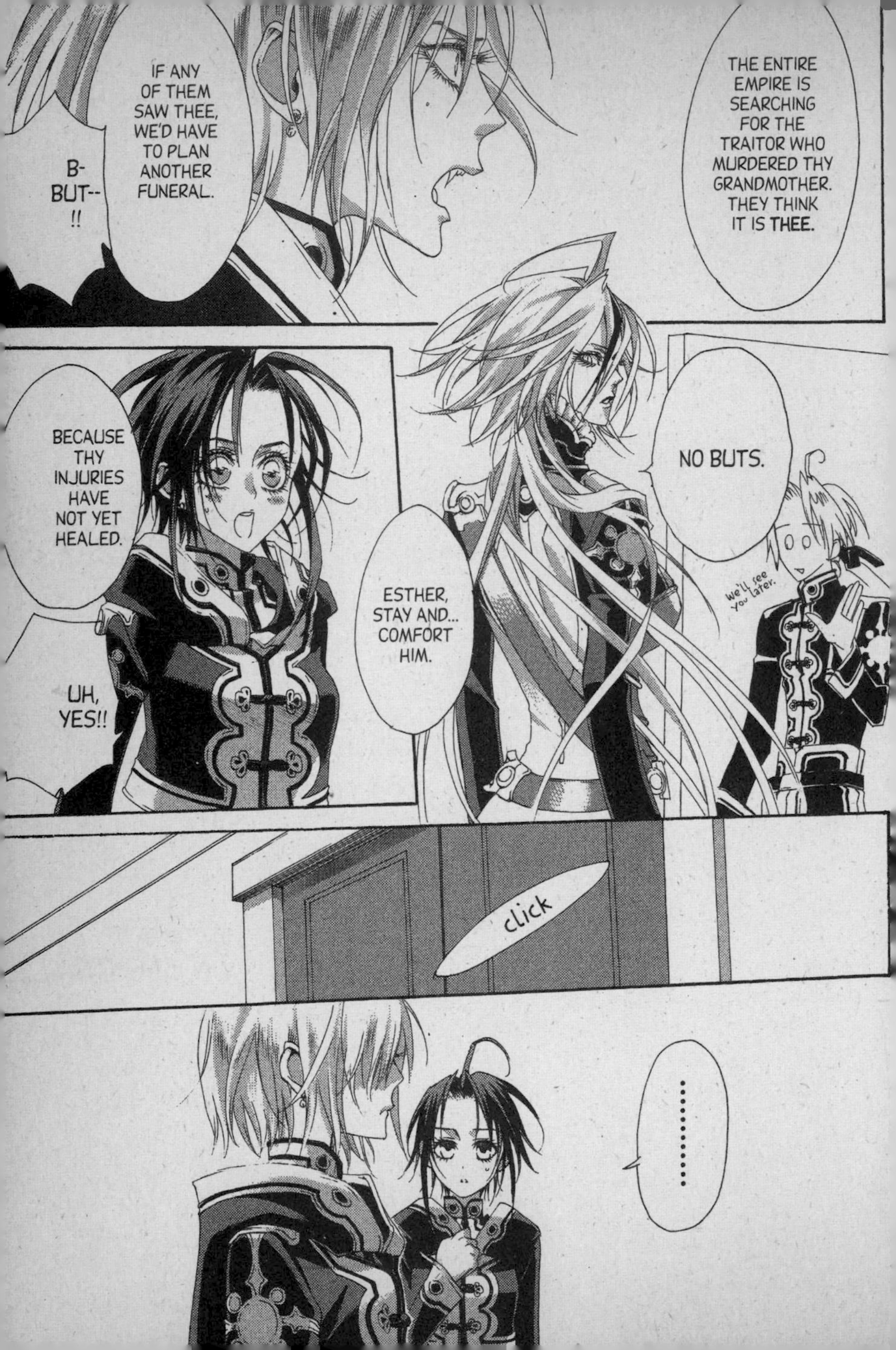
THE ENTIRE EMPIRE IS SEARCHING FOR THE TRAITOR WHO MURDERED THY GRANDMOTHER. THEY THINK IT IS THEE.
IF ANY OF THEM SAW THEE, WE'D HAVE TO PLAN ANOTHER FUNERAL.
B- BUT-- !!
BECAUSE THY INJURIES HAVE NOT YET HEALED.
NO BUTS.
we'll see you later.
ESTHER, STAY AND... COMFORT HIM.
UH, YES!!
click
.........

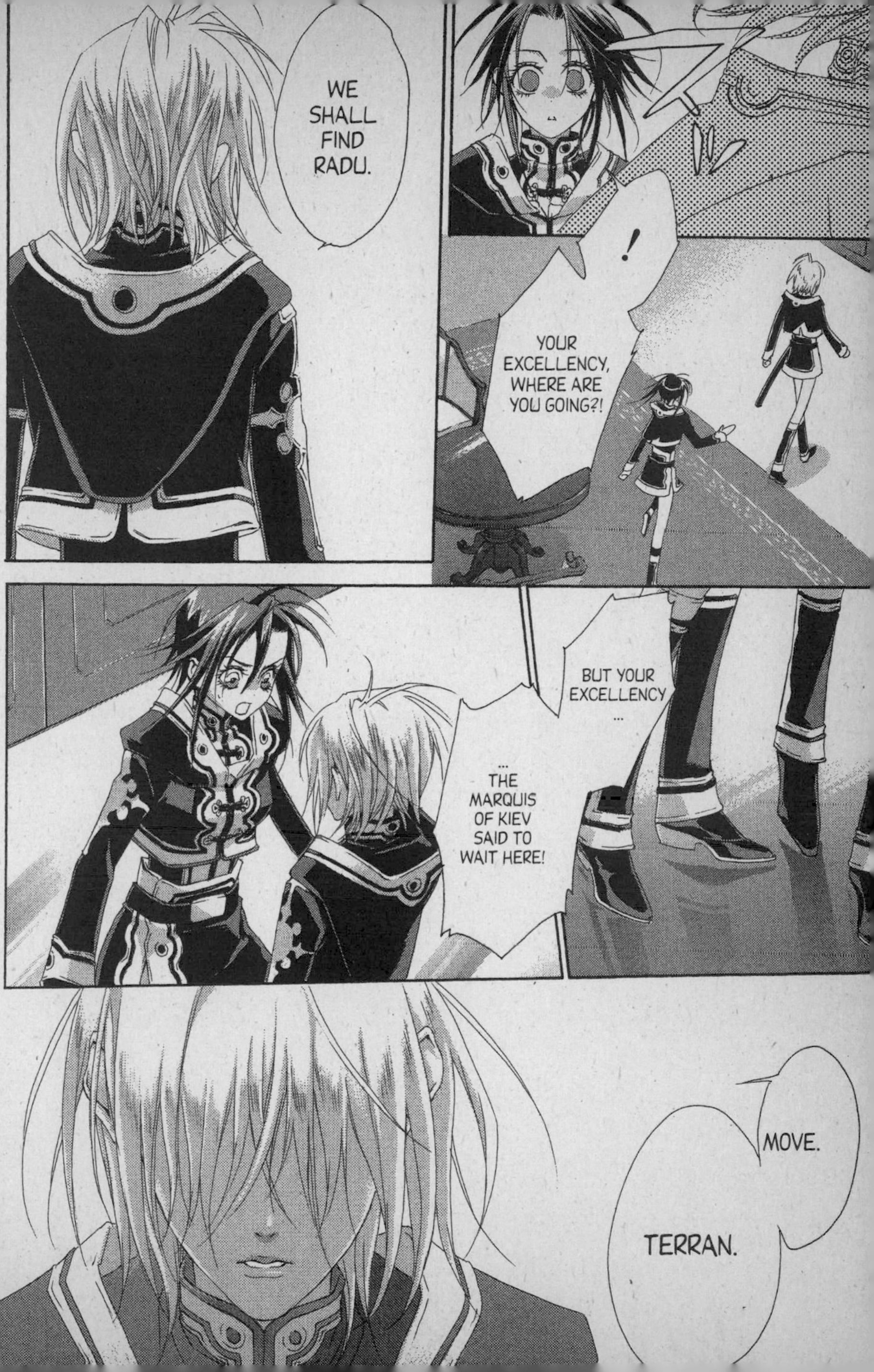
!
YOUR EXCELLENCY, WHERE ARE YOU GOING?!
WE SHALL FIND RADU.
BUT YOUR EXCELLENCY ...
... THE MARQUIS OF KIEV SAID TO WAIT HERE!
MOVE.
TERRAN.

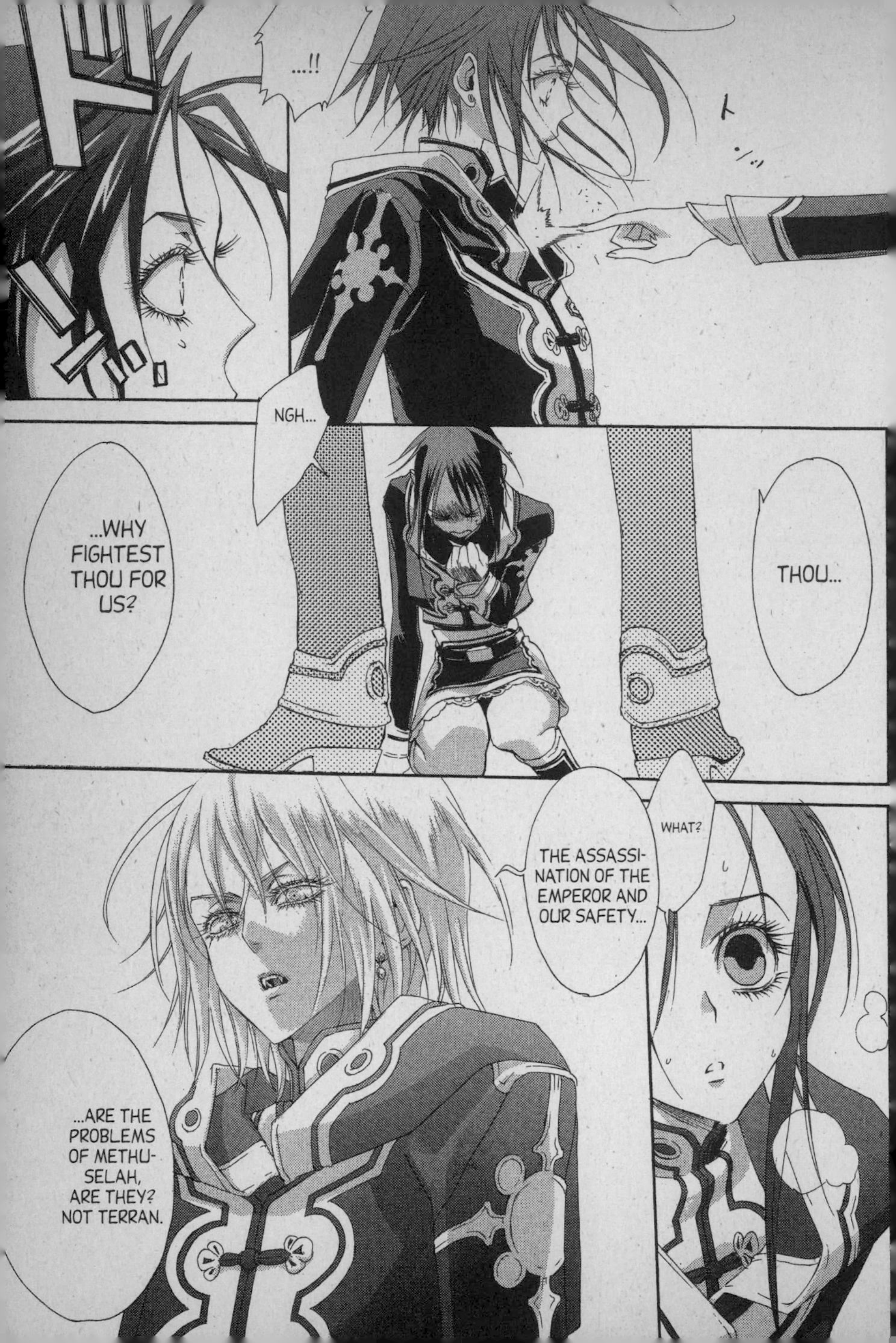
...!!
NGH...
THOU...
...WHY FIGHTEST THOU FOR US?
WHAT?
THE ASSASSINATION OF THE EMPEROR AND OUR SAFETY...
...ARE THE PROBLEMS OF METHUSELAH, ARE THEY? NOT TERRAN.

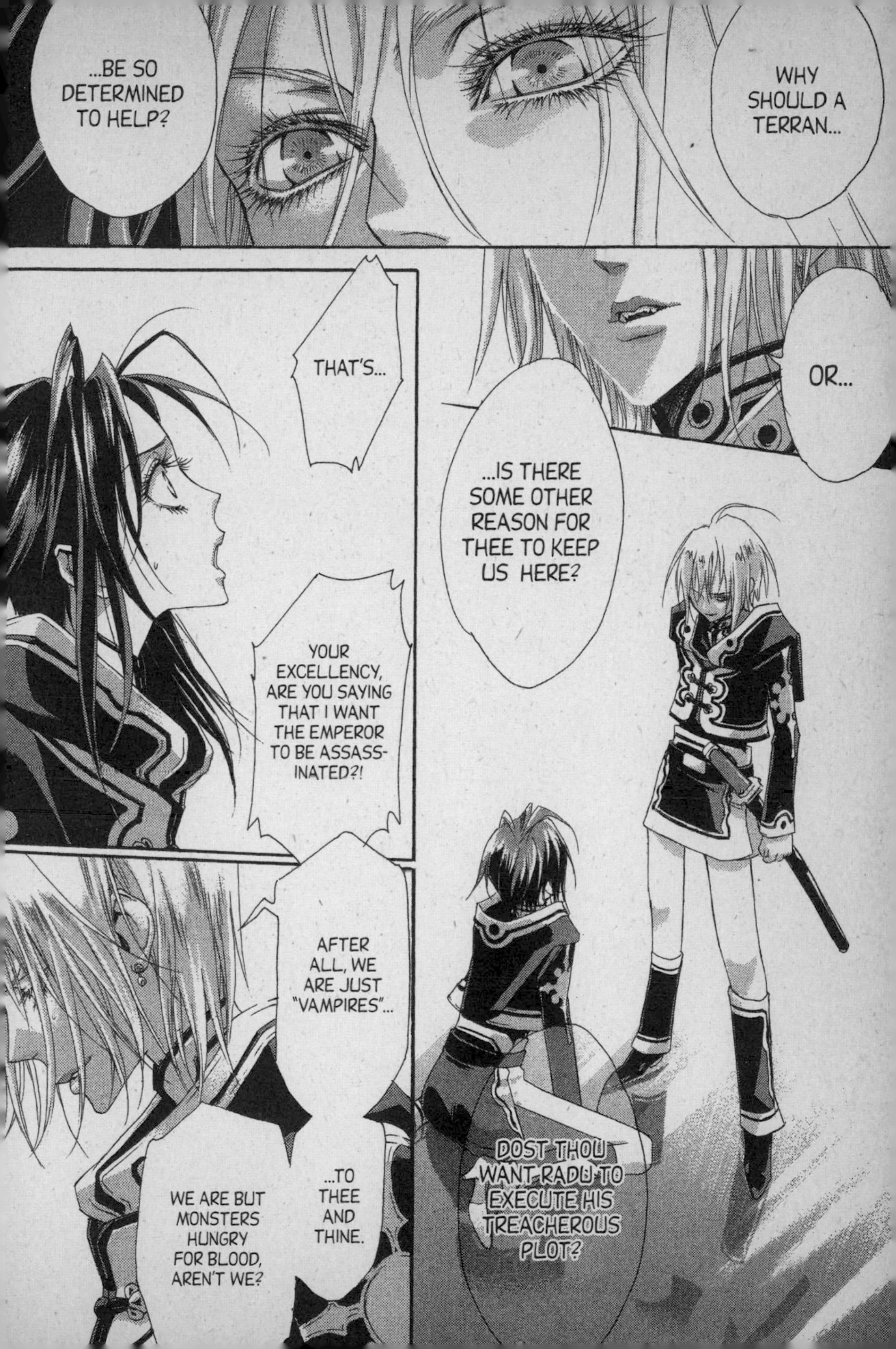
WHY SHOULD A TERRAN...
...BE SO DETERMINED TO HELP?
OR...
...IS THERE SOME OTHER REASON FOR THEE TO KEEP US HERE?
DOST THOU WANT RADU TO EXECUTE HIS TREACHEROUS PLOT?
THAT'S...
YOUR EXCELLENCY, ARE YOU SAYING THAT I WANT THE EMPEROR TO BE ASSASS-INATED?!
AFTER ALL, WE ARE JUST "VAMPIRES"...
...TO THEE AND THINE.
WE ARE BUT MONSTERS HUNGRY FOR BLOOD, AREN'T WE?

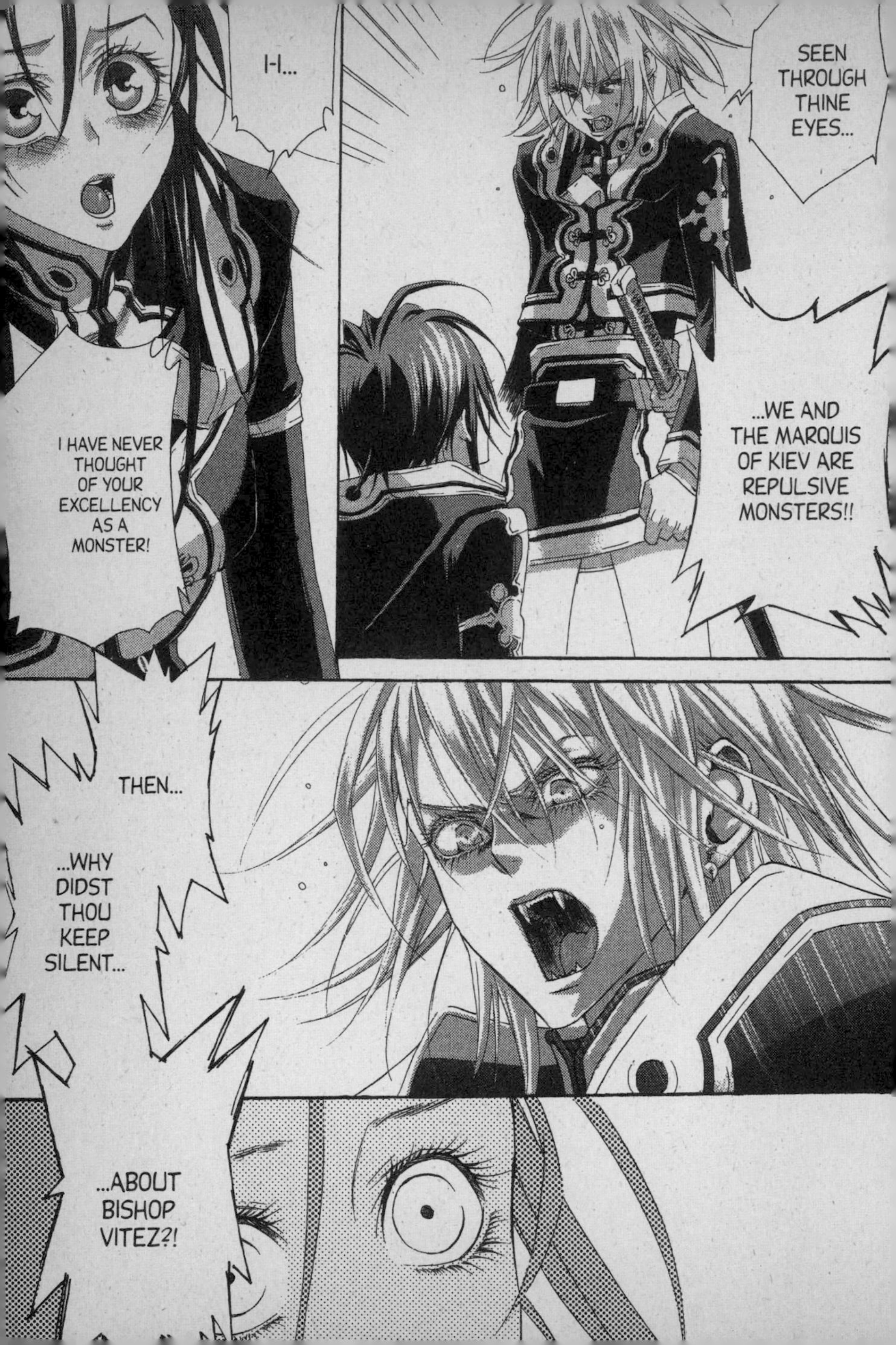
SEEN THROUGH THINE EYES...
...WE AND THE MARQUIS OF KIEV ARE REPULSIVE MONSTERS!!
I-I...
I HAVE NEVER THOUGHT OF YOUR EXCELLENCY AS A MONSTER!
THEN...
...WHY DIDST THOU KEEP SILENT...
...ABOUT BISHOP VITEZ?!

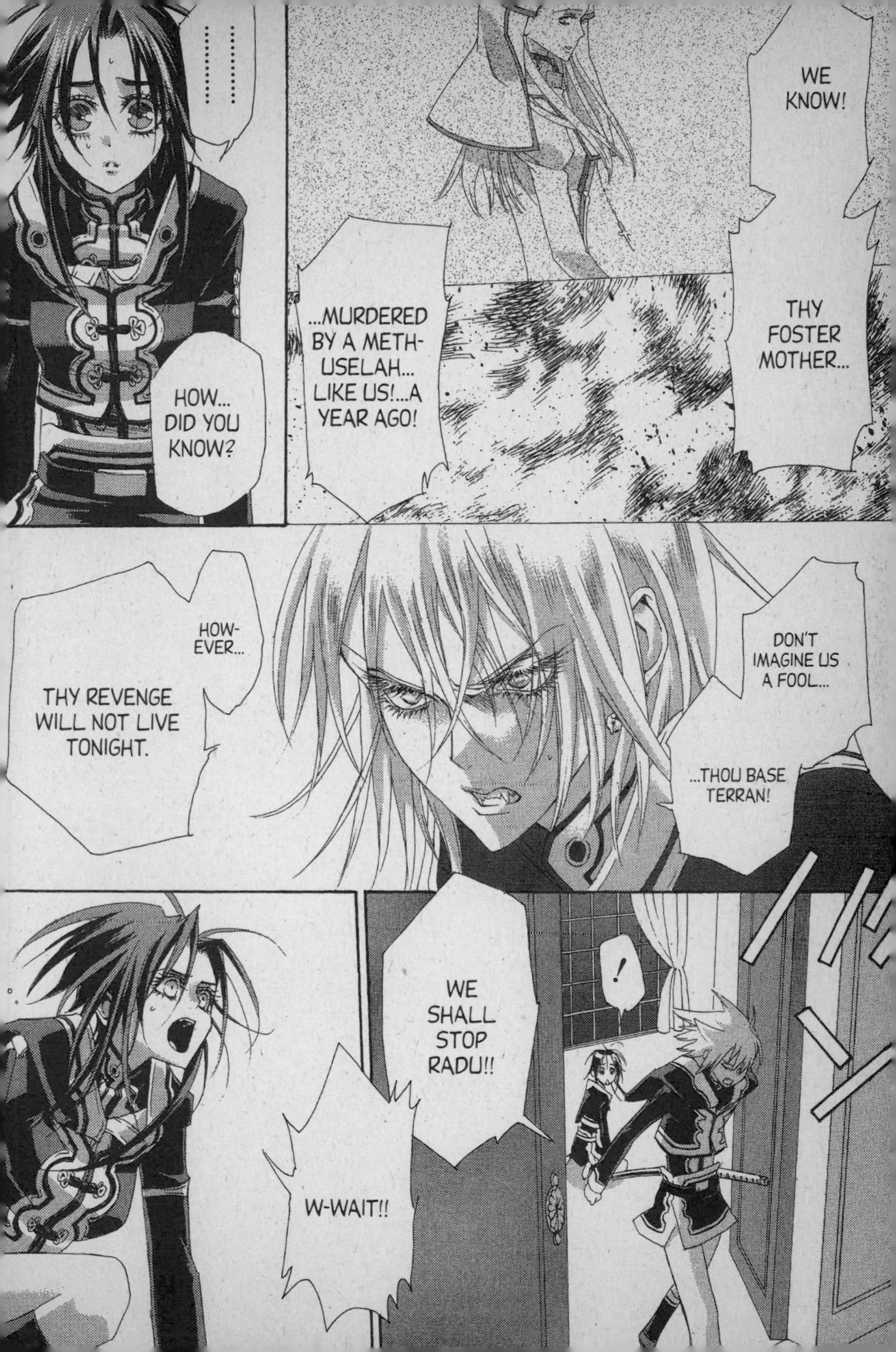
WE KNOW!
THY FOSTER MOTHER...
...MURDERED BY A METH-USELAH... LIKE US!...A YEAR AGO!
......
HOW... DID YOU KNOW?
DON'T IMAGINE US A FOOL...
...THOU BASE TERRAN!
HOW-EVER...
THY REVENGE WILL NOT LIVE TONIGHT.
WE SHALL STOP RADU!!
!
W-WAIT!!

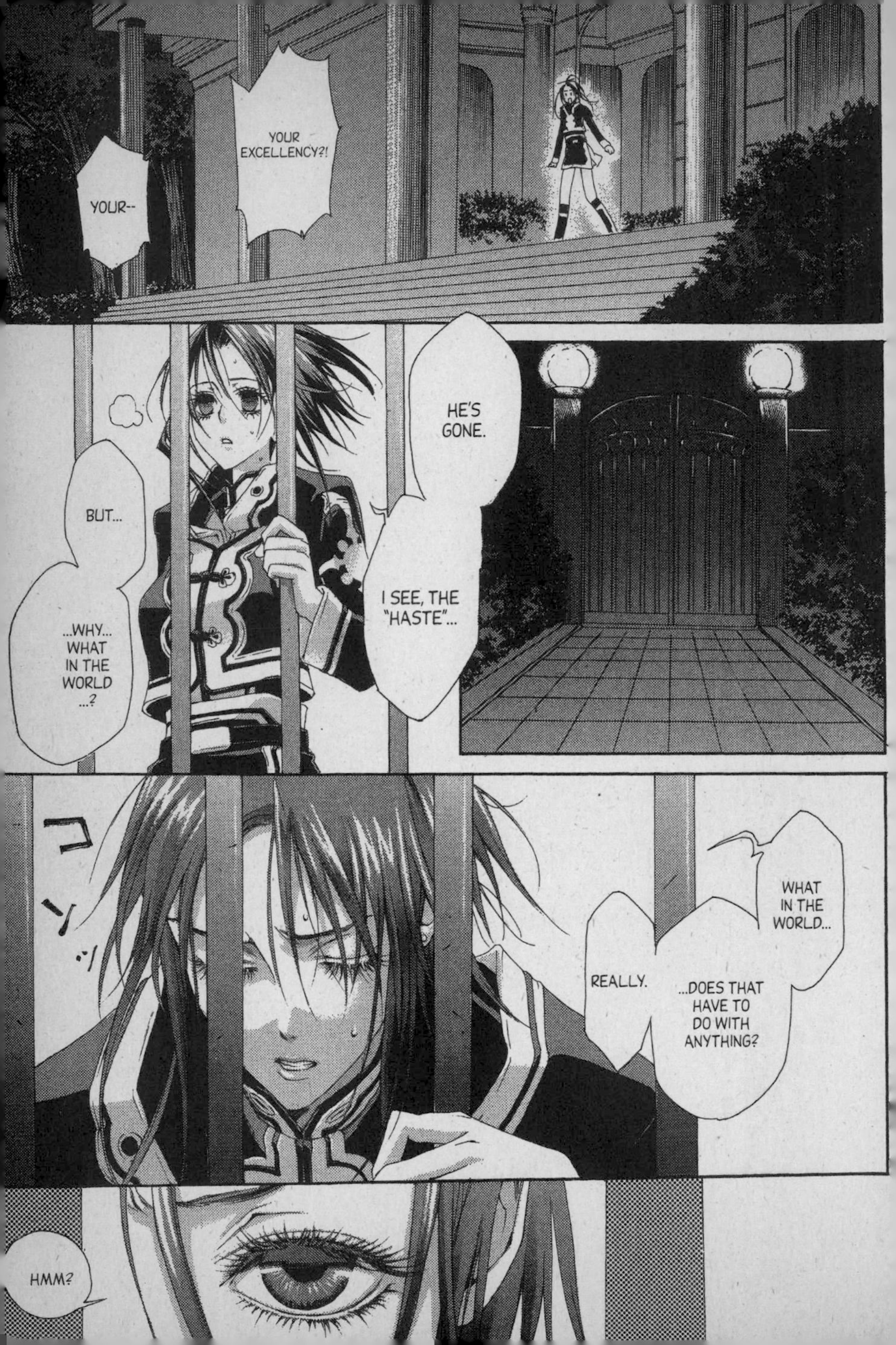

YOUR EXCELLENCY?!
YOUR--
HE'S GONE.
I SEE, THE "HASTE"...
BUT...
...WHY... WHAT IN THE WORLD ...?
WHAT IN THE WORLD...
...DOES THAT HAVE TO DO WITH ANYTHING?
REALLY.
コンッ
HMM?

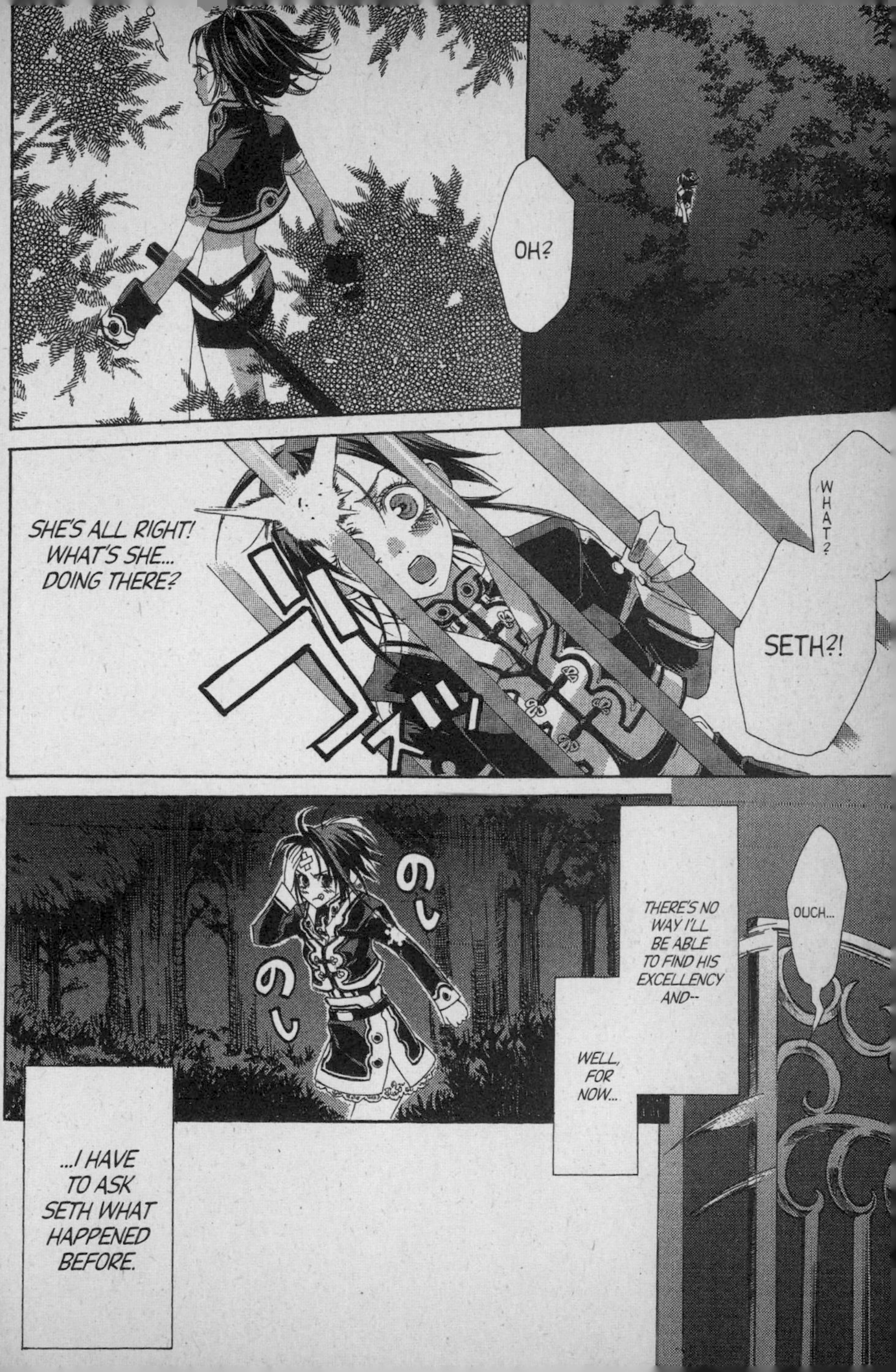
OH?
WHAT?
SETH?!
SHE'S ALL RIGHT! WHAT'S SHE... DOING THERE?
OUCH...
のしのし
THERE'S NO WAY I'LL BE ABLE TO FIND HIS EXCELLENCY AND--
WELL, FOR NOW...
...I HAVE TO ASK SETH WHAT HAPPENED BEFORE.

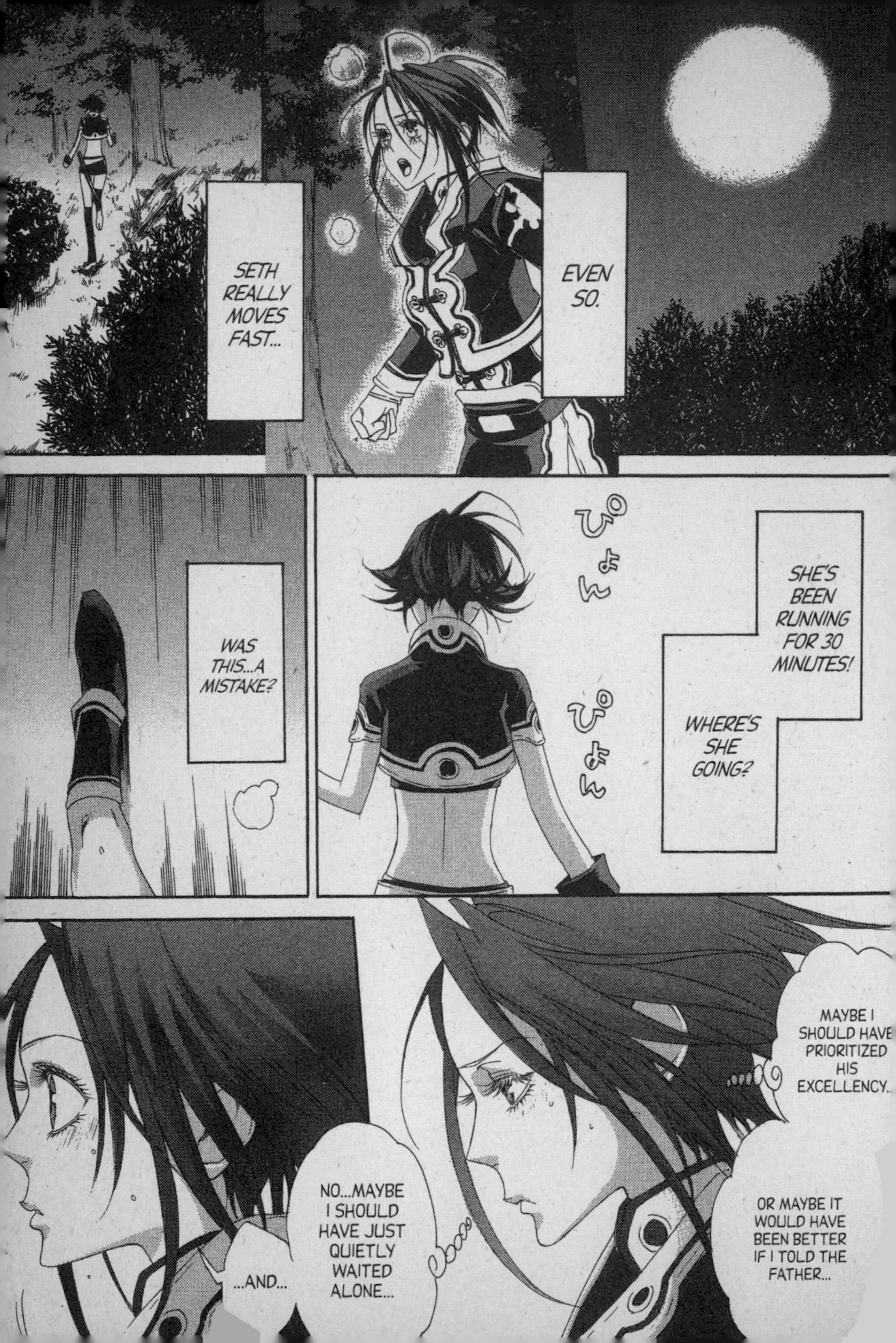
EVEN SO.
SETH REALLY MOVES FAST...
SHE'S BEEN RUNNING FOR 30 MINUTES!
WHERE'S SHE GOING?
ぴょん
ぴょん
WAS THIS...A MISTAKE?
MAYBE I SHOULD HAVE PRIORITIZED HIS EXCELLENCY...
OR MAYBE IT WOULD HAVE BEEN BETTER IF I TOLD THE FATHER...
NO...MAYBE I SHOULD HAVE JUST QUIETLY WAITED ALONE...
...AND...

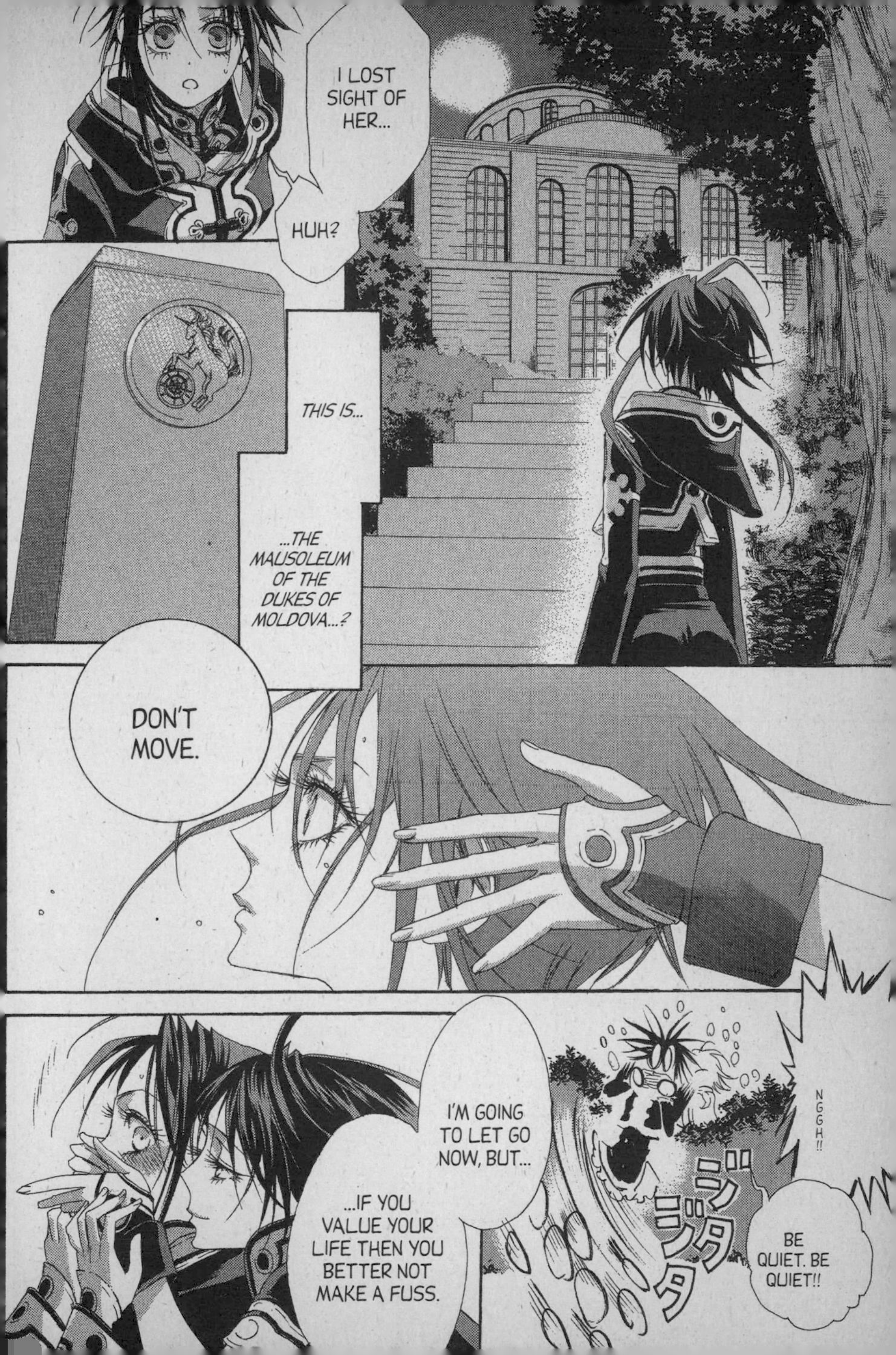

I LOST SIGHT OF HER...
HUH?
THIS IS...
...THE MAUSOLEUM OF THE DUKES OF MOLDOVA...?
DON'T MOVE.
NGGH!!
ジタジタ
BE QUIET. BE QUIET!!
I'M GOING TO LET GO NOW, BUT...
...IF YOU VALUE YOUR LIFE THEN YOU BETTER NOT MAKE A FUSS.

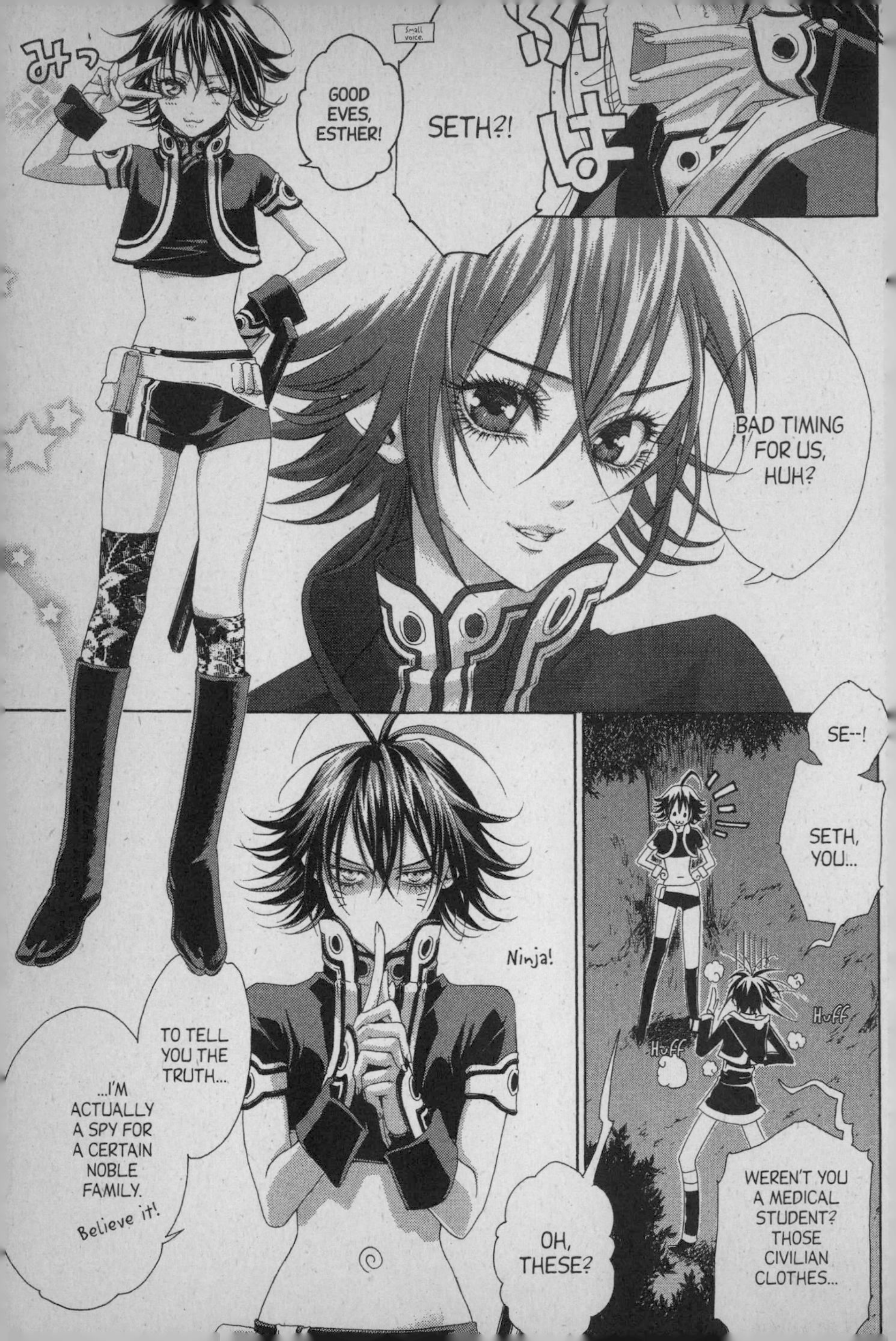
SETH?!
Small voice.
GOOD EVES, ESTHER!
みっ
BAD TIMING FOR US, HUH?
SE--!
SETH, YOU...
Huff
Huff
WEREN'T YOU A MEDICAL STUDENT? THOSE CIVILIAN CLOTHES...
OH, THESE?
Ninja!
TO TELL YOU THE TRUTH...
...I'M ACTUALLY A SPY FOR A CERTAIN NOBLE FAMILY.
Believe it!

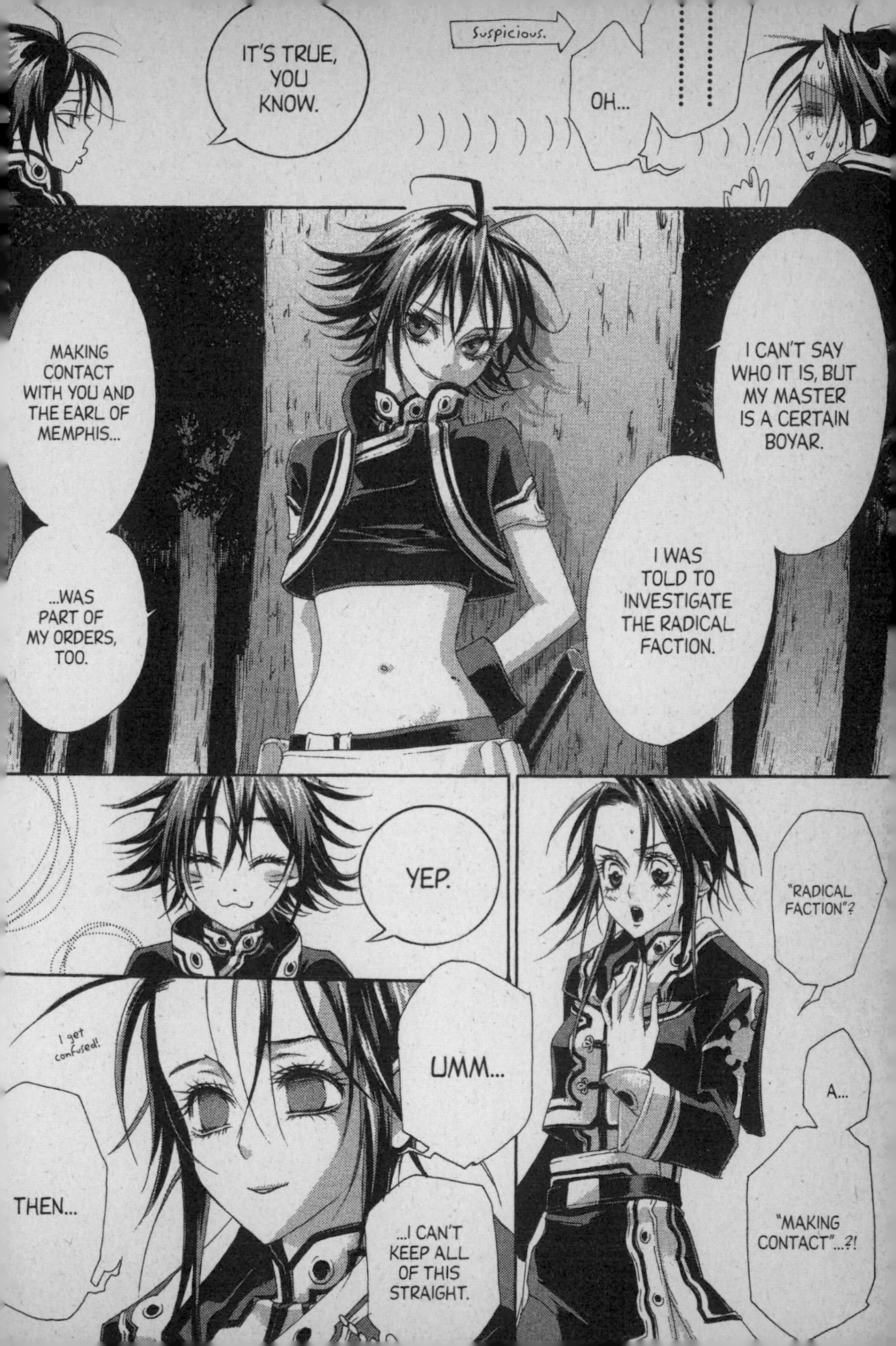
Suspicious.
OH...
IT'S TRUE, YOU KNOW.
I CAN'T SAY WHO IT IS, BUT MY MASTER IS A CERTAIN BOYAR.
I WAS TOLD TO INVESTIGATE THE RADICAL FACTION.
MAKING CONTACT WITH YOU AND THE EARL OF MEMPHIS...
...WAS PART OF MY ORDERS, TOO.
"RADICAL FACTION"?
YEP.
A...
"MAKING CONTACT"...?!
UMM...
...I CAN'T KEEP ALL OF THIS STRAIGHT.
THEN...
I get confused!

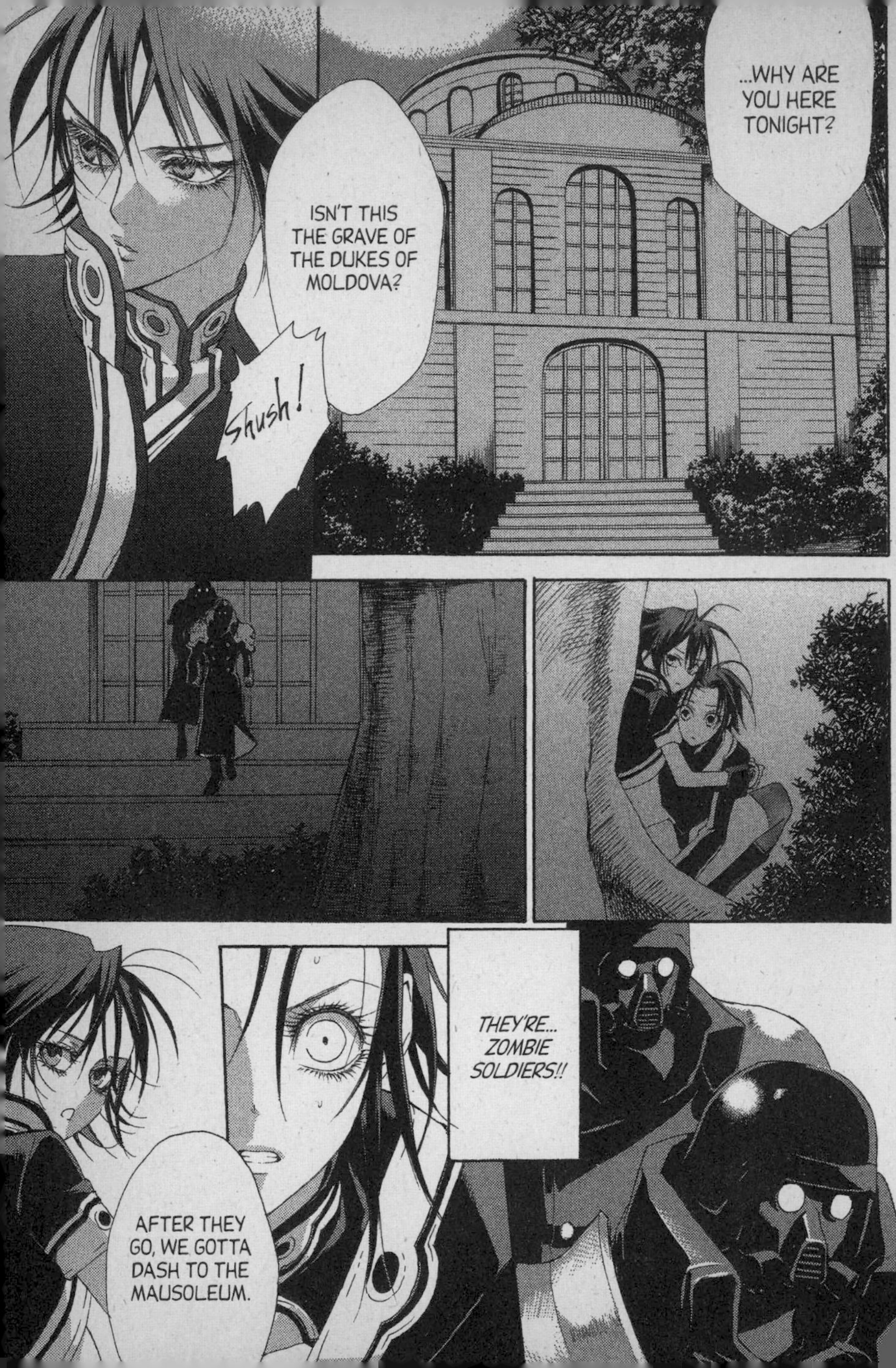
...WHY ARE YOU HERE TONIGHT?
ISN'T THIS THE GRAVE OF THE DUKES OF MOLDOVA?
Shush!
THEY'RE... ZOMBIE SOLDIERS!!
AFTER THEY GO, WE GOTTA DASH TO THE MAUSOLEUM.

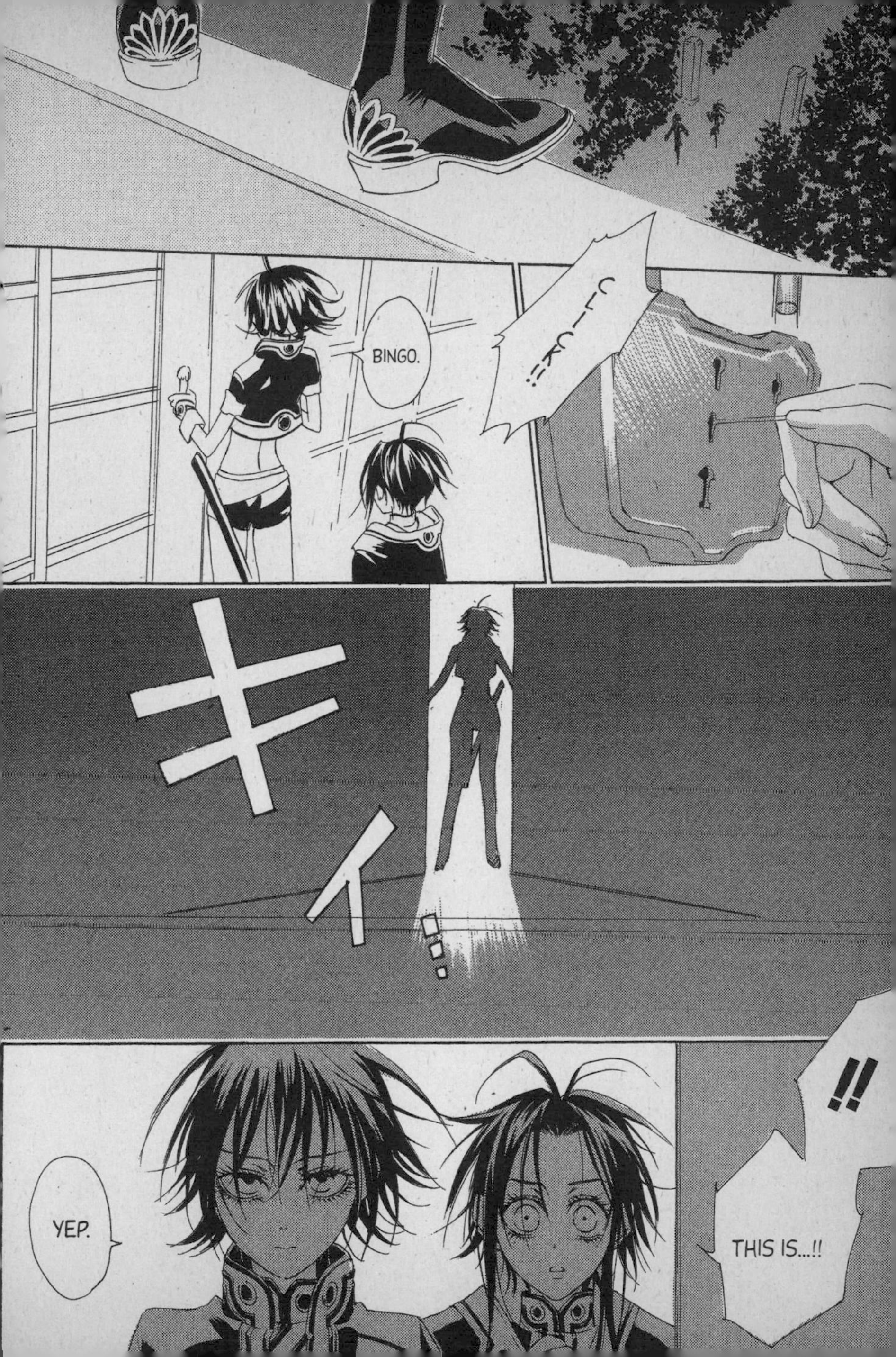
CLICK!!
BINGO.
キイ
!!
THIS IS...!!
YEP.

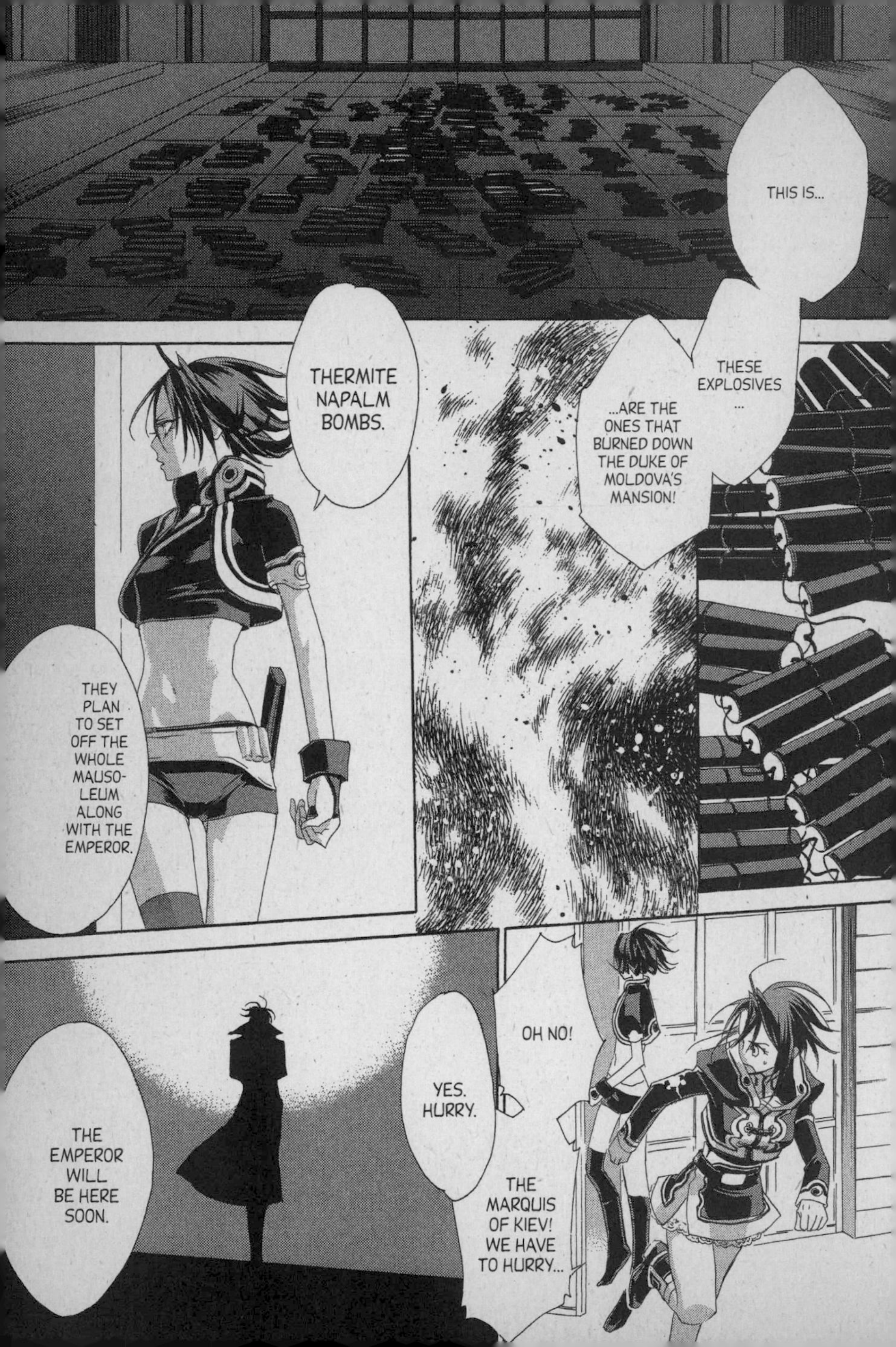
THIS IS...
THESE EXPLOSIVES ...
...ARE THE ONES THAT BURNED DOWN THE DUKE OF MOLDOVA'S MANSION!
THERMITE NAPALM BOMBS.
THEY PLAN TO SET OFF THE WHOLE MAUSO-LEUM ALONG WITH THE EMPEROR.
OH NO!
THE MARQUIS OF KIEV! WE HAVE TO HURRY...
YES. HURRY.
THE EMPEROR WILL BE HERE SOON.

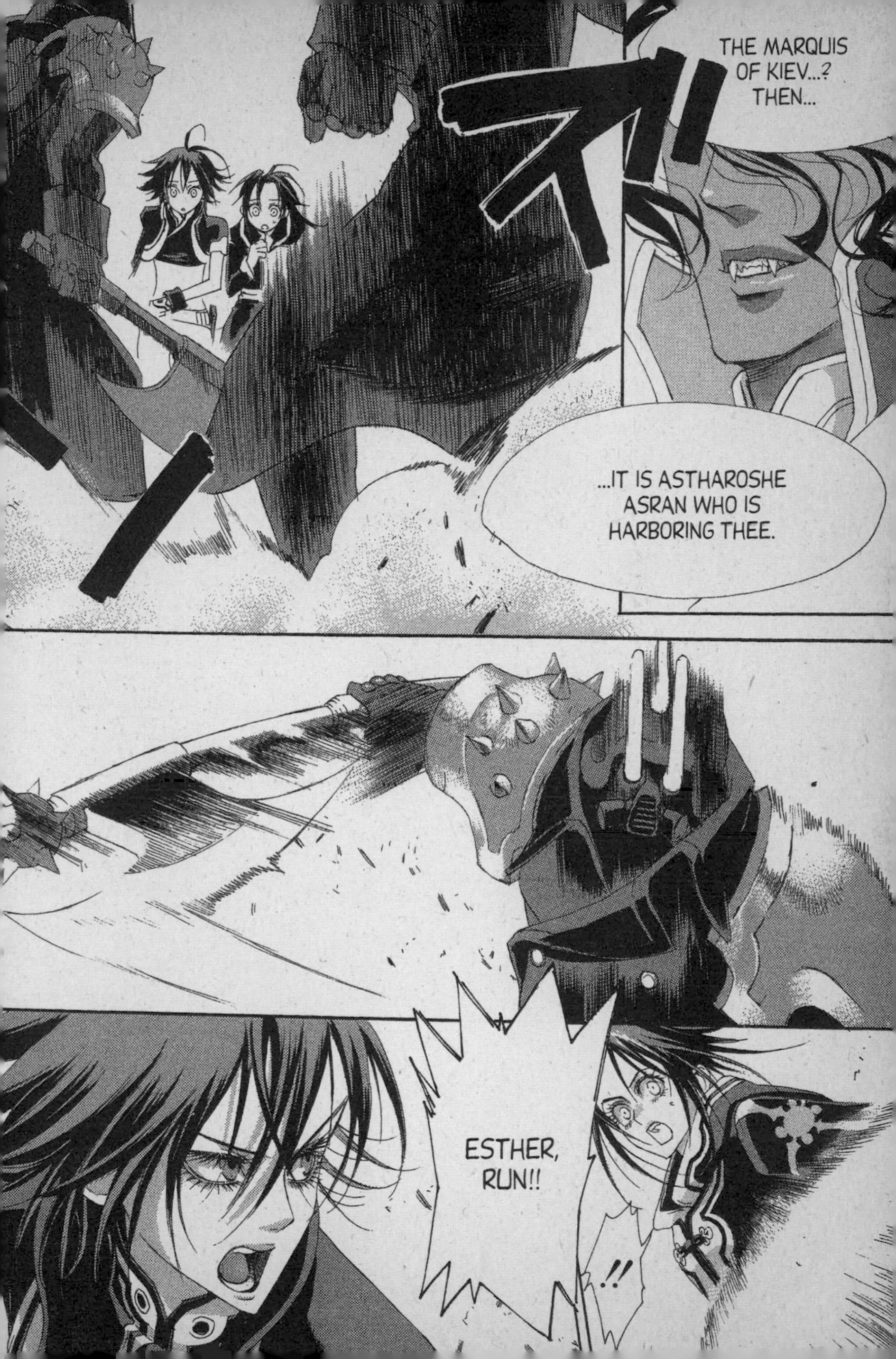

THE MARQUIS OF KIEV...? THEN...
...IT IS ASTHAROSHE ASRAN WHO IS HARBORING THEE.
ESTHER, RUN!!
!!

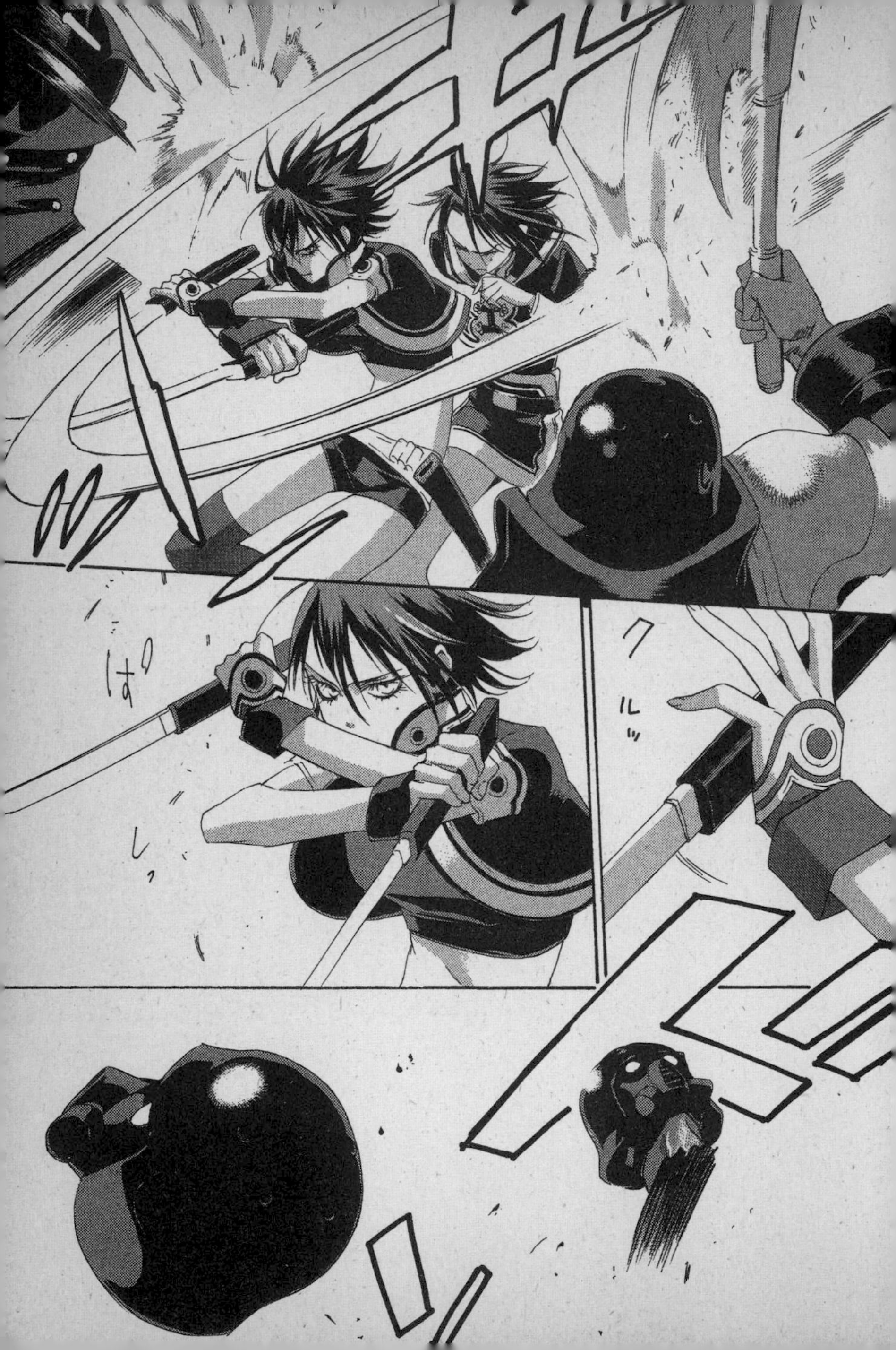
クルッ
はっ
しっ

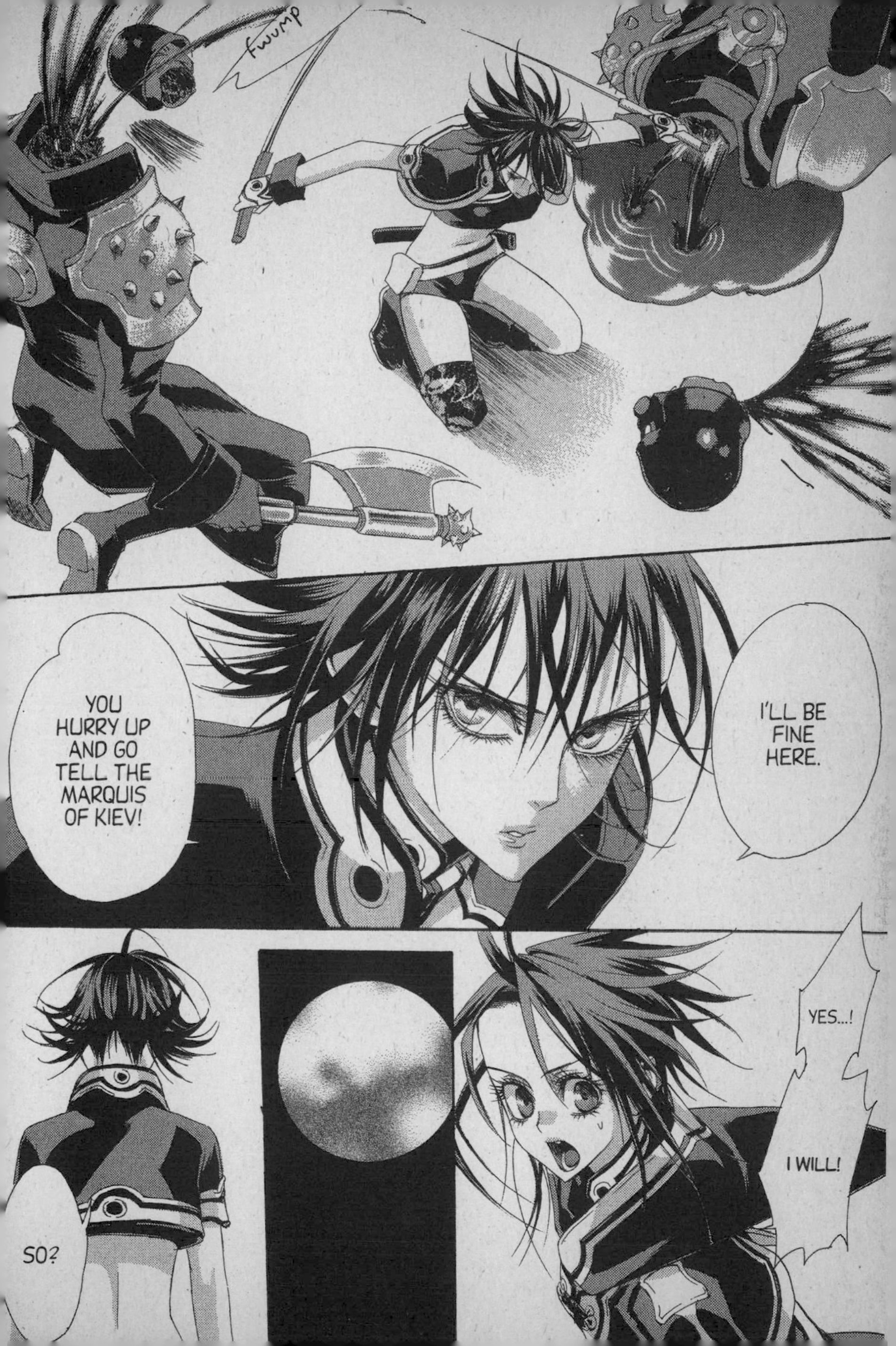
fwump
I'LL BE FINE HERE.
YOU HURRY UP AND GO TELL THE MARQUIS OF KIEV!
YES...!
I WILL!
SO?

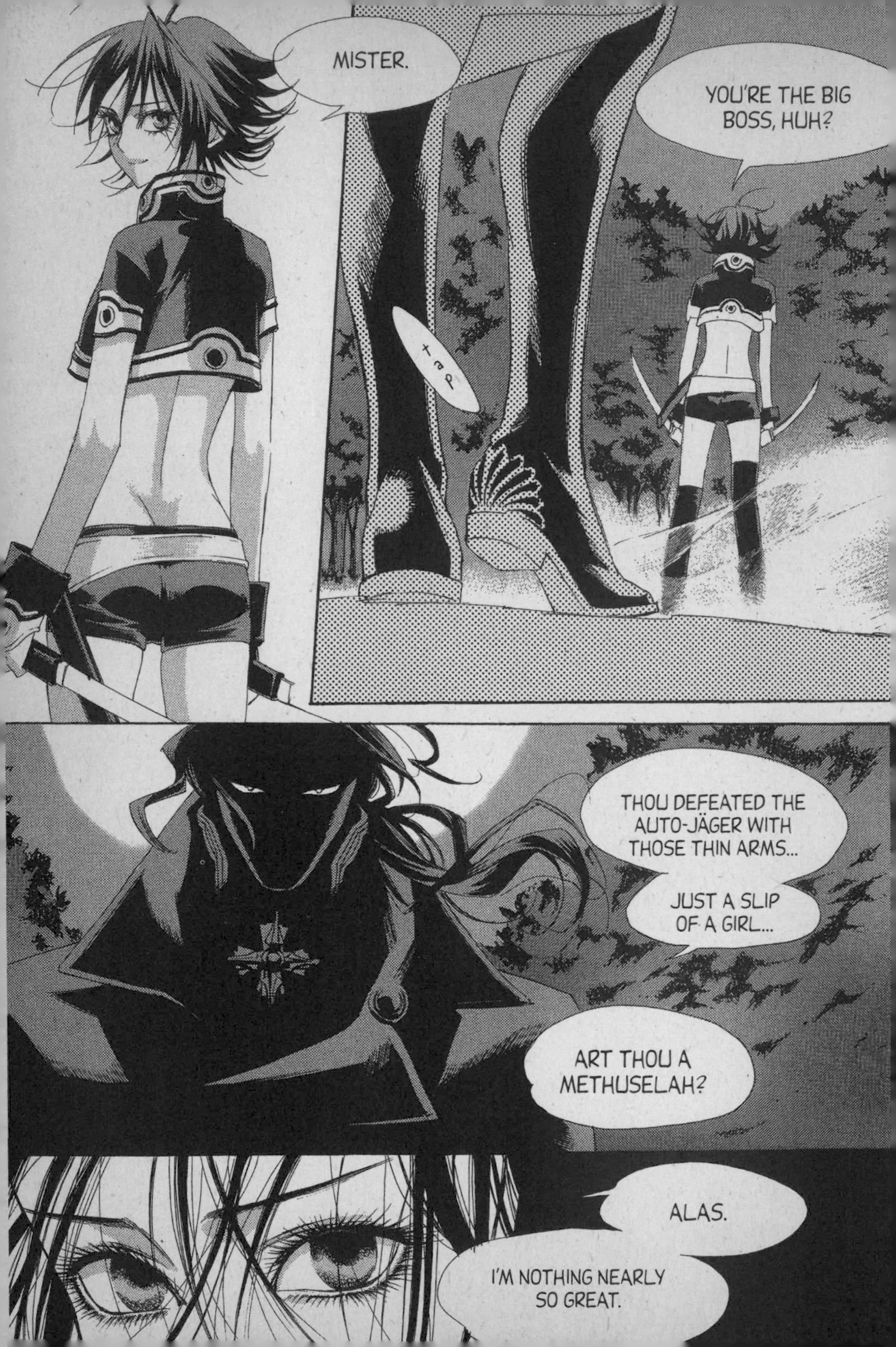
MISTER.
YOU'RE THE BIG BOSS, HUH?
tap
THOU DEFEATED THE AUTO-JÄGER WITH THOSE THIN ARMS...
JUST A SLIP OF A GIRL...
ART THOU A METHUSELAH?
ALAS.
I'M NOTHING NEARLY SO GREAT.

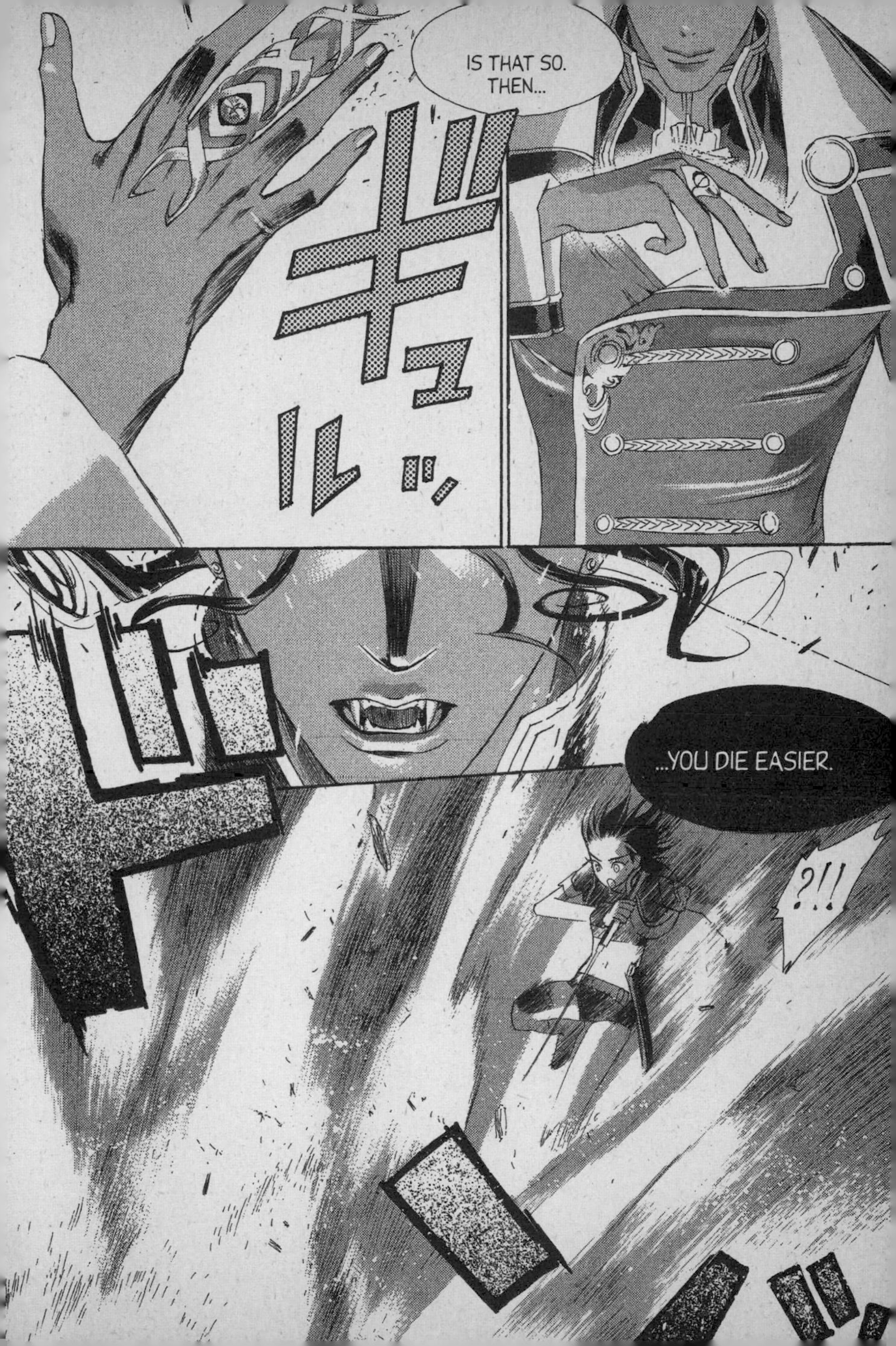
IS THAT SO. THEN...
ギュルルッ
...YOU DIE EASIER.
?!!

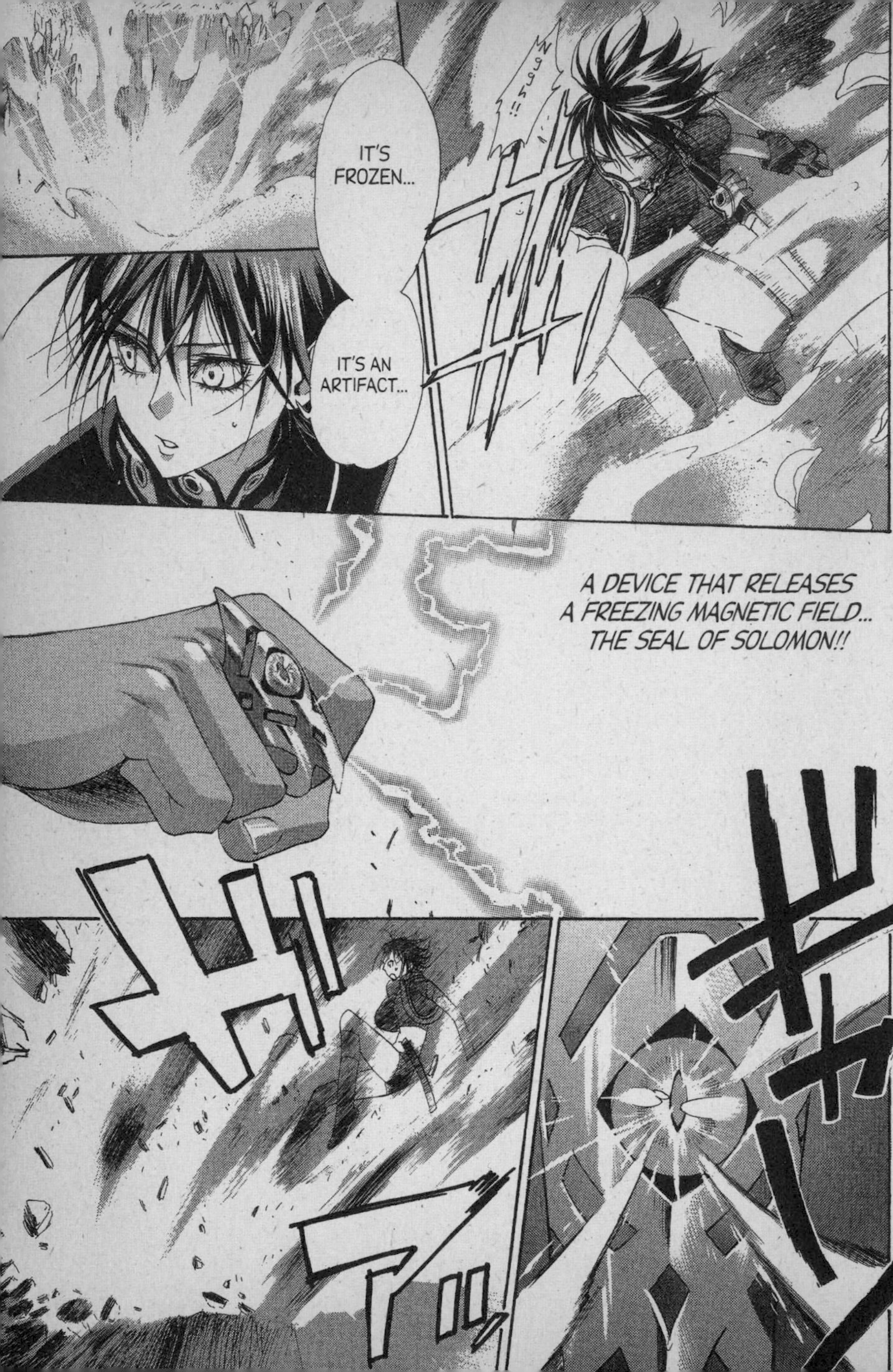
IT'S FROZEN...
IT'S AN ARTIFACT...
A DEVICE THAT RELEASES A FREEZING MAGNETIC FIELD... THE SEAL OF SOLOMON!!

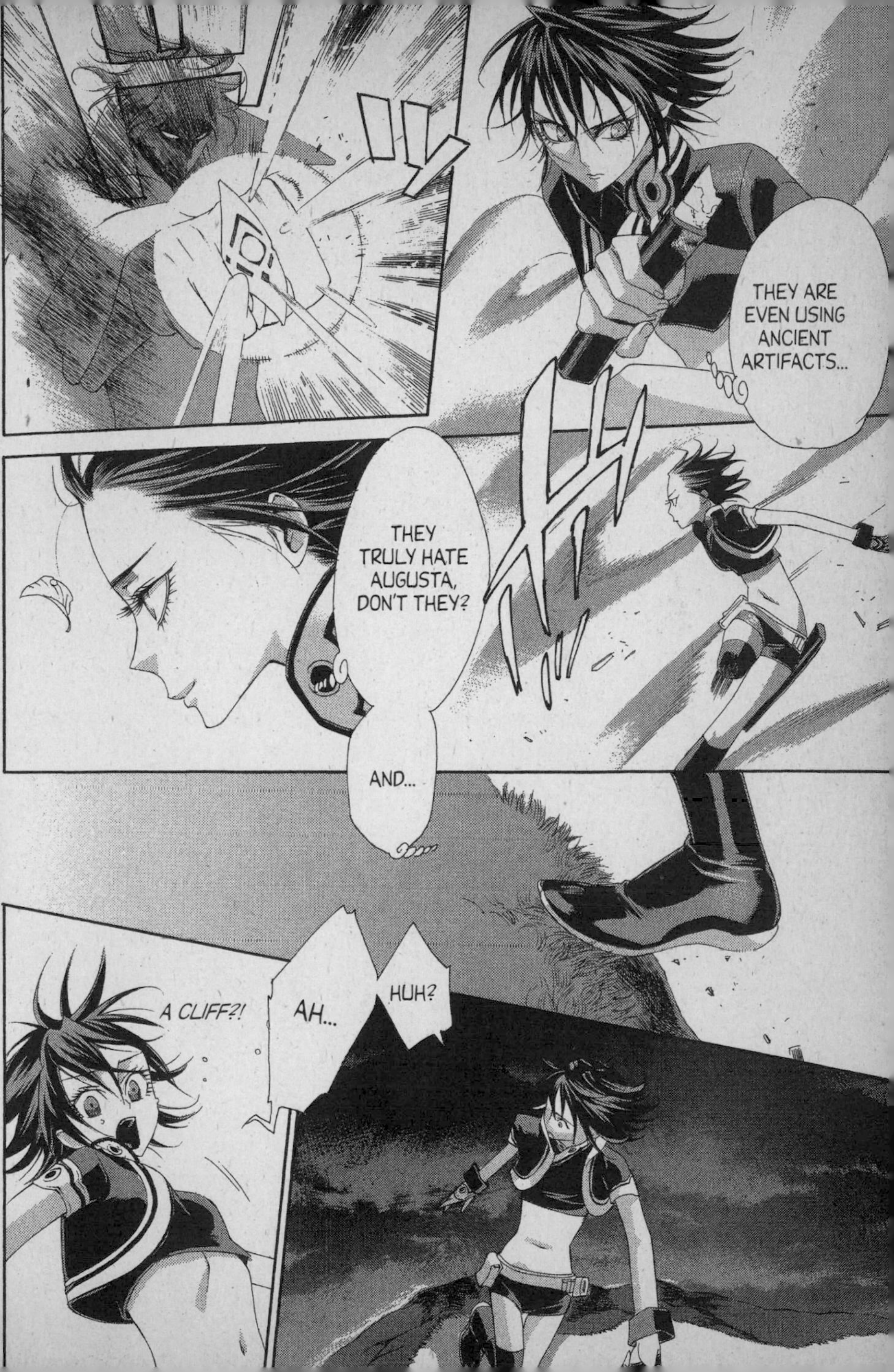
THEY ARE EVEN USING ANCIENT ARTIFACTS...
THEY TRULY HATE AUGUSTA, DON'T THEY?
AND...
HUH?
AH...
A CLIFF?!

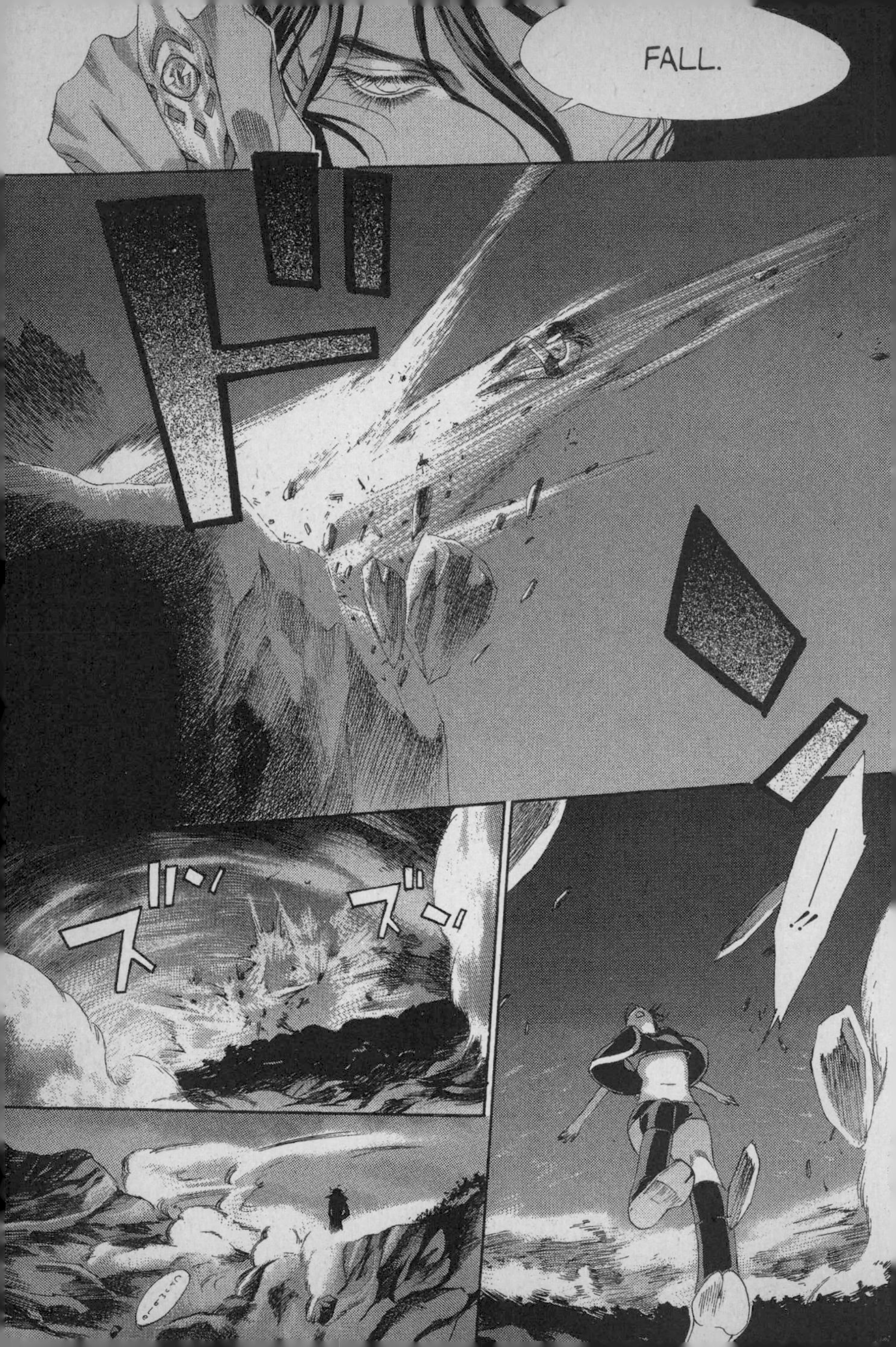
FALL.
!!

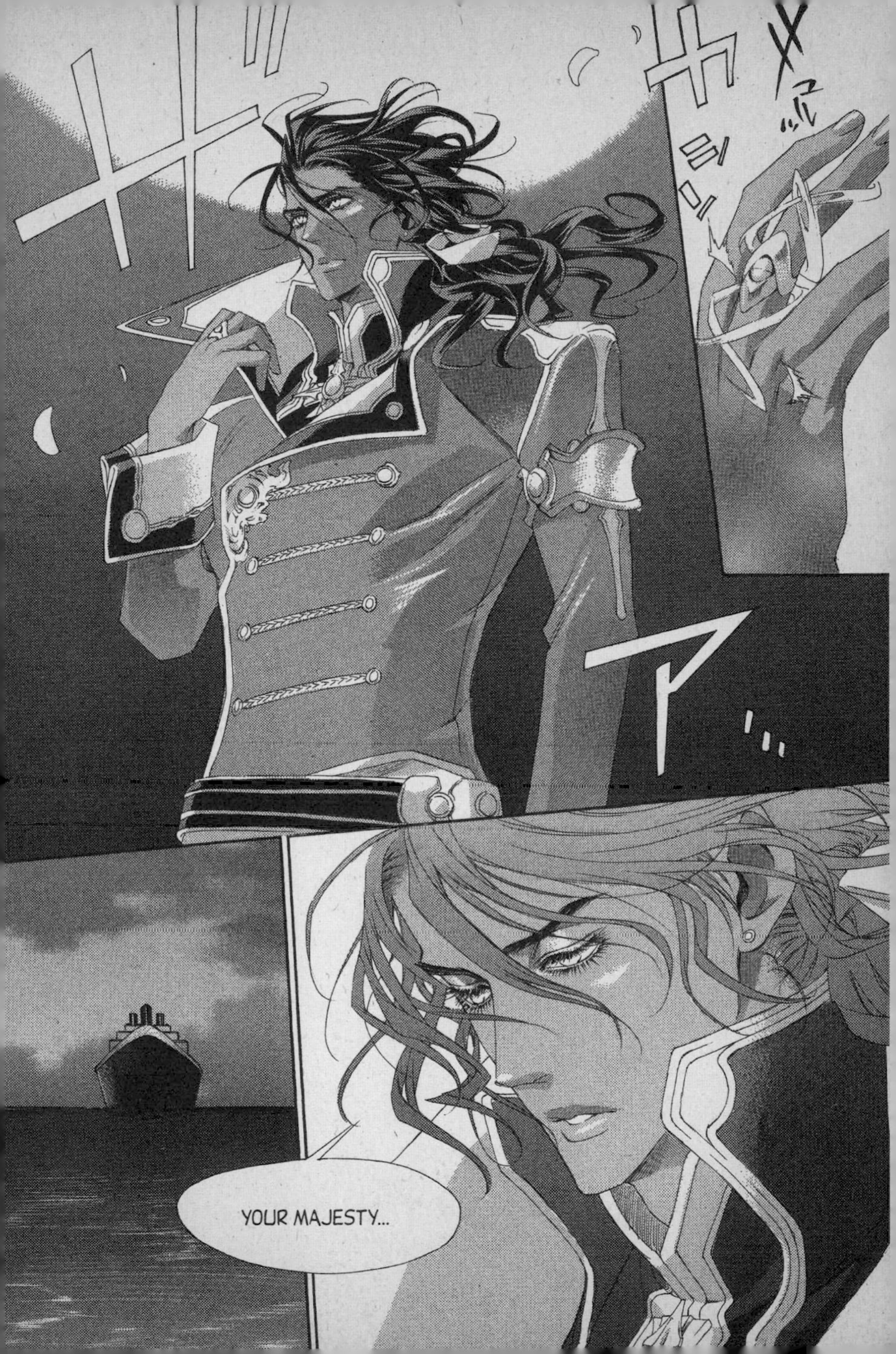
YOUR MAJESTY...

act.28

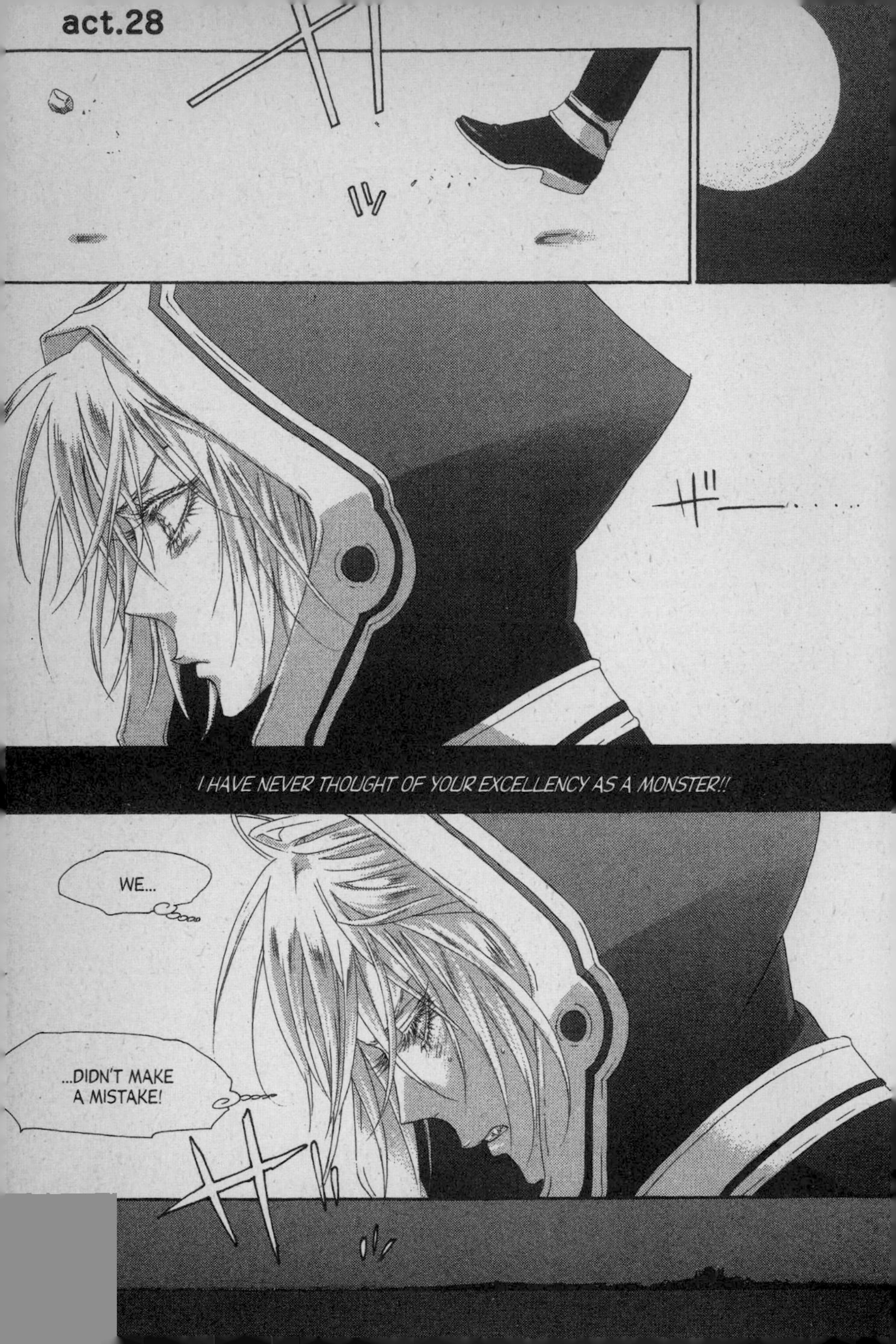

I HAVE NEVER THOUGHT OF YOUR EXCELLENCY AS A MONSTER!!
WE...
...DIDN'T MAKE A MISTAKE!

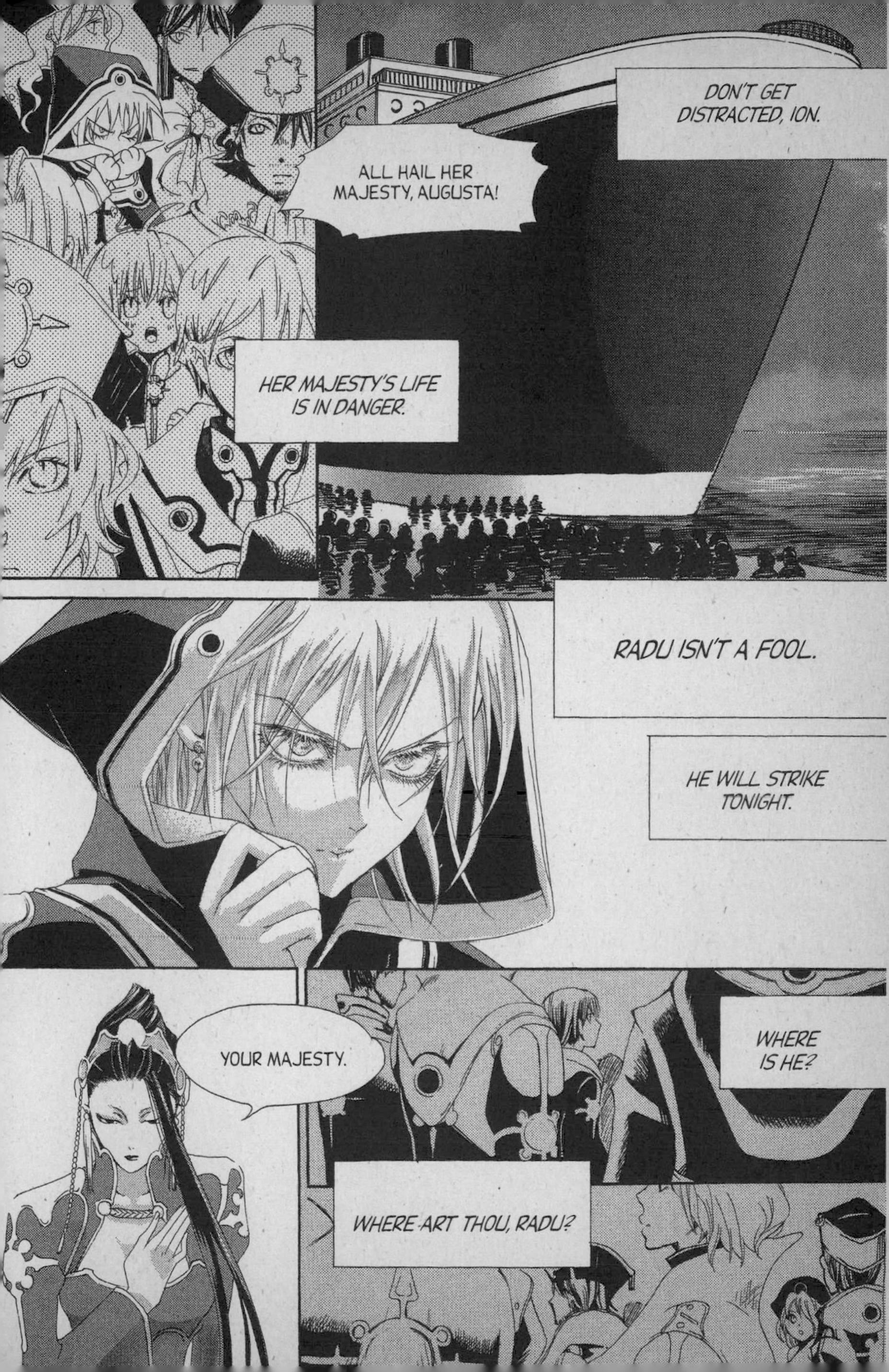
DON'T GET DISTRACTED, ION.
ALL HAIL HER MAJESTY, AUGUSTA!
HER MAJESTY'S LIFE IS IN DANGER.
RADU ISN'T A FOOL.
HE WILL STRIKE TONIGHT.
WHERE IS HE?
WHERE ART THOU, RADU?
YOUR MAJESTY.

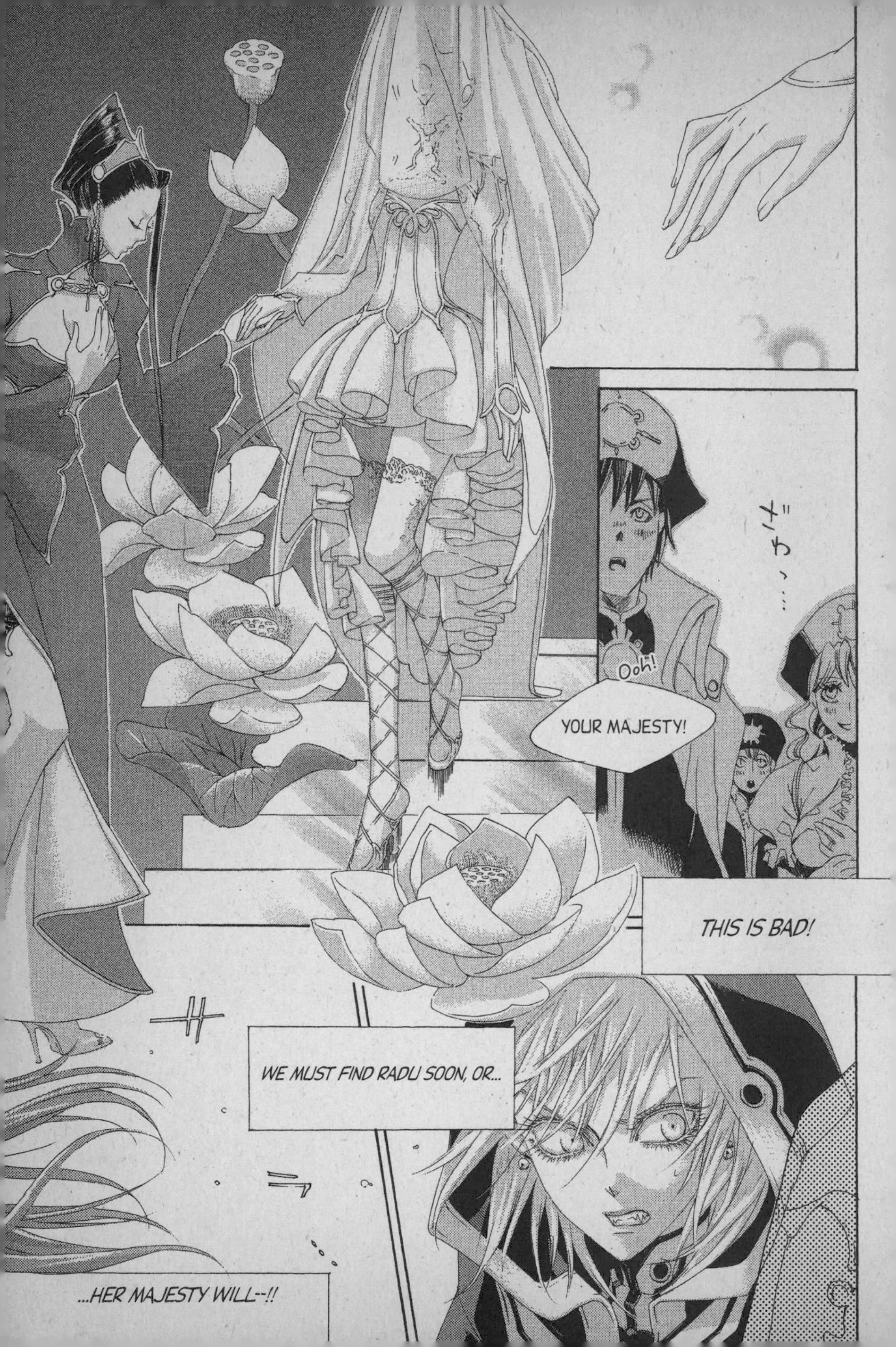

Ooh!
YOUR MAJESTY!
THIS IS BAD!
WE MUST FIND RADU SOON, OR...
...HER MAJESTY WILL--!!

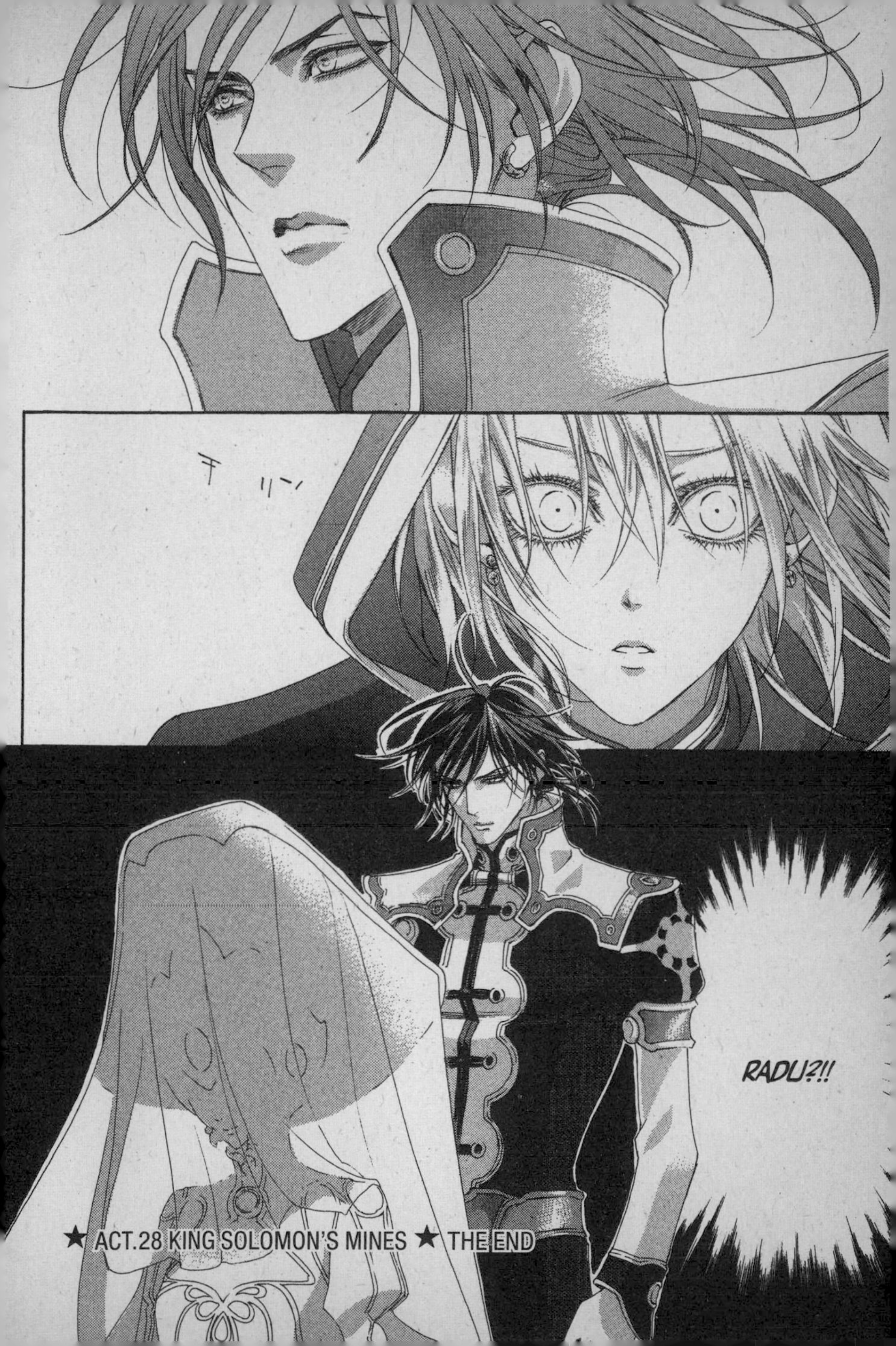
チ リーン
RADU?!!
★ ACT.28 KING SOLOMON'S MINES ★ THE END

Battle Maiden

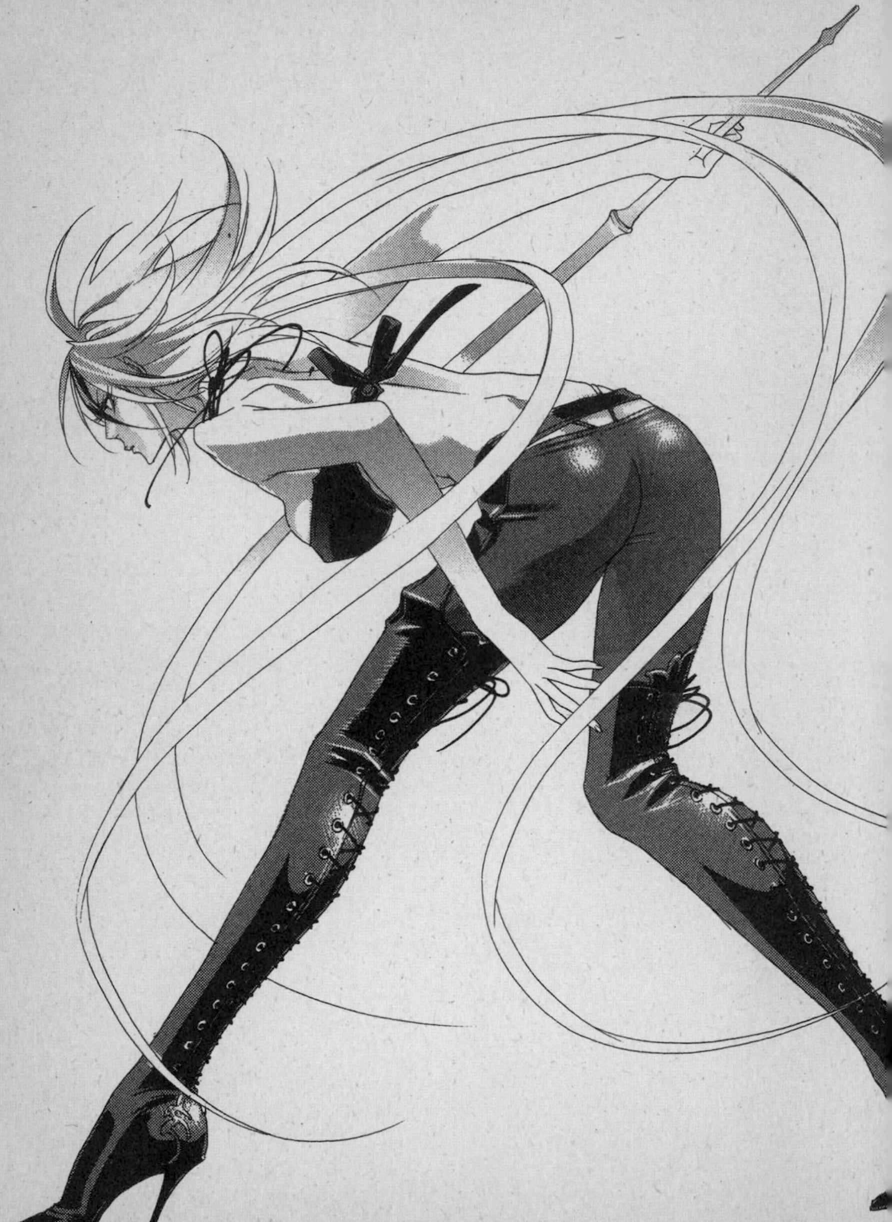

## This is Probably the Real Radu

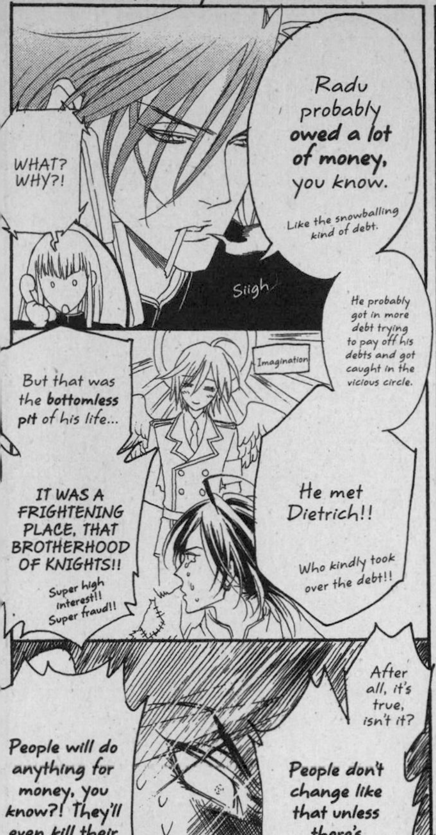

Radu probably owed a lot of money, you know.
Like the snowballing kind of debt.
WHAT? WHY?!
Siigh
He probably got in more debt trying to pay off his debts and got caught in the vicious circle.
Imagination
But that was the bottomless pit of his life...
He met Dietrich!!
Who kindly took over the debt!!
IT WAS A FRIGHTENING PLACE, THAT BROTHERHOOD OF KNIGHTS!!
Super high interest!! Super fraud!!
After all, it's true, isn't it?
People don't change like that unless there's money involved!
People will do anything for money, you know?! They'll even kill their friends!
Umm, you know, Aki-chan...
...Did something happen?
...
I lost tens of thousands of yen on slots.


Based on that, when I reread "Hot Sands," it's totally plausible.

## Flamberg Akira--G-Pen of Flames!

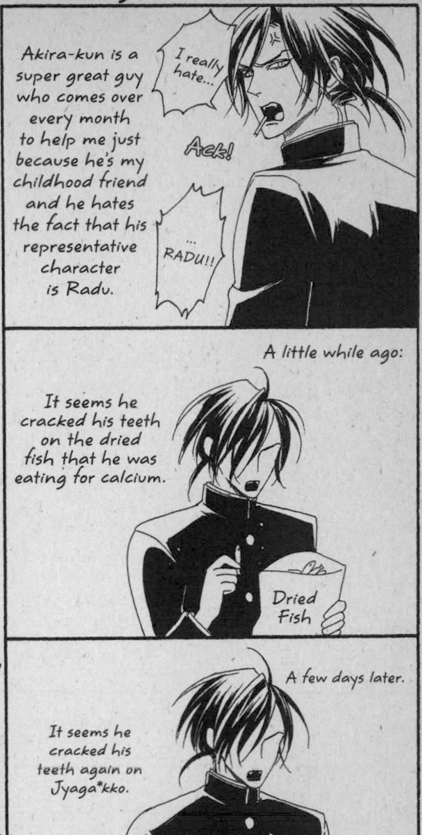

Akira-kun is a super great guy who comes over every month to help me just because he's my childhood friend and he hates the fact that his representative character is Radu.
I really hate...
Ack!
...RADU!!
A little while ago:
It seems he cracked his teeth on the dried fish that he was eating for calcium.
Dried Fish
A few days later.
It seems he cracked his teeth again on Jyaga*kko.
It seems Akira-kun has begun to like Radu a little.
Ha ha.
You know it seems...
...like I'm starting to understand how Radu feels.


Please stay healthy. I'm begging you.

This time it's a Radu Special!!

Flamberg = Akira-kun

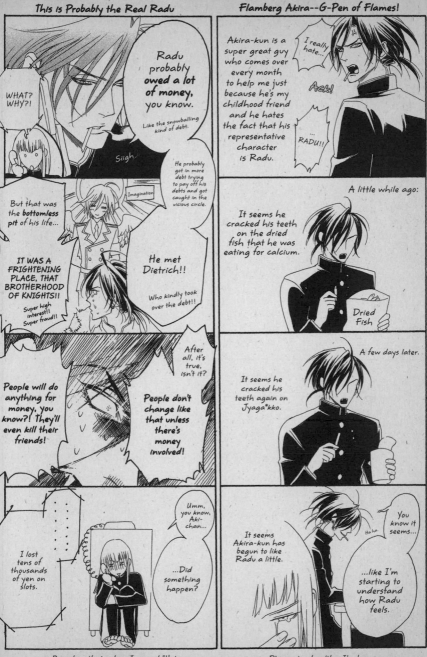

## This is Probably The Real Radu 2

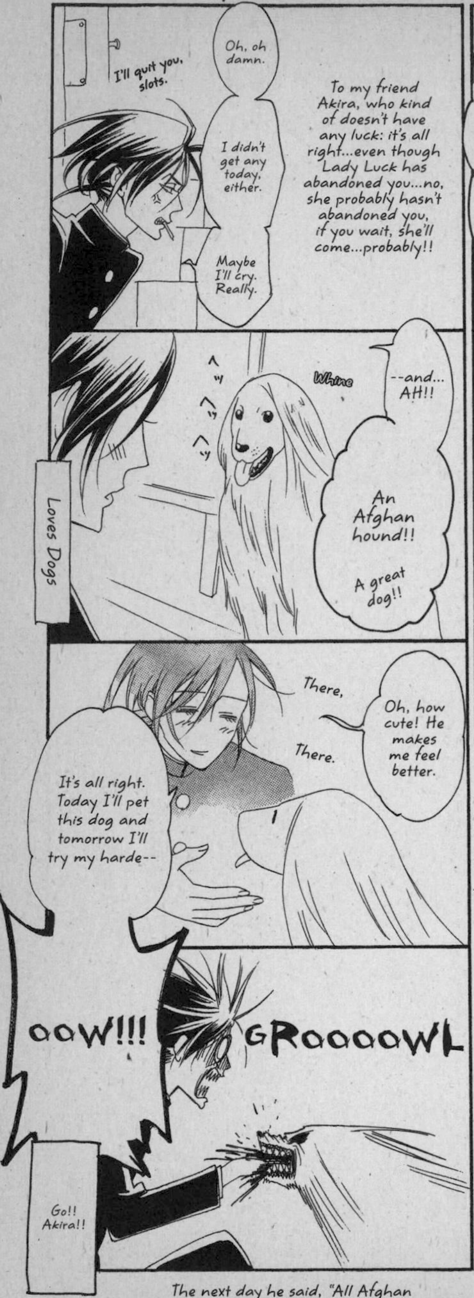
I'll quit you, slots.
Oh, oh damn.
I didn't get any today, either.
Maybe I'll cry. Really.
To my friend Akira, who kind of doesn't have any luck: it's all right...even though Lady Luck has abandoned you...no, she probably hasn't abandoned you, if you wait, she'll come...probably!!
Whine
--and... AH!!
An Afghan hound!!
A great dog!!
Loves Dogs
There,
There.
Oh, how cute! He makes me feel better.
It's all right. Today I'll pet this dog and tomorrow I'll try my harde--
aaW!!!
GRaaaaWL
Go!! Akira!!

The next day he said, "All Afghan hounds should die."

## Massage-assistant S-ko

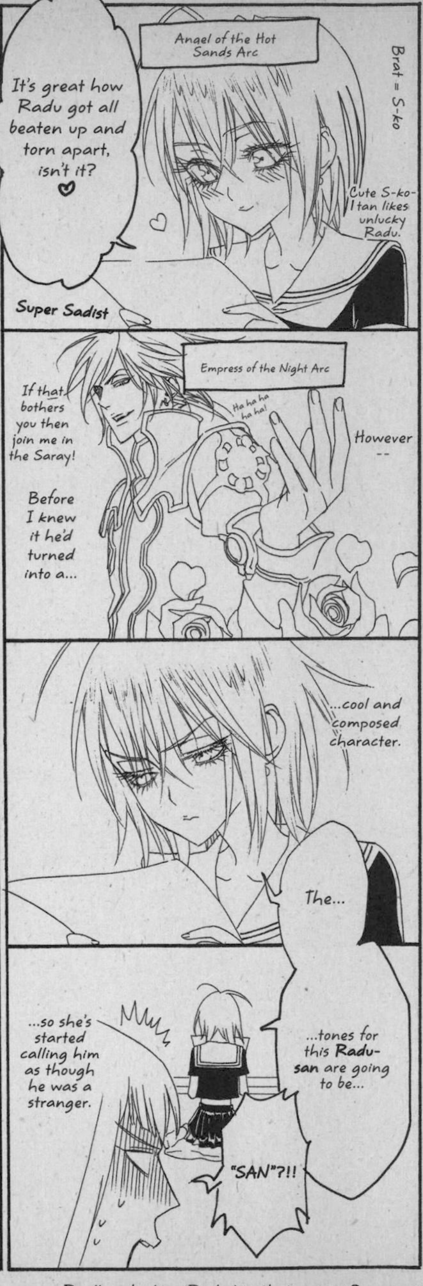
Angel of the Hot Sands Arc
It's great how Radu got all beaten up and torn apart, isn't it?
Brat = S-ko
Cute S-ko-tan likes unlucky Radu.
Super Sadist
Empress of the Night Arc
If that bothers you then join me in the Saray!
Ha ha ha ha ha!
However --
Before I knew it he'd turned into a...
...cool and composed character.
The...
...tones for this Radu-san are going to be...
...so she's started calling him as though he was a stranger.
"SAN"?!!

Really, who likes Radu like that anyway?

# ♥OUTRO♥

It's summer, isn't it? Is everyone being swallowed by the waves at the beach? I'm swallowed by my deadlines. Kyujyo wants to grab on to a parasol and get blown away to the bar in front of the station right now. Up! Up! It's summer.

It's finally volume 7. It's a great number! Thank you, everyone! I was able to come this far by continuing to cause a more-than-necessary amount of trouble for the people of the editorial department and the people who helped me. It's already been two years since the last time I saw Sunao Yoshida-sensei. It's a strange feeling, kind of like, "It's already been two years," and also like, "It's only been two years." To tell you the truth, I've had to continue to face Toribura so much to write the manga that sometimes I feel like I've forgotten about it. It's an amazing story. If I get to continue the serialization one year after this, two years after this, I think I'd say the same kind of thing... it's the original work!! I'll be happy if we meet again in the next volume. Kiyo Kyujyo.

Thanks

**Tsukasa** "Dick Mickey" **Kyouka** Moby Dick.

We did it...we did it, didn't we...that's good, huh! Every once in a while!! And from now on...right!! Best wishes!!

**Akira** "Yellow Ranger" **Ootaki** DJ

Really, you know, you. I got it already, you know, so enough already~. Let's live... strong, okay?!! Both of us!!

**Shouko** "What's San" **Kitamura** san

Somehow...I'm really sorry for a lot of things!! Next time let's go somewhere where like our meat and bags will get all squishy or something. Seriously! Meat, okay!

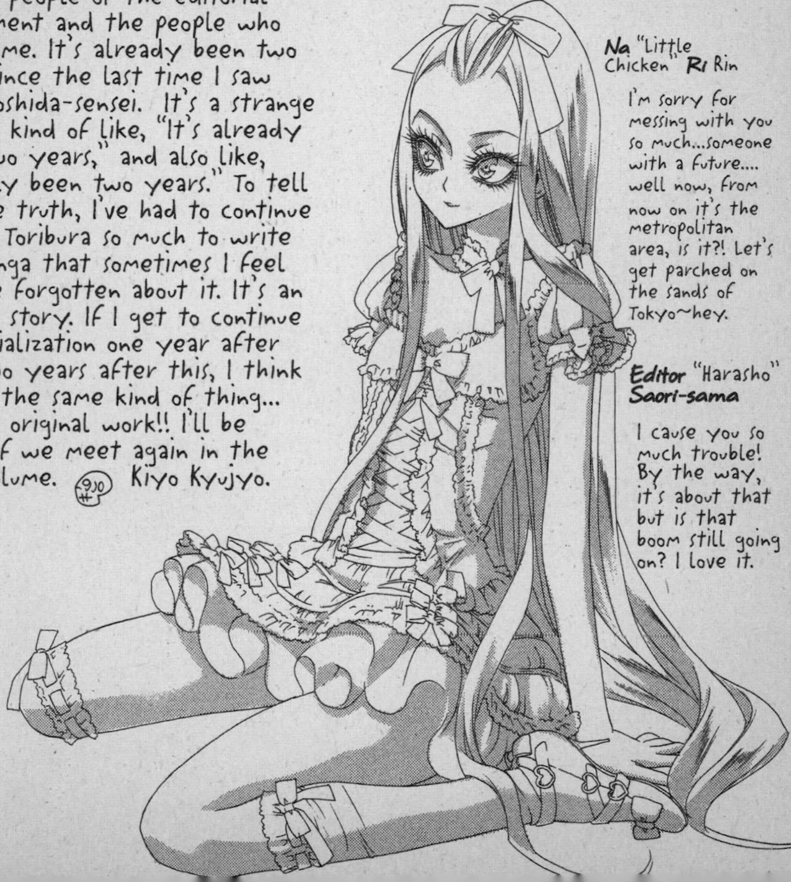

**Na** "Little Chicken" **Ri** Rin

I'm sorry for messing with you so much...someone with a future.... well now, from now on it's the metropolitan area, is it?! Let's get parched on the sands of Tokyo~hey.

**Editor** "Harasho" **Saori-sama**

I cause you so much trouble! By the way, it's about that but is that boom still going on? I love it.

# IN THE NEXT VOLUME OF

# TRINITY BLOOD™

The plot to assassinate the Methuselah Emperor is revealed at last, but instead of the malicious Radu, Ion and Esther are imprisoned for the crime! Astharoshe struggles with her own immortality and how feelings of loyalty and love can change over the course of centuries, and Dietrich has yet another cruel twist of fate in store for his beloved Esther...

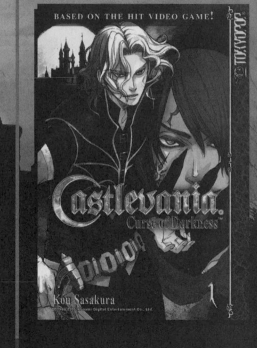

## GAKUEN ALICE VOLUME FOUR

Mikan's daring rescue of Natsume has earned her an upgrade to One-star rank!

Mikan's upgrade to One-star rank has come just in time for the School Festival, and it's even more spectacular than Mikan ever dreamed. But what will happen when Mikan and Natsume get locked in the haunted house together?!

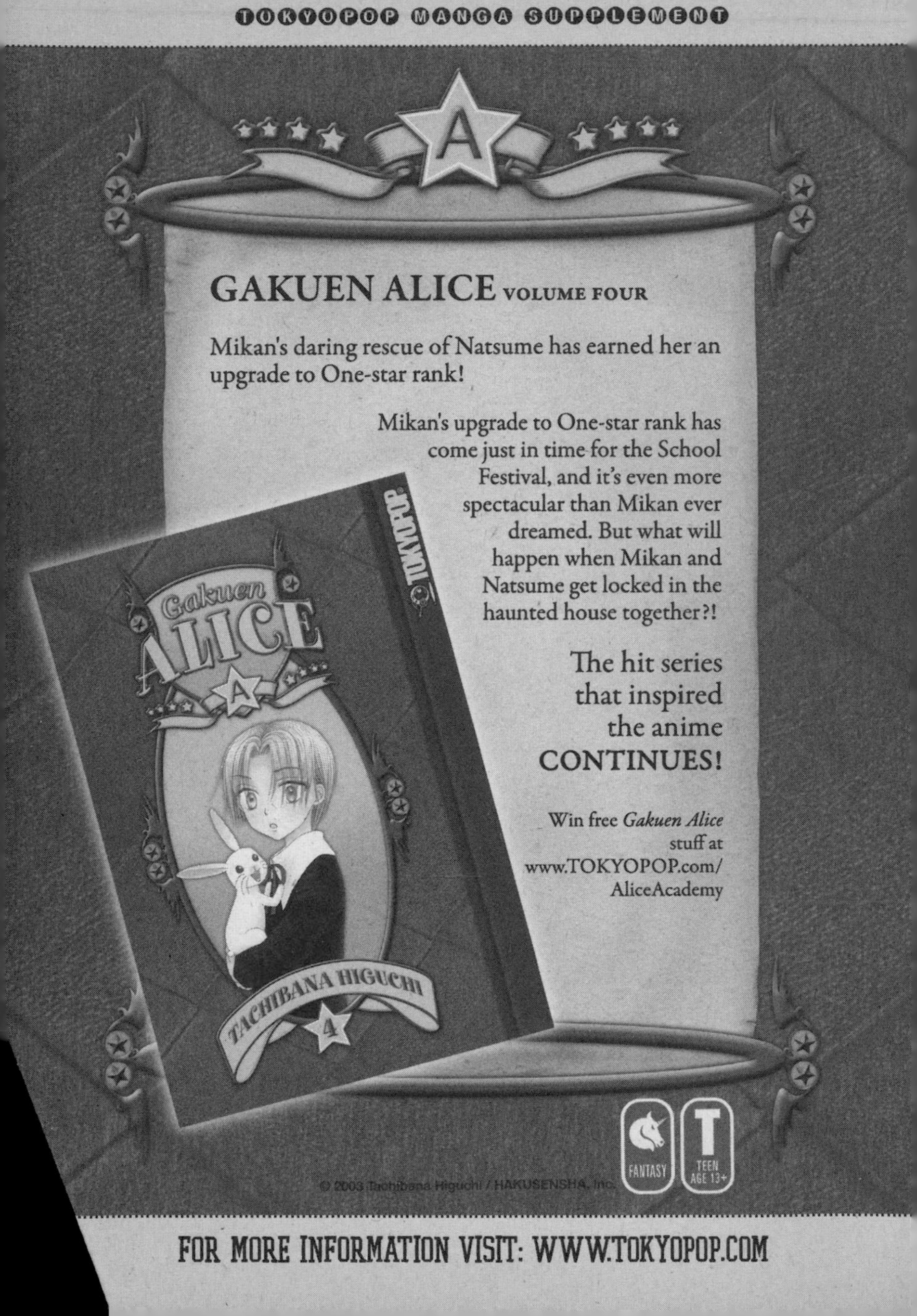
TOKYOPOP
Gakuen
ALICE
A
TACHIBANA HIGUCHI
4

The hit series that inspired the anime **CONTINUES!**

Win free *Gakuen Alice* stuff at www.TOKYOPOP.com/AliceAcademy

FANTASY

T TEEN AGE 13+



FOR MORE INFORMATION VISIT: WWW.TOKYOPOP.COM

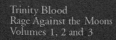

る時は
ゃいだ！

9/08
3/10
3/11 3/10-1
4/12 3/11
1/22 - 6 (7/15)

# You w ing!

This bool t-to-left
format. S ers
get to ex en
asking fo ss,
and far m

s a

p

k for
a

8 7

10